914

Hoy

AN OUTLINE OF THE
HISTORY OF MUSIC

BY

KARL NEF
LATE PROFESSOR OF MUSICOLOGY
UNIVERSITY OF BASEL

TRANSLATED BY

CARL F. PFATTEICHER
DIRECTOR OF MUSIC AT PHILLIPS ACADEMY
ANDOVER, MASSACHUSETTS

NEW YORK : MORNINGSIDE HEIGHTS
COLUMBIA UNIVERSITY PRESS

COLUMBIA UNIVERSITY
STUDIES IN MUSICOLOGY

BOARD OF EDITORS

Translated and Enlarged from the Second German Edition; also from the Second French Edition (Edited by Yvonne Rokseth)

COPYRIGHT 1935
COLUMBIA UNIVERSITY PRESS, NEW YORK

First printing 1935
Second printing 1938
Third printing 1939
With additional bibliographic material
Fourth printing 1944
Fifth printing 1946
Sixth printing 1947

Published in Great Britain and India by Geoffrey Cumberlege, Oxford University Press, London and Bombay

MANUFACTURED IN THE UNITED STATES OF AMERICA

INTRODUCTORY NOTE

The publication in America of a series entitled "Studies in Musicology" calls for comment. The very word "musicology," used to denote the scientific, philosophic, and historic approach to the art of music, has only recently been added to the legitimate vocabulary of the English language. Although much has been written about music, a large part of this literature is purely technical, dealing with the theory of music and of composition from a practical point of view. Other books on music have been written from the standpoint of the artist dealing with his art. But the application to musical studies of purposive, systematic methods of research has been left to a comparatively small number of scholars.

Minute scholarly research in the field of music had been cultivated in Europe many years before signs of the same type of activity became evident in America. The time is ripe for the establishment of a series of musicological studies comparable to the various series which have been established in Europe. Our universities and colleges, our music schools and conservatories, are beginning to awaken to the fact that there is a place for musical scholarship in our system of education.

This series inaugurated by the Columbia University Press is intended to meet the needs of the English-speaking student for the crystallization of various phases of musical knowledge around which the rapidly expanding material may be oriented.

The choice of the first volume of the series was dictated by the desire to provide an introductory manual which would be of interest to the beginner in musical history, since a scholarly view of the development of the art must be the foundation of scholarly research into special problems. The *Outline of the History of Music* by the late Professor Nef of Basle is such a work. It was written by a trained musicologist of broad tastes, who was reliable in his judgments concerning recent developments in musical history and also of its early phases. It should be of real service to students as well as to general readers.

Other volumes in the series will be planned to include studies in more limited fields and of a more specific character.

Cornell University,   Otto Kinkeldey
Ithaca, N. Y.,
July 31, 1935

FOREWORD TO THE ENGLISH TRANSLATION

The translator knows of no work on the history of music quite comparable to Professor Nef's *Outline of the History of Music*. There are, of course, more encyclopedic works, but they are not well adapted either for general reading or for classroom use. There exist also more popular works, but they lack scholarliness. Professor Nef's book is brief, yet comprehensive; readable, yet scholarly. The general reader may omit, or treat cursorily, the footnotes containing biographical and bibliographical material; so also the general bibliographical section. For the serious student in musicology, these will be indispensable. If the modern field may seem to have been treated in too summary a manner, this treatment is due to the fact that the field is already comparatively familiar to the average person interested in music, as well as to the fact that the literature on this period is easily accessible. Moreover, it is highly important that the average reader and the student should be made to realize strongly that the history of music does not begin with the Vienna classicists nor even with Bach.

In addition to the collections of examples cited by Professor Nef in his foreword (the *Musikgeschichte in Beispielen*, by Riemann, and the *Musikgeschichtlicher Atlas*, by Steinitzer) mention should also be made of the two short collections, the one by Einstein, Teubner, 1930, the other by Wolf, Vieweg, 1932, and especially of the comprehensive collection *Geschichte der Musik in Beispielen*, by Arnold Schering, Breitkopf & Härtel, 1931. In connection with these collections of musical illustrations the use of the tables of musical historical data offered in Arnold Schering's *Tabellen zur Musikgeschichte* (4th ed., Breitkopf & Härtel, Leipzig, 1934) will prove extremely helpful.

By arrangement with M. Payot, the publisher, and Mme. Rokseth, the editor, it was possible to include the numerous musical examples and other additions found in the French edition.

The question might be raised whether the English edition of Professor Nef's work should not have contained still more supplementary material relating to the subject of both English and American music. With regard to this, two answers may be made: in the first place, the book purports to present the development of music in its broad and important aspects, to present it from an international and not a national point of view, and it must be admitted that the author has pursued this end in a fair and impartial manner. Moreover, it may also be said that for the reader who wishes to delve more deeply into the English or the American field there are comprehensive, easily obtainable books at hand. With regard to the English field, it is only necessary to mention such works as: *History of English Music*, by Henry Davey, J. Curwen & Sons, 2d edition, 1921; and *A History of Music in England*, by Ernest Walker, Oxford University Press, 2d edition, 1924. With regard to the American field, the reader will doubtless find all the material he desires in the recently published work: *Our American Music*, by John Tasker Howard, T. Y. Crowell Co., 1930.

In conclusion, the translator may allow himself to express the hope, that a book which is used as extensively as is Professor Nef's work in Europe (Switzerland, France, Germany—a Norwegian translation has also recently appeared), a book which has merited the commendation of that distinguished musicologist, André Pirro of the Sorbonne, will also be serviceable in the early studies of the ever increasing number of students of musicology in America.

It is the writer's pleasure to express sincere thanks to the German musicologist, Willibald Gurlitt, professor at the University of Freiburg i/Br., for many hints and suggestions with regard to the most recent researches and developments in the musicological field; also, for valuable assistance with regard to bibliographical details, to Professor Otto Kinkeldey, librarian of Cornell University and professor of musicology, formerly professor of musicology at the University of Breslau, Germany; to Professor Paul H. Lang, professor of musicology at Columbia University; to Professor Edgar Refardt of the University of Basel, Switzerland; to Dr. Carlton Sprague Smith, librarian of the Music Department of the New York City Public Library; to Mr. Richard G. Appel, librarian of the Music Department of the Boston Public Library; to Dr. Harold Spivacke, of the Music Department of the Library of Congress, Washington; and to Mr. Richard S. Angell of the Music Library of Columbia University. For reading the entire manuscript and offering many stylistic suggestions, the writer wishes to thank Mr. Edwin Tenney Brewster of Andover. Carl F. Pfatteicher

Andover, Mass.,
January 31, 1935

FOREWORD BY THE AUTHOR

The previous brief compendia of the history of music were, as a rule, specifically intended as books for classroom instruction; the present work, in addition to the purpose mentioned, aims to present the material in a form understandable by all; in other words, it purposes to be not merely a reference book, but a book for the general reader as well. It endeavors to show the main features in their significance for general culture, and their connection with universal history; moreover, it desires to conduct the reader to the music itself, to reveal to him that which shines forth in eternal beauty but unfortunately has become obscured or completely forgotten. In addition to this, there are references for singers and musicians to compositions which are especially worthy of a revival in the concert hall and the home. In order not to remain limited to general phrases, I have occasionally added musical examples, and in order to make possible for each one some acquaintance with old music, I have chosen for more detailed discussion selections which are printed in the following two works: H. Riemann, *Musikgeschichte in Beispielen* (Leipzig, Breitkopf und Härtel) and M. Steinitzer, *Musikgeschichtlicher Atlas* (Freiburg, i/B., Ruckmich). These two collections present the old compositions in easy piano arrangements for two hands, so that in this way a bridge is projected for all friends of music, or for musicians themselves, who, either through lack of knowledge or lack of time, do not familiarize themselves with the old scores.

The history of music is still a young science which had first to solve many technical problems. From this fact doubtless arises the dread of it with which most educated people are still obsessed, as if they were to deal with a black-art. It is an error and a prejudice which must be overcome. The fruits of music history are for all, and in connection with our modern mass-cultivation of music, one can only wish that they be thoroughly appropriated in order that one may find both anchorage and depth.

The following presentation would like to serve as a general stimulus to this end; it is an attempt to fulfil this in general. In order, however, that it may not hover in mid-air, and that thoroughness may not be sacrificed, a special section is appended at the bottom of the page

in smaller type, which gives the bibliography, short biographies of the
most outstanding musicians, and some more detailed explanations, as
well as furnishing all that is requisite for one desirous of pursuing more
explicit studies. The little book, accordingly, would also like to serve as
a basis for the studies of both students and conservatory pupils. It has
evolved from the experiences which the editor has acquired during
many years as teacher in conservatory and university.

Karl Nef

Schwyz,
October, 1919

CONTENTS

ABBREVIATIONS

Allg. MZ.	*Allgemeine Musikzeitung*
Ambros	Ambros, *Geschichte der Musik*
Arch. f. MW.	*Archiv für Musikwissenschaft*
art.	article
B. & H.	Breitkopf und Härtel
D.T.B.	*Denkmäler der Tonkunst in Bayern*
D.d.T.	*Denkmäler deutscher Tonkunst*
D.T. OE.	*Denkmäler der Tonkunst in Oesterreich*
E.B.	*Beispielsammlung zur Musikgeschichte* (Einstein)
ed.	edition and edited
Enc. Lav.	*Encyclopédie de la musique* (Lavignac et de la Laurencie)
Eng.	English
enl.	enlarged
Ger.	German
Hdb.	Handbuch
J.P.	*Jahrbuch der Musikbibliothek Peters*
Km. JB.	*Kirchenmusikalisches Jahrbuch*
MG.	*Musikgeschichte*
Monatsh. f. MG.	*Monatshefte für Musikgeschichte*
MS	Manuscript
M.T.	*Musical Times*
Mus. Quart.	*Musical Quarterly*
MW.	*Musikwissenschaft*
O.U.P.	Oxford University Press
p.	piano
P.D.M.	publications of ancient music by the Deutsche Musikgesellschaft
P.S.M.	publications of the Société française de musicologie
Publ. Eitner	publications of the Gesellschaft für Musikforschung (R. Eitner)
R.B.	*Geschichte der Musik in Beispielen* (H. Riemann)

ABBREVIATIONS

R.M.	*Revue musicale*
R.M.I.	*Rivista musicale italiana*
R. Musicol.	*Revue de musicologie*
S.I.M.G.	*Sammelbände der Internationalen Musikgesell-schaft*
S.A.	*Musikgeschichtlicher Atlas* (Max Steinitzer)
S.B.	*Geschichte der Musik in Beispielen* (Schering)
tr.	translation and translated
Viertelj. f. MW.	*Vierteljahrsschrift für Musikwissenschaft*
W.B.	*Sing- und Spielmusik aus älterer Zeit* (Wolf)
Z. f. MW.	*Zeitschrift für Musikwissenschaft*

PART ONE

MONOPHONIC MUSIC
Until the Latter Part of the Middle Ages

I

ANTIQUITY

The Origins of Music [1]

IT would be instructive to know the beginnings of music, inasmuch as we could infer from these its actual nature. For this reason numerous philosophers, e.g., Spencer, Nietzsche, Hausegger, have evolved hypotheses concerning its origin.

In still more recent times, the quest for the origin has been pursued by a more reliable path through the investigation of the musical practices of primitive, savage, and half-savage peoples. The French were the first to show interest in primitive music, J. J. Rousseau in his *Dictionnaire de la musique*, 1767, and de Laborde in his *Essai sur la musique ancienne et moderne*, 1780. The English, a travelling people, next furthered this investigation, and most recently the Germans broadened and deepened the search under the title: the comparative science of music, or comparative musicology.

The Berlin philosopher, Karl Stumpf, wrote a book entitled: *Die Anfänge der Musik* (The Beginnings of Music), 1911, in which he recognizes the origins of music in the signals employed for communication. From these the independent art of music is supposed to have evolved. Musical practices of different tribes are so characteristic, that we are able to recognize racial relationship from them. Even in the case of peoples on a very low level of culture, the rhythmical sense is often highly developed. Among certain Negro tribes, the drummers, beating their instruments simultaneously, combine various rhythms in so skillful a manner, that they produce a rhythmical polyphony that is more complicated than anything our music can show in the way of rhythmical combinations. [2] Everywhere the develop-

[1] BIBLIOGRAPHY: Karl Bücher, *Arbeit und Rhythmus*. E. Reinicke, Leipzig, 6th edition, 1924.—R. Lach, *Studien zur Entwicklungsgeschichte der ornamentalen Melopöie*. C. F. Kahnt Nachfolger, Leipzig, 1913.—Karl Stumpf, *Die Anfänge der Musik*. J. A. Barth, Leipzig, 1911.—Stumpf and von Hornbostel, *Sammelbände für vergleichende MW*. Drei Masken Verlag, Munich, 1922 ff.—Rich Wallaschek, *Die Anfänge der Tonkunst*. Barth, Leipzig, 1903. Wallaschek's most important works on music were published in London: "On the Origin of Music," *Mind*, 1891; *Natural Selection and Music*, 1892; *Primitive Music*, Longmans, Green, 1893; and "On the Difference of Time and Rhythm in Music," *Mind*, 1895. The above-mentioned German work is an expansion of the last-named article.
[2] Cf. E.B., No. 1.

ment of the tonal sense and of melody reveals itself as dependent upon the instruments used. This is still true of the popular music of European peoples.[3]

Through investigations among primitive peoples, the political economist Karl Bücher likewise arrived at a significant theory concerning the origin of music, which he expounded in his book *Arbeit und Rhythmus* (Work and Rhythm). All uniform bodily work has the tendency to express itself rhythmically. Rhythm simplifies the work. Therefore it is employed even where it is not necessarily required. It is attained through song. Bücher points out in the case of the most diverse peoples numerous work songs for grinding, spinning, weaving, lace making, plaiting, lifting and bearing of burdens, rowing, etc. Among the most primitive, only the melody with its rhythm is fixed; the text is improvised. Where several unite their efforts in the same task, a leader improvises, and the others sing a definite, fixed refrain. Bücher sees therein the beginnings of dramatic art, in the rhythmical movements accompanying work, the incitement to all music and poetry. This view seems more plausible, when one recalls that the oldest drama presents a close union of poetry, music, and dance. In the early period of art, poetry and music were always combined, and supported by rhythmical, bodily movements. Specialization of the individual departments of art takes place only in the further course of development. It is also certain that the rhythm of the body and that of music stand in correlation to one another, and that rhythm is the original element of music. "In the beginning was the Rhythm," said Bülow. Richard Wagner again cemented the union in his music drama; children in their games never lost sight of it; and musical education, incited by Jaques Dalcroze, today again properly takes rhythm as its point of departure.[4]

[3] The influence which musical instruments exert upon song can still be observed in the songs of the Swiss mountaineers, in which occurs the so-called "alphorn-fa," the augmented fourth of the natural scale of wind instruments. The composer Ferd. Huber has preserved this in his song *Der Ustig* (The Ascent), which begins as follows:

Der Us‑tig wott cho. der Schnee zer‑geit scho‑

and Brahms uses it in his well-known C Major melody for horn in the finale of his first symphony, in C minor.

[4] Cf. G. Becking, *Der musikalische Rhythmus als Erkenntnisquelle.* B. Filser, Augsburg, 1928.

MUSIC IN ANCIENT CIVILIZATIONS [5]

Early civilizations laid the foundations of our modern music. In prehistoric days the Chinese, through acoustical measurements, determined the tonal system which we still use today. By progressing in fifths, they established the five-degree scale: G A C D E, a scale lacking both semitones and leading tones. Many songs are still based upon this pentatonic scale, even though the seven-degree scale has long been in use. Scotch folk song has clung to it, and even the Gregorian choral in part rests upon it. Our seven-degree diatonic scale was likewise established by the Chinese, about 1500 B.C. This nation possessed a highly developed musical theory, which, however, is more mystical than musical, occupying itself with musical symbols and the like. It survived in Pythagoras, in the Greek doctrine of the harmony of the spheres, and in the musical theory of the Middle Ages.

The Egyptians, according to the numerous representations which have been preserved, were passionately devoted to music. They possessed highly developed stringed instruments, harps, as well as lutes. In the latter, the entire musical gamut is produced by the shortening of the strings by means of a finger board, whereas the harp requires a special string for every note. The traverse flute was also known.

Musical records of the Egyptians have not been preserved. On the other hand, numerous compositions of the East Indians have been transmitted to us. It is apparent that the latter are very musical, but it is not certain that their melodies, agreeable to our European ears, date from prehistoric times. The old national instrument of India is the *vina*, a large, sonorous lute.

The Israelites were distinguished for their love of music. They were forbidden to make images, but, as if to compensate, they developed

[5] BIBLIOGRAPHY: Ambros, *Geschichte der Musik*, Vol. I (only the *first* edition is to be used).— Enc. Lav.: "Assyria," by Virolleaud; "China and Japan," by M. Courant; "Egypt," by U. Loret; "Greco-Roman," by Maurice Emmanuel; "Hebrews," by A. Cahen; "India," by J. Grosset. — H. Gressmann: *vide* text. — A. Z. Idelsohn, *Hebräisch-orientalischer Melodienschatz I. Gesänge der Jemenischen Juden.* B. & H., Leipzig, 1915.—L. Laloy, *La Musique chinoise*, Laurens, Paris, 1910.—The two German investigators O. Abraham and E. von Hornbostel have won distinction in the domain of comparative musicology through their researches into the present music of the Japanese, East Indians, etc. That the study of extra-European and ancient music can also produce practical results may be observed in numerous scores which reveal borrowings from Turkish, Arabian, and Indian music. Cf. Mozart, *Die Entführung aus dem Serail* (The Abduction from the Seraglio); Weber, *Oberon:* Saint Saëns, *Samson et Dalila* (Samson and Delilah); Grieg, *Peer Gynt;* Verdi, *Aida.* Specialists in the employment of exotic sounds are: Félicien David, Delius, and, in a certain sense, also Debussy.

poetry and music to the highest degree. Genesis iv. 21 mentions Jubal as "the father of all such as handle the harp and organs," or, as Luther translates "of fiddlers and pipers." The Psalms are genuine songs. Some of them contain directions as to the method of their musical rendition. The fourth, e.g., is to be performed with accompaniment of stringed instruments. In the service, the music was developed in a most elaborate manner. In II Chronicles v. 12–14 it is stated that under Solomon the Levites sang "having cymbals and psalteries and harps," while beside them there were "an hundred and twenty priests sounding with trumpets." Concerning David, it is even reported that he had four thousand singers praise the Lord with stringed instruments. However, concerning the actual nature of the music of the Israelites, we know nothing; what has been written and asserted concerning this, especially in pious books of the eighteenth century, is pure fiction. The sources are too vague to permit one to learn anything that is definite. This has been shown by H. Gressmann in his illuminating investigation *Musik und Musikinstrumente im Alten Testament* (Music and Musical Instruments in the Old Testament).[6] The author attempts, through comparisons with the known Greek music, to determine the probable facts.

Semitic music differs fundamentally from Indo-Germanic music in its predilection for chromatic intervals. This still manifests itself strongly at the present day among the Arabs who even distinguish quarter tones. To the European, this music appears whining and howling, while it affects the Arab in a sensual, even intoxicating manner. This may be the reason why in Assyrian and Babylonian representations music frequently appears in connection with feasts and orgies.

The Music of the Greeks [7]

Reports of the music used by the Greeks stand on a somewhat firmer basis. For the first time, some remnants of compositions have

[6] J. Ricker, Giessen, 1903.

[7] BIBLIOGRAPHY: H. Abert, "Die Antike," in Adler's *Handbuch.*—F. Bellermann, *Die Tonleitern und Musiknoten der Griechen.* Foerstner, Berlin, 1847.—Gevaert, *Histoire et théorie de la musique de l'antiquité.* 2 vols., Annoot-Braeckmann, Ghent, 1875 and 1881.—Gevaert and Vollgraff, *Les Problèmes musicaux d'Aristote.* 3 vols., Hoste, Ghent, 1903.—K. von Jan, *Musici scriptores graeci* (the appendix contains, both in original notation and in transcription, the melodies that have been preserved). 2 vols., Teubner, Leipzig, 1895–99.—R. von Kralik, *Altgriechische Musik, Theorie, Geschichte, und sämtliche Denkmäler* (Theory, History, and Complete Monuments). Roth, Stuttgart, 1903 (Popular.)—Louis Laloy, *Aristoxène de Tarente et la musique de l'antiquité.* Société française d'imprimerie et de librairie, Paris, 1904.—H. S. Macran, *The Harmonics of Aristoxenus.* Clarendon Press,

been preserved in notation. Furthermore, we are reliably informed concerning their theory. The Greeks possessed a tonal system based on an acoustical foundation, a system of notation, and a special musical esthetics. The last-named is still of value, not because of its specific content, but because of its suggestiveness and example.

In their tonal system the Greeks distinguished between three families, or genera, the diatonic, the chromatic, and the enharmonic. The diatonic system virtually corresponds to that of the present day; in the chromatic, as in our present system, semitones prevail; completely different from the present conception is the enharmonic. Characteristic of this system are the quarter tones; it exhibits Oriental-Semitic influence.

The diatonic scale divides the octave into whole tones and semitones, as in the modern system in C major. On the other hand, while we form only one additional independent scale beside the major, namely, the minor, and limit ourselves to transposing these two types, the Greeks formed a new scale or tonal system on every tone of our C major scale. The most important, named according to the Greek tribes, were: Dorian: e f g a b c d e; Phrygian: d e f g a b c d; Lydian: c d e f g a b c; Mixolydian: b c d e f g a b. The scales based on the remaining tones were viewed as derived from the principal scales: A–a, Hypodorian; G–g, Hypophrygian; F–f, Hypolydian.

The wealth of scales is much greater than in the modern system; but one must note that the old scales did not serve as foundations for harmony, as do our present ones, but that they merely determined the limits of the melody. They form a framework within which the melodies move. The Greeks did not possess harmony in the modern sense of the word. What has been written about Greek "harmony" belongs to the realm of fable. The word "harmony" which frequently occurs in the Greek writers, signifies for them "melody," i.e., change of degree in rhythmic order. The sounding together, or accord, of two tones the Greeks designated by the term "symphony."

Supported by acoustical investigations they developed a theory of consonances according to which they designated the octave, the fifth, and the fourth as consonances; the third and the sixth, on the other

Oxford, 1902.—D. B. Monro, *Modes of Ancient Greek Music.* Clarendon Press, 1894.— Théod. Reinach, "La Musique des Hymnes des Delphes" in *Bulletin de correspondance hellénique.* Thorin et Fils, Paris, 1893–96; by the same author, *La Musique grecque,* Payot, Paris, 1926.—H. Riemann, *Handbuch der Musikgeschichte,* Vol. I.—C. F. Abdy Williams, *The Aristoxenian Theory of Musical Rhythm.* Cambridge University Press, 1911.

hand, they considered as dissonances. This latter view became disastrous for a subsequent era. When polyphony was developed in the Middle Ages, composers hesitated to apply thirds and sixths, because the teachings of the Greeks still enjoyed universal authority, and as a result of this the development of polyphonic music was checked and restrained for centuries. The practice of the composers of the sixteenth century of omitting the third in the final chord is based upon the authority of the Greeks, according to which it was not allowable to conclude with a dissonance. A last remnant of the old teaching survived in instruction books in harmony, which until recently were in general use, in the designation of thirds and sixths as "imperfect" consonances, as contrasted with the "perfect" ones, the octave, the fifth, and the fourth.

Greek musical notation employed the letters of the Greek alphabet for the designation of the tones. By this means it becomes completely clear and precise, but it has the disadvantage of not being perspicuous to the eye, and was therefore incapable of being further developed. The beginnings of our musical notation first appear in the Middle Ages.

Greek music was vocal in its nature. It was homophonic, and the tone was completely subservient to the poetry. Its chief function was always merely to support and vivify the poetic text through close union with the melodic and rhythmic nuances of the language itself. The dependence was so great that the rhythm of the melody was completely subject to the meter of the verse; the three-part time arose from, and was filled out with, iambuses and trochees; the four-part time, with spondees, anapaests and dactyls; the five-part time, with the paeon. That meant that a short syllable signified one beat, a long syllable, two beats; the iambus, accordingly, consisting of a short and a long beat, signified three-part time.

There was in fact no poetry without music, and no music without poetry. Poet and composer were always united in one person. If, occasionally, instrumental music occurred, it was program music; independent instrumental music, in the modern sense, the imaginative and plastically sensing Greeks did not know. In the year 586 B.C. the aulos player, Sakadas, was victorious in the Pythian games at Delphi with a composition (*nomos*), which represented the battle between Apollo and the dragon; and some two hundred years later, Timotheus of Miletus (417–357 B.C.) represented a storm at sea in his composition *Nautilos*.

Even in those days scoffers were not wanting; the parasite Dorion surmised that he had experienced in many a bubbling cooking pot more violent storms than the one in the *Nautilos* of Timotheus.

As a rule the singing was accompanied by instruments. These did not always play along in unison, but other tones which lay above, not below, the melody were chosen according to rules, definite indeed, but strange and incomprehensible to us. However, this procedure did not result in what we today should call a harmonic accompaniment. In the first place, the music was only two-voiced; furthermore, the instrumental tones purposed only the accentuation and amplification of the rhythm. This is always placed in the foreground by the theoreticians as by far the most important element; they treat the tonal element, the *melos*, as much more subsidiary.

The accompaniment was played either on a stringed or a wind instrument. The former, the lyre (with bellied sounding box) or the cithara (with flat sounding box) had, in the classical period, only seven strings; at a later time, eleven at the most, and no finger board. Its musical effect, therefore, must have been quite primitive. Owing to its restrained tone it was the instrument of the pure Apollonian cultus. The wind instrument, the aulos, was a kind of shawm, belonging to the family of reed instruments, related in sound to the modern oboe, sharp and penetrating. Therefore it was considered as stirring, adapted to the expression of passion, and was the instrument of the cult of Dionysus.

The sharp distinction in the character of the instruments leads to the subject of esthetics, which consisted primarily in the so-called doctrine of the ethos. It was established by the Pythagoreans, was further developed by Plato and Aristotle, and later through the schools of the Peripatetics and the Stoics. The doctrine of the ethos rests upon the view, held by all the above-named philosophers, that the external movements, capable of being translated into hearing, stand in immediate relationship to the movements of the soul; upon the belief that certain tonal successions are capable of calling forth quite definite emotions of the soul. If this doctrine is true—and the Greek philosophers were fully persuaded of its truth—music has great ethical influence, and is therefore also important in the instruction of youth. In order to verify the good or bad effect of each tone, the Greeks organized rigorous experiments. This was possible only because of the comparative simplicity of Greek music; but even if the principle no longer appears capable of being carried through in this manner at the present day, the principle in itself is nevertheless true, and the Greek doctrine of the ethos still has its great value as a prototype for our time. In spite of a Hanslick, for whom music was only an arabesque-like play of tones, or a kaleidoscope,[8] it still produces its psychological effects, and the recognition of this should be the chief end of all music instruction. In its lofty conception of the art, the music teaching of antiquity stands high above the modern, which expends and dissipates itself almost entirely in technical instruction. The eighteenth century had something in common with the antique doctrine of the ethos in its so-called doctrine of the affections (*Affekten-lehre*) which discussed the expression of the emotions. The French school of *ideologues* also treats of the expression of the emotions among its favorite themes.[9] Later, however, this portion of the doctrine of the Greeks was entirely forgotten. H. Kretzschmar has evoked a revival in his "Anregungen zur Förderung musikalischer Hermeneutik" in the *Jahrbuch der Musikbibliothek Peters*, 1902.

The doctrine of the ethos, moreover, even among the Greeks, was not simple. The ethos of a song was dependent upon manifold circumstances. Of greatest importance was always the rhythm; then followed the tonality, the accompaniment, etc. With regard to the Dorian tonality, the Greeks believed that it steeled the character, and taught courage in danger, and resignation in misfortune; the Phrygian, on the other hand, was viewed, like the aulos accompaniment, as exciting, inspiring. It was the tonality of the dithyramb. Greater detail may be found in the delightful book of H. Abert, *Die Lehre vom Ethos in der griechischen Musik* (The Doctrine of the Ethos in Greek Music), 1899.

---

[8] *Vom Musikalisch-Schönen; ein Beitrag zur Revision der Ästhetik der Tonkunst.* R. Weigel, Leipzig, 1854 (15th ed., B. & H., Leipzig, 1922); Eng. tr., *The Beautiful in Music*, by Gustav Cohen. Novello & Co. Ltd., London, 1891.

[9] Stendhal, the most accessible popularizer of that school, declares that "music awaits its Lavoisier. That man of genius will make experiments on the human heart and on the organ of hearing as well . . . After this he will deduce the rules of music from his experiments. In his work, under the word 'anger,' he will present to us the twenty songs which seem to him best to express the sentiment of anger; he will do the same with regard to jealousy, happy love, the torments of absence . . . Will these airs be more effective with or without accompaniment? To what degree can one complicate their accompaniments? All these great questions, resolved *by experiments*, will finally establish a true theory of music, based on the nature of the human heart in Europe and on the uses of the ear." (*Vie de Rossini*, Boulland et cie., Paris, 1824; Germ. tr. by A. Wendt, L. Voss, Leipzig, 1824, reprinted 1892; Eng. tr. by H. S. Edwards, *Life of Rossini*, Hurst & Blackett, London, 1869; condensed in "Great Musicians," 1881; new French ed. by H. Prunières, Calmann-Lévy, Paris, 1892.)

Of Greek compositions only some ten have survived, and a number of these are fragmentary. They are: 1. The first Pythian victory ode of Pindar, 478 B.C.; 2. Chorus from the *Orestes* of Eurypides (mutilated), 408 B.C.; 3. Two Delphic Apollo hymns, c. 138 and c. 128 B.C., engraved in the wall of the Treasure-House of the Athenians at Delphi; 4. Epitaph of Seikilos of Tralles in Asia Minor, first century A.D.; 5. Three hymns of Mesomedes of Crete (To the Muse, To Helios, To Nemesis), c. 130 A.D.; 6. Vocal fragments from Contrapollinopolis, c. 160 A.D.[10]

The most valuable piece is the great Delphic Apollo Hymn. Even though only preserved in fragmentary condition, it nevertheless shows masterful adaptation of the word to the tone, and lofty, majestic flight. Almost equally significant, but differing in its style, is the epitaph which Seikilos dedicated to his wife Euterpe, and had chiseled, with the notes, upon her tombstone. The Greeks distinguished between recitative and melodic song. The only example of the latter kind which has been preserved is this epitaph, a short, serious song with symmetrical melody. It sounds strange to us, but after listening to it sympathetically, we seem to feel something of what it wishes to express.[11]

The arrangements for several voices of the Greek musical fragments which have been presented numerous times are to be rejected as humbug. The old songs must be sung by a single voice, if one really wishes to approach their true nature. To be sure, the scanty remnants are unable to convey to us a genuine idea of the antique music. One may still cherish the hope, that a happy discovery will yet open to us a more thorough knowledge.

The Romans took their music from the Greeks. They brought about the separation of poetry and music. We no longer hear that the poems of the Roman poets were sung, as were poems, at least in classical times, among the Greeks. The high esteem which music enjoyed among the Hellenes, it lost among the Romans. That is sufficiently attested by the

[10] The treasury of ancient music was recently enriched through the discovery of a Christian hymn in Greek notation from the third century, No. 1786 of the *Oxyrhynchus papyri*, Part XV, edited by B. P. Grenfell and A. S. Hunt, transcribed by H. Stuart Jones. Quaritch, Ltd.; Kegan Paul, Trench, Trubner & Co., Ltd., London, 1922. See also: H. Abert, "Ein neu entdeckter frühchristlicher Hymnus," in Z. f. MW., IV, 1922, pp. 524–29. All the fragments of Greek music that have been preserved may be found in the book of Th. Reinach already mentioned. For the beginning of Pindar's first Pythian victory ode, see also E.B., No. 2.
[11] S.B., No. 1.

fact that its cultivation was left to the slaves. It was frequently employed for the enhancing of sensual pleasure; monster performances were instituted; an extravagant virtuosity was developed. All these manifestations of an unhealthy musical mania are familiar from the life history of the emperor Nero.

II

THE CHRISTIAN ERA

Beginnings of Church Music.—Christianity brought with it a spiritualization which was necessarily advantageous to the development of music, which indeed first loosed its wings and set it forth upon its lofty flight. We know from the Gospels and the Apostolic Epistles that the Christians sang in their assemblies from the very beginning (cf. the hymn of praise at the Last Supper before the journey to Gethsemane). The Jewish writer Philo of Alexandria and the Roman Pliny (in his letter to Trajan in which he defends the Christians) also testify that the first Christians sang in their convocations. Likewise, various church fathers speak of the singing of Psalms and hymns, for example, Clement of Alexandria, Tertullian, Basil the Great, Gregory of Nyssa. Records of such songs have not been preserved. For the first four centuries we are solely dependent upon literary records. These have been compiled most accurately by Forkel in his *History of Music* (Vol. II, 1801).

Psalter and Psalmody the Christians took over from the Jews, and, according to their example, the canonical hour, especially its oldest form, the vigil, received the emphasis at first. The sacrifice of the Mass was elevated to its central position only at a later period. Alongside the Psalms and biblical canticles, the Christians, quite early, placed newly created hymns. When the Christian Church became victorious, and after it had struggled through to freedom, from the year 323 on, its jubilation resounded in the Alleluia song. The monastic orders in Syria and Egypt won for themselves the honor of having first developed a musical liturgical ritual.

In the Occident, an important protagonist of church music arose in Ambrose, Bishop of Milan (374–97). The facts regarding his services are well established, even though they have been exaggerated in legendary manner. This much is certain, that he introduced a liturgy into his church according to Oriental model, i.e., he prescribed the music to be used in

---

[1] BIBLIOGRAPHY: N. Forkel, *Allgemeine Geschichte der Musik* (to the end of the Middle Ages). 2 vols., Schwickert, Leipzig, 1788, 1801. Founded on Hawkins, Burney, and Marpurg.—A. Machabey, *Histoire et évolution des formules musicales du Ier au XVe siècle.* Payot, Paris, 1928.

connection with the regularly recurring festivals of the church year. Innovations comprised the two-choir, antiphonal singing and hymns. Ambrose, himself, is mentioned as author and composer of a large number of hymns, including: *Aeterne rerum conditor, Deus creator omnium, Jam surgit hora tertia, Intende qui regis Israel*. The *Te Deum* is called the Ambrosian Hymn of Praise, although, to be sure, recent investigation denies to Ambrose the authorship of just this particular song, assigning it to Nicetas, Bishop of Remesiana in Asia Minor. A pretty legend recounts the origin of the *Te Deum* as follows: At the baptism of St. Augustine, Ambrose is reported to have begun singing: "Te Deum laudamus," to which Augustine replied: "Te Dominum confitemur," whereupon Ambrose continued: "Te aeternum patrem omnis terra veneratur," and so forth, through the entire hymn. Even if this story has sprung from pious imagination, we nevertheless know definitely that Augustine was an admirer of the Ambrosian song, of which he speaks with enthusiasm in his *Confessions* (ix. 6. 14).

Gregorian Chant.[2]—At the end of the sixth century the Occidental Christian song was reformed by Pope Gregory the Great (Bishop of Rome, 590–604). The impetus to this movement was given in the form of complaints of abuses, of too great artifice, of sentimentality, and especially

[2] BIBLIOGRAPHY: Maurice Emmanuel, *Traité de l'accompagnement modal des Psaumes.* Janin, Lyon, 1913.—A. Gastoué, *Cours théorique et pratique de plaint chant romain grégorien.* Bureau d'édition de la Schola cantorum, Paris, 1901–4; 1917; by the same author, *L'Art grégorien.* Alcan, Paris, 1911; and *Le Graduel et l'Antiphonaire romains.* Janin, Lyon, 1913.—P. Dominicus Johner, *Neue Schule des gregorianischen Gesanges.* Pustet, Regensburg, 1906; Eng. tr. by H. S. Butterfield, Pustet, Regensburg & N. Y., 1906; 3d ed., 1925; by the same author, *Der gregorianische Choral.* J. Engelhorns Nachfolger, Stuttgart, 1924.—Kienle, *Choralschule. Ein Handbuch zur Erlernung des Choralgesanges.* 3d ed., Herder, Freiburg i/Br., 1899.—L. Lambillotte, *Antiphonaire de Saint Grégoire,* 1851. (Facsimile edition of the St. Gall antiphonary.) Greuse, Brussels, 1851.—Dom A. Mocquereau, *Le Nombre musicale grégorien.* 2 vols., Société de Saint Jean l'Evangeliste, Desclée et cie., imprimeurs, Rome and Tournay, 1908–27; Eng. tr. by Aileen Tone, *A Study of Gregorian Musical Rhythm,* Vol. I, Part 1. Desclée et cie., Tournai, 1932.—*Paléographie musicale,* the collection founded by Dom A. Mocquereau, continued by the Benedictines of Solesmes: 1st series, reproduction of MSS in facsimile, with introductions, 13 vols. actually published; 2d series, documentary, 2 vols. have appeared. Imprimerie St. Pierre, Solesmes, 1889–1900.—Dom J. Pothier, *Les Mélodies grégoriennes d'après la tradition.* Imprimerie liturgique de Saint Jean l'Evangeliste, Desclée, Lefebvre et cie., Tournay, 1880.—Peter Wagner, *Einführung in die gregorianischen Melodien.* Veith, Fribourg (Switzerland), 1895; 2d ed., Part 1, 1901–05; also B. & H., Leipzig, 1911–21; 3d ed., as *Ursprung und Entwicklung der liturgischen Gesangsformen bis zum Ausgange des Mittelalters.* B. & H., Leipzig, 1911; French tr. by the Abbé Bour, *Origine et développement du chant liturgique.* Desclée, Lefebvre, et cie., Tournay, 1904; Eng. tr. of the 2d ed., Part I, by Agnes Orme and E. G. P. Wyatt, *Introduction to the Gregorian Melodies: A Handbook of Plainsong.* Plainsong and Medieval Society London, 1901; Part 2, *Neumenkunde.* O. Gschwend, Fribourg (Switzerland, 1905,

of divergencies in different localities. Gregory collected and sifted the extant treasure of melodies, made alterations, created new tunes, and determined precisely in what manner and at what place in the service the music was to be rendered. Thus he laid the foundation for a strictly regulated, diversified liturgy. Arranged according to the church year, the chants were recorded in the so-called antiphonary which was laid upon the altar of St. Peter, and fastened to it with a golden chain. For all time it was to serve the music of the Roman Church, as irrevocable norm and foundation.

This intention has been fulfilled to the present day in a magnificent and amazing manner. The Gregorian chant still serves the church as the musical foundation upon which everything rests, as the center about which everything turns. The faithful still find it the purest and most exalted means for the expression of religious feeling. And still further, it has become the foundation of all European music in general. It is the trunk from which branched forth the entire new development, a root from which music ever and again draws new nourishment.

The Gregorian chant served polyphonic music as a support by which the latter learned to walk in its slow development through a lengthy period of childhood. In the great choral period it nourished the imagination of composers with its inexhaustible wealth of melody. When Luther set about his work of reform he strove eagerly to preserve it in his church as the valuable parent stock. The Anglican High Church has also diligently preserved it. In J. S. Bach its influence manifests itself freely. The Credo of his *Mass in B Minor*, for example, is built upon a Gregorian intonation. Even the Reformed Churches, still sing a Gregorian chant, without knowing it, namely, a Gloria melody, in the hymn *Allein Gott in der Höh' sei Ehr'* (All Glory Be to God on High). The famous concluding fugue in Mozart's *Jupiter Symphony* rests on a Gregorian motif. Berlioz made the Dies irae the center of the finale of his *Symphonie fantastique*. Saint Saëns's *Symphony in C Minor* (with organ) received inspiration from the Gregorian chant. Vincent d'Indy (2d quartet, *Légende de saint Christophe*, etc.) and his school have used Gregorian themes extensively. Ottorino Respighi has written a *Concerto gregoriano* for

2d ed., 1912; Part 3, *Gregorianische Formenlehre, eine choralische Stilkunde*, B. & H., Leipzig, 1921; by the same author, *Elemente des gregorianischen Gesangs*. F. Pustet, Regensburg, Rome, New York, and Cincinnati, 1909; 2d ed., 1917; by the same author, *Einführung in die katholische Kirchenmusik*. L. Schwann, Düsseldorf, 1919.—For examples of Gregorian music cf. E.B., Nos. 3–4; and W.B., Nos. 1–2; also S.B., below.

violin and orchestra, 1921. In brief, throughout the centuries one finds everywhere the fertile influence of the Gregorian choral. It would be a rewarding task to pursue this influence and to sketch it in broad outlines; the foregoing examples will at least serve to call attention to it.

The Gregorian chant is the most perfect efflorescence of monophonic song, its classical perfection. Its excellence springs from the beauty, the abundance, and diversity of its melody. A part of its individuality and strength also lies in its rhythm. But as this is treated freely in the delivery, it is difficult to isolate it and to determine its value. On the other hand, one at once recognizes the finely graduated relations of the melodic phrases.

In German, the Gregorian chant, like the Protestant hymn tune, bears the name choral. In reality, however, the chant differs widely from the hymn, and one should not confuse the two things bearing the same name. The Gregorian chorales are not hymn tunes, but are recitatives, or at least songs which are closely related to the modern recitative.

The name choral comes from the *chorus* of singers whose function it is to execute the chant, and this chorus, or choir, was stationed in church in the place to which it later gave its name. The laity were originally not excluded from participating in the service. The congregation sang the Kyrie, in some localities also the Sanctus and the Agnus Dei. Gradually, however, the rendition became exclusively the function of the priests and of the choir trained in special schools for singers. The French call the Gregorian chant "plain chant," the English, "plain song," from the Latin *cantus planus*, which designation arose as contrast to the later *cantus figuralis*, or the so-called *musica mensurata*. The German Catholics today speak briefly of the "choral."

Its language is Latin. The melodies are not divided into measures, but the delivery is in a free recitative manner, such as an orator would use in declaiming Latin prose. The majority of the texts, too, are prose, taken from the Bible; the hymns, which Ambrose had placed in the foreground, while not altogether lacking, assume a minor rôle.

The older teachers of the Gregorian chant divided the melodies, with regard to their delivery, into two categories, the *accentus* and the *concentus*. Later teachers distinguish between "syllabic" and "melodic" songs. In the first category the executant recites on one note, and only the conclusions are marked by slight melodic variations, as is shown on page 17.

To this category belong the readings from the Epistles and the Gos-

pels, the Psalmody, the Orations (prayer-like appeals), the Versicles; the *Pater Noster* also belongs to the liturgical recitatives which are chiefly syllabic. Despite its simplicity, this clearly reveals the unusual melodic power of the Gregorian chant. Within the narrow compass of only four notes, an astounding diversity of melody is revealed which prevents all feeling of monotony. Only once, and that doubtless not without intention, the narrow circle of the four notes is broken through, in the case of the petition "And lead us not into temptation," whereby this petition receives a deeply moving emphasis:

To the category of the *concentus,* or in other words, to the melodic songs, belong the antiphons and the hymns, especially also the chief songs of the Mass. Among these, again, those are most highly developed which are not the same in every Mass (as are the Kyrie, Gloria,[3] Credo, Sanctus,[4] Benedictus, and Agnus Dei), but which change according to the festival season, as the Gradual,[5] the Alleluia, and Offertory melodies. The following Alleluia from the Mass for the Pontifical Martyrs may serve as an example. This reveals not only that inspired flight of melody, which characterizes these songs but even thus early exhibits the tripartite form A B A, the threefold division which seems to be an original element of music, and which occurs again and again in its later development. Examples are the *da capo aria* of the eighteenth century; the alternation between minuet and trio; their successor, the scherzo; the modern military march; numerous homophonic songs and many small instrumental pieces (Schubert, Chopin); and in a profounder manner, also the sonata form:

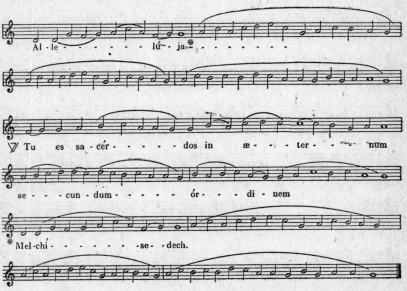

The chant of Gregory still lives, although his antiphonary has been lost. It was formerly thought that we still possess a copy of this in a manuscript of the monastery library in St. Gall, but it has become evident that the St. Gall antiphonary dates from a much later time. How-

---

[3] Cf. S.B., No. 2, a.   [4] *Loc. cit.,* No. 2, a.   [5] *Loc. cit.,* No. 2, b.

ever, the Gregorian melodies have been handed down since the ninth century in manuscripts which are preserved in the great ecclesiastical and state libraries of Europe. As musical notation, they employ the so-called "neumes." Unpractical as these originally were, they nevertheless represented progress when compared with the Greek alphabetical notation, in so far as they endeavor to present a clear picture of the inflections of the melody, and therefore contain within themselves the possibility of development. While nothing corresponding to our complicated music could ever have evolved from the Greek notation, our modern system did develop from the neumes, although after toilsome growth through a period of centuries.

The word "neume" is derived from the Greek νεῦμα, meaning a "nod" or "sign." This kind of sign is supposed to have originated in the Greek *chironomy*, that art, still practiced in the Middle Ages, according to which the precentor, through motions of the hand, indicated to the others the rising or falling of the melody. From this arose the accents of the written word, as the French still employ them, and the tonal signs, the neumes, related to these accents, and originally like them in appearance. The dots and small strokes, were, of course, able to give to the singer only an approximate hint as to the course of the melody. The chief indication had to be imparted through oral tradition, and the notational signs could merely serve to give external support to the memory.

The situation became different when it occurred to a scribe to draw a line and by this means to fixate a tone. It was but a small step from the first to the second line, and thus the way was opened to our present system which is capable of fixating our many-voiced complicated music. It has been correctly said that one could not sufficiently praise the monk who drew the first line, if his name were known.

The lines first appear in Italian manuscripts of the eleventh century. A red line was first drawn to designate the tone F, then a second, a yellow line, for the tone C. From these there developed later, from the twelfth century on, the modern F and C clefs, the G clef being added later. A special service to the further development of the musical notation was rendered by the famous theorist, Guido of Arezzo. In the year 1026 he presented to Pope John XIX his new doctrine, according to which a third line was added for the tone A.

The melodies of the Gregorian chant are built upon the tonal system of the ecclesiastical modes, as they are called today. Four modes form the basis of the whole. Originally only these four were established; at a later time four more were added. The first were called the chief, or *authentic* modes, the latter the derived, or *plagal* ones. The following table will give an insight into their range and designation:

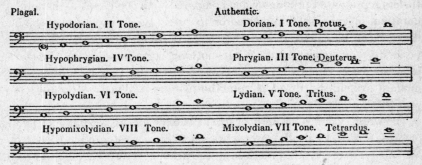

Originally, the four chief modes were designated as *protos, deuteros, tritos,* and *tetrardos* (first, second, third, and fourth tones). Later, the chief and subordinate modes were numbered consecutively in such manner that the authentic modes received the numbers 1, 3, 5, and 7, the plagal, 2, 4, 6, and 8. In the Roman choral books of today every melody still bears a Roman numeral which indicates its tonality. One recognizes this by the concluding tone, though the authentic and the corresponding plagal modes have the same "final," the lowest tone of the chief mode: i.e., Dorian and Hypo-Dorian, D; Phrygian and Hypo-Phrygian, E; Lydian and Hypo-Lydian, F; Mixolydian and Hypo-Mixolydian, G.

It is striking that no principal mode is built upon the two tones, C and A, from which the modern tonal system takes its departure. The tonality on A occurs in quite isolated instances (Psalm 114: In exitu Israel) and is therefore designated as *tonus peregrinus.* The secular musicians are reported to have had, even at an early time, a special predilection for the tonality on C. But for this very reason it was looked at askance by the ecclesiastical teachers and designated as *tonus lascivus.* The itinerant musicians were more progressive than the theorists.

It was the humanist Glarean, who, in his *Dodekachordon,* which appeared in Basel in the year 1547, first adopted the modes on A and on C as chief tones in his system, thereby rounding it off and completing it. He called the mode on A, Aeolian; that on C, Ionian.

The Gregorian chant was originally intended for male voices, according to the ancient rule of the Church: *Mulier taceat in ecclesia*, to which the pope still adheres in principle. On glancing over the table given above, one perceives that the ancient system corresponds to the range of the male voices, from A to g'. The low G was subsequently added to these fourteen tones, and was designated with the Greek letter Γ (gamma); hence, still, the designation of the scale by the French as a *gamme*.

If one wishes to gain a clear conception of the character of the ecclesiastical modes, one must especially remember that they do not serve, as does our tonal system, as a foundation for the harmony, but merely for the melody. They are schemata, patterns, within which the monophonic songs move. The semitones occur at different places in the different modes; the cadences differ from one another, and it is evident that the melodies will assume a somewhat different character according to their tonality. In order to impress upon the pupils the characteristics of each individual mode, model melodies for each tonality were invented in the Middle Ages, and the so-called *tonarii* presented compilations of songs arranged according to tonalities.

The Gregorian choral is fundamentally diatonic; chromatic alterations, which play so prominent a part in modern music, do not occur, with one single exception: the B is often changed to B♭, e.g., in the Lydian and the Dorian tonalities. In the former, the augmented fourth from F to B

was felt to be difficult for the singer, and the lowering of the B must readily have suggested itself. Even today the leap from F to B is excluded from a good vocal style and is employed only for characterization. Every friend of music knows it from the "Song of the Dragon" in R. Wagner's *Siegfried*. One can readily understand that in the Middle Ages, when especial attention was paid to the vocal quality of music, the attempt was made to avoid this interval by lowering the B to B♭. The interval is commonly known as the *Tritonus*, i.e., the interval consisting of three whole tones. Its inversion, the so-called *Quinta falsa*, or diminished fifth, was also forbidden in pure ecclesiastical music.

The application of the letters to the notes arose at the time of the origin of the plagal modes. The lowest note of the system, i.e., the lowest note of the Hypo-Dorian tonality, was designated as A, the successive ones as B, C, D, etc. When they began to lower the B, they distinguished between B *quadratum*, ♮ (whence our natural sign), and B *rotundum*, ♭. Later, in German usage, only the latter retained the designation B, while the B *quadratum* was called H. Consequently, in German-speaking countries one finds an unpractical transposition of the letters of the alphabet. After children have with difficulty learned in school A, B, C, they must unlearn this order in their music-lesson and substitute A, H, C. In French, the B *quadratum* has been contracted into *bécarre*, meaning "natural," and the B *molle*, as the French called the B *rotundum*, into *bémol*, meaning "flat."

The Spread and Further Development of the Gregorian Chant.[6]—Not all of that which we today designate as Gregorian choral goes back to its founder; a considerable element has developed through the course of several centuries, and in part outside of Rome. With the extension of the Roman Church its chant also spread abroad, at first especially to Britain. The monasteries of Ireland contributed significantly to its further development. In France and in Germany it was finally naturalized through Charlemagne, who, striving after unity in his great kingdom, for political reasons, sought to use the ecclesiastical chant also as a unifying bond. Among the bishops who supported him firmly in his undertaking, Haiton of Basel (814–827) is especially mentioned.

The monasteries of Metz and St. Gall, where famous schools arose, became chief centers for the cultivation of the Gregorian choral. To be sure, our ancestors originally seemed to have shown little talent for the Roman chant. John Diaconus, the biographer of Gregory the Great, is of the opinion that the Gauls and the Alemanni were hindered from grasping this in its purity by their native uncouthness, and furthermore insists that they always added some elements from their own songs. Their raucous voices, says he, bellowing like thunder, were incapable of any gentle modulation, because their hoarse throats, addicted to

[1] BIBLIOGRAPHY: H. Abert, *Die Musikanschauung des Mittelalters.* Niemeyer, Halle, 1905.—E. de Coussemaker, *Scriptores de musica medii aevi.* 4 vols. Durand, Paris, 1864–76; photographic reprint, Durand, Paris, 1908; facsimile reprint by Bolletino bibliografico musicale, Milan, 1931.—Martin Gerbert, *De cantu et musica sacra.* Typis San Blasianis, 1774; by the same author, *Scriptores ecclesiastici de musica sacra.* 3 vols., Typis San Blasianis, 1784; facsimile reprint by Bolletino bibliografico musicale, Milan, 1931.—J. Handschin, "Über Estampie und Sequenz," Z. f. MW., 1929–30.—N. Rousseau, *L'école grégorienne de Solesmes.* Desclée et cie., Tournay and Rome, 1910.—P. Anselm Schubiger, *Die Sängerschule St. Gallens vom 8. bis 12. Jahrhundert.* Benziger, Einsiedeln, 1858.—Ferd. Wolf, *Über die Lais, Sequenzen und Leiche.* C. F. Winter, Heidelberg, 1841.

drink, did not produce those nuances which a more gentle melody demands; their repellent voices could only produce tones that were similar to the rumbling of a truck rolling down from the heights, and instead of moving their hearers, filled their hearts with abhorrence.

The situation cannot have been quite so bad, otherwise Metz and St. Gall would not have blossomed forth into brilliant centers for the Gregorian chant. Other monasteries followed: Reichenau, Fulda, Würzburg, Eichstätt. At the cathedral and parochial schools the chant was cultivated no less diligently, e.g., in Mainz, Aachen, Cologne, Trier, and Worms. In France, Saint Denis, the Abbey Saint Martial in Limoges, Soissons, Rheims, and Paris became centers for its cultivation.

St. Gall won especial importance because a great number of poets and composers labored here, and because new species of chant here found acceptance. A symbolical legend relates the origin of the school of St. Gall as follows: At the request of Charlemagne, the Pope sent to Metz two singers, Petrus and Romanus, with an authentic copy of the antiphonary. They journeyed across the Stelvio, but owing to the hardships of the journey, Romanus was taken ill. He was kindly received and well attended by the monks of St. Gall. In gratitude for this he remained there and allowed Petrus to continue the journey to Metz alone. In this manner the monastery is reported to have come into the possession of a copy of the Roman antiphonary, and through this the foundation was supposed to have been laid for the development of the song-school of St. Gall. Even though some of the account of its history given by Ekkehard may be legendary, poetic embellishment, it is nevertheless certain that the school blossomed forth greatly, and that its renown shone through the centuries. Indeed the most ancient and most precious manuscripts of the Gregorian chant since the ninth century are preserved at the Abbey of St. Gall.[7] As distinguished poets and composers of melodies, there labored there the well-known monks Iso, Marcellus, the two Notkers, the Ekkehards, and Tuotilo, all names familiar from Scheffel's romance *Ekkehard*.

The most distinguished were Notker Balbulus and Tuotilo, to both of whom is ascribed the introduction of new types of song. They were contemporaries, and personify one of the most distinguished periods of

[7] Rombaut van Doren contests the extent of the influence of St. Gall in his work: *Étude sur l'influence musicale de l'abbaye de Saint-Gall* (8th to 11th century). Uystpruyst, Louvain. 1925.

the monastery, the second half of the ninth century. Notker Balbulus died in 912, Tuotilo c. 915.

The name of Notker Balbulus is associated with the introduction of the "sequence," or "prose." This originated in the Oriental Church, but Notker, through his creations, won for it recognition in the Occident. It came into being in a strange manner. It had become customary in connection with the Alleluia to indulge in a so-called *Jubilus* on the final syllable "*a*," i.e., to allow the jubilation to flow forth in a broad coloratura or melisma. In order that one might the better retain in memory the long wordless melodies which rolled along on the syllable "*a*," Notker supplied words for them. Thus he himself explained the origin of his sequences on presenting a collection of them to a friend of the monastery, Luitwart of Vercelli, the chancellor of Charles the Fat.[8] The words, though not in measured verse form, nevertheless, at times approach this, and at all events have a religious-poetic content. Notker himself appears not always to have used existing *jubilus* melodies, but sometimes composed new ones. Evidence of this is found in the fact that in one of his sequences, according to his own assertion, he imitated the rolling of a mill wheel, and thus even at this period indulged in tone painting. And even if it should be true that this remark was merely attributed to him, and that he did not make it, it is nevertheless significant, in so far as it shows that the Middle Ages were thoroughly familiar with the connection between music and the tones and noises of the external world, and reproduced these, even in ecclesiastical compositions.[9]

In the course of its development, the sequence, in the hands of Notker's successors, reveals more and more an approach to the musical form of the hymn. Soon rhymes and rhythmic verse forms were introduced.[10] Many sequences arose during the course of the centuries for the Church festivals of different localities, and they soon became the most popular of all the songs of the Gregorian choral. Among the creators of sequences, Adam of St. Victor, who labored in Paris in the twelfth century, was one of the most fertile and most famous. However, after the Council of Trent, Pope Pius V excluded from the official Church song all of the great number that had been gradually introduced into

[8] Credit for this innovation of the application of words to the *jubilus* melodies doubtless belongs to the monks of the Abbey of Jumièges in Normandy. One of their antiphonaries was carried to Notker after the sack of Jumièges by the Normans in 851.
[9] A sequence by Notker will be found in S.B., No. 4; cf. also, E.B., No. 5.
[10] Cf. S.B., No. 5.

the Church except five which still hold their place in the liturgy. At Easter is sung *Victimae Paschali laudes*, by Wipo, Chaplain at the court of Conrad II and Henry III (eleventh century); [11] at Whitsuntide *Veni sancte spiritus*, [12] ascribed to Pope Innocent III (d. 1216); at Corpus Christi, *Lauda Sion Salvatorem* by Thomas Aquinas (d. 1274); at the Festival of the Seven Sorrows of Mary, *Stabat Mater dolorosa*, by the Franciscan, Jacopone da Todi (d. 1306), but recently ascribed to St. Bonaventura; interpolated in the *Requiem* Mass is the *Dies irae, dies illa* by the Spanish Franciscan, Thomas of Celano (thirteenth century). It is doubtless no mere coincidence that four of these sequences which have been incorporated into the treasure of the Gregorian choral arose in the thirteenth century, the most brilliant period of the Church.

While these sequences still live and resound from year to year, that type of song which Tuotilo fathered, the trope, has completely disappeared. This variety of liturgical song was an addition or interpolation in the official songs. The tropes were often used so lavishly that they entwined the original text as does the ivy the tree. The Mass songs, especially "Kyrie," "Gloria," etc., were embellished with them. They were written in prose or in verse, and were appropriate to the character of the feast at which they were sung. They became of especial historical importance because from them developed the liturgico-dramatic celebrations from which in turn sprang the spiritual drama. [13]

The mention of this root of a great art form suggests still another from which a musically important species evolved, namely, the "Passion." [14] Originally, the text of the Passion history was treated like the Gospel lessons, and was recited by the deacon. From the thirteenth century, it received greater significance by being treated dramatically. From that time, one priest sang the words of Christ, a second the account of the Evangelist, a third or several together the words of the throng (disciples, Pharisees, *turba*). The delivery takes place in the lesson tone, which, to be sure, is treated somewhat more ornately than usual, as is shown on page 26.

At one point, however, even the old liturgical Passion has already replaced the reciting or only slightly embellished delivery with copious

[11] See S.B., No. 6.   [12] See S.B., No. 5.

[13] A trope by Tutilo or Tuotilo will be found in S.B., No. 3. A liturgical play presenting the story of The Resurrection will be found in S.B., No. 8.

[14] See H. Kretzschmar, *Führer*, II, Part 1, Ecclesiastical Works, Passions, Masses, Hymns, Psalms, Motets, Cantatas. 5th ed., 1921.

Cantor or Chronista:

Pássio Dómini nostri Je‑su Chris‑ti   se‑cún‑dum Mat‑‑thǽ‑‑‑‑um.

First Priest (Christ):

Tu‑‑‑‑‑‑‑‑di‑‑‑‑‑‑‑‑‑‑‑‑‑‑‑cis.

Succentor (Turba):

Cru‑ci‑‑fi‑‑gá‑‑‑‑‑‑‑‑‑‑‑‑‑tur.

melody, namely, in the case of the *Eli, Eli, lama asabthani!* An example of this agonizing cry of Christ will serve once more to show what beauty lies concealed in the vocal nuances of the Gregorian choral: [15]

E‑‑‑‑‑‑‑‑‑‑‑‑‑li,   E‑‑‑‑‑‑‑‑‑‑‑‑

‑‑‑‑‑‑li,   la‑ma a‑sab‑tha‑‑‑‑‑‑‑ni!

[15] ULTERIOR DEVELOPMENT OF THE GREGORIAN CHANT: The end of the development of the Gregorian chant falls in the time of the great theorist, Guido of Arezzo, who died about 1050. Both humanism and polyphony had a deleterious effect upon its cultivation. Humanism despised the church Latin of the Middle Ages as barbarian, while the polyphony of the sixteenth century misunderstood and also frowned upon monophony. The choral was "reformed," i.e., it was simplified by abbreviating and pruning away its rich melodic nuances. A witness to this reform is the *Graduale medicaeum,* which appeared in Rome in 1614 and 1615. Later centuries also were little favorable to the choral, so especially the period of the Illumination. When finally, under the influence of Romanticism, which brought about a reawakening of the historical sense, interest in the choral also revived, only "reformed" choral books were at first employed. A choral edition which was published in the year 1868 with the approbation of Rome by the publisher Pustet in Regensburg was based, so far as the gradual was concerned, on the *medicaeum.* The Regensburg edition was declared to be the official one, and the firm of Pustet was granted a thirty year publishing license. Meanwhile a mighty movement for the study of the choral had set in. The most important work was done by the Benedictine monks of Solesmes in France. Their abbot Guéranger set up the principle: If a large number of the oldest manuscripts from different countries agree among themselves, they contain the original version of the Gregorian choral. From the diligent work of numerous scholars, whose more important works have been mentioned previously, it became evident that the reform choral books presented the choral melodies in a corrupted form. The head of the Church also could not remain indifferent to this conclusion, and after the license granted the firm of Pustet had expired in the year 1900, Pope Leo XIII permitted the reintroduction of the newly won old melodies, and expressed his public commendation to the Benedictines of Solesmes in a *breve* addressed to their abbot on May 17, 1901. Pius X completed the work that had been initiated by his predecessor. Immediately on beginning his pontificate, he recalled all the testimonials granted the *Medicean* books, and arranged for the introduction of the traditional choral in a *motu proprio* of the 22d of November, 1903, and the

THE SECULAR MUSIC OF THE MIDDLE AGES: TROUBADOURS, TROUVÈRES, MINNESINGERS, AND MEISTERSINGERS

Troubadours and trouvères.[16]—The Gregorian choral is the song of the clergy. Even if the laity originally had a share in it, it nevertheless soon developed into an esoteric art of the ecclesiastical singers. In the early Middle Ages the clergy were the sole bearers of education and culture. When, as the result of the crusades, knighthood blossomed forth, it created its own art, the troubadour song and minnesong. And when the burghers gained prominence in the cities they established the meistersong.

Great movements in the life of peoples stimulate the joy in singing and awaken vernal seasons of song. The crusades were the real cause for the origin of the art of the troubadours. As the crusades themselves appear enveloped in a strange poetry, so also the singer who proceeded from them. His songs are silent, but his proud knightly form lives on in the poetry of other times and peoples, so that it is no coincidence that the beginnings of the new romanticism are to be sought in the revival of the troubadour poetry in France in the eighteenth century.

Southern France, above all, Provence, is the home of the troubadours.

---

decree of the Congregation of Rites of the 8th of January, 1904. Pius X introduced the expression *cantus traditionalis*, which has now been officially adopted. It is meant to designate the traditional choral, as it has been restored by comparison of numerous manuscripts, in contrast to the "reformed" choral. Concerning the traditional choral, Pius X says, it is the actual song of the Church, which it has inherited from the fathers and has preserved zealously during the centuries in its liturgical books, and which it presents to the faithful as its own and indeed exclusively prescribes for certain parts of the liturgy. D. Pothier had already published a *Liber gradualis* in the year 1884. Pius X decreed that on the basis of this a new typical and official edition should be prepared. This *Editio Vaticana* was declared obligatory for the entire church through the decree of April 8, 1908. A large number of publishers obtained the privilege of reprinting it.

[16] BIBLIOGRAPHY: P. Aubry, *Trouvères et Troubadours*, in the collection "Les Maîtres de la musique." Alcan, Paris, 1909; by the same author, *Le Chansonnier de l'Arsenal.* Geuthner, Paris, 1909 (facsimile and transcription of the melodies of the trouvères of the 13th century).—J. Beck, *Die Melodien der Troubadours.* Trübner, Strassburg, 1908; by the same author, *La Musique des troubadours*, in the collection "Les Musiciens célèbres." Laurens, Paris, 1910; by the same author, *Le Chansonnier Cangé.* 2 vols., in "Les Chansonniers des troubadours et des trouvères," facsimile and transcription, Univ. of Pennsylvania Press, 1927; H. Champion, Paris, 1927.—Joseph Bédier et P. Aubry, *Les Chansons de Croisade.* Champion, Paris, 1909.—De Coussemaker, *Oeuvres complètes du trouvère Adam de la Halle.* Durand et Pédone-Lauriel, Paris, 1872.—A. Gastoué, "La Musique mesurée," in *Enc. Lav.*—F. Gennrich, *Rondeaux, Virelais und Balladen.* 2 vols., Gesellschaft für romanische Literatur, Dresden, 1921 and 1927.—F. Ludwig, "Die geistliche nicht liturgische und weltliche einstimmige und die mehrstimmige Musik des Mittelalters bis zum Anfang des 15. Jahrhunderts," in Adler's *Handbuch der Musikgeschichte.*

In the north of France, also, the art was cultivated, the singers there calling themselves trouvères in distinction from the southern troubadours. The name has its origin in *trovar, trouver*, to find, discover, invent. Count William IX of Poitiers (1087–1127) is mentioned as the first troubadour; the best known is doubtless Bertran de Born, who flourished from c. 1180 until 1195 and died before 1215. Special mention must be made of Marcabrun, Bernard de Ventadour (1145–95), Rambaut de Vaqueiras (d. 1207), and Gaucelm Faidit. Among the North French, trouvères are to be found even among kings, for example, Richard Cœur de Lion (d. 1199) and Thibaud of Navarre (1201–53). Especial importance also attaches to Raoul de Couci and to the last one, Adam de la Halle (d. 1287), who has become especially famous through his song plays (*jeux*), and who with his motets and *rondeaux* entered upon the field of polyphonic music. The courts, where refined culture and knightly spirit were nurtured, were centers for the art of the singers, as, e.g., those of the counts of Provence, Toulouse, Poitou, and Flanders, of the dukes of Brabant, of the kings of France, England, Aragon, and Castile, especially the French court at the time of Louis VII as the result of the activity of the artistic queen, Eleonore of Aquitaine.[17]

The troubadours and the trouvères for the most part did not sing their songs themselves, but had this done by their *jongleurs* or *ménestrels*, wandering minstrels who sprang from the old order of secular, itinerant performers (*Spielleute*). The best-known among these is Blondel de Nesle, the minstrel of King Richard Lionheart. The names of the imprisoned master and the faithful servant at once recall to memory the whole poetic atmosphere of the troubadours and their singing messengers. These letters in the form of songs are characteristic of the romantic sentiment of the time, and breathe a peculiar enchantment, it matters not whether the subject be a message for a king pining in a dark tower, as in the legendary story of Lionheart and Blondel, or a love message to an honored dame.

The minstrels carried with them an instrument, as a rule the *vielle* or *viole*, the ancestress of the violin. This is the first time that bowed instruments appear and play an active rôle. They were probably invented not long before this period, although their origin is enveloped in com-

[17] Examples by Rambaut de Vaqueiras, Thibaut of Navarre, and Adam de la Halle will be found in S.B., Nos. 11, 13, 14, respectively; cf. also E.B., No. 7.

plete darkness. The earlier Middle Ages seem to have given preference to the harp, which was still used among the troubadours, and has, of course, remained in favor among wandering minstrels to the present day.

For a long time no one knew how to read the melodies of the troubadours, and they were misinterpreted. They are recorded in the square choral notation, which is a continuation of the old neumes and is still employed in the Catholic choral books. It was thought, accordingly, that the troubadour songs were to be delivered in a free, recitative style, like the Gregorian choral; or else the notes were read as mensurable, according to the rules of the slightly later mensural music, i.e., definite values were assigned to them. Neither method produced a satisfactory result. Only in recent times was it established, through the researches of J. Beck, P. Aubry, and F. Ludwig, that the rhythm of the music is dependent upon that of the verse, and that the so-called *modi* are applicable to these, as they are to the oldest polyphonic music. These modi are rhythmical schemata for the construction of melodies. They are six in number, and can be indicated in modern notation by the following rhythms:

First Modus = Trochæus = ♩ ♪ = ♪ ♪ | ♪ ♪ | ♪ . etc.

Second Modus = Iambus . = ♪ ♩ = ♪ ♪ | ♪ ♪ | ♪ . etc.

Third Modus = Dáctylus = ♩ ♪ ♪ = ♪· ♪ ♪ | ♪· ♪ ♪ | ♪· . etc.

Fourth Modus = Anapæstus = ♪ ♪ ♩ = ♪ ♪ ♪· | ♪ ♪ ♪· | ♪ . etc.

Fifth Modus = Spondeus = ♩ ♩ = ♪· ♪· | ♪· ♪· | ♪· . etc.

Sixth Modus = Tribrachys = ♪ ♪ ♪ = ♪ ♪ ♪ | ♪ ♪ ♪ | ♪ . etc.

Thus interpreted, the melodies gain real meaning, and true pearls are discovered among them. Two examples, culled from the suggestive little book of J. Beck, *La Musique des troubadours*, will serve to demonstrate this. The first of the two is in the first, or trochaic, rhythmic mode, as is shown on page 30.

This little love song, as fresh as spring, requires no explanation. Beck gives the following French translation:

Quand le rossignol chante—qui nous charme par son chant—
Pour ma belle, douce amie—Je vois mon cœur rossignolant—
Jointes mains je la supplie—Car jamais je n'aimai tant;—
Je sais bien, que, si elle m'oublie—C'en est fini de mon bonheur.

The second, of especial interest, is the following *plainte* on the death of King Richard Lionheart (1169–99), by Gaucelm Faidit; the example is the first of seven strophes: [18]

[18] TRANSLATION: What immense grief and what cruel misfortune, For all his friends, what sorrow without equal! And I, instead of weeping and lamenting, Am obliged to sing and tell my suffering. Because he, the prince and the chief of valor, The good, the great Richard, king of the Angles, Is dead. Oh God! Sorrows for ever and ever! Death! the frightful word, so terrible to hear! Hard, indeed, is he who hears it without trembling.

es!   Quant es - trangz   motz,quan sal · vatge   a   au ∗ zir!
mais!   Mort! L'af·freux   mot, si   ter·rib·le   a   ou' · ir!

Ben a dur cor   totz hom   qu'o   pot   suf · frir.
Bien dur ce · lui   qui l'en - - · -tend   sans   fré · mir.

One can view this *plainte* as a precursor of the *lamentos* and *tombeaux*
that were in vogue in the seventeenth and eighteenth centuries. A great
and singular power lies in the irregular melody of Faidit. One is irre-
sistibly reminded of certain equally original melodies of Berlioz who,
like the troubadours, sprang from the south of France.

The only other *plainte* of which the music has been preserved is the
one written by Guiraut Riquier (1254–92), the last of the troubadours,
on the death of Amauric IV of Narbonne.[19] There are two chansons by
the same author, harmonized, in the work of P. Aubry, *Chansons de
troubadours*, which also contains the celebrated Provençal ballad *A l'entrada del tems clar* (beginning of the thirteenth century).

The minnesingers.[20]—The art of the German minnesingers was evoked
by the same influences as those which brought forth the troubadours.
The heyday of the troubadours was in the twelfth century, while that
of the minnesingers began with the thirteenth. There can be no question that the troubadour influenced the minnesinger, although the
latter, as was inevitable on account of the very difference of language, soon went his own way. Even among the troubadours not
all belonged to the knightly rank; Marcabrun was a foundling, some of
those of lower station were at the same time jongleurs and poets, as the

---

[19] Cf. Higini Anglès, *Les Melodies del trobador Guiraut Riquier.* Institut d'estudis catalans;
Biblioteca de Catalunya, Vol. XI, 1926, pp. 1–78. Barcelona, 1927.
[20] The word "minnesinger" is compounded of two words from the German of the Middle
Ages: *Minne* = love and *Singer* = singer. BIBLIOGRAPHY: G. Holz, F. Saran, Ed. Bernoulli,
Die Jenaer Liederhandschrift. 2 vols., reproduction and transcription, C. L. Hirschfeld,
Leipzig, 1901.—Oswald von Wolkenstein was a late comer among the minnesingers. He
already leads the way to polyphony, but is distinguished by wealth of melody. His works
have been published by O. Koller in the D.T. OE., IX, 1, 1902.—F. A. Mayer und H.
Rietsch, *Die Mondsee-Wiener Liederhandschrift,* Acta Germanica, Vol. III, No. 4, & Vol.
IV. Mayer & Müller, Berlin, 1894–96.—Melodies by Walther von der Vogelweide were
not known hitherto, but recently it is surmised that such have been discovered in the
Münster fragments; cf. R. Molitor, S.I.M.G. XII, 3.—P. Runge, *Die Sangesweisen der
Colmarer Handschrift und der Liederhandschrift Donaueschingen.* B. & H., Leipzig, 1896.
—A history of the minnesong from the musical standpoint has been presented for the
first time by H. J. Moser, *Geschichte der deutschen Musik,* Vol. I, 1st ed., 1920, and in subsequent editions.

trouvère, Blondel de Nesle. Among the minnesingers, likewise, one finds representatives of the burgher class, or such as stood near that class, for example, the burgher of Eisenach, Heinrich von Ofterdingen, who was one of the most distinguished contestants at the famous singing tournament on the Wartburg in the year 1207. A popular strain often breaks through in the songs of the minnesingers, as everyone knows from the songs of their most famous representative, Walther von der Vogelweide.[21] The Germans did not employ jongleurs, they sang their own songs.

The minnesongs, as one readily discerns from their very length, are, in general, no true *Lieder*, no folk music, but art songs. The most prevalent form is a couplet (two *Stollen*) and a conclusion (*Abgesang*). The two lines of the couplet are metrically alike, and are sung to the same melody, while the conclusion has its own new melody. At a later time the meistersingers also took over this form, which indeed was already to be found among the troubadours, and which remained the rule for the *Lied* of the sixteenth century, especially of the spiritual song. The repetition of the first part satisfies the musical craving for symmetry. This form, built on the pattern A A B, is a basic type that may be compared with the already mentioned A B A. The latter finally won the victory, and is doubtless the superior form. An adumbration of this can already be found in individual minnesongs. It occasionally happens that the couplet melody is repeated at the conclusion of the *Abgesang*, the whole being then constructed according to the pattern A A B A. With the meistersingers this pattern actually became the rule. Viewed carefully, the sonata-allegro form, the highest form of music which has been evolved up to the present time, represents this pattern, though, to be sure, in an enriched and deepened manner.

Like the melodies of the troubadours, those of the minnesingers also are recorded in the square choral notation. But again, as with the troubadour melodies, it has been discovered only in recent times that these songs are not to be delivered after the manner of the Gregorian choral, but that their rhythm is determined by the meter of the verse, as was the case with the Greek music. The only fundamental difference between the two lies in the fact that in the German verse it is not the number of syllables and their quantity which are considered, but the

[21] Two songs by Walther von der Vogelweide will be found in S.B., No. 12; cf. also E.B., No. 8.

accented and unaccented syllables. Accordingly, the accent determines the musical rhythm. Expressed in modern terms, every accent falls on a strong beat; the unaccented syllables, and the notes which often appear in greater numbers than the syllables, are arranged between these strong beats, with shorter notes if necessary. Only through the discovery of this method of delivery have the melodies become esthetically understandable. In general, they impress one as somewhat less interesting than those of the troubadours. Concerning most of them one must confess that they possess no intrinsic significance, and that for richness of melodic invention they cannot be compared with the later German song, although they do supplement and clarify the text. The following simple, manly melody admirably fits the straightforward verse of Spervogel (twelfth century, according to the edition of the Jena Lieder manuscript, by Holz, Saran, and Bernoulli): [22]

1. Swa eyn vrivnt dem an - dern vrivu - - de bi - ge - stat mit gan-tzen

tru - wen gar an al - le mis - se - tat. 2. Da ist des vrivn-des hel - fe gût. dem

er sie wil-lich-li-che tût 3. Daz sie ge-hel-lent vn-der in. dem me-ret

sich daz Kvn-ne 4. Swa vrivnde an - der we-ge sint, daz ist ein mi - - chel wun - - ne
eyn-

Individual minnesingers tower high above the average as inventors of melody, for example, Masters Alexander and Witzlav of Rügen (c. 1300). Severe and not very flexible is the following spring song of Witzlav. It has not yet attained the singableness and overflowing richness of the folk songs which appeared shortly after, but it nevertheless reflects genuine vernal atmosphere in its melody, which unites itself closely to the words, wings its way to greater heights, and calmly sub-

---

[22] TRANSLATION: When a friend stands by his friend with perfect fidelity, even in all his errors, then is the friend's help good for him upon whom he bestows it voluntarily. Because when they are united their welfare prospers. When two friends dedicate themselves to one another, their joy is great.

sides as it nears its conclusion. The very chastity of its expression is its attraction: [23]

1. Der walt vnde an-gher lyt ghe-breyt mit wůn-nen-ri-gher var-men
2. Se v̊-ben e-ren sů-ze(n) scal vro-li-chem her-tzen v̊ ber

cleyt . . . ., reyt . . . .-sin der sů zen voghe-lin do . . . ne
al . . . . mal . . . .-ich des vin-de an blo-men sco . . . ne

3. Ho, vro 'so stet des mey-ien blů-te, ghů-te, sůte ich mer-ke

vroy-den vol in ang-her vnde vph al - - ben wyt-int-hal - - ben

The dance songs of Nithart are delicious in their joviality, as may be seen from the following, which also glorifies the spring (Riemann's version): [24]

Mai hat wun-nik-lich ent-spros-sen Berg und tal dar zuo die grue-ne
liegt das veld mit touw be-goz-zen. Al-ler cre-a-tur ist nie-mer

hei--de. Da man brach der vi--ol un-ge-zalt. Dez
lei--de, Schon ge-zie--ret steht der grue-ne walt.

Man sieht gein der sun-ne gle-sten Niu-we bluet uf-drin-gen;
O--ben in des wal-des e-sten Hoert man vog-lin sin--gen; Ein

jeg-lich dier hat vröu-den lank: Des hab der wün-ne-bern-de mei--e dank.

The meistersingers.[25]—The art of the minnesingers bloomed in the thirteenth century; it fell into decay in the first half of the fourteenth.

[23] TRANSLATION: The forest and the meadows lie clothed in charming colors; the young birds are disposed to sing their sweet tones. With joyful heart they practice their sweet songs on all sides. I find beautiful flowers. How gladsome stands the bloom of May! Goodness and sweetness I joyfully feel everywhere in the meadows and the fields.

[24] TRANSLATION: May has charmingly sprung forth from hill and vale and the green heath where one gathers the violets unnumbered. The field lies covered with dew. No creature suffers sorrow any more. Beautifully adorned stands the green forest. One sees new blossoms sprouting forth to the glistening sun. Up in the branches of the trees are heard the little birds. Every creature feels great joy, for which be praised the happiness-bestowing May.

[25] BIBLIOGRAPHY: R. Jonas, *Adam Puschmann, Gründlicher Bericht des deutschen Meistergesanges zusammt der Tabulatur*, 1571; new ed. Niemeyer, Halle, 1888.—G. Münzer, *Das*

The burghers with their meistersinger schools took over the heritage of the knights. The origin of these schools is closely connected with the rise of the cities, in which the burghers, organized into guilds, appear as a new and important class. Mainz is considered as the cradle of the meistersinger art, and in the fourteenth century was its chief seat. At an early period Strassburg, Frankfurt, Würzburg, and Zwickau followed in its footsteps; in the fifteenth and sixteenth centuries, Colmar, Augsburg, Nuremberg, Munich, Ratisbon, as a matter of fact, most of the cities of Germany up to the Baltic Sea. The schools were associations with strict rules, the school order and the tablatures. How the members were distinguished according to rank is evident from the following rule:

He who does not yet thoroughly understand the tablature becomes a pupil; he who knows everything in the same, a school friend; he who can sing forth several tunes, about five or six, becomes a singer; he who composes texts according to other melodies, a poet; he who originates a tune is called a Master.

It is significant that the invention of a new tune was considered the highest accomplishment.

The meistersingers treated their melodies just as we treat some of ours, writing new verses to old tunes. Names were given to the melodies to distinguish them. One of the most beautiful, by Hans Sachs, had the poetic designation *Silberweis* (Silvertone). But among the great number of names that were required, some were very prosaic or outlandish, as for example, Red Tone, Blue Tone, Tailed-Ape Tone, Sad Bun Tone, Fat Badger Tone, and Little Glass Half-Jug Tone.

The treatment of the material was similarly uncouth. Both sacred (especially biblical), and secular subjects were chosen, not infrequently quite crude ones. It is especially offensive to good taste that the poets merely counted syllables without regarding accents. To be sure, it has become evident to-day that the roughness, the bad accentuation, which thus arose, was to a considerable extent compensated for by the vocal rendition. The meistersong is somewhat better than its reputation. Information with regard to it has until lately been obtained from the book of J. C. Wagenseil, *Von der Meistersinger holdseligen Kunst Anfang, Fortübung, Nutzbarkeiten und Lehrsätzen* (Concerning the Origin, Progress, Utility and Principles of the Charming Art of the Meistersingers),

---

Singebuch des Adam Puschmann (with numerous meistersinger melodies). B. & H., Leipzig, 1906.—The "Morgenweis" by Hans Sachs will be found in E.B., No. 9; for the "Silberweis" by Sachs, see below.

which appeared at Altdorf in 1697, when the heyday was already past. Richard Wagner also took this for the basis of his information.

The meistersongs were delivered slowly. In their style they remind one of the Protestant choral in its present unrhythmic form. They are, however, more artful than this, on account of their coloratures, the "flowers" (*Blumen*), as the meistersingers called them, with which they are often overladen. The performance of these songs not infrequently offers difficulties, and this fact evokes a certain respect for the ability of the meistersingers. The Protestant hymn tune of the sixteenth century has manifestly been considerably influenced by their melodies. In the above-mentioned beautiful *Silberweis* of Hans Sachs one finds a motif which appears in Luther's *A Mighty Fortress Is Our God:*[26]

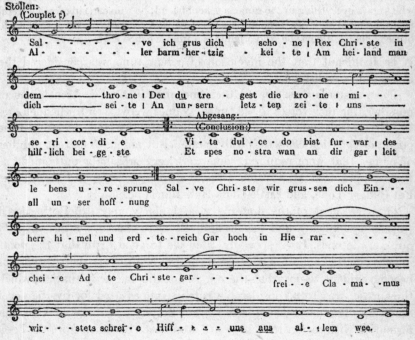

[26] TRANSLATION:

> Hail! I greet thee heartily, King Christ, upon the throne,
> Who mercifully bearest the crown; Sweet life, thou truly
> art the origin of life! All merciful, a Saviour one doth call thee,
> In our last hour support us with thy help. Thou our hope,
> in thee lies all our confidence. Hail, Christ, we greet thee,
> Lord of heaven and earth, High in the Hierarchy;
> To thee, Christ, we freely cry: Help us from all our woe!

In Italy, in the thirteenth century, the monodic song took the form of *laudi*, while in Spain, Alfonso the Wise, king of Castile and Leon from 1252 to 1284, wrote numerous *Cantigas de Santa Maria*.[27] These spiritual songs all adopt the form of the virelay from the refrain of the French troubadours.

FOLK SONG [28]

The romanticists believed that the folk song was created by the entire nation, and the brothers Grimm also entertained this view. Later, how-

[27] Cf. H. Anglès, *Les "Cantigas" del rei N'Anfós el Savi*. E. Subirana, Barcelona, 1927.— Fr. Ludwig, art. in Adler's *Handbuch der Musikgeschichte*, pp. 176 ff.—J. Ribera, *La música de las cantigas*. Vol. III of the "Cantigas de S. Maria," published by the Real Academia Española, Tipografia de la Revista de archivos, Madrid, 1922; Eng. tr., abridged, by Eleanor Hague and Marion Leffingwell, *Music in Ancient Arabia and Spain*. O.U.P., London, 1929.

[28] BIBLIOGRAPHY: P. Aubry, *Esquisse d'une bibliographie de la chanson populaire en Europe*. A. Picard et Fils, Paris, 1905.—W. Bäumker, *Das Katholische deutsche Kirchenlied in seinen Singweisen*. 4 vols., Herder, Freiburg, 1883–1911.—F. M. Böhme, *Altdeutsches Liederbuch*. B. & H., Leipzig, 1877 (reprint, 1913).—Chappell, *Popular Music of the Olden Time*. Cramer, Beale, and Chappell, London, 1855–59; 2d ed., 1892.—G. Doncieux, *Le Romancero populaire de la France*. Bouillon, Paris, 1904.—Erk-Böhme, *Deutscher Liederhort*. 3 vols., B. & H., Leipzig, 1893–94.—Walter Keller, *Das toskanische Volkslied* (Basel dissertation), 1908.—Aug. Reissmann, *Das deutsche Lied in seiner historischen Entwicklung*. O. Bertram, Cassel, 1861; by the same author, *Geschichte des deutschen Liedes*. J. Guttentag (D. Collins), Berlin, 1874.—J. Tiersot, *Chansons populaires, recueillées dans les Alpes françaises*. H. Falque, & F. Perrin, Grenoble, 1903 (with music); by the same author, *Histoire de la Chanson populaire en France*. Plon, Nourrit, et cie., Paris, 1889; by the same author, *La Chanson populaire et les écrivains romantiques*. Plon, Paris, 1931; by the same author, *Mélodies populaires des provinces françaises, recueillées et harmonisées*. Heugel, Paris, 1887–94; by the same author, *Noëls français, transcrits et harmonisés*. Heugel, Paris, 1901.—H. E. Wooldridge, *Old English Popular Music*. Chappell and Co., London, 1893.

The Best Collections of Folk Songs

BASQUE COUNTRIES: Ch. Bordes, *Archives de la tradition basque*. Rouart, Lerolle, Paris, 1910. ENGLAND, IRELAND, AND SCOTLAND: A. Moffat, *English Songs of the Georgian Period: 200 Songs*. Bailey and Ferguson, London, 1920; *The Minstrelsy of England*. Bailey and Ferguson, London, 1901; *The Minstrelsy of Ireland*: 206 Irish songs. 4th enlarged ed. Augener, London, 1897; *The Minstrelsy of the Scottish Highlands*. Bailey and Ferguson, London, 1901.—For a fuller bibliography of collections of folk songs of Great Britain, see under English music, Part 2, Chapter V. FRANCE: L. Branchet and J. Plantadis, *Chansons populaires du Limousin*. H. Champion, Paris, 1905.—V. d'Indy and J. Tiersot, *Chansons populaires du Vivarais et du Vercors*. Reprinted from the *Revue de traditions populaires*, Vol. VII, 1912.—J. Tiersot, *Chansons populaires harmonisées;* collections of French folk songs under the editorship of J. Tiersot have been published in America by O. Ditson, and G. Schirmer; see *Sixty Folksongs of France*, edited by J. Tiersot. "Musicians Library," Vol. I, Oliver Ditson Co., Boston, 1915.—*Forty-four French Folk-Songs and Variants from Canada, Normandy, and Brittany*, ed. by J. Tiersot. G. Schirmer, N. Y., 1910. HUNGARY: Béla Bartók and Z. Kodály, *Folksongs: Transylvanian Hungarians*. Popular Literary Society, Budapest, 1921. ITALY: Eugenia Levi, *Fiorita di canti tradizionali*. R. Bemporad et

ever, it was realized that an individual is always required for the composition of either verse or music, the mass cannot compose. Yet on the other hand, the mass often does change the songs; it simplifies them, adapts or modifies them, sometimes spoils them, at times even improves them, especially in their melodic part, the melody often becoming more singable in the mouths of the people. John Meier, in his instructive little book, *Kunstlieder im Volksmund* (Art Songs from the Lips of the People), sees the chief characteristic of the folk song to be the fact that the mass views it as its own, treats it freely by altering it, whether by additions, omissions, or otherwise. When the mass at large in this manner assumes a position of lordship over a song, when a song has become "popular" in the sense of having become current among the people, then it has become a genuine folk song, no matter by whom it was created. In this way songs by master poets and by professional composers have also become actual folk songs, numerous examples of which are given by J. Meier.

It is, therefore, as futile to seek the precise date of a folk song as it is to endeavor to find its author. The songs of the Middle Ages in particular, of which there are very few remains, afford us no indications as to a precise date or authorship. The oldest of the German folk songs which have been preserved with their melodies come from the twelfth century. The still familiar *Christ ist erstanden* (Christ Is Arisen) is the oldest known. Still other spiritual songs might be mentioned.

Fils, Florence, 1895; 2d ed., 1926. LITHUANIA: A. Jaszkiewicz, continuator Kolberg, *Melodje ludowe litewskie* (Lithuanian songs). Wydanictvo Akademji miejetuosci, Krakow, 1900. POLAND: Kolberg, *Songs of the Polish People*. 1865.—Adam Wieniawski, *Polskie Piesni Ludowe* (Chansons populaire Polonaises). 2 vols. Gebethner & Wolff, Warsaw, 1926. RUSSIA: M. A. Balakirew, *Harmonized Songs*. 1891.—*Recueil de chants populaires russes;* Fr. tr. by J. Sergennois. Belaïeff, Leipzig, 1898.—d'Istomine-Nekrassov, *Songs of the Russian People*. (Collections from 1895 on.) SLAVS OF THE SOUTH: Ludvik Kuba. COLLECTIONS: Slovanstvo ve svých zpěvech (The Slavs in Their Songs). Hudebni Matice, Prague, 1384–95.—Kuhač-Koch, Franjo Š., *Južno-slovjenske narodne popievke* (Chansons nationales des Slavs du Sud). U. Albrecht, Zagrebu, 1878–81. Mrs. Natalie (Curtis) Burlin has published the songs of the Negroes in Hampton Series, *Negro Folksongs*. G. Schirmer, New York and Boston, 1918–19; and in *Songs and Tales from the Dark Continent*. G. Schirmer, New York and Boston, 1920.—Marguerite Béclard d'Harcourt has collected American Indian songs in *Mélodies populaires indiennes d'Amérique*. Ricordi, Milan, 1923.—M. and R. d'Harcourt, *La Musique des Incas*. Geuthner, Paris, 1925–26. For a fuller bibliography of collections of Negro and Indian music, see under American music, Part 2, Chapter V. In the case of the folk song one should attach less importance to the collections noted, in which the songs are always treated more or less arbitrarily by the transcriber, than to good gramophone records taken at the sources.—Musical research would be greatly profited if it would occupy itself with a comparative study of the folk songs of the different nations.

Secular ones are traceable only to a later time. When these appear, no difference between them and the spiritual can be determined; until the sixteenth century both are carved from the same block. The same melodies are also frequently used for both spiritual and secular texts. Although the opposite has often been asserted, it must, nevertheless, be stated, as the result of the greater knowledge which we possess at the present day, that the secular songs are based musically upon the ecclesiastical modes, and hence it follows that for the folk song, also, the Gregorian chant was a fostering mother.

The music of our forbears of pre-Christian times has completely disappeared; no trace of it can be found. Such very early music as has been preserved can have grown up only under the influence of the new culture which was created by the Carolingian Empire; and, as remarked, the oldest that can be discovered is spiritual.

This spiritual folk song is reported to have arisen in the following manner: From olden times the laity were permitted to join in the singing of the Kyrie Eleison. The custom was especially prevalent in the case of funerals, processions, and similar ceremonies. Salzburg statutes of the year 799 explicitly prescribe this. The Kyrie Eleison cry thereby became the song of the people; the farmer behind his plow, the artisan in his workshop, is reported to have sung it. Words in the vernacular were gradually set to the Kyrie Eleison melodies, and thus arose the oldest spiritual folk songs. Because of the manner of their origin, they were called *Leisen* in German. In olden times they regularly concluded with the Kyrie Eleison cry, for example, the above mentioned *Christ ist erstanden* (Christ Is Arisen), and the *Gelobet seist du Jesu Christ* (Praised Be Thou, Lord Jesu Christ), which also belongs among the very oldest, and many more.

In the twelfth century, spiritual folk songs were also created through the translation of Latin hymns. An example of this class, still revered, and frequently sung by both Protestants and Catholics, is the *Komm, Gott Schöpfer, heiliger Geist* (Come Holy Ghost, Creator God), a paraphrase of the hymn ascribed to Gregory the Great, *Veni creator spiritus*. Many versions of the song *O filii et filiae* (O Sons and Daughters), differing in their rhythm, have been taken from the sequence or prose of the ninth century, *Victimae Paschali laudes*. The crusades also inspired the people. The crusaders sang *Nu helfe uns das heilige Grab* (Now Help Us Gain the Holy Grave), and in connection with the preaching of the crusade by St. Bernard of Clairvaux in the year 1146, it is reported that the Germans sang *Christ uns genade* (Christ show us mercy).

While we can trace the spiritual folk song back to the twelfth century, we gain more explicit information concerning the secular only in the thirteenth and early fourteenth centuries. No earlier melodies have been preserved. While it is true that one always assumed, and probably correctly, popular influence in the case of the troubadours and the minnesingers, this influence cannot be demonstrated. On the other hand, we can readily observe how the minnesong influenced the folk song to the perfecting of its rhyme. It is probable, indeed virtually certain, that there was folk song before the times of the knightly song, but this folk song has been transmitted to us only after it was influenced by the song of the knights.

The majority of the folk song melodies of the Middle Ages are in the ecclesiastical modes, the Dorian and the Phrygian approaching the modern minor, the Lydian and Mixolydian, the modern major. They are also related to the Gregorian chant in not recognizing the chromatic element. As a result, they often appear to us as somewhat austere; but at the same time they are also free from all sentimentality. The expression of pain, whether it be the anguish of love or any other type, is often so realistic that there is not the slightest indication of effeminacy. An abundance of the chromatic element in a melody arouses the impression of whining, of which there is not the slightest trace in the old folk song.

The earliest information concerning folk music is furnished by the tractate of Johannes de Grocheo,[29] which belongs to the beginning of the fourteenth century. The author distinguishes two groups of songs, and designates these as *cantus* and *cantilenae;* the latter embrace the popular songs. The *rotunda* (roundel) was sung in Normandy by maidens and youths on occasions of festivals and feasting. The *stantipes* is so difficult of execution that it serves to restrain the youths from wicked thoughts; it can also be executed by instruments only. The *ductia* is a light and rapid, rising and falling song, intended for choirs of youths and maidens.

[29] JOHANNES DE GROCHEO was perhaps professor at the Sorbonne in Paris. His interesting tractate, written in the Latin language, has been published by Johannes Wolf, with a German translation, in the S.I.M.G., I., 1899.

The folk song is distinguished by the richness and the diversity of its poetic content. This is scarcely the place to depict this in detail, but it may be permitted, as an indication of this wealth and variety, to give the general summary which F. M. Böhme presents in his *Altdeutsches Liederbuch:* narrative songs, ballads and romances, day songs, equestrian songs, watchmen's songs; songs of love, parting, wandering, enigmas, wishing, lying, drinking, carousing, history, soldiers, and hunting; songs dealing with different ranks or classes; humorous, satiric, and obscene songs; also children's songs. One may add to this list slumbersongs (*berceuses*), Christmas songs (*noëls*), dance songs, and songs for special festivals.

The subjects of the songs are treated in a remarkably similar manner in different countries—Brittany or Provence, Scotland, England, Catalonia, and even Denmark; [30] there are always love scenes in the fields, stories of young women discontented with their aged husbands, reminiscences of war, and so forth. But the poetic forms, and consequently also the musical forms, differ according to the different regions. Conversely, the same melody may be found joined to one text in Flanders, to another in Poitou.

The Limburg Chronicle of the chronicler Johannes, which also contains a number of poems from the years 1347 to 1380, reports concerning the German folk song, which is much better known than that of other countries and has been made the subject of numerous investigations. The Chronicle relates, concerning the year 1370, that a leprous, barefooted monk who lived on an island in the Main "wrote the best songs and roundels in the world, from the point of view of both words and music," and that "what he sang all the people sang gladly, and all masters piped, and other strolling players led in the song and the verse." Songs which he invented are recorded; for example, the following one in which he apparently laments his own sorrow: *Ich bin ausgezählet, man weiset mich Armen vor die Tür, Untreu ich spür nun zu allen Zeiten* (I am branded; wretched one, I am shown the door; Faithlessness I now feel at all times).

The records of this Chronicle show us how the folk song arose at that time, how it spread and was valued by all. The first great heyday of the German folk song is to be placed in the fourteenth century; a second,

[30] However, England specialized in ballads; Spain, in epic romances; Russia, the European country richest in folk songs, sang epic songs from the twelfth century.

which, of course, was only a continuation of the first, falls in the sixteenth, inspired by the great spiritual movements of humanism and especially the Protestant Reformation.

Endowed with higher artistic qualities, with greater intrinsic merits than the meistersong, the folk song supplanted the disintegrating minnesong. Naturally, its blossoming forth is also related to the advent of the new burgher class. But the folk song is not only the song of the burgher, like the meistersong; its significance at that time lay in the fact that the entire people, the entire nation participated and expressed in it, its sorrow and its joy. When at the present day we occupy ourselves with the folk song, we, as it were, condescend to it, and oppose to it the art song of the educated classes. But in the period from the fourteenth century to the sixteenth century there were no such differences. The knights had ceased to be a special class distinguished by education and culture, at least they no longer possessed their own art. At that time there was only one song, the folk song, in which beggar and king equally participated, and in which the plowman, the learned clerk, the huntsman and the fisher, the artisan, the soldier and the student, the priest, the monk and the nun, the noblewoman and the page, the charlatan and the vagabond, husband and wife, and old and young, all rejoiced. For all of these, the folk song was *the* song; it reflected the general life of the day. For this reason, too, it attained at that time a significance and a beauty greater than in any subsequent period. In the period in question it became truly classic.

Characteristic of all the folk songs is the stanza form. Every song consists of several stanzas or couplets which are sung to the same melody. The oldest German song strophe consists of two long verses or four half verses, which are connected by rhyme. Every line has a definite number of accents, as a rule, three or four; the unaccented syllables may vary in number. The inequalities which arise on account of this, and which would be more or less disturbing in reading or reciting, are obviated in the singing by the melody, as is still the case with the folk song.

The classical folk song, much more than the minnesong, is characterized by a strong joy in singing. Frequently, as a final discharge of ebullient spirits, a colorature is employed at the end, a most beautiful example of which is found in the case of the well-known song *Innsbruck*

ich muss dich lassen (Innsbruck, I Now Must Leave Thee),[31] by Heinrich Isaak: Furthermore, to satisfy the mere joy in singing, nonsense syllables are often interwoven, as *dölpel*, *dölpel*, or *pumperleinpum*, and so forth. Otherwise the melody is closely wedded to the text, and mirrors and corroborates with finesse the niceties of the verse and rhyme structure. As the result of this, a finely proportioned architecture often results, which, in spite of all its simplicity, yet bears evidence of genuine art. The rhythm is vigorous and manifold; change of time takes place frequently. The present day has come to realize that there is an inexhaustible, primal power in these spontaneous rhythmic creations. Vocal music having become too uniform, as the result of the influence of instrumental music, which is dependent upon a certain regularity, it is again allowing itself to be inspired by the mobility of the old folk song. Two examples will illustrate the points mentioned: (1) *Es fuhr ein Maidlein übern See* (A Maiden

[31] TRANSLATION:

> Innsbruck, I now must leave thee,
> I journey on my way
> To strange lands afar;
> All joy is taken from me,
> I know not what awaits me
> Where I shall live in misery.

Journeyed o'er the Lake),[32] the melody of which has been adapted to
the 141st Psalm in the Dutch collection *Souter-Liedekens*, 1540:

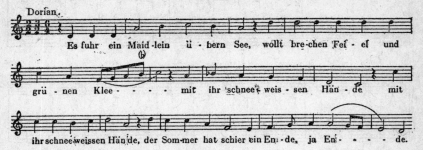

and (2) *Und wollt ihr hören neue Mähr* (And Would You Hear a Story
New), the song of the Box Tree and the White Willow,[33] from the
songs of Heinrich Finck, 1536:[34]

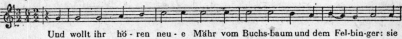

A pearl which Brahms honored is the song: *All' mein Gedanken, die
ich han* (What Thoughts Soe'er I Call My Own)[35] from the Lochheimer
Liederbuch. With its major tonality it does not impress one as anywise
strange, but on the contrary, immediately creates an impression of
familiarity:

[32] TRANSLATION:

> A maiden journeyed o'er the lake
> To pluck some violets and clover green
> With her snow-white hands;
> The summer is almost gone, yes gone.

[33] TRANSLATION:

> And would you hear a story new
> Of the box tree and the willow:
> They journeyed on together,
> They warred with one another.

[34] For further examples see R.B., No. 26 *et sq.;* also S.B., Nos. 85, 87, 88 a & b.

[35] TRANSLATION:

> What thoughts soe'er I call my own, all are with thee.
> My consolation, thou alone, be still with me.
> Thou, thou shalt think of me forever.
> Were each wish within my pow'r,
> From thee would I swerve never.

All' mein Ge-dan-ken die ich han', die sind bei dir, Du aus-er-wel-ter
einz-ger Trost bleib stet bei mir. Du, du, du, sollst an mich ge-den ken;
hat ich al--ler Wunsch ge-walt, von dir wolt ich nit wen---ken.

In France, the folk song employed a system of versification based
upon assonance. Its form was not fixed, but there is found most frequently a refrain of one or two verses which sometimes make no sense,
the singers having contented themselves with repeating syllables of comic
effect. In view of the existing scarcity of songs which are of authentically
popular origin, we can rely on the presence of such a refrain in a song,
in forming our judgment as to whether it really has the character of a
folk song. Thus the *pastourelle* of the thirteenth century reproduced in
the work of P. Aubry, *Les Plus Anciens Monuments de la Musique
Française*, carries a refrain which allows us to regard it as constructed
after the manner of a folk song: [36]

1. L'au-trier m'en a-loi-e che-vau-chant par-mi une ar-
2. Trou-vai pas-to-re-le qui en chan-tant de-me-noit grant

broi-e lez l. pen-dant. 3.En son chief la be-le cha-pel out mis
joi-e por son a-mant.

de ro-se nou-ve-le si di-soit toz dis Chi-be-ra la chi-

-be-le douz a--miz hi-be-ra la chi-be-le soiez jo-lis.

One should note the initial formula with which the *pastourelles* fre-
quently begin, and, indeed, in a general way, many of the ancient airs.
That leap of a fifth is one of the typical turns of the music of the Middle
Ages, having previously been employed in the Gregorian chant. Many

[36] *Op. cit.*, pl. XII, facsimile of MS 847 of the Bibliothèque Nationale of Paris; transcription in modern notation.

an introit, antiphon, or offertory begins with that skip to the upper fifth.

Certain fragments of songs can be reconstructed, on the one hand, from the refrains which the troubadours intercalated in their courtly songs, examples of which may be found in the study of K. Bartsch, *Altfranzösische Romanzen und Pastourellen des 12. und 13. Jahrhunderts* (Old French Romances and Pastourelles of the 12th and 13th Centuries), Leipzig, 1870. On the other hand, a great number of polyphonic compositions, from the thirteenth century to the sixteenth century, take for their theme "tenors" of a popular origin. The celebrated manuscript of Montpellier makes us acquainted with certain of these tenors. A collection of French compositions for three and four voices, dating from the fourteenth century to the fifteenth century, is preserved at the library of the Liceo Musicale at Bologna, and contains a piece established on a tenor, the text of which presents a frankly popular character:

> La triquotée est par matin levée,
> La triquotée, la triquoton, la belle triquotée,
> Se i'ay du mal i'aray lyesse
> Toutes les fois qu'il vous plaira . . .

The music of the tenor is doubtless likewise of popular origin: [37]

Josquin Desprez has written one of his songs for four voices on the theme of a soldier's song which was very popular in the various provinces of France, and which Heinrich Isaak transcribed freely for organ: [38]

Transcribed by Th. Gérold [39]

A Dieu, mes a-mours, à Dieu vous com-mant à Dieu mes a-mours jus-ques au prin-

[37] According to Torchi, "I monumenti dell' antica musica francese à Bologna," *R.M.I.*, 1906.

[38] The beginning of the instrumental transcription which H. Isaak made of this chanson will be found in the section on the music of the organ in the sixteenth century, p. 140.

[39] Th. Gérold, *Le Manuscrit de Bayeux*, text and music of a collection of songs of the fifteenth century. Imprimerie alsacienne, Strasbourg, 1921.

-temps. Je suis en sou - cy de quoy je vi - vray la rai-son pour-quoy je vous le di-

-ray: je n'uy point d'ar-gent vi - vrai - je de - vent? Se l'ar-gent du

Roy ne vient plus sou - vent, à Dieu mes a - mours, à Dieu vous com - mant.

Josquin's polyphonic transcription of this chanson will illustrate in an interesting way the manner in which the composers utilized the popular melodies or folk songs:

The folk songs, as remarked just above, owe their survival primarily to the fact that the composers began to arrange them polyphonically. So long as they were sung homophonically they were transmitted chiefly through oral tradition. The wandering singers and musicians, doubt-less also the itinerant monks and clerics, spread them abroad. Like the Gregorian chant, so also the folk song inspired the musicians to develop it polyphonically. The first German collection of this kind is the manuscript known as the Lochheimer Liederbuch, in which three-voice arrangements were recorded between the years 1450 and 1454, and which contains veritable pearls of song melodies, such as, *Ich fahr dahin* (I Journey Hence) and the already-mentioned *All' mein Gedanken, die ich han, die sind bei dir*. Numerous further collections of polyphonically arranged folk songs followed. In the sixteenth century large printed editions also appeared. Further mention of these will be made in connection with the discussion of the polyphonic song.[40]

Since the invention of the art of printing, folk songs—to be sure for the most part without the melody—were issued singly with the date of publication as is still done. Many melodies of secular songs have been preserved owing to the fact that sacred words were set to them, a practice that was frequently followed in the Reformation period, as well as in previous times. The recast poems, through which many an old melody has been saved for us, were called *contrafacta*. The same thing happened as the result of the strange custom, which composers observed, of using in their church music, especially in the Masses, a secular song as *cantus firmus*, instead of melodies from the Gregorian choral. The lute collections have also preserved folk melodies for us.

CONCLUSION OF THE MONOPHONIC PERIOD

The monophonic song reached its highest development in the fourteenth century. This fact makes it evident that although polyphony had already existed for several centuries, the artistic feeling of the majority was still under the spell of monophony. There was as yet no great desire for polyphony, which meanwhile had been grafted upon music as an artificial shoot. As a matter of fact, this can easily be explained. Viewed esthetically, the monophonic folk song stands on a higher plane than the contemporaneous polyphony. The leaf is turned only about the middle of the fifteenth century, when, from a curious artificial specialty, polyphony becomes a developed art form, destined to lead and to take over the hegemony.

In the Middle Ages the monophonic song constituted the most important and the most artistic form. It found its classical fruition in the Gregorian choral and in the folk song. The Orient has clung to monophony to the present day. It seems to retain an insuperable aversion to polyphonic music. The credit for having developed the latter

---

[40] Cf. also, S.B., Nos. 44–47 inclusive.

belongs to Western Europe, and this development surely belongs among the greatest cultural achievements of all time. In its special manner, however, monophony retains its value; that it is still effective for definite purposes is proved by the music of later composers, from Handel to Wagner and the most modern.

PART TWO
POLYPHONIC MUSIC

III

THE ARS ANTIQUA AND THE ARS NOVA IN THE MIDDLE AGES[1]

THE BEGINNINGS OF POLYPHONY: ORGANUM, DISCANTUS, FAUXBOURDON

A SPRINGTIDE of ecclesiastical musical art, full of creative power, developed in the ninth century, in the late Carolingian period. There arose at that time, as we have seen, the sequences, the tropes, and the liturgical drama. At the same time the "organa" appeared, the first attempts at polyphonic music. The strange designation "organum" is derived from certain passages in the Vulgate, the Latin Bible, for example, "Canentes domino in organis" (1. Par.[2] xxiii, 5), from which the meaning of festive song arose for the word organum in the Christian Church. Thus the attempts to sing polyphonically seem from the very beginning to have been viewed as something festive.

The earliest unambiguous record of the organum comes from the philosopher Scotus Erigena, who was probably born in Ireland and died c. 880. In the *Musica enchiriadis*, which was formerly, though incorrectly, attributed to the theoretician Hucbald (c. 840–930), Benedictine monk in St. Amand in Flanders, there occurs a detailed exposition of the new polyphonic art. The doctrine of the organum is further developed by Guido of Arezzo (c. 995–1050), Benedictine in Arezzo in Italy. These two famous musicians, who among other things had also rendered good service in the field of musical notation, were elevated to a kind of mu-

[1] BIBLIOGRAPHY: Coussemaker, *Histoire de l'harmonie au moyen âge.* V. Didron, Paris, 1852.—J. Handschin, "Zur Geschichte der Lehre vom Organum," Z. f. MW., 8. Jahrg., 1926; by the same author, "Über Voraussetzungen, sowie Früh- und Hochblüte der mittelalterlichen Mehrstimmigkeit" in *Schweizer. Jahrb. f. MW.*, II, pp. 1–42. H. R. Sauerlaender & cie., Aarau, 1927.—Fr. Ludwig, *Die mehrstimmige Musik des 11. und 12. Jahrhunderts*, report at the congress of the I.M.G. in Vienna, 1909; by the same author, "Die geistliche nicht liturgische und weltliche einstimmige und die mehrstimmige Musik des Mittelalters bis zum Anfang des 15. Jahrhunderts," in Adler's *Handbuch der Musikgeschichte.*—H. Riemann, *Geschichte der Musiktheorie.* Max Hesse, Leipzig, 2d ed., 1920.— According to the most recent investigation, Guido of Arezzo is supposed to have come from the neighborhood of Paris, a fact of especial interest because France deserves the chief credit in the early development of polyphony. Guido was educated in the monastery of S. Maur des Fossés near Paris; later he went to Pomposa near Ferrara, whence he is reported to have been driven by the jealousy of the monks, in consequence of which he fled to Arezzo.
[2] Chronicles.

sical sainthood of the Middle Ages. In legendary manner the reports
exaggerated their accomplishments, so that all innovations and progress
were attributed to them. Guido, e.g., was also reported to have invented
the clavier. But though this and other reports belong to the realm of
legend, it does remain true that both of them left behind important
theoretical works, and especially also the doctrine of the organum.

The organum was improvised; a second part was sung to a melody
of the Gregorian chant. In the oldest organum the improvised voice
lay beneath the Gregorian melody, which latter was designated as the
cantus firmus, or the "tenor" (from *tenere* = to hold). Two varieties
of organum were distinguished. The following method was probably
the older: both voices are in unison at the beginning; they then diverge
stepwise until they reach the interval of a fourth; then they continue in
parallel fourths, returning again at the conclusion to the unison, e.g.:

Gerbert, I, 169, quoted according to Riemann.

Rex cœ - li do - mi - ne ma - ris un - di - so - ni.

The stationary voice at the beginning of this example is noteworthy.
It is possible that instrumental music suggested this method. In the
old bowed instruments, the *vielle* and the still older *rota*, the strings lay
flat beside one another, and it is quite possible that in playing a
melody, an open string often sounded simultaneously. The hurdy-gurdy
(*chiffonie* or *vièle à roue*) which too was known in the Middle Ages (represented in the stone sculptures of the church of Boscherville in Normandy) [3] had accompanimental open strings, just as the more recent
bagpipe has its drone bass notes.

The second kind of organum requires parallel movement in fourths
without touching other intervals. When the voices are doubled, the following form arises:

Tu pa - tris sem - pi - ter - nus es fi - li - us.

or progression in pure fifths is also demanded.

The author of the *Musica enchiriadis* was still under the influence

---

[3] The capital which bears these sculptures is now in the museum of Rouen.

of the Greek theory. Inasmuch as the latter recognized only the octave
and the fifth as pure consonances, he evidently believed that the pro-
gressions would have to take place only in consonances, which, of course,
produces a horrible cacophony. The organum is valuable and interesting, because for the first time it suggested and brought to realization
the idea of letting two voices sound together. In the similar progression of the two voices it was still primitive.

Beside the word "organum," the word "diaphony" is also used as a
designation for many-voiced music. The word "diaphony," as a matter
of fact, is frequently found in the writings of the Anglo-Saxon Bishop
Aldhelm (d. 709), so that the first attempts at two-part singing had
perhaps already been made in the seventh century.

The form of polyphony designated by the term "*discantus*" made its
appearance in the twelfth century—that is to say, quite long after
the organum—and it developed during the course of the thirteenth
century, when the life and art of the Church took on new vitality. The
progress made in other domains seems to have powerfully stimulated
both the theoreticians and the composers of music. They cultivated the
polyphonic field with great ardor.

The term "*déchant*" arose in the twelfth century in France, which
country merits the highest credit for the development of polyphonic
music. One of the oldest methods of *déchant, Quiconques veult des-
chanter*, is written in French. The *déchant* also, at first, was not noted
but was improvised; here, however, the added, improvised voice lay
higher than the choral melody upon which one descanted. It is of the
greatest significance that at this time, in *déchant* as well as in organum
(two forms which it is difficult to distinguish), the principle of parallel
motion is abandoned in favor of contrary motion, which latter is, and
will remain, the only true principle of many-voiced music. The rule for
déchant says that the counter voice must sound alternately the octave
and the fifth of the fundamental voice, and should do so in contrary
motion. The following clear example is taken from the handbook
of Riemann. It will be observed that occasional parallel fifths still
occur in *déchant*, and indeed these continue to appear for a long time:

Quem æ-the-ra et ter -ræ at-que ma-re non præ-va-lent to-tum cap-ta - re.

The rules allowed embellishments, and with the addition of these, the foregoing illustration may have sounded considerably better. For example:

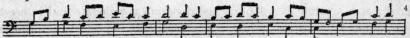

The fauxbourdon (*falso bordone* = false bass) is a special kind of *discantus*, which is first described in English tractates of the fifteenth century, though it is probably much older. Its great significance lies in the fact that it not only employs parallel thirds, but is actually based on these. By the acceptance of these the ban was removed which hindered the further development of polyphony. What is accepted today as a matter of course, and is done quite spontaneously by musical children, i.e., singing in thirds, had to be achieved with difficulty in the development of polyphony. It seems that the English first came upon the idea. At any rate, at the end of the thirteenth century an anonymous writer asserted that in that part of England which is called West-cuntre, thirds had long been used as consonances. At about the same time, the English theoretician Walter Odington favored the recognition of thirds as consonances. A special manner of singing, the gymel (*cantus gemellus* = twin singing), proceeding in thirds, which was used in England, seems to have been employed there in very old times. Perhaps the fauxbourdon has developed from this.[5]

Fauxbourdon was so called because it was noted differently from its sound. One imagined thirds placed below the cantus firmus, but then sang them an octave higher than they were imagined. The fauxbourdon, like the *discantus* not recorded, was improvised in the following manner:

Conceived:

Rendered:

As a rule the fauxbourdon was three-voiced. Thirds were added above the cantus firmus, sounding as written:

[4] Cf. S.B., No. 9.

[5] It is probable that the English have only imitated the Scandinavians in that point; the Viking colonists, established in Scotland and in England in the eleventh century, would be the ones who would have taught the peoples of those countries the singing in thirds. Cf. V. Lederer, *Über Heimat und Ursprung der mehrstimmigen Tonkunst.* Vol. I., C. F. W. Siegel, Leipzig, 1906.

The fauxbourdon practice maintained itself in the Church for a long time, and indeed, one can still hear so-called *falsi bordoni* sung in Rome. These, however, do not correspond accurately to the older form, but are quite simple recitations for several voices.

THE DEVELOPMENT OF POLYPHONIC MUSIC IN FRANCE AND IN ENGLAND [6]

The oldest forms of polyphonic music appear under the names organum, discantus, and fauxbourdon. The term organum is the most general, the most inclusive. At first, polyphony, as remarked, was improvised. Naturally the attempt was also made at an early period to fixate this by notation. One of the earliest manuscripts is the Winchester Troper, which contains ecclesiastical songs in two-voice arrangements.[7] Unfortunately, however, they are recorded in neumes without lines. This gives only a general indication of the melodic progress, and can not be deciphered at the present day. All that can be definitely determined is that the voice which is added to the given Church song lay above the cantus firmus, and that, despite the contrapuntal form of note against note, independence of voice leading did exist. Indeed, unrestrained independent voice leading was and remained for a long time the outstanding characteristic of polyphonic music. This was carried to such an extent that even crossing of voices, which in later decades was forbidden, at any rate for the upper voices, was indulged in without scruple by the composers of the Middle Ages. In the freedom of the individual voices lies the attraction of the early art. To be sure, the one who himself participates in the rendition of the music will feel this the most keenly; the ear of the listener, on the other hand, must put up with much harshness, since little or no attention is paid to the harmonic euphony.

France won the distinction of having for the first time brought po-

[6] BIBLIOGRAPHY: Fr. Ludwig, *Repertorium organorum recentioris et motetorum vetustissimi stili.* Vol. I (Classified Catalogue of the Sources). Niemeyer, Halle, 1910.—*Oxford History of Music.*—Johannes Wolf, *Geschichte der Mensural-Notation von 1250–1460.* 3 vols., Vol. II (containing music pieces in facsimile), Vol. III (transcriptions). B. & H. Leipzig, 1904.
[7] Facsimiles in the edition of the Troper published under the editorship of W. H. Frere-Henry Bradshaw Society, London, 1894.

lyphony to a higher form of development, definitely assuming a leading
position from the eleventh to the fourteenth century. The compositions
which were created there spread throughout Europe and served as
models. One of the oldest nurseries of this music was the Abbey of
St. Martial in Limoges. Here arose a kind of organum in which the Church
melody, the cantus firmus in the lower voice—metrical poems are chiefly
employed—is expanded into long-sustained notes, while the upper voice
moves in a more lively manner; for every note in the lower voice there
is a greater number of short notes in the upper voice. Expressed
in modern terms one might call this a kind of pedal-point style. The
school of Chartres also played an important rôle, in the eleventh century,
in the elaboration of polyphonic music.

About the middle of the twelfth century, the Parisian school took over
the lead. For the first time, names of composers are mentioned. About
1160 Magister Leoninus, who wrote a large liturgical work, the *Magnus
liber organi de Gradali et Antiphonario*, was choirmaster at Notre
Dame. This work was renewed by his successor Perotinus Magnus. As
the result of the establishment of the university by Robert de Sorbon
(1202–74), Paris became an intellectual center. The new seat of learn-
ing, at which there were professors of music, contributed its share to the
development of the new art.[8]

Polyphony which first appeared in the old organum, had contented
itself for centuries with conducting the supplementary voice in the
same rhythm as the cantus firmus. But now the effort made itself
more and more felt to have each voice rhythmically independent, just as
we have observed that in the compositions of Limoges a larger number
of notes of shorter values were already coupled with a long note.

But these new rhythms called for a more precise method of notation.
Inasmuch as the transmitted system of notation, the system of the
neumes, was incapable of indicating rhythmic values, i.e., had no means
of indicating the time value of a note, recourse was at first had to the
so-called *modi*, based upon Greek metrics, which determined the rhythmic movement of a voice uniformly for its entire course, according to the
scheme of the ancient metrical feet. According to the prescribed *modus*,
a song moved uniformly throughout in trochaic, iambic, dactylic, or
anapaestic rhythm.

[8] Cf. A. Pirro, "L'Enseignement de la musique aux universités françaises," *Bull. de la soc.
intern. de musicologie*, II (1930), Nos. 1 & 2.

Soon, however, came the actual measuring of the individual note. Mensural, or measured, music arose. This was another long forward step. Fundamentally, all modern music, except the recitative and the free cadenza, is mensural music, but it is customary to limit the term to the period in which it arose. Time has not brought about any fundamental modification in the laws laid down by the first theoreticians. Those who were chiefly concerned in the origin and establishment of mensural notation were Johannes de Garlandia, the elder, who was born about 1190 in England, and labored in Paris and at the University of Toulouse; and besides him two writers who both bear the name of Franco, and are distinguished as Franco of Paris and Franco of Cologne. The last-named was also distinguished as a composer. Among famous composers one must cite also Petrus de Cruce of Amiens, designated as *optimus notator*, and the trouvère, *Adam de la Halle*, already mentioned.

Until the thirteenth century, the Parisian school enjoyed the leadership. The compositions of Leoninus are still similar to those of the school of Limoges, except that they are composed on liturgical prose-texts, and, what is quite characteristic, that the newly or freely invented upper voice is molded more or less definitely according to a rhythmic scheme, in three-part rhythm, according to the manner of the modes. During the period of the activity of Perotinus, who directed the music at Notre Dame from about 1183 to 1236, there arose a new type known as the *conductus*. This has a metrical poem as text. The new element lies in the fact that the cantus firmus, for which heretofore an already existing melody was regularly used, is now freely invented as an original composition. Furthermore, it does not consist of long-sustained notes, but is rhythmically animated. The supplementary upper voice, so far as the rhythm is concerned, is fundamentally similar to it.[9]

The highest excellence was achieved by Perotinus in his three- and four-voiced organa, which already enjoyed great fame during his life. While in the case of the two-voice organum with its long-sustained cantus firmus the upper voice pursues its course in an improvisatory manner, in the compositions of Perotinus, when two or three supplementary upper voices are present, these are rhythmically uniform, as in the conductus.

From the organa proceeded a form that is both historically and artistically significant, namely, the *motet*. In order to avoid misunderstanding, it should immediately be pointed out that the medieval motet,

[9] Cf. E.B., No 6, and S.B., No. 16.

called *motetus*, is something different in its form from that which is understood by the word since the sixteenth century. For the upper voice of an organum a new text is composed, one syllable to every note, which is related to, and elucidates, the text of the cantus firmus. The proceeding is the same as that which in monophonic music gave rise to the trope several centuries before. From this procedure the word *motetus* also receives its explanation: the content of the word, of the saying, is further elaborated in the text of the upper voice.

But this was not the ultimate stage of the development. The textual connection between the contrapuntal part and the cantus firmus was soon dissolved, the upper voice becoming as independent textually as it had become melodically. Indeed, it became the practice to add secular texts, to accompany the ecclesiastical cantus firmus with a trouvère melody or a popular refrain. Thus there arose for the first time a secular polyphonic art. Furthermore, halt was not made at one secular voice; a second voice was added, or, indeed, if we go back to the origin, three-voiced organa were also transformed into motets. In a word, organa for three voices were converted into compositions in which the two upper voices had a non-liturgical text. The name motet at this time bore the double signification of the ensemble of the entire work and also that of the voices which were placed immediately above the tenor. The highest voice, having become the third, was called the triplum (triple, hence *treble* in the old French texts; this is also the probable derivation of the English word "treble"). When still a fourth voice was placed above the triplum it took the name of quadruplum.

The three-voice motet reached a high degree of development. Numerous examples are found in the frequently cited Codices of Montpellier and of Bamberg,[10] as well as in others. The fundamental voice, the tenor, is still taken from the Church song, and a strange intermixture of the spiritual and the secular thus arises. Thus two love songs will be grafted upon an ecclesiastical trunk. To be sure, the matter is not quite as bad as appears at first sight. The chorale sounds in such long notes that it is scarcely recognizable; only a small portion, which is repeated several

---

[10] Fifty examples from the Montpellier MS have been reproduced by Coussemaker, *L'Art harmonique aux XII*e *et XIII*e *siècles.* A. Durand, Paris, 1865. Cf. on that subject: Ludwig, "Die 50 Beispiele Coussemakers aus dem MS. Montpellier," S.I.M.G., 1904.—The Bamberg MS has been published entirely in facsimile, with modern transcription, by P. Aubry, *Cent motets du XIII*e *siècle.* A. Rouart, Lerolle et cie., Paris, 1908.—For further examples of motets, see E.B., No. 10, and W.B., Nos. 3 & 5.

times, is presented; and—the chief mitigating circumstance—as a rule it was not sung at all, but was played by an instrument. This early motet, accordingly, is, in fact, a one- or two-voiced song, accompanied by an instrumental part. It could scarcely have been otherwise than that the tenor was executed by an instrument, for the simple reason that the lung power of a singer would scarcely have sufficed to sustain the long tones.

Moreover, it should be added that already in the thirteenth century motets occur which have a secular song in all three voices, i.e., including the tenor. There were also peculiar mannerisms, the most important of which was the hocket or *hoquetus* (*hoketus*). It consisted in a rapid alternation of the different voices. The following ever fresh dance song, *Prenes i garde*, from the Codex of Montpellier, is an example of motet with three secular songs:

One will observe the imitations by which the two higher voices present the same motif, while the instrumental bass (announced by three words of the text only) is totally different from the upper voices. The motet is of the greatest importance in the evolution of music, because it is the soil in which first flourished that procedure of imitation between voices which subsequent ages raised to an unequaled estate.

In a special form of imitation, the *rondellus*, we recognize the beginnings of the canon. In England, where singing in canon was still quite popular in the days of Elizabeth, as everyone knows from the comedies of Shakespeare, this strict form of imitation seems to have found a high degree of development at an especially early period. A rondellus, *Sumer is icumen in*, of surprisingly mature form has been transmitted to us.[11] It is of early date, c. 1240, and is ascribed to a monk of Reading, John of Fornsete. It is a double canon for four tenors and two basses. The harmony rests on two chords which recur regularly from the beginning to the end, with, however, surprisingly good effect. There is no monotony. A veritable spring song, with cuckoo call, is heard. The example stands quite solitary, but it corroborates the supposition that a significant rôle in the development of polyphony is to be assigned to England.

THE ARS NOVA IN FRANCE AND ITALY [12]

In the fourteenth century, in the years from c. 1330 to 1340, a renewal of art took place which is designated by no less a title than the *ars nova*. The bishop of Meaux, Philippe de Vitry (d. 1361) gave this proud title to one of his works, and from this the entire epoch received its name. In the theoretical investigations of Vitry and his colleagues, there appears for the first time the prohibition of parallel fifths and octaves; in fact, the rules for pure part writing are here given.

Only a few of Philippe de Vitry's compositions have survived. The chief master of the *ars nova* is Guillaume de Machaut, distinguished also as a poet. Jehan de Lescurel and Chaillou de Pestain whose compositions, in the beginning of the fourteenth century, were inserted in the *Roman de Fauvel*, an epic work of moral content, can be designated as his precursors. The motets of this time are characterized by a high pathos. They are of especial historical interest because they frequently refer to contemporaneous events. The coronations of secular and ecclesiastical princes are accompanied with felicitations and admonitions; the abuses of the order of the Templars are excoriated; famous composers, among them also Machaut, are praised; the vices of the singers are deprecated.

Machaut was already recognized during his lifetime as master of the masters. Eustache Deschamps celebrated him in numerous ballads;

[11] The rondel may be found in the general histories of Burney and Hawkins, in Coussemaker, *L'Art harmonique au moyen âge* (with the original notation), No. XX, 20; in G.M.B., No. 17; in Grove's *Dictionary of Music and Musicians;* and in Riemann's *Beispiele*, No. 1.
[12] See H. Besseler, "Studien zur Musik des Mittelalters," Arch. f. MW., Vol. VII.

King René erected an epitaph for him in the Roman de la Queste. He came from the Champagne. At an early period he came to the court of King John of Bohemia in Prague. Here, and at the courts of John of Normandy and Charles V of France, he seems to have led a brilliant life. He died as Canon of Rheims, probably in the year 1377.

His work is equally important in the secular and the ecclesiastical fields. Especially noteworthy is a four-part Mass which has but one precursor in polyphonic music, the Mass of Tournai. We have also from Machaut Latin and French motets, virelays, ballads, and *rondeaux*.[13] The virelays, although only monophonic, are examples of beautiful melody. Machaut was the last master who still worked in the field of monophonic music. The ballad must be accounted as the most important secular form. With Machaut, the tenor, which, as in the old motet, is conceived as instrumental, is now original, an important innovation. Sometimes he adds a contra-tenor as a second instrumental voice. In this case we are confronted by a ballad for one voice accompanied by two instrumental voices. Machaut reveals both great skill and great imagination in the melodic conduct of the voices.[14]

An interesting observation which reveals Machaut's conception of art has been transmitted to us. He says: "Qui de sentement ne fait, son dit et son chant contrefait," i.e., he who writes and composes without feeling spoils both his words and his music. That Machaut put his heart into his ballads may be clearly observed from the following opening portion of one of them:

Edition Ludwig, I. 35.

Pas de tor en thi-es pais etc.

Influenced by France, but soon developing an independent character, the *ars nova* appears also in Italy, chiefly in Florence, in the third decade of the fourteenth century.[15] The efflorescence of the intellectual life in

[13] The complete musical works of G. de Machaut have been edited by Fr. Ludwig in 3 vols., P.D.M., Leipzig, 1926 ff.

[14] Cf. S.B., Nos. 26 & 27; E.B., Nos. 11 & 12; and W.B., No. 5.

[15] BIBLIOGRAPHY: G. Gasperini, "La Musique italienne aux XIVe et XVe siècles," in Enc. Lav., 1912.—Fr. Ludwig, "Die Entwickelung der mehrstimmigen Musik im 14. Jahrhundert, S.I.M.G., IV, 1903.—A. Schering, *Studien zur Musikgeschichte der Früh-*

Italy also led to the development of polyphony. Through the French troubadours, poetry had received a strong impetus, which made itself felt in the twelfth century. In the thirteenth century there developed at the court of Frederick II (1212–50) in Sicily a literature in the Italian vernacular. Quittone d'Arezzo, Guido Guinicelli, and Jacopone da Todi are its chief representatives. The fourteenth century is dominated, at its threshold, by Dante (1265–1321), and by Petrarch (1304–74), and Boccaccio (1313–75).

Dante himself was of a highly musical nature. In his *Purgatory* he erected a monument to his friend, the composer Pietro Casella, who was considered the earliest composer of madrigals—that form in which the Florentines were distinguished. Casella, inasmuch as he died before Dante, doubtless belonged to the first half of the fourteenth century. At about that time Johannes de Florentia (Giovanni da Cascia), organist at the Cathedral in Florence, later, from 1329–51, in the service of Mastino della Scala II in Verona, and Giacopo da Bologna established the new style in Italy. The most famous, and perhaps also the greatest of all, was the organist at St. Lorenzo, Francesco Landino (Franciscus caecus de Florentia), who was born, c. 1325, in Florence, the son of a painter. He became blind in childhood as the result of the smallpox, and in music sought comfort for the loss of his sight. He played the lute, the guitar, the flute, and keyboard instruments, especially the organ. He was decorated with the highest honors; at Venice in 1364 he was feted as poet, composer, and performer. He was crowned with the laurel by the king of Cyprus in the presence of Petrarch. The musicians, evidently asserted their position beside the other artists, a fact only recently discovered by history.

Still more than the compositions of the French do those of the Florentine *ars nova* impress one as veritable works of art. The crude successions of fifths and of octaves have disappeared, the thirds and sixths have been definitely accepted, a harmonic system has become preponderant which is acceptable even to modern ears, while the richness of the melody bears witness to the special gift of the Italians for song.[16]

It has been demonstrated that in this epoch instrumental playing was cultivated with ardor. Both the literature and the painting of the

renaissance. C. F. Kahnt, Leipzig, 1914.—Joh. Wolf, "Florenz in der Musikgeschichte des 14. Jahrhunderts," S.I.M.G., III, 1902.

[16] Cf. S.B., Nos. 22 & 23. A madrigal by Landino will be found in W.B., No. 6.

time bear witness to this fact. Frequently the compositions of the Italian *ars nova* were not only sung, but also played by instruments; concerning this there is no longer any doubt. As to what the instruments were, or what their precise nature was, we are not certain. Analysis of the works seems to indicate that they were either entirely intrusted to instruments, or were divided between these and the voice. In the latter case the instruments simply reinforced the ensemble of voices, which they accompanied from beginning to end.

Florence, Bibl. Laur. Pal. 87.
Transcribed by J.Wolf, *Gesch.Mensural-Notation.* III, 94.

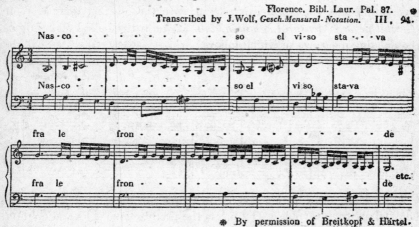

* By permission of Breitkopf & Härtel.

To the old forms of the motet and the rondo the Florentines added three new ones, the *madrigal*, the *ballata*, and the *caccia*. The two former were derived from the troubadour poetry, but the caccia is an innovation. The madrigal [17] was originally a pastoral poem, but it soon expanded to the idyll, in the broader sense of the term, and even the more serious problems of life are occasionally discussed. One of its characteristics is its compact form; each stanza contains but two or three rhymes, the number of stanzas varying from six to thirteen. The madrigal, *Nascoso el viso*, of John of Florence presents a typically Italian subject: "The youth entranced spies upon his beloved at a spring, clad as she was at her birth." The composition is for two voices, as are many of the Florentine ones. The upper voice moves in rich florid passages, the second adds a kind of supporting bass. The piece can be played on instruments; when sung *a cappella* by two male voices, a resonant tenor

[17] With regard to the derivation of the word "madrigal," cf. Rassegna bibliografica della letteratura italiana, October, 1898, published at Pisa: the essay by Leandro Biadene, Professor of Neo-Latin Literature at the University of Pisa.

in the upper voice, it will not fail even today to produce a charming impression with its ebullient, almost exuberant invention, even though harmonic lacunae at times offend our ears. The madrigal begins as is shown on page 65.

The ballata, originally a dance song, consists in its simple form of a *ripresa*, or refrain, sung at the beginning; a middle portion consisting of two halves, the so-called *piedi*, indicated with repeat marks, but having a double text; a repetition of the refrain, now called the *volta*, with new text; and finally the *ripresa*, or refrain, with the opening text. J. Wolf (*Geschichte der Mensural-Notation*, No. 52) cites the ballad of Landino, the opening measures of which follow:

The caccia is a hunting song which presents pictures of the much-beloved aristocratic chase. Doubtless the promiscuous calls and counter calls of the voices and the horns led to the particular musical form of the caccia, which is that of the canon. Two voices are carried through canonically; at times a third one is added as a kind of supporting bass. How realistic and lively this music is may be seen from the beginning of a caccia by Ghirardellus de Florentia: "As soon as the morning of the beautiful day appears, the huntsman awakes." The entire piece is reprinted in Riemann's *Handbuch*. Male choruses should not neglect to revive this charming picture of old Florentine life, as shown on page 67.[18]

The Supremacy of the Netherlanders in the Fifteenth Century [19]

The Style.—In the fifteenth century the shifting leadership in music passes to the Netherlanders. "These are the true masters of music"

---

[18] A further example of the caccia will be found in W.B., No. 7.
[19] Bibliography: Ambros, *Geschichte der Musik*, Vol. III and Vol. V (Examples).— R. Ficker, "Die früheren Messkompositionen der Trienter Codices," *Studien zur MW.* (Beihefte der *D.T. OE.*), XI; *vide* also *loc. cit.*, Vols. II and VII, B. & H., Leipzig, 1913.— A. Orel, "Die mehrstimmige geistliche Musik von 1430–1600," in Adler's *Handbuch der*

says the sixteenth-century Italian historian, L. Guicciardini. He assures us that they brought music to perfection, and is of the opinion that in the Netherlands musical ability is so generally innate, that men and women sing in time correctly, with much charm and melody.

The term "Netherlands" must be taken in a broad sense. It includes not only Belgium and Holland, but also a large portion of Northern France. With respect to its value and significance, the music of the time is not inferior to the contemporary painting, even though it does not assume equal importance among the educated, and unfortunately is very seldom performed. No one will be surprised that music could develop so highly in the Netherlands. The degree of culture which sprang up as the result of centuries of commerce is well known. The living together in large cities necessarily furthered the art of music. Music is a social art; it has never flourished in the open countryside, where people live in manors far apart. In the large cities of the Netherlands there were brilliant festivals, ecclesiastical, as well as secular, at which music was a welcome assistant.

Musikgeschichte.—Riemann, *Handbuch der MG.*, Vol. II, Part 1.—H. E. Wooldridge, *Oxford History of Music*, Vol. II, 1905.—A large collection of compositions of the period is contained in the *Trent Codices* (Trienter Codices), ed by G. Adler, Koller, Loew, Schegar, Ficker, Orel, in the D.T. OE., VII, 1; XI, 1; XIX, 1; XXVII, 1; and XXXI.—Transcriptions for organ of 12 compositions by A. Schering, *Alte Meister aus der Frühzeit des Orgelspiels.* Edition Breitkopf. No. 3938.

An important medium for the cultivation of music were the chapels of choristers. The old papal chapel in Rome, which employed both French and Flemish singers in great numbers, served as model for the ecclesiastical chapels. One of the most important, certainly the most famous in the north, was the one in Cambrai. But the churches were not the only possessors of such chapels; the princes also began to maintain these at their courts. The chapel of the dukes of Burgundy, under Philip the Good and Charles the Bold, was especially famous.

With the rise of the princely chapels there begins a new epoch in the history of the cultivation of music. These princely institutions became for centuries the most important bearers of musical culture. Originally, as noted, these institutions were primarily choral chapels (they were called in German *Kantoreien*); the instrumentalists at first held a secondary position. Only at a much later period, at the end of the eighteenth and in the nineteenth century, was the emphasis placed upon the orchestra. Emperor Maximilian set up a royal chapel in Innsbruck after the model of the Burgundians—it is pictured in Hans Burgkmair's Triumphal Procession of Maximilian. With this he laid the foundation for the brilliant cultivation of music by the Habsburgs.

In the time of the Netherlanders, the composers, almost without exception, were singers or masters (*Maîtres de chapelle, Kapellmeister*) in a chapel, even the greatest among them, like Dufay and Josquin Desprez. From this one must conclude that the level of their performances was exceptionally high. Where such talent and genius worked, mediocrity was excluded. The choruses were small, of from twelve to twenty-four men; but they consisted entirely of professional musicians, and this gives an indication of the manner in which one should at the present day again seek to revive the old art, not with our great dilettante organizations, but with small ensembles of professional singers.

The so-called "artifices" of the Netherlands composers have been much discussed and greatly decried. Because of exaggerated accounts the impression was formerly prevalent that their accomplishments were more of the nature of mathematical problems than of genuine music. To be sure, there are compositions which create the impression of being the product of the mind of an arithmetician rather than of an artist, especially through the exaggerated application of the artificial forms of the canon, e.g., cases in which a second voice does not merely repeat what the first one has sung, but where, as in the so-called crab canon, it sings backwards, i.e., from the end of the theme to the beginning; or in the mirror canon, where the second voice so alters the intervals that they are sung as they appear in a mirror; or else, where it repeats the theme in notes of smaller or larger time values; or where these procedures are combined; or where too many voices participate in the canon. Such artifices even the greatest of the masters allowed themselves. Thus there is a thirty-six voiced *Deo gratias*, ascribed to Okeghem (reprinted in Riemann's Handbook) which is in ninefold canonical form, i.e., nine voices repeat from time to time, each at the interval of one measure, one and the same melody! It is evident that in such a case not much latitude is left for artistic expression.

But the fact must be emphasized that such compositions constitute the exception, forming but a very small fraction of the sum total of the school's creations. Furthermore, one ought not take too serious umbrage at the masters' desire now and then to carry things to extremes. Such procedures were a veritable necessity; the final consequences had to be drawn.

Only he who has mastered the greatest difficulties moves everywhere with assurance and ease. The Netherlanders performed their work for all time. After the value of thematic development had been recognized, they pursued this with all the means available, in stricter and freer form, and all later epochs learned from them; the polyphony of Bach, the thematic development of Haydn and Beethoven, as well as the quite different art of variation of Brahms and Liszt rest, in the last analysis, upon the accomplishments of the Netherlanders.

In a word, the Netherlanders brought the art of counterpoint to its highest perfection. Counterpoint is the combination of several voices, or still better, of several melodies. Accordingly, it is the natural ultimate fruition of the first attempts at polyphony, which from the beginning aimed at allowing two melodies to sound at the same time. Chordal development or formation, the accompaniment of a melody with simple chords, was unknown at that time. This first appeared at the turn from the sixteenth to the seventeenth century, and was indeed given a theoretic basis by Rameau only in the eighteenth century.

Through their practice in the most difficult problems of musical setting, the Netherlanders attained a freedom and virtuosity in the combination of several melodies that is not to be confused with that which is generally called counterpoint at the present day, the stiff contrapuntal studies of our music pupils. Their freedom and virtuosity, moreover, have scarcely been attained by our modern masters. The Netherlanders really understood *faire chanter les parties le plus plaisamment*, as the French theoretician Michel de Ménehou demands.[20]

It is to be emphasized that this method, which lets every voice sing a melody, is the only proper one for choral singing. Man is too intelligent a creature to keep reiterating a few tones only, as is often demanded by some modern choral compositions. On the other hand, the danger exists that the principle, which is good in itself, will be exaggerated. Then the text suffers, the words become unintelligible, the poetry is deprived of its rights. This is often the case in the Netherlands compositions, and this also led to opposition on the part of the Church, which was justly unwilling to allow the words to lose their significance completely. The Council of Trent seriously discussed the complete banishing of polyphonic music from the Church on account of its disregard for the words. As is well known, it was Palestrina who saved it by allowing both the devout text and the musical art equally to come into their own in his clarified compositions. He and the entire Italian school mollified the frequently severe style of the older Netherlanders, and bestowed upon it, without prejudice to its dignity, a higher grace and beauty.

The Older Netherlands School.[21]—The head of the Older Netherlands School was William Dufay. Born c. 1400 at Chimay in Hainaut, he entered the papal chapel in Rome as a singer in the year 1428.[22]

[20] *Nouvelle instruction familière*, 1558; ed. by H. Expert in facsimile. A. Leduc, Paris, 1900.

[21] COLLECTIONS: E. Droz, Y. Rokseth, and G. Thibault, *Trois chansonniers français du XVe siècle.* 3 vols., E. Droz, Paris, Vol. I, 1927.—E. Droz and G. Thibault, *Poètes et musiciens du XVe siècle.* G. Jeanbin, Paris, 1924.—K. Jeppesen and V. Brondal, *Der Kopenhagener Chansonnier.* B. & H., Leipzig; Levin and Munksgaard, Copenhagen, 1927.

[22] After having received his early education in the choir of the cathedral of Cambrai, W. Dufay was a member of the papal chapel, 1428–37. From 1433 to 1435 he accompanied Eugene IV to Pisa and to Florence. Then he probably returned to Paris. From 1442 to 1449 he was in the service of the antipope Felix V (Amadeus VIII of Savoy). He died in Cambrai, where he was a canon, on the 29th of November, 1474. BIBLIOGRAPHY: Ch. van den Borren, *Guillaume Dufay, son importance dans l'évolution de la musique au XVe siècle.* Académie royale des sciences, des lettres, et des beaux-arts. M. Lamertin, Brussels, 1926.— Fr. X. Haberl, *Bausteine zur Musikgeschichte*, I, *Wilhelm Dufay.* 3 vols., B. & H., Leipzig, 1885–88.—A. Pirro, criticism of the last-named work in the R.M., VII, 321 ff. — John Stainer, *Dufay and His Contemporaries* (with many examples). Novello & Co., London, 1898. NEW EDITIONS: H. Besseler is preparing a complete edition of the works of Dufay for the *Publikationen älterer Musik.*—REPRINTS: H. Besseler, 12 nos. in Blume's *Chorwerk.* Kallmeyer, Wolfenbüttel & Berlin.— Riemann's *Handbuch.* B. & H., Leipzig, 2d ed., 1919, Vol. II, 1, 3 nos.—S.B., nos. 38–40.—W.B., No. 12.—J. Stainer, *Dufay and His Contemporaries*, 19 nos.—Trent Codices in D.T. OE.

He is, therefore, a contemporary of the painters Hubert and Jan van Eyck, the creators of the altar of Ghent. The efflorescence of music and of painting begins at the same time. Doubtless Dufay was influenced by the somewhat older John Dunstable (d. 1453), an Englishman, who together with Lionel Power and some other masters had brought counterpoint to a high degree of development in the British Isles at an early time. After the great victory of the English over the French at Agincourt, in the year 1415, a lively intercourse arose back and forth across the Channel, and it appears that as a result of mutual fructification a brilliant period of music developed under Henry V in England and Charles VII in France.

D.T.Œ., Vol. VII.

Dunstable [23] is especially significant as composer of spiritual songs or hymns. He entwines ecclesiastical melodies with a second and third voice in rich and phantastic manner, and varies the different strophes freely and characteristically. Of especial interest from a historical point of view is the appearance of the variation form. One hundred and fifty years later the English gain the distinction of founding the variation form in clavier music also. The most valuable element in Dunstable's work is the rich melody in which he clothes his voices.

[23] Nothing certain is known concerning the life of John Dunstable. He is supposed to have been born about 1370, perhaps at Dunstable (Bradford). He died on the twenty-fourth of December, 1453, and was interred in St. Stephen's Church, Walbrook, London. Some scholars surmise that he was identical with Lionel Power.—Cf. Cecie Stainer, "John Dunstable," S.I.M.G., II (1900). Reprints: Ambros, II, *O rosa bella;* S.B., Nos. 34–36; Trent Codices in D.T. OE.; W.B., No. 11; Wooldridge, *Early English Harmony,* 2 vols., B. Quaritch, London, 1897–1913.—A composition by Lionel (Power) will be found in W.B., No. 9.

In this characteristic William Dufay is not only comparable to Dunstable, but even surpasses him. In both the influence of the monophonic period of the Gregorian choral with its fecundity of inflections or nuances still betrays itself. Note, e.g., the flight of the melody in the Sanctus of the Mass *Se la face ay pale*, as is shown on page 71.

The Benedictus which follows this presents a short canon for soprano and alto on the words *in nomine Domini*. Far from impressing one as being artificial, it reveals a kinship with pleasing folk song:

The entire piece reveals in how masterly a manner Dufay understood how to utilize the alternation between high and low voices, between soli and chorus.

These fragments of a Sanctus are taken from an entire Mass. From this time on it became customary to compose polyphonically the so-called *Ordinarium Missae* (the Ordinary of the Mass), the five regularly recurring parts of the Mass, the Kyrie, Gloria, Credo, Sanctus, and Agnus Dei. The Mass became the chief form of composition. As a kind of *Leitmotiv*, as a support and melodic-thematic band of union, the composers employ some melody of the Gregorian choral as *cantus firmus* in the tenor, according to ancient custom. The motifs of this *cantus firmus* melody are then utilized and carried through in the different voices in the most diverse manner. By this means a unity is imparted both to the individual numbers and to the whole, which considerably deepens and spiritualizes the composition. A peculiar mystery pervades such a unity in variety. Even though the hearer may not be fully conscious of these relationships, they nevertheless seem to be effective; they are organic, and therein lies their power.

Strangely enough, the composers frequently use, instead of a Gregorian choral melody, a secular song as *cantus firmus*, as in the example cited, the song *Se la face ay pale*. The custom is a strange one, but scarcely affected the churchliness of the compositions, because we merely have to do with melodic turns, which for the most part lose their specifically secular character, inasmuch as the artistic structure concealed them in the tenor where they occur chiefly in notes of long time value, to say nothing of inversions and other altered forms.

Of course, the situation was worse when the secular text was actually sung in the midst of the polyphonic web. Even though it was for the most part not recognizable, one can understand why the Council of Trent rebelled against this abuse. We are the gainers by this practice, since in this way, as already pointed out, many a folk melody has been preserved which would otherwise have been lost.

Bibl. nat., nouv. acq. fr. 4379 fol. 50,
transcribed by Stainer.[24]

Characteristic of the school of Dufay, as also of the contemporaneous English school, is the preference shown the upper voice, which, both melodically and rhythmically, is treated in a more lively manner than the lower ones.[25] However, even though the bass voice is limited, for the most part, to somewhat longer time values, it nevertheless never becomes a merely harmonic bass, but remains a melody, a fact carefully to be observed. The partiality toward the upper voice is also noticeable in secular compositions, for example, in the ballad *Amours merchi de*

[24] *Dufay and His Contemporaries*, p. 69.
[25] The same partiality toward the upper voice is noticeable also in the folk-tune-like rondeau by Johannes Legrant, *Laissies moy coy, je vous en prye*, which Riemann gives in his *Beispiele*, No. 8.

trestout mon pouvoir, by Gilles Binchois,[26] which with its terse declamation so characteristically reveals the French spirit, as is shown on page 73.

Besides Dufay, Gilles Binchois was one of the leading masters. Unfortunately we know little more concerning his life than that for a long time he was chapel singer at the court of Philipp the Good, of Burgundy. The examples cited show that besides the principal forms which the Netherlanders cultivated in their compositions, the Mass, the spiritual song, and the motet, in the modern sense of the word, that is, a free composition of a Psalm or Bible verse, they also understood how to write secular music, the chief form being the chanson. But the style which they applied to these diverse forms was virtually the same. The following is a fragment of a Gloria attributed to Binchois in which the tenor, being instrumental, does not have any text:

MS Trent 93,
D.T.Œ., XXXI, 55.

Ho - - mi - - ni - bus bo - - naevo - lun - ta - - tis   Lauda-mus te etc.

The Younger, or Second, Netherlands School.—A triple constellation of names shines over the younger Netherlands school: Jean de Okeghem [27]

---

[26] Probably born at Mons c. 1400, chorister in the chapel of Philipp the Good, Duke of Burgundy. He became canon of St. Wandru in Mons, and died at Lille on the 20th of Sept., 1460. The "Publications de la société française de musicologie" plan a complete edition of his preserved works. A great number of his compositions have appeared in the D.T. OE. (Trent Codices).—See also E.B., No. 13; S.B., Nos. 42 & 43; and W.B., No. 13.

[27] JEAN DE OKEGHEM (also Ockenheim, Okergan, etc.) (b. c. 1430, d. Tours, 1495) was a choir boy in the cathedral at Antwerp from 1443 to 1444. From 1446 to 1448 he was in the service of the Duke of Bourbon at Moulins. C. 1450 he was probably a pupil of Dufay. He in turn was the teacher of Josquin Desprez, Pierre de La Rue, Brumel, Loyset Compère, so that one may observe, that, although these Netherlanders wandered far abroad in the world, they nevertheless formed a unified school. In 1453 he came to Paris to the court of Charles VII; in 1459 he was elevated to the dignity of *trésorier* of the Abbey of St. Martin of Tours. In 1461 he is again in Paris, and becomes master of the king's chapel in 1465. In 1469 he journeyed to Spain at the expense of the king, and in 1484 to Flanders. NEW EDITIONS: A complete edition of the works of Okeghem is in course of publication under the editorship of Dragan Plamenac; there has already appeared Vol. I (8 masses), *P.D.M.,* 1927.—Blume's *Chorwerk,* Motets and the *Missa mimi,* ed. by Besseler; D.T. OE., XIX, 1, 2 masses and a chanson; S.B., No. 52; and W.B., No. 14.—Cf. Michel Brenet, *Jean de Ockeghem, maître de chapelle des rois Charles VII et Louis XI.* Nogent-le-Rotrou, Imprimerie Daupeley-Gouverneur, Paris, 1893.

(Ockenheim, c. 1430–95), Jakob Obrecht [28] (Hobrecht, c. 1450–1505), and Josquin Desprez [29] (1460–1521). All three led an active life, carried their art into foreign parts, and won fame and honor during their lifetime. Okeghem labored as first chaplain and composer to Charles VII and Louis XI at the court in Paris. Obrecht was master of the chapel in the cathedral at Utrecht, later at the court of Hercules of Este in Ferrara, then again in various positions in Utrecht, Cambrai, Bruges, Antwerp. After returning to Italy in 1504 he was overtaken by the plague, to which he succumbed. He is reported to have instructed the great humanist Erasmus of Rotterdam, in music. Josquin Desprez was at the court of the Sforzas in Milan in 1471, was a singer in the papal chapel in Rome between 1486–1494, and died as prior at Condé.

In the younger Netherlands school the four-voice setting, to which Dufay had already given the preference, became the rule in contrast to the three-part setting formerly favored. The four voices frequently divided into alternating parts of two and two voices. The preference given to the upper voice disappeared, all had equal status, and there developed the so-called "continuous imitation" (*imitation continue, durchimitierender Stil*). When the different voices successively sang the same words, they employed for these, in imitative manner, the same music. This is a practice which seems to us today to be quite natural and

[28] JAKOB OBRECHT (b. Utrecht, c. 1430; d. Ferrara, 1505), in 1456 was appointed master of the cathedral choir in Utrecht; 1474, chapel singer at the court of Hercules of Este at Ferrara, then again in Utrecht where Erasmus of Rotterdam is reported to have enjoyed his instruction; 1483–85, at the cathedral at Cambrai; 1489, cantor, and 1490, master of the chapel at St. Donat in Bruges; 1492, successor of Jakob Barbireau as master of the chapel at Notre Dame in Antwerp; 1498, again at St. Donat; 1500, provost at St. Peter's at Thourout; 1501, again in Antwerp; 1503 in Innsbruck; 1504, in Italy where he died in 1505 of the plague. NEW EDITIONS: A complete edition of the works of Obrecht under the editorship of Joh. Wolf. Amsterdam, Alsbach & Cie.; Leipzig, B. & H., 30 fasc. See S.B., No. 54.—Cf. O. J. Gombosi, *Jakob Obrecht, eine stilkritische Studie.* B. & H., Leipzig, 1925, with an important musical supplement.

[29] JOSQUIN DESPREZ (also Després and des Prés) (b. c. 1450, d. 1521) was perhaps born in Condé where he died on the 27th of Aug., 1521, as proprietor of a house and provost of the cathedral chapter. Jósquin, Joskin, is a familiar name for Joseph. Although he was honored by his contemporaries as the "Prince of Music," but little has been transmitted concerning his life. After 1474 he lived in Milan, 1484–86 and 1489–94 in Rome, 1495–99 director of the cathedral choir in Cambrai, 1499 in Modena, 1500 probably in Paris, 1503 in Ferrara, and finally was canon prebendary at Condé. Josquin was instrumental in transplanting musical activity from Flanders to Italy. NEW EDITIONS: A complete edition of his works is in process of publication under the editorship of A. Smijers. Alsbach, Amsterdam; 14 numbers have appeared up to 1930.—Masses: Blume's *Chorwerk*, 1929 and 1932; S.B., No. 59. Motets: Blume's *Chorwerk*, 1932; Publ. Eitner, Vol. V; Riemann's *Handbuch*, Vol. II, pp. 258 ff.; S.B., No. 60. Chansons: Blume's *Chorwerk*, No. 3; S.B., No. 61. Instrumental Nos.: S.B., No. 62, a & b; W.B., No. 19.

obvious, but which has only become generally prevalent since the time
of Okeghem. Obrecht, even more than Okeghem, presented consistent
imitations without free intervening parts. He also distinguished himself
through an extremely expressive style. In the Credo from the Mass
Ave regina coelorum, he followed the text with never-failing power and
warm feeling. Its beginning presents a clear example of the division
of voices by twos, and of the practice of imitation:

The alternations of the two groups follow one another, one group repeating the fragment just announced by the other; the episodes correspond. But at the words *et incarnatus est*, the depth of the sentiment
demands a warm and full writing for four parts:

Do these few measures not contain a profound sorrow and a heartfelt
devotion? If one follows the entire composition carefully, one will
discover everywhere fine relations between the text and the music.

Okeghem also frequently treated as two pairs the soprano and alto, and the tenor and bass, e.g., in the Sanctus of his Mass *Pour quelque peyne*. But his procedures are infinitely varied, as one may judge from the beginning of the Sanctus of the Mass *Au travail suys:*

One will find a great dignity or nobility of rhythm in the Sanctus of the Mass *L'Homme armé* of Josquin Desprez:

At the Osanna a cheerful rhythm is introduced, as is shown on page 78.

While the later composers show a predilection for a majestic tone for the Sanctus, the older ones seem to have interpreted the acclamations as a knightly act of devotion, a chivalric act of homage, according to the spirit and forms of their time. It is worthy of note how Okeghem and Josquin endeavored to paint the very heavens in the music for the words *Pleni sunt coeli*, while they chose for the Benedictus a more gentle, but artistic, canonic two-voice setting. One should also observe in the case of both the carefully chosen gradation of two-, three-, and four-voice settings.

Josquin has ever been considered the greatest master of his school. He is one of the greatest of all times. Never has lament escaped from a burdened heart with greater feeling or greater power than in his *De profundis*, the beginning of a motet:

One need only sing the melody of the upper voice to feel the spirit-breath of genius. That other masters also knew how to combine profound expression with the high art of polyphonic composition, may be demonstrated, among many other examples, by the Agnus Dei of the Mass *Mente tota*, by Antoine Févin (Antonius Fevim),[30] a contemporary

[30] Antoine Févin was born at Orléans, probably in 1473, and probably died c. January, 1512. The extent to which anthologies of the time included his works proves his reputation.

of Josquin. The Mass *Mente tota* was printed, with two other Masses of Févin, for the first time by the Italian editor, Antico, in 1516, in his *Liber quindecim missarum electarum*. It was edited by H. Expert, in 1899. The opening measures of the Agnus Dei are:

Beside the Masses of Févin, there appeared in the same collection, the Mass *Alma Redemptoris Mater*, of the pupil of Josquin, Jean Mouton,[31] the beginning of whose Agnus Dei is:

[31] Jean Mouton, probably born at Hollingue, near Metz, lived in Paris, was a chapel singer of the French kings Louis XII and Francis I, and died Oct. 30, 1522, as canon of Thérouanne, near Saint-Quentin.—Cf. G.M.B., No. 66.

Mouton distinguished himself as a singer in the chapel of the Kings of France, while as a composer he deserves to be placed among the heads of his school. The Mass *De beata Virgine* by another contemporary of Josquin, Antoine Brumel,[32] is built on a Gregorian theme taken from the Office of the Virgin, and shows how well the Netherlands composers knew how to adapt their polyphonic constructions to the *cantus firmus* of their choice.

It is only possible to mention here the names of a few other musicians who contributed to the grandeur of the school: Carpentras, Clemens non Papa,[33] Loyset Compère, Mathieu Gascongne, Pierre Moulu, Pierre de la Rue.[34] They belong to the first half of the sixteenth century.

The German *Lied*

At the time of the supremacy of the Netherlanders, German composers also entered the competition. At first there were only isolated instances, as the original Adam von Fulda, Thomas Stoltzer, master of the chapel at the Hungarian court, and Heinrich Finck,[35] who spent his youth in Poland. Soon, however, they formed a school themselves, having for its centers the Imperial Chapel of Maximilian at Innsbruck, and the ducal chapels at Munich and Stuttgart. Maximilian's court composer, Heinrich Isaak,[36] though a born Netherlander, must also be credited to this school. It reached its height in his pupil and successor, the later Bavarian court composer, Ludwig Senfl,[37] a native of Switzerland.

[32] Cf. S.B., No. 64.

[33] Cf. Bernet-Kempers, *J. Clemens non Papa und seine Motetten.* B. Filser, Augsburg, 1928.—H. Expert in *Les Maîtres musiciens de la Renaissance* (M. Sénart, Paris, 1894–1908) has edited a certain number of the works of the musicians mentioned. See also the motets published by Y. Rokseth in *Treize motets et un prélude pour orgue,* 1531. P.S.M., Paris, 1930.

[34] Cf. S.B., No. 65.

[35] Cf. S.B., No. 87.

[36] HEINRICH ISAAK (b. before 1450; d. Florence, 1517) came to Florence c. 1480 as organist of Lorenzo the Magnificent; 1484 he was at the court of the Archduke Sigismund at Innsbruck. The remainder of his life was spent in diverse residences in Italy, Germany, and Austria. Reprints of his works are to be found in the D.T. OE.: part I of the great motet collection, the *Chorale Constantinum,* in Vol. V, 1, ed. by Bezecny and Rabl, and Vol. XVI, 1, ed. by A. von Webern; secular compositions in Vol. XIV, 1 (Supplement XVI, 1), ed. by J. Wolf.—A complete edition of the masses of Isaak is in preparation under the editorship of H. Birtner for the D.T. OE.; the *Missa Carminum,* in Blume's *Chorwerk,* 1932; six instrumental movements, ed. by O. Dischner. Bärenreiter Verlag, Kassel; S.B., Nos. 55, 56. —Cf. H. Rietsch, "H. Isaak und das Innsbrucklied," J.P., 1917.

[37] LUDWIG SENFL (b. Zürich, or Basel, c. 1492, d. c. 1555, probably at Munich) always designated himself as Swiss. As a boy he entered the royal chapel in Vienna, where he became a pupil of Isaak, of whom he speaks with great respect in an autobiographical poem which he set to music. After Isaak's death he became his successor as court composer to

In the Mass and the motet these Germans vied with the Nether-landers. In the German *Lied* they cultivated a field of their own. Whereas the French *chanson*, even at an early period, was developed freely, i.e., without a *cantus firmus*, the German *Lied* of this time was still consistently based upon the old German folk song. The composers took as their basis a folk melody which they employed as tenor, and then, as it were, wove the three other voices about it. Thematically this was chiefly done in such a way that the soprano, alto, and bass, took up and developed principal motifs of the *cantus firmus*.

In these polyphonic settings the diversity of view, the depth, and the frankness of the old monophonic folk song are renewed. They signify a new springtide of *Lied* composition. Because we, today, have a different harmonic sense, it causes us some difficulty to understand this art. But we shall again learn to hear with those artists, just as we have again learned to see after the manner of their contemporaries. As we again rejoice in the pictures of the old German schools of painting, we shall again allow ourselves to be delighted with the pure charms of the old Ger-man choral song (*Chorlied*). One pearl, at least, has again become popular at the present day, the parting song: *Innsbruck ich muss dich lassen*, already-mentioned (p. 43), which Isaak set, and which legend attri-butes to King Max. Many others deserve to be sung again. They should be revived in the intimate circle of friends of music, just as they were originally performed.

It seems that the humanists often edified themselves with these settings. At any rate, one of them, Bonifacius Amerbach of Basel, uni-versally known through the portrait by Hans Holbein, left a rich collec-tion of choral compositions of his day, and we know that many scholars maintained lively relations with the musicians. The epistolary col-lection of the humanist and reformer of St. Gall, Vadian, gives a clear picture of this relationship. That Luther was a passionate devotee of music is well known; less well known is the fact that Zwingli also distin-guished himself as a musician, and himself played the lute. Even the strict Calvin recognized with fine words the power of music. It has already

---

Maximilian until the time of the latter's death in 1519. From 1530 he was master of the royal chapel in Munich, where he died c. 1555. Luther was a great admirer of Senfl, even though the latter remained true to the old faith. The D.T.B. plan a complete edition of Senfl's works. There has already appeared in this edition, III, 2, a volume of *Magnificats* and *Motets*, edited by Th. Kroyer.—Cf. E.B., No. 15; S.B., Nos. 76, 84, 85, 86; and W.B., No. 28.

been mentioned that Erasmus was instructed in music by Obrecht. Several humanists were also theoreticians, at their head, the distinguished Glarean; and at all universities there were chairs for music. Never have the learned displayed a greater devotion to this art than at the time of humanism. The Greeks were their ideals, and because the Greeks honored music so highly, their disciples followed, unconcerned that their music was something quite different from that of their exemplars. They did, indeed, exert themselves to create Roman song to the extent of urging the composers to make choral settings of the odes of Horace in the meters of the originals.[38] But these attempts remained pedagogical experiments, even though such masters as Senfl and Hofhaimer participated in them.

The oldest collection of concerted German *Lieder* is the manuscript already-mentioned dating from the middle of the fifteenth century, known as the Lochheimer Liederbuch. Numerous others, such as the Munich and the Berlin books, followed. When the art of printing music had been invented, a lively activity developed in the publication of great *Lieder* collections. We possess the collection published by Oeglin in Augsburg in 1512; that by Schoeffer in Mainz in 1513; the great *Auszug guter alter und neuer teutscher Liedlein* (Selection of Good Little German Songs, both Old and New) by G. Forster in Nuremberg, who between the years 1539 and 1556 published not less than 380 *Lieder* in five instalments; the collection of *115 gute und neue Lieder* (115 Good and New Songs) published in 1544 by H. Ott in Nuremberg; and the *Lieder* of Heinrich Finck which appeared in 1536. A modern selection of old folk songs, some in monophonic, some in concerted settings, which presents the most beautiful of the beautiful, and which indeed may be called classic, has been compiled by Rochus von Liliencron in his book *Deutsches Leben im Volkslied um 1530* (German Life in Folksong around 1530), "Kuerschner's Deutsche Nationalliteratur," Vol. XIII.[39]

The Song by Paul Hofhaimer, *Meins traurens ist ursach* (The Cause of My Sorrow)[40] will show with what simplicity the old masters, standing

[38] S.B., Nos. 73 & 74.

[39] New editions of collections of *Lieder:* "Das Lochheimer Liederbuch," edited by Arnold, in Chrysander's *Jahrbücher für musikalische Wissenschaft*, Vol. II, 1867; facsimile edition by K. Ameln, Wölbing Verlag, Berlin, 1925.—Oeglin, Ott, Heinrich Finck, and Forster (Part 2), in the Publ. Eitner, Vol. IX, 1–4, 7, 29.—H. Leichtentritt, *Meisterwerke deutscher Tonkunst, Mehrstimmige Lieder alter deutscher Meister.* B. & H., Leipzig, 1905.

[40] See H. J. Moser, *Paul Hofhaimer*. Cotta, Stuttgart, 1929.—For an example by Hofhaimer, cf. also W.B., No. 25.

upon the old *Lied*, knew how to express true and heartfelt sorrow:[41]

The opening phrase with the intervals of the fifth is that of the Protestant choral *Aus tiefer Not schrei ich zu Dir* (Out of the Depths I Cry to Thee) which is familiar from the Bach cantata and the Bach choralpreludes. That interval of the fifth occurs frequently at the beginning of the chants of the Reformed Church in the sixteenth century (cf. the sixty-fifth Psalm), and we have already noted that it occurs in Gregorian music. It belongs to those stereotyped turns of old music, which, like certain word expressions of the folk song, although constantly

[41] TRANSLATION: The cause of my sorrow is my lack of one to whom I can lament that I would, believe me, rather elect death than thus to leave you.

recurring, yet never lose their effect. Moreover, Hofhaimer employs it in a masterly imitative manner in all voices. The natural, spontaneous independence of the voice leading compels admiration. The Phrygian tonality is clearly evident.

Senfl's *Es jagt ein Jäger geschwinde* (A Huntsman Pursues with Speed) [42] is exhilaratingly lively despite its strict imitation, as its first part shows:

Riemann, *Beispiele,* p.69.*

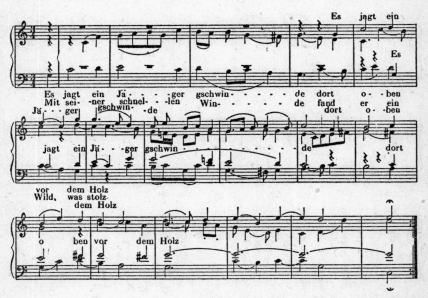

* By permission of Breitkopf & Härtel.

As a characteristic creation of this second period of bloom of the German folk song, one may mention *Ach Elslein, liebes Elselein* (Ah Elsbeth, Dearest Elsbeth) [43] which in its text presents a variation of the old legend of Hero and Leander. In a four-part setting, Senfl gives the melody

[42] TRANSLATION:
    A huntsman pursues with speed up yonder next the wood,
    With his swift winder he found some prey, was proud.

[43] TRANSLATION:
    Ah Elsbeth, dearest Elsbeth mine
    Would I were now with thee!
    But two deep waters are flowing between thee and me.

in the treble, and combines with it the melody *Es taget vor dem Walde* (Day Breaks outside the Wood): [44]

From Liliencron: *Deutsches Leben im Volkslied um 1530.**

The following additional songs by the greatest of these song composers, Senfl, will still further illustrate his versatility: *Dich meiden zwingt* (Constrained I Am to Shun Thee); *Ich armes Keuzlein kleine* (Poor Little Innocence I); *Die Brünnlein die do fliessen* (The Brooklets Which Do Flow); *Von erst so well wir loben* (Foremost Let Us Be Praising);

[44] TRANSLATION:

> Day breaks outside the wood,
> Arise, little Kate!
> The hares will soon be running,
> Arise, little Kate, dear love!
> Be up!
> Thou art mine and I am thine!
> Arise, little Kate!

Mit Lust tet ich aussreiten (With Joy Would I Ride Forth); *Nun grüss dich gott, du edler saft* (Now Greet Thee God, Thou Precious Juice); *Ein abt den wöll wir weihen* (An Abbot We Would Consecrate).

The songs of Heinrich Finck, Sixtus Dietrich,[45] Benedict Ducis, examples of which may be found in Riemann, *Beispiele*,[46] impress one as similarly artistic and at the same time heartfelt. Other distinguished composers to be mentioned are Arnold Bruck and Lorenz Lemlin.

Music Notation and Music Printing [47]

The invention of music printing, which of course was of the greatest importance for the further development of music, falls in the time of the Netherlanders. Before discussing this, we shall take a brief glance at the development of musical notation. We have noted how from the neumes there developed the chorale notation with lines. Concerted music gave the impetus for further development. At first, a solution was attempted by means of the modi already-mentioned, which were used also by the troubadours, i.e., the rhythm of the music depended upon the meter of the verse. A great advance took place when the rhythm was made independent of the text, and notes of definite time value were introduced. Thus arose in the thirteenth century the notation of mensural music. Its creators were the followers of Perotinus: Robertus de Sabilone, Petrus de Cruce, called "optimus notator," Johannes primarius de Garlandia, Franco of Paris, Franco of Cologne, and others.

It strikes us as strange at the present time that the notes were subdivided into threes instead of into twos, as appears natural to us at the present day. In other words, the triple measure was adopted as the normal measure. This was based upon the Holy Trinity. Musical theory was still transfused with a mystical, scholastic spirit. Only the longest note, the *maxima*, was divided into two portions:

$$\text{maxima (duplex longa)} = 2 \text{ longæ}$$

The *maxima*, however, was employed only exceptionally. The unit value

---

[45] Cf. Hermann Zenck, *Sixtus Dietrich*, P.D.M., III, 2. B. & H., Leipzig, 1928.

[46] Nos. 26, 27, 32, 38.

[47] Bibliography: Heinrich Bellermann, Die Mensuralnoten und Taktzeichen des XV. und XVI. Jahrhunderts. 2d ed. Georg Reimer, Berlin, 1906.—A. Pirro, "La Notation proportionnelle," *Tribune de Saint-Gervais*. Paris, 1895, Nos. 3, 4, 5.—H. Riemann, *Notenschrift und Notendruck*. Röder, Leipzig, 1896; by the same author, *Kompendium der Notenschriftkunde*. F. Pustet, Regensburg, 1910.—Johannes Wolf, *Handbuch der Notationskunde*. 2 vols., B. & H., Leipzig, 1913 and 1919.

of the measure was the *longa* which equalled three *breves*, the *brevis* three *semibreves:*

> ¶ longa = 3 breves ■
>
> ■ brevis = 3 semibreves ◆

The *brevis* was the counting unit, like our quarter note today. Accordingly, the customary measure was tripartite, consisting of a long or three breves.

If several longs follow one another, each one constitutes a measure. In this case they are called perfect:

$$\text{¶ ¶ ¶} = \tfrac{3}{4} \ | \ \text{♩·} \ | \ \text{♩·} \ | \ \text{♩·} \ |$$

Likewise when three breves follow a long:

$$\text{¶ ■ ■ ■} = \tfrac{3}{4} \ | \ \text{♩·} \ | \ \text{♩ ♩ ♩} \ |$$

If, however, only one or two breves stand between the longs, they are reckoned together with these, they make these imperfect, " *imperficiunt*," as the old musicians were wont to say. There are definite rules concerning this "imperfecting," which can best be understood from examples:

$$\text{¶ ¶ ■ ¶} = \tfrac{3}{4} \ | \ \text{♩·} \ | \ \text{♩ ♩} \ | \ \text{♩·} \ |$$

In the preceding example, the breve "imperfects" the preceding long: it forms with this a *perfectio*, an entire measure. The situation is different when a dot is placed between the notes, the so-called *punctum divisionis.* In the following example the dot designates that the breve is to be reckoned with the following long, thus:

$$\text{¶ ¶ ■ ¶} = | \ \text{♩·} \ | \ \text{♩·} \ | \ \text{♩ ♩} \ |$$

The following examples explain themselves. It may be noted that under certain circumstances the brevis is also prolonged by one beat:

$$\text{¶ ■ ■ ¶ ¶} = | \ \text{♩·} \ | \ \text{♩ ♩} \ | \ \text{♩·} \ | \ \text{♩·} \ |$$

$$\text{¶ ■ ■ ¶ ¶} = | \ \text{♩ ♩} \ | \ \text{♩ ♩} \ | \ \text{♩·} \ |$$

$$\text{¶ ¶ ■ ■ ■ ¶} = | \ \text{♩·} \ | \ \text{♩ ♩} \ | \ \text{♩ ♩} \ | \ \text{♩·} \ |$$

$$\text{¶ ¶ ■ ■ ¶} = | \ \text{♩·} \ | \ \text{♩·} \ | \ \text{♩ ♩} \ | \ \text{♩ ♩} \ |$$

The shorter values, the breves and semibreves, are treated in a similar manner.

In the year 1309 Marchettus of Padua set up the so-called *prolations*, and the custom of dichotomizing, or dividing into halves arises. The unit value of the measure has now gone over to the brevis. A circle O at the beginning of a composition denotes three-part measurement of the brevis, i.e., that the brevis is to be divided into three parts; a semi-circle C that it is to be divided into two parts. The semicircle continues to live in our notation as the "C," with which we designate even, or common, time. A point within the circle or semicircle indicates that the subdivision of the measure is tripartite; if the dot is lacking the sub-division is dual. The following table will explain these old time designations more clearly than further words:

Tempus perfectum,	prolatio maior	⊙ =	a measure in	$\frac{9}{8}$ time
Tempus perfectum,	prolatio minor	O =	a measure in	$\frac{3}{4}$ time
Tempus imperfectum,	prolatio maior	⊂· =	a measure in	$\frac{6}{8}$ time
Tempus imperfectum,	prolatio minor	⊂ =	a measure in	$\frac{4}{4}$ time

By the beginning of the fourteenth century colored notes appeared, to indicate a change in time value; i.e., on occasion notes were written in red instead of black. Later they were often left unfilled, in which case there were white notes instead of red ones. The red or the unfilled notes had imperfect value, i.e., they were to be dichotomized. In other words, if the brevis in the composition had the value of three semibreves, it was given the value of two semibreves by being colored red or left white, i.e., unfilled, as in the following example:

About 1430 it became the custom to alter this system as a matter of convenience; most notes remained white, while black notes were employed to indicate shortened value. Blackening a note reduced its value to three-quarters of that of a white note. The list of the forms used at that period is shown on page 89.

From the brevis we still say *alla breve*, when the counting time passes from the quarter- to the half-note, from the black to the white.

As was already the case with the neumes, so also in the mensural notation it became customary to bind several notes together in so-called "ligatures." Special intricate rules again apply to these, and make the reading of mensural notation decidedly complicated and difficult.

Maxima	⊓	Minima	♦
Longa	⊓	Semiminima	♪
Brevis	▫	Fusa (filled)	♩
Semibrevis	◊		

In this way, musical notation gradually attained definiteness and the ability to present complicated time relationships. It strikes one all the more strange therefore that in the time of the Netherlanders the composers practiced occultism in their recordings, and made sight reading more difficult for the singers through all kinds of baffling indications. This was a playing with hindrances, which apparently edified composers as well as singers, but which strikes us today as quite incomprehensible. For example, instead of writing out the canons, they would indicate through some mysterious word, a Latin distich or something similar, that the voice was to begin anew, and was to be sung in notes of larger tone values, or of smaller ones, or from the end to the beginning, or in some other new form.

Ottaviano dei Petrucci invented the art of printing music with movable metal types in Venice in the year 1498. He himself published a number of ecclesiastical and secular works of the Netherlands school and of contemporary Italian composers. His first book appeared in the year 1501. It is a collection of thirty-three three-voiced motets by Josquin, Loyset Compère, and Brumel, to mention only the most distinguished names.

For a long period Venice remained the center of music publishing in Italy. The new invention spread comparatively rapidly. As early as 1512, the younger Peter Schoeffer produced good music prints in Mainz. P. Haultin made an important improvement in Paris in 1525 with a composite type, whereby separate types are not used for the lines and the notes, but the two are united. The Paris publishers, Attaingnant and Ballard availed themselves of the improvement. Paris gained world fame as a center of music printing and music publishing. At Lyons, beginning with 1532, Jacques Moderne brought out a great number of French and Spanish works. Amsterdam became preëminent in the

Netherlands, while Nuremberg was the center for Germany in the sixteenth and seventeenth centuries, later to be supplanted by Frankfurt and Leipzig, which gained preëminence through their fairs. In the nineteenth century, Leipzig, as is well known, absorbed the music publication, and established a veritable monopoly.

In the eighteenth century, printing music from type was almost completely superseded by engraving. Simone Verovio in Rome (1586) is mentioned as the first one to employ the new method. Printing with movable types had become so completely obsolete, that Immanuel Breitkopf of Leipzig, familiar to the readers of Goethe's *Dichtung und Wahrheit*, almost invented it anew. He improved upon older methods by making types that could be divided into small parts. A new revolution in music printing resulted from the invention of zinc engraving with puncheons or burrs, by Cluer and Walsh in England about 1730. At the present day the notes are usually engraved on metal plates. With the aid of transfer paper an impression of the engraved plate is conveyed to a zinc plate having a finely grained, roughened surface, which takes ink like a lithographic stone. This zinc, on a flat bed or on a rotary press, is moistened with water and inked as in the lithographic process, and is printed on paper with or without the interposition of a rubber "offset" blanket. Printing with movable types is employed only for songbooks which have extensive word-texts, as hymn books, school books, etc.

IV

THE SIXTEENTH CENTURY

Palestrina and Orlando di Lasso

In the course of the sixteenth century, the Italians became the peers of the Netherlanders, and indeed assumed the supremacy. The development of church music culminated in Palestrina. His music has become the symbol of the entire period. One speaks of the Palestrina style, when referring to the clarified *a cappella* choir style of the sixteenth century. While in the case of the Netherlanders one must assume an extensive coöperation on the part of the instruments, in the Italian period, there developed a style so purely vocal, that the addition of instruments would appear a crime. This style was brought to its perfection by Palestrina.[1] One must not think the Roman master contributed anything completely new. He joined himself to the Netherlanders and

---

[1] Giovanni Pierluigi da Palestrina (b. Palestrina, probably 1525; d. Rome, 1594). The family name was Pierluigi; the name of his natal village was later added to this. Palestrina dedicated both his works and his life entirely to church music. In his youth he was organist and master of the chapel of the principal church of his native village; from 1544 to 1551 he was instructor in singing and leader of the boy choir at the Cappella Julia in St. Peter's at Rome. In 1555 he became papal chapel singer in the Sistine Chapel under Julius III and Marcellus II. Because he was married, Pope Paul IV dismissed him in the very same year, a severe blow to Palestrina. He fell sick, but in the same year, so full of agitation for him, he received the appointment as master of the chapel at St. John Lateran; 1561–71 he was master of the chapel at Santa Maria Maggiore. In 1571, finally, he obtained the high position of master of the chapel at St. Peter's. Bibliography: G. Baini, *Memorie storico-critiche della vita e dell' opere di Giovanni Pierluigi da Palestrina.* 2 vols., Dalla Società tipografica, Rome, 1828; German tr. by Kandler and Kiesewetter, B. & H., Leipzig, 1834.—Michel Brenet, *Palestrina.* Alcan, Paris, 1906.—R. Casimiri, *Giovanni Pierluigi da Palestrina: nuovi documenti biographici.* Edizione del "Psalterium," Rome, 1918 and 1922; by the same editor, the quarterly *Note d'archivio per la storia musicale.* Ed. del "Psalterium," Rome, 1924 ff.—K. G. Fellerer, *Palestrina.* Pustet, Regensburg, 1930.—K. Jeppesen, *Der Palestrinastil und die Dissonanz* (Vienna inaugural dissertation). Levin & Munksgaard, Copenhagen, 1923; Eng. tr., *The style of Palestrina and the Dissonance,* by Margaret W. Hamerik, with an introduction by E. J. Dent. Levin and Munksgaard, Copenhagen, and O.U.P., London, 1927.—Zoe Kendrick Pyne, *Giovanni Perluigi da Palestrina: His Life and Times.* John Lane, London, 1922.—F. Raugel, *Palestrina.* Laurens, Paris, 1930.—Eug. Schmitz, *Palestrina.* B. & H., Leipzig, 1914. Works: Complete edition in 33 vols., containing 950 compositions, ed. by Witt, Espagne, Commer, and Haberl, B. & H.—From the same house, practical editions of numerous Masses, motets, of the Stabat Mater, etc., ed. in modern notation by H. Bäuerle.—Selections for male voices, by the same house.—Six numbers in *Frauenchöre alter Meister,* ed. by Leichtentritt, also B. & H.—Some works in the popular ed., "Anthologie des maîtres religieux primitifs" of the "Répertoire des Chanteurs de Saint-Gervais," edited by Chas. Bordes. Bureau d'Edition de la Schola cantorum, Paris.—S.B., Nos. 121, 122.

mastered all their arts. But he employed them in a manner which has
stripped off everything artificial, and which is at the same time adapted
to the most perfect and most sensitive of all musical organs, the human
voice.

In one direction Palestrina did achieve an improvement which approaches something new, namely, in his chordal, harmonic, declamatory
style. Whereas in the case of the Netherlanders, the chords still arose in
a more or less fortuitous manner, as the result of the combination of
melodies, with Palestrina appeared the feeling for harmonies in the modern sense. In their application he was ingenious. In the place of all
further explanation it is only necessary to remind the reader of the
beginning of the *Stabat Mater*, whose wonderfully arranged triads have
become typical, and have been used as late as by Liszt as a chief means
of mystical expression:

This method also assisted Palestrina in saving church music, which the
Council of Trent investigated, because the words sung could not be
understood. In the year 1564, Pope Pius IV appointed a commission of
cardinals and singers to look into the matter. This body consulted with
Palestrina, who, in his *Missa Papae Marcelli* and other compositions,
had solved the problem in a musically satisfactory manner, and thereby
assisted in retaining polyphonic music in the Church. The *Missa Papae
Marcelli* is not his greatest Mass, but it is distinguished by its clarity.
The following brief example may serve to characterize its style. We
select the four-voiced *Crucifixus*—the remainder of the Mass is for six
voices—which will also show how skillful Palestrina was in combining
most beautiful melody with the declamation:

After Palestrina, the churchliness of the *a cappella* style named after him was never again doubted; on the contrary, he serves as its pure exemplar. Properly so, for his style is suited to give solemn expression to the religious feelings of a congregation of believers. There is no place in him for the passion of the individual, and all superficial worldly glamor is far removed. One can understand Palestrina's music only when one remembers that his entire activity was devoted to the service of the Church. He wrote 93 Masses and approximately 350 motets. These are the chief forms of his artistic genius. One of his most beautiful Masses, of incomparable sublimity as well as mildness, is the *Assumpta est Maria* which has the antiphon on this text as its *cantus firmus*. Restricted in its means of expression, composed for female voices only, the motet *Ave regina coelorum* reveals the incomparable contrapuntal and melodic art of the master who at an early period was already compared to Raphael:

Orlando di Lasso,[2] a native Walloon, exhibits the survival of the Netherlands school in the midst of the Italian period of *a cappella* music.

[2] ORLANDO DI LASSO (Orlandus Lassus), b. Mons in Hainaut c. 1532; d. Munich, 1594. He received his first education as choir boy at the Church of St. Nicholas in Mons; at the age of twelve he was taken to Sicily and later to Milan by the viceroy Ferdinand Gonzaga. These early migrations explain the international character of Lassus, the ease with which he adapted himself to different styles. Having reached maturity he spent two years in Rome, made great journeys to England and France, sojourned two years in Antwerp, and

The Netherlanders maintain themselves on an equal footing with the Italians until the close of the sixteenth century. Lassus does not yield to Palestrina in the power of his genius, though his figure is carved from different timber. He is one of the brilliant international characters of the surging century. He is master of all styles in equal degree, and occupies a position of first rank in the art of several countries. From the beginning, his fame as a composer rested upon his religious compositions (Masses, motets, lections, the Psalter of Marot, hymns, including the Stabat Mater, etc.), in particular, upon his moving Penitential Psalms. Their style is free, lively, expressive; images abound; not that Lassus, after the manner of Jannequin, sought these as an end in themselves; he merely gave them a subordinate and ornamental place. The movements of the melody are simple and powerful; the various voices, treated in complete independence of one another, do not submit to the despotism of the upper voice. In narrowest confines, the motet *Alme Deus* offers a picture of that intensely nervous, lively, impulsive art of composition. Lassus did not allow any idea of the poetic text to escape; he painted the "clouds" and the "valleys" by appropriate inflexions of the melody:

finally, at the end of the year 1556, was called to Munich to the court-chapel by Duke Albert V, becoming master of the same in 1560. He retained that post until his death. His compositions number more than two thousand. Bibliography: Ch. van den Borren, *Orlande de Lassus.* Alcan, Paris, 1920; 3d ed., 1930; by the same author "Orlande de Lassus et la musique instrumentale." R.M., May, 1922.—Ad. Sandberger, *Beiträge zur Geschichte der Hofkapelle in München unter Orlando di Lasso.* 3 vols., Drei Masken Verlag, Munich, 1894–95; by the same author *Ausgewählte Aufsätze. zur Musikgeschichte.* Drei Masken Verlag, Munich, 1921.—Eug. Schmitz, *Orlando di Lasso.* B. & H., Leipzig, 1914. Works: Complete edition in 60 vols., ed. by Adolf Sandberger; until 1934, 21 vols. have appeared. B. & H., Leipzig.—Some works in the "Répertoire des chanteurs de Saint-Gervais."—H. Bäuerle, *Die "Sieben Busspsalmen" des Orlando di Lasso* (The Seven Penitential Psalms of Orlando di Lasso), in modern edition, B. & H., Leipzig, 1906.—Selections in the collections of Proske and Commer.—S.B., Nos. 125–27.

He did not overlook the chromaticism which was just then arising and was greatly agitating the musical world. The concluding words of this motet offered him precisely the occasion for employing these recently acquired splendors:

The thought in that little composition seems almost too abounding in content; the force of invention, the imagination in Lassus are inexhaustible.

We shall meet Lassus again as a composer of French chansons and in connection with Italian and German madrigals.

Beside him, one must give a place to his compatriot, Philippe de Monte (1521–1603), whose inspiration is akin to that of Palestrina and Lassus. His art is serious and substantial. He has written Masses and a quantity of motets.[3]

THE ROMAN SCHOOL

In Italy two schools became especially prominent during the *a cappella* period, the Roman and the Venetian. The name of Palestrina obviously dominates the first. It was formerly believed that the Frenchman C. Goudimel was his teacher, but this has been shown to be erroneous. An actual school was founded by Palestrina's pupil, G. M. Nanino (1545–1607), who has again become known today, especially through his childlike, naïvely joyful motet *Hodie Christus natus est*. To this circle, belongs also M. A. Ingegneri (1545–92), whose *Responses* for Holy-Week were long considered to be a work of Palestrina. They would not have been unworthy of him. Ingegneri is a master of the harmonic, declamatory style. His *Tenebrae factae sunt* offers a good example of this:

[3] The works of Philippe de Monte are being published under the editorship of the Canon van Nuffel and Ch. van den Borren. Desclée, de Brouwer et soc., Bruges. 1930 ff. Cf. G. van Doorslaer, *La Vie et les œuvres de Philippe de Monte*. M. Hayez, Brussels, 1921.

The Chanteurs de Saint-Gervais have popularized these responses in France.[4]

A number of compositions of F. Anerio (1560–1614), among them the well-known *Adoramus te Christe*, were likewise formerly considered as compositions of Palestrina. One must mention also Fr. Suriano (1549–1620), and G. Allegri (1582–1652), whose world-renowned *Miserere* has already been noticed. Closely related to the Roman school, are the Spaniards, Morales and Vittoria, the latter a friend of Palestrina.

THE VENETIAN SCHOOL

Just as the brilliant republic of Venice later became of decisive importance in the development of opera, so it already possessed in the *a cappella* period an important and influential school which reflects in its style the glory of its home. This school developed the double-chorus form of composition, and made it a specialty. The Netherlanders had already made occasional attempts, of an experimental nature, at composing for an unusually large number of voices. We heard of a *Deo gratias* for thirty-six voices by Okeghem; Desprez wrote a *Qui habitat* for twenty-four voices. But the brilliant compositions for eight, twelve, and more voices became the rule in Venice.

It was a Netherlander who founded the school, Adrian Willaert (d. 1562), who received the title of Master of the Chapel at St. Mark's in 1527. The school was continued and advanced to its highest stage through the two Gabrielis, both native Venetians, Andrea [5] and his

---

[4] A motet by Ingegneri will be found in W.B., No. 41.

[5] ANDREA GABRIELI (b. Venice, c. 1510; d. there, 1586), a pupil of Willaert, was a singer in the chapel at St. Mark's from 1536 to 1566. In the latter year he received the position of organist of the second organ, as successor to Merulo. He was the teacher of his nephew

nephew, Giovanni.[6] With the death of the latter, in 1612, the school lost its peculiar character even in Venice itself—other ideals arose—but during the second half of the sixteenth century it exercised the greatest influence. Students came from Germany and Denmark to receive their instruction in Venice. Hassler and Schütz were developed there; Jacobus Gallus, Aichinger, and Sweelinck were influenced by it.

A short *Agnus Dei* of Andrea Gabrieli, even though the number of voices does not exceed five, will serve to illustrate the brilliant effect which the Venetians achieved through the antiphonal singing of groups of voices:

Proske, *Musica Divina*, Vol. I.

Giovanni and of Hans Leo Hassler. Reprints: Carl von Winterfeld, *Johannes Gabrieli und sein Zeitalter*, Vol. III, Schlesinger, Berlin, 1834.—Torchi, Vols. II and III.—J. W. Wasielewski, *Geschichte der Instrumentalmusik im 16. Jahrhundert.* J. Guttentag (D. Collin), Berlin, 1878.—S.B., No. 130.

[6] Giovanni Gabrieli (b. Venice, 1557; d. there, 1612), a pupil of his uncle Andrea, spent the years from 1575 to 1579 at the court of Munich, under Orlando di Lasso, then returned to

In rendering compositions for double chorus, the choirs were placed in different galleries. The splendid effect of song reverberating in the wide spaces of the cathedral was resorted to freely. In recent times it was Berlioz who first again hit upon these beautiful effects. He has been unjustly attacked and accused of superficiality on this very account.

The Venetians were also the founders of an independent form of organ and orchestral composition, in which their system was transferred from the voice to the instruments. The *Sonata pian e forte*, and the *Canzone* for two violins, two cornetts, and two trombones by Giovanni Gabrieli are good illustrations of the pomp which they developed, of the sublimity of their tonal effects. The *Canzone* begins thus:

PROTESTANT CHURCH MUSIC

The German Masters.[7]—In the second half of the sixteenth century most of the German masters are under the influence of the Reforma-

Venice where he was chosen first organist in 1586, as successor to Merulo. He was the teacher of Heinrich Schütz. The influence of Venice upon German music is obvious from the numerous personal relationships between the two. BIBLIOGRAPHY: O. Kinkeldey, *Orgel und Klavier in der Musik des 16. Jahrhunderts.* B. & H., Leipzig, 1910.—Carl von Winterfeld, *Johannes Gabrieli und sein Zeitalter.* 2 vols., and one volume of musical extracts, Schlesinger, Berlin, 1834. REPRINTS: G. Benvenuti, *Istituzioni e monumenti dell' arte musicale italiana; I,* 1–2: "Andrea e Giovanni Gabrieli e la musica strumentale di S. Marco." Ricordi, Milan, 1931, 1932.—Blume's *Chorwerk,* three motets.—G.M.B., No. 148.—R.B., No. 52.—Torchi, Vol. II & III.

[7] BIBLIOGRAPHY: C. von Winterfeld, *Der evangelische Kirchengesang.* 3 vols. with numerous musical examples. B. & H., Leipzig, 1843–47.—A great collection of Protestant church music may be found in Ludwig Schöberlein's *Schatz des liturgischen Chor- und Gemeindegesangs.* 3 vols. Vandenhoeck & Ruprecht, Göttingen, 1865–72.—A new edition of Schöberlein is in process of publication under the title *Handbuch der deutschen evangelischen Kirchenmusik.* Vandenhoeck & Ruprecht, Göttingen. The Protestant chorale became a basis for evangelical church music up to the time of Bach, as the Gregorian choral had been for the Catholic Church. All the melodies which have passed into church usage as

tion, and cultivate the forms inspired by it. Among the greatest, one only is to be named among those who did not follow the new faith, namely, Jacobus Gallus (Handl),[8] a native of Carniola, who died as cantor at St. John's Church in Prague in the year 1591. He is one of the most distinguished of all composers, called, perhaps with exaggeration, though not without reason, the German Palestrina. His extensive collection of motets: *Opus musicum harmoniarum*, reveals as great a wealth of invention as of artistic skill. The motet *Ecce quomodo moritur* is one of the very few pieces of the literature of the sixteenth century which Germany has preserved to the present day in its repertoire of sacred music. With its gentle flow and appealing harmony, and its popular refrain, this music still lives in the hearts of many thousands of friends of music:

Proske, *Musica Divina*, IV, 151.

congregational tunes have been compiled, together with hymnals and the biographies of the composers, in the work of Johannes Zahn, *Die Melodien der deutschen evangelischen Kirchenlieder.* 6 vols., C. Bertelsmann, Gütersloh, 1889–93.

[8] JACOBUS GALLUS (b. Reifnitz in Carniola, 1550; d. Prague, 1591). Gallus is the Latin translation of the German name Handl. The *Opus musicum harmoniarum* has been published anew in the D.T. OE. by Bezecný and Mantuani, VI, XII (1), XV (1), XX (1), XXIV, XXVI.—The motet "Mirabile mysterium," reprinted in Riemann's *Handbuch*, Vol. II, 1, p. 435, is a composition remarkable for the boldness of its harmonization.—See also: S.B., No. 131; selections by I. Mitterer, *Praktische Chorsingschule*, B. & H., Leipzig, 4th ed., 1908; and Schöberlein, *Schatz des liturgischen Chor- und Gemeindegesangs*, 18 nos.

-, tis sub- -la -tus est jus-tus. Et e -rit in pa -ce me -mo -ri -a e - -jus.

Luther was a passionate devotee of music, and in no wise did he wish to have it banned from the Church. Quite to the contrary, he did all in his power to raise its estate, and retained all existing forms, even the Mass, in his service, although the latter in somewhat altered form. However, by making the congregational hymn, which to be sure had been cultivated in the Catholic Church but had not been received into the liturgy, the very center of the musical portion of the service, much was changed, and new branches burst forth from the tree of church music.

Above all else the folk song blossomed forth. Not only was the old treasure cultivated, but many new songs arose, which are among the most beautiful of all time. One need only remember *Ein feste Burg ist unser Gott* (A Mighty Fortress Is Our God) by Luther himself.[9] Inasmuch as the church hymns were not only sung by the congregation in unison, but at times also by the choir, polyphonically, the necessity arose for polyphonic arrangements. These were composed simply or more elaborately, always with dignity, and often very appealingly by such men as Johann Walter [10] (1496–1570), the friend and musical adviser of Luther; Seth Calvisius [11] (1556–1615), the Leipzig cantor, who was also distinguished as musical theoretician; the pastor Erhard Bodenschatz (1576–1636); the cantor at Frankfurt on the Oder, Bartholomäus Gesius (1557–1613); and Michael Praetorius [12] (1571–1621), renowned equally as theorist and composer. Of especial beauty are the *Geistliche Lieder auf den Choral mit fünf Stimmen* (Spiritual Songs on the Choral with Five Voices), 1597, by the Königsberg Kapellmeister, Johannes Eccard,[13] who is indeed to be considered as one of the greatest of the

[9] See also S.B., No. 77.
[10] See Willibald Gurlitt, *Johannes Walter und die Musik der Reformationszeit*. Reprint from the *Lutherjahrbuch*, 1933. Chr. Kaiser Verlag, Munich.—See S.B., No. 80.
[11] See S.B., No. 160.
[12] His works are in course of publication under the editorship of Fr. Blume, A. Mendelssohn, and W. Gurlitt. Kallmeyer, Wolfenbüttel and Berlin.—For details concerning M. Praetorius, see Chapter V, footnote No. 40, p. 172.
[13] JOHANNES ECCARD (b. Mülhausen in Thuringia, 1553; d. Berlin, 1611). After having been a pupil of Lassus in Munich, he was first employed by J. Fugger, the merchant-prince of Augsburg, who vied with the other princes in the cultivation of music. In 1580 he be-

Protestant masters of tone. The choral melody lies in the soprano, and can be sung by the congregation in unison, while the remaining voices interpret the content poetically, in contrapuntal manner, and reënforce the impression by well-chosen harmonies.

Similarly are to be reckoned among the pearls of Protestant church music the *Psalmen und christliche Gesäng mit 4 Stimmen auf die melodeyen fugweis komponierl* (Psalms and Christian Songs composed frugally upon the melodies, for 4 voices) (Nuremberg, 1607) by Hans Leo Hassler,[14] the great Nuremberg master, the most highly gifted of the entire movement. How splendidly the polyphonic arrangement of *Ein feste Burg* (Riemann, *Beispiele*, p. 116) depicts the proud defiance of the opening words, how well it delineates the "cruel enemy," and in what a beautifully flowing line it calmly draws to its conclusion!

Not less beautiful, though of course more unassuming, are the simple four-voice arrangements of the church melodies which Hassler published in 1608. This is golden treasure which the church choirs should ever cherish. Even he who stands far removed from a genuine musical appreciation can surmise what depth of spirit lay in this master who wrote the melody *O Haupt voll Blut und Wunden* (O Sacred Head Now Wounded). To be sure he did not sing it for the Church, but set it for a love-song *Mein G'müth ist mir verwirret, das macht ein Mägdlein zart* (Confused

---

came second master of the chapel in Königsberg, and in 1608, master of the chapel at the court in Berlin.—Works: A modern edition in Publ. Eitner, Vol. XXV.—*Geistliche Lieder auf den Choral*, G. W. Teschner, 1860; B. & H., Leipzig, c. 1898.—New edition of the *Geistliche Lieder* by Fr. v. Baussnern. Kallmeyer, Berlin, 1928.—The *Preussische Festlieder* have been edited by Teschner, 1858.—Numerous settings in Schöberlein, *Schatz des evang. Chor- und Gemeindegesangs.*—S.B., No. 159.

[14] HANS LEO HASSLER (b. Nuremberg, 1564; d. Frankfurt on the Main, 1612). In 1586 Hassler became organist of Count Octavian Fugger in Augsburg; also organist at the cathedral. From time to time he sojourned at the court of the Emperor Rudolf II in Prague, and was knighted by him. In 1601 he became organist of the Frauenkirche in Nuremberg, and in 1604, at Ulm. In the year 1608 Prince Christian II of Saxony called him to Dresden. In the suite of Prince George I he journeyed to Frankfurt on the Main to the coronation of the Emperor Matthias, where he died. See Ad. Sandberger, "Biographische Bemerkungen über Hans Leo Hassler und seine Brüder." D.T.B., Vol. V, 1. New edition of religious works: *Cantiones sacrae* of 1591, 1597, and 1607, D.d.T., Vol. II; *Sacri Concentus*, D.d.T., Vols. XXIV–XXV (Auer); Masses, D.d.T., Vol. VII; *Psalmen und christliche Gesänge fugweis*, 1607, ed. by Ph. Kirnberger, 1777, new ed. by R. v. Saalfeld, Bärenreiter, Kassel; *Kirchengesänge, vierstimmig simpliciter*, ed. by Teschner, 1865, new ed. by R. v. Saalfeld, Bärenreiter, Kassel; cf. also Publ. Eitner, Vol. XV. The secular works will be found in the D.T.B., Vol. V, 2: *Canzonette* and *Neue teutsche Gesäng;* Vol. XI, 1: Madrigals; Publ. Eitner, Vol. XV contains the *Lustgarten;* a selection from the last-named has been ed. by A. Mendelssohn, Peters.—Selections in Schöberlein, Proske, Commer; R.B., Nos. 61, 62; S.B., Nos. 152, 153; Leichtentritt, *Meisterwerke deutscher Tonkunst.* B. & H., 1905.

are all my feelings; A tender maid's the cause),[15] but like *Innsbruck ich muss dich lassen* it has had power to survive the centuries, and to remain popular in its ecclesiastical home:

Hassler was the first German musician to journey across the Alps to seek his higher education. From this time on, Italy became the land of longing for German composers. Each one set this goal before him, that he might drink at the assumed fountain of music. These pilgrimages continued until the end of the eighteenth century. Hassler, as noted, was a pupil of Andrea Gabrieli in Venice. In his 5–12 part *Sacri concentus* he brought the brilliant style of his master to Germany. His Masses are highly esteemed for their melodic wealth, and he achieved delightful results as composer of madrigals and secular songs. Concerning this, more will be said later on.

[15] TRANSLATION:

> Confused are all my feelings;
> A tender maid's the cause.
> Bewilderment comes o'er me,
> Pain at my heartstrings gnaws
> By day, by night, I rest not,
> At all times much lament.
> I sigh and weep forever,
> With grief and sorrow spent.

Composers of the Reformed Church in France.[16]—Though the strict Calvin did not completely exclude music from the Church, as Zwingli did in Zürich, he allowed only the unison singing of Psalms. He himself had attempted to arrange Psalms for this purpose, but probably did not feel sufficient poetic ability for this work. Consequently he adopted for his church the Psalm versifications of Clément Marot, together with those of Theodor Beza, who had completed the cycle. They were sung to melodies which doubtless sprang chiefly from the folk song. As the Lutheran composers practiced their art on the chorales, so the Reformed composers exercised theirs on these Psalms. The outstanding example is a four-part arrangement by Claude Goudimel in simple setting, note against note, with the melody in the tenor. It appeared in 1565, in the same year in which the Königsberg jurist, Ambrosius Lobwasser, had completed a German translation of the Marot-Beza texts, with exact retention of the meter. This was published with the settings of Goudimel, in Leipzig, in the year 1573. This Lobwasser-Goudimel Psalter became the material for the congregational song in the German-Swiss Reformed Church in the seventeenth century, for this church could not permanently maintain its hostility to music. It was, as a matter of fact, ultimately adopted in all the Reformed churches, was translated into all languages, and thus became a spiritual bond for the Reformed of all tongues.

Goudimel, however, did not content himself with these simple arrangements, but elaborated the Psalm-tunes, as did Eccard and Hassler the Lutheran chorales, into works of consummate art. At times the original melody was retained with circumambient counterpoint; at times, quite after the manner of the motet, the melody itself was dissipated into the figuration. A profound religious sentiment animates the LXIX Psalm, with its passionate supplication at its beginning, as is shown on page 105.

Goudimel did not intend these settings to be performed in the Church

[16] BIBLIOGRAPHY: O. Douen, *Clément Marot et le Psautier huguenot.* 2 vols., Imprimerie nationale, Paris, 1878–79.—Chr. J. Riggenbach, *Der Kirchengesang in Basel seit der Reformation;* with new elucidations on the beginnings of the French psalm-singing. Basler Beiträge, Georg, Basel, 1870.—Modern editions: H. Expert, *Le Psautier huguenot du XVIe siècle.* Fischbacher, Paris, 1902; by the same editor, *Psaumes de Goudimel,* in three parts, 1895, 1896, 1897, in *Les Maîtres Musiciens de la Renaissance française.* Leduc, Paris.—Th. Gérold, *Psaumes de Clément Marot avec les mélodies.* Bibl. Romanica, Heitz, Strasbourg; G. E. Stechert & Co., New York, 1913, 1919.—Chr. J. Riggenbach, and R. Löw, *Ausgewählte Psalmen Goudimels.* Schneider, Basel, 1868.

—the preface to the simple settings of 1565 clearly proves this. They were intended only for edification in the home circle. But once introduced into the chapels of the Protestant princes, they soon became popular and beloved, not only in France, but in Germany as well.

Psalter of 1580, ed. Expert.

Protestant music in France had as its creator, in addition to Goudimel, his contemporary and coreligionist, Claude Le Jeune. Both of them, however, also composed Masses.[17]

THE FRENCH CHANSON [18]

The contrast between troubadour song and minnesong first revealed the difference between Romance and Germanic. It shows itself much more strongly in the chanson and the folk song of the fifteenth and sixteenth centuries. Nothing is more enlightening for one who desires to penetrate the spirit of the two nations than to compare their musical productions in that period. The French chanson reveals, from the first

[17] Several masses by Goudimel have been published by H. Expert, Senart, Paris.
[18] A great number of French chansons have been edited by H. Expert in the collection *Les Maîtres Musiciens de la Renaissance.* 23 vols., Senart, Paris, 1894–1908; and in the collection *Monuments de la musique française au temps de la Renaissance.* Senart, Paris, 1924 ff.; cf. by the same, the article in *Enc. Lav.,* III, pp. 1261–98.—*Loc. cit.,* P. M. Masson, "Le Mouvement humaniste," pp. 1298–1342.—There are 60 French chansons in the Publ. Eitner, Vol. XXVII.

polyphonic attempts, the typically French sense for pregnant rhythm and declamation. In the Renaissance period that gift is united with a masterly skill in counterpoint. Already in the works of Busnois [19] the independence of the voices was attained without prejudice to the good effect of the ensemble, as the following serious composition will show:

D. T. Œ., VII, 246,

Busnois, poet and musician, was a contemporary of Okeghem, and acknowledged himself to be his disciple and continuator. The influence of Okeghem appears very pronounced in the works of Pierre de La Rue (d. 1518; see in particular, in the collection Expert, his Mass *Ave Maria*). In his chansons, the counterpoint of P. de La Rue acquires an elegance and a clarity without any sacrifice of profundity. One will be able to judge this by the chanson *Au feu d'amour*, the intensity of which grows to the very end:

Publ. Eitner, Vol. XXVII.

[19] ANTOINE BUSNOIS was from 1467 to 1477 musician to Charles the Bold, then to his

The significance which the chanson attained in the French musical life of the sixteenth century can be seen from the fact that the publisher, P. Attaingnant, in the years between 1535 and 1549, issued not less than thirty-five books of four-part chansons. His example was followed by A. Le Roy, in Paris, and J. Moderne, in Lyon, with the publication of great collections. While the German concerted *Lied* in the second half of the sixteenth century changes character as it comes under the influence of the Italian madrigal, the French chanson maintains its character, and indeed develops it still more, putting forth new blossoms.

It appears in manifold forms, both small and large, sung and declaimed, burlesque and ecclesiastical, simple, note against note, and pregnant with artistry, set with all the devices of counterpoint. There are little jests of a few bars, and motet-like pieces of 50 and more pages. A tendency which appears repeatedly in French music later on, forces itself upon the attention here for the first time, namely, tone painting.

By resorting to this device, Clément Janequin [20] introduced a species

daughter, Mary of Burgundy.—Cf. *Trois chansonniers français du XVe siècle*, by E. Droz, Y. Rokseth, and G. Thibault, Vol. I.

[20] CLÉMENT JANEQUIN (probably b. at Châtellerault, c. 1485; d. c. 1560) was supposedly a soldier at the battle of Marignano in the service of Ronsard's father; c. 1520 he was in Paris; 1529, in Bordeaux in the service of the cardinal of Lorraine and chaplain of the Duke of Guise; 1545–58, curate at Unverre; in a dedicatory poem of the year 1559 he

of portraiture chanson, which give precious illustrations of the life of
the day. Well known is his *Bataille de Marignan* (Battle of Marignano),
which paints with realism the entire course of events. Indeed, the realism
goes so far, that at the close the voices of the defeated Swiss suddenly
resound in a Swiss German dialect, as the French understand it: *Toute
frelore bigott* (All Lost, by God). In *La Chasse* we are present at a court
hunt. At the end, the king dispatches the deer with his own hand. In
Le Chant des oiseaux we hear a piquant bird concert, of starlings and
nightingales; also something similar, intermixed with references to the
gallant life, in *L'Alouette*. The following few measures will show how
the little cries of the lark are expressed:

Les Cris de Paris is a theme which modern orchestral composers have
again taken up. The title *Le Caquet des femmes* scarcely savors of gallantry; its execution demands, above all, great lingual facility. In their
vivacity and joviality, with their characteristic tonal effects, these
creations are thoroughly original. Through them, Janequin, as a true
national composer, has expressed a vein of French national genius. It is

bewails poverty and his age. He was a pupil of Josquin Desprez. Although his compositions
created the greatest interest and made him famous, the mystery which surrounds his life
occasioned the surmise that he was identical with another master, and it was suspected
that this might have been the master of the chapel at the cathedral at Antwerp, Clemens
non Papa, a hypothesis, however, which has little probability. BIBLIOGRAPHY: M. Cauchie,
"Clément Janequin." R. M., VII, 1923, pp. 13 ff.—The chansons of Janequin form Vols. V
and VII of the collection *Les Maîtres Musiciens de la Renaissance*, by H. Expert. Paris,
1927.—Another collection, *Trente chansons a 3 et 4 voix*, has been published by M. Cauchie.
Rouart-Lerolle, Paris, 1928.—New editions of *Le Caquet des femmes* and *La Jalouzie*
by M. Cauchie. Rouart-Lerolle, Paris, 1924.—Cf. also Riemann's *Handbuch*, II, 1,
pp. 365 ff. and 407 ff.

scarcely necessary to observe that Janequin's and his contemporaries' conception of nature is quite different from that of the German composers. A study of this difference, as well as of the differences of the underlying texts, would be an interesting task.

The subjects of the chansons are as varied as the music. They embrace all kinds of satire, scenes of gallantry, anecdotes, and conviviality. There are, moreover, also elegies, songs of triumph, vocational songs, and some moral songs. A pleasing love lament is to be found in the simple homophonic setting of the Paris *maître de chapelle*, Claudin de Sermisy,[21] *Au joli bois* (*Trente et une chansons musicales*, Attaingnant, 1529; edited by H. Expert, 1897).

The *C'est a grand tort* by Nicolas Gombert [22] reveals a sure craftsmanship, is pregnant with meaning, and possesses a clarity that is characteristic of the French nature. The *Quand je vous ayme* of Jacques Arcadelt (b. 1514; d. c. 1560) begins with the following moving phrase:

Among the masters of the chanson one must also mention Claude Le Jeune,[23] Costeley,[24] and Passereau. The international genius Orlando

[21] CLAUDIN DE SERMISY was a singer in the royal chapel until the death of Louis XII; in 1532 he became second master of the chapel of the Sainte-Chapelle of the Palace; in 1547, Henry II made him first master. He died in Paris in 1562.
[22] NICOLAS GOMBERT (b. at Bruges), a pupil of Josquin, carried the art of the Netherlanders to Spain, whither he went with 20 singers in 1537, and where he is reported to have risen to the position of master of the chapel to Charles V in Madrid. See S.B., No. 102.
[23] CLAUDE LE JEUNE (b. Valenciennes 1528, d. c. 1600), is designated in his books of Psalms (the first of which appeared in 1564), as court composer to the king.—His *Psaumes* in measured verse, and his *Printemps* have been edited by Expert in "Les Maîtres musiciens de la Renaissance," Vols. XI–XIV, XVI, XX–XXII; his *Octonaires de la vanité et inconstance du monde* is also edited by Expert in the collection "Monuments de la musique française," Vol. I. See S.B., No. 144.
[24] COSTELEY was organist to the kings Charles IX and Henry III until 1592.

di Lasso employed the French style as competently as he did the Italian and the German, and has left behind chansons of an enduring charm.

A unique new branch that was engrafted upon this trunk was the *chanson mesurée* [25] which was written for the poems of Ronsard and Baïf, which were constructed according to antique models. The *chanson mesurée* was composed note against note, i.e., the syllables of the verse were sung simultaneously by all the voices, and it was composed according to strict scansion. In spite of the monotony which threatens as the result of the constantly recurring rhythm, the French composers were able to bring the *chanson mesurée* to distinction, doubtless chiefly for the simple reason that the sharp accentuation of simple rhythms is compatible with the character of French music. The *chanson mesurée* places in relief the little accented rhythms of the French language. The following is an example taken from Jacques Mauduit [26] as found in his *Chansonnettes mesurées* on verses of Baïf, in which each of the various stanzas is based on the following group of rhythms:

First strophe:

Vous me tu - ez si dou - ce-ment A - vec que tour mans si bé - nins

Que ne scay cho - se de dou - ceur Plus dou - ce qu'est ma dou - ce mort

---

[25] On the music *mesurée*, see the article by P. M. Masson already cited.

[26] JACQUES MAUDUIT (b. Paris, 1557; d. there, 1627) was a friend of the poet Ronsard, in whose memory he composed a *Requiem* for 5 voices. He was celebrated as a player of the lute.

Claude Le Jeune wrote, according to the same principles, an important collection of chansons, *Le Printemps* (collection Expert, Vol. XII), and of Psalms. The *Psaumes en vers mezurez* of Claude Goudimel [27] also belong to that genre of *musique mesurée à l'antique*. The *chanson mesurée*, like the opera in Italy, was a fruit of the Renaissance; but while the latter proceeded upon entirely new paths, the former remained upon the foundation of the old choral art.

One must accord a special place in the second half of the sixteenth century to Antoine de Bertrand whose works of vocal polyphony (*Premier livre des amours de Ronsard, Second livre des amours,* and *Troisième livre des chansons*) [28] were published by Le Roy and Ballard in 1576 and 1578. At times they present intimations of the Italian madrigal; at times their brusque modulations already anticipate those of Monteverdi (cf. the beginning of the piece *Amour donne moy paix,* or of *Les Deux Yeux bruns,* in the first book of *Amours*).

THE SPANISH MASTERS [29]

Spain, with its old culture, also possesses valuable church music, which up to the present time has been all too little known. At the time of the Netherlanders, from the fifteenth century on, there were Spanish masters whose sonorous and original settings merit them a place among the best. Their romances and ballads are rhythmically pregnant, re-

[27] CLAUDE GOUDIMEL (b. Besançon, c. 1505; d. Lyons, 1572). The monograph on Goudimel by M. Brenet (1898) has definitely refuted the legend that Goudimel was the teacher of Palestrina. Goudimel probably never saw Italy, having resided in Paris, Metz, Besançon, and Lyon. Like Le Jeune he cultivated in a brilliant manner, besides the *chanson mesurée,* the Huguenot music; he was assassinated as a Huguenot in the massacre of Lyons (August 28–31, 1572) which followed the massacre of St. Bartholomew in Paris. BIBLIOGRAPHY: G. Becker, *Goudimel et son œuvre.* Société de l'histoire du protestantisme français; 3d series, 4th year, No. 8, 1885.—M. Brenet, *Claude Goudimel.* P. Jacquin, Besançon, 1898.—New editions by Maldeghem and Bordes; also by Expert in *Les Maîtres Musiciens de la Renaissance.* 1897.—See S.B., No. 142.

[28] Edited by H. Expert, *Monuments de la musique française.* Vols. IV, V, VI.

[29] New editions of the Spanish works: Fr. As. Barbieri, *Cancionero musical de los siglos XV y XVI,* published by the Academy of Madrid. Tip. de Los Huerfanos, Madrid, 1890.—Miguel Hilarion Eslava, *Lira sacro-hispana.* 10 half-vols. M. Martin Salazar, Madrid, 1869.—F. Pedrell, *Hispaniae schola musica sacra.* 8 vols., J. B. Pujol, Barcelona, 1894–98.

calling the dance and the march; but at the same time they are serious
and passionate, so that one already perceives in these early creations
the characteristic Spanish nature. One of the examples best fitted to illustrate this music is the ballad, *Mi querer tanto*, by Enrique (c. 1480):

Barbieri, *Cancionéro Musical*, No. 21.

Everyone knows from Cervantes' *Don Quixote* that a jovial life reigned
at the Spanish universities. Music, with its direct power of suggestion,
presents us with a living picture of that youthful gaiety in the drinking
song for four voices by Juan Ponce (c. 1500):

Barbieri, *Cancionéro Musical*, No. 414.

These Spanish compositions frequently impress one as more modern than many other contemporary ones.

In the Palestrina period, the Spaniards stood in personal contact with the Roman school, as we have already seen. Two names should be mentioned especially: Cristobal Morales [30] (a charming Christmas motet by him will be found in Riemann, *Beispiele*, p. 62) and the great Tomás Ludovico da Victoria.[31] A number of Victoria's sublime, hymn-like motets have again become common property, for example, *Jesus dulcis memoria* and *O vos omnes*. His full significance, like that of his friend Palestrina, is revealed in his Masses. A little motet from the office of Holy-Week, *Tenebrae factae sunt* (Riemann, *Beispiele*, p. 88, also edition Pedrell), is characteristic. Despite the independence of the voices, these are no longer conducted without regard to the general consonance, as was the case with the Netherlanders, but, as with Palestrina, the harmonic, chordal effect is taken into consideration and carefully weighed. A severe seriousness is achieved through the limitation to male voices and a strong emphasis upon minor tonality. Despite this, however, the composition is not wanting in a strong tonal appeal and in intense passion. In brief, the few measures reveal the Spanish character with its vacillation between asceticism and sensual ardor.

The Italian Madrigal [32]

Beside the French *chanson* and the German *Lied*, there developed in the sixteenth century a new form which represents the supreme perfec-

[30] CRISTOBAL MORALES (b. Seville, c. 1500; d. Malaga, 1553). His works have been published in the first volume of *Hispaniae schola musica sacra*, F. Pedrell, 1894. BIBLIOGRAPHY: R. Mitjana, "Cristobal Morales," in *Estudios sobre algunos músicos españoles del siglo XVI*. Libreria de los sucesores de Hernando, Madrid, 1918.—J. B. Trend, "Cristobal Morales" in *Music and Letters*. Wessex Press, Taunton, Engl., 1925.

[31] TOMÁS LUDOVICO DA VICTORIA (b. Avila in Old Castile, c. 1540; d. Madrid, c. 1613) came to Rome in his youth, where the papal chapel singer Morales became his teacher. In 1573 he became master of the chapel at the Collegium Germanicum, and in 1575 at Sant' Apollinare. He left Rome in 1589 and became chaplain to the Empress Marie, sister of Philippe II, in Madrid.—See Henri Collet, *Victoria*. Alcan, Paris, 1914.—NEW EDITIONS: A complete edition of his works has been published in 8 vols., under the editorship of F. Pedrell, by B. & H., Leipzig, 1902–04.—Cf. S.B., No. 128.

[32] BIBLIOGRAPHY: Th. Kroyer, "Die Anfänge der Chromatik im italienischen Madrigal des XVI. Jahrhunderts," Supplements of the I.M.G., 1902.—A. Pirro, "Les Frottole et la musique instrumentale," R. Musicol., Paris, March, 1922.—Rud. Schwartz, "Die Frottole im 15. Jahrhundert," Viertelj. f. MW., II, 1886.—P. Wagner, "Das Madrigal und Palestrina," Viertelj. f. MW., 1902.—The series "Raccolta nazionale delle musiche italiane" contains several volumes of madrigals. Istituto ed. Italiano, Milan, 1914 ff.—For examples of Frottole, see E.B., No. 14; and W.B., Nos. 20, 21, 22, 23.—For a Villanella, see W.B., No. 42.—For Madrigals, see W.B., Nos. 38, 48.

tion of polyphonic music in its secular aspect. To be sure, the madrigal is not absolutely new. We have already discovered it in the *ars nova* of the Florentines, which, in turn, had borrowed it from the troubadours. Nevertheless, it now assumed a new form, as it sprouted forth afresh from seeds latent among the rank and file.

At the end of the fifteenth century, the *frottola* (little fruit) made its appearance, a little song of amorous or sportive content, set for four voices, note against note, with the melody in the soprano, and severe in harmony with its parallel fifths and octaves. This product of the soil is probably descended from the popular dance song, as its normal meter, the octosyllabic trochaic, seems to indicate. To be sure, the eleven syllable iambic, the *strambotto*, was also popular. The *frottola* was cultivated diligently in northern Italy. Marco Cara [33] and Bartolomeo

Munich Library.

Joannes B. Tessa.

[33] See S.B., No. 72.

Tromboncino,[34] both laboring at the court of Mantua, were its chief composers. Petrucci, the inventor of the art of music printing, published, between 1504 and 1509, no fewer than ten books of *frottole*. One of the dances taken from the seventh book is shown on page 114.[35]

Bald. Donati.
Canzon villanesche alla napolitana. a 4.   Venice, Gardane, 1558.

[34] See S.B., No. 69, and W.B., No. 22.

[35] An edition of the books of the *Frottole* published by Petrucci, according to the copy preserved at Munich, has been announced in the P.D.M. (Rud. Schwartz).

G. Gastoldi,
Vilanella napolitana, a 5.

According to the edition of 1626
(Paris, Conserv.)

The South Italian sister of the *frottola* was the *villanella*, which appeared about 1545, and became gradually refined until it took on an elegant form. The preceding two are very typical examples of Neapolitan *villanelle*, the one by Baldassare Donati, the other by Giovanni Gastoldi.

Finally, the madrigal [36] belongs to the same family as the *frottola* and the *villanella*, being the most aristocratic of the members. It is a short piece, sharply accented, with a subject, for the most part, of a trifling nature. Little by little, however, the madrigal extended its domain, as did the French chanson, until it included all possible subjects. Beside

[36] MODERN EDITIONS OF MADRIGALS: W. Barclay Squire. *Ausgewählte Madrigale und mehrstimmige Gesänge berühmter Meister des 16.–17. Jahrhunderts* (Collection of Madrigals and Part-Songs of Famous Masters of the 16th and 17th centuries). B. & H., Leipzig, 1903–13.—Torchi, *L'Arte musicale in Italia*, Vols. I–III. Ricordi, Milan, 1900 ff.—F. Wüllner, *Chorübungen der Münchener Musikschule*, 3d stage. T. Ackermann, Munich, 4th ed., 1900.—For collections of English madrigals, see below, p. 126.

the principal category of love songs, there are also religious and moral madrigals (*madrigali spirituali*). Their structure is always free, without *cantus firmus*. They are generally divided into parts constructed on different motifs, into sections that are thematically developed; but the text is composed throughout, i.e., it is not treated strophically. In the classical period, the sixteenth century, five-part settings became the rule.

It was the Netherlanders who founded the madrigal in Italy. At their head stands Adrian Willaert, as founder of the Venetian school a landmark in musical history; beside him Philippe Verdelot [37] and Jacques Arcadelt.[38] The compositions of the latter seem to have contributed much to establishing the form. His madrigals which appeared in the year 1539 attained sixteen editions within thirty years. One of his most famous madrigals is that of the dying swan, *Il bianco e dolce cigno cantando more*. It flows forth in so gentle a stream that one can imagine that one is seeing a swan describing his circles in the water. The various thoughts of the text are reflected in the music with scrupulous care. At the conclusion of the composition an impressive climax is gained through a short *fugato*. The composition was so highly esteemed in its day as a universally known model, that Orazio Vecchi set to the same text a new, more elaborate madrigal, based upon Arcadelt's music.

The classical period of the Italian madrigal art reaches its climax in the triple constellation, Luca Marenzio,[39] Giovanni Gastoldi,[40] and Baldas-

[37] PHILIPPE VERDELOT (b. at the end of the 15th century; d. between 1560 and 1565), probably spent a great part of his life in Italy. He was master of the chapel at San Giovanni in Florence c. 1530. See S.B., Nos. 97 & 98.

[38] JACQUES ARCADELT (b. probably in Flanders, c. 1514; d. Paris, after 1557). One finds him first in Florence, then, in 1539, member of the Cappella Julia in Rome. From 1540 to 1549 he continued as singer of the papal chapel with the sole exception of a journey to Paris. In 1553, Arcadelt followed the Duke of Guise to Paris, where in 1557 he bore the title of *regius musicus*. See S.B., No. 100.

[39] LUCA MARENZIO (b. Coccaglio, near Brescia, c. 1560; d. Rome, 1599) lived in Brescia, Rome, Ferrara, Florence, and at the court of Sigismund of Poland. He was finally attached to the papal court at Rome. The Italians called him *il più dolce cigno*, and he is doubtless the leading madrigal composer. He corresponded with J. Dowland and strongly influenced the English madrigalists. He probably died of chagrin on account of a love affair, because insurmountable obstacles interposed between himself and his beloved. Such romantic stories related concerning the lives of the composers testify to the important rôle played by these heroes in the popular imagination. NEW EDITIONS: A complete edition of the madrigals of Marenzio has begun to appear in the P.D.M. (Alfred Einstein); the first volume appeared in 1929; three volumes have appeared so far (1934), B. & H., Leipzig.— See Blume's *Chorwerk*, folio 8; H. Engel, selection of the *Villanelle*, Bärenreiter, Kassel; by the same editor, the volume of *Motets*, Universal Edition, Vienna; E.B., No. 19; S.B., Nos. 140, 165.

[40] GIOVANNI GIACOMO GASTOLDI (b. Caravaggio, c. 1556; d. Mantua, 1622) was master of the chapel at the court at Mantua. See W. Herrmann, selections. Vieweg, Berlin.—

sare Donati.[41] All the best elements of their style will be found in the madrigal of Marenzio: *Parto o non parto:*

Il nono libro de madrigali di Luca Marenzio, a 5 voci.

Edition of 1601 (Paris, Bibl. nat.)

Jöde, *Staatliches Jugendliederbuch*, 12 nos. Peters, Leipzig, 1930.—E. Kiwi, *Spielstücke für zwei Melodieinstrumente* (Pieces for two Melody Instruments). Bärenreiter, Kassel, 1933.— Cf. also, E.B., No. 21, and W.B., No. 47.

[41] BALDASSARE DONATI, a Venetian (d. Venice, 1603) was at first singer at St. Mark's, and after 1590 first master of the chapel. See Jöde, *Staatliches Jugendliederbuch*. Peters, Leipzig, No. 362: cf. also W.B., No. 46.

The composer utilizes his vocal resources with a complete freedom, allowing to each voice its full development, its individual life; one does not know which to admire more, the intimate, spiritual expression, or the dramatic force, the effect upon the sensibilities.

Toward the end of the sixteenth century and at the beginning of the seventeenth, the Italian madrigal experienced a further bold development through the introduction of a dramatic element. As a reaction against the old, restrained, diatonically self-sufficient choral art, the great fermentation began from which the new harmony evolved, and from which also the opera and the oratorio proceeded.

The ingenious explorers, the discoverers of new land, who may be contrasted with the afore-mentioned triple constellation, are Cipriano de Rore, Gesualdo Prince of Venosa,[42] Orazio Vecchi,[43] and Claudio

[42] CARLO GESUALDO, Prince of Venosa (b. c. 1560; d. Naples, 1614). BIBLIOGRAPHY: C. Gray and Ph. Heseltine, *Gesualdo*. K. Paul, Trench, Trubner and Co., Ltd., London, 1926.— F. Keiner, *Die Madrigale des Gesualdo von Venosa* (Leipzig dissertation; with examples). O. Brandstetter, Leipzig, 1914. NEW EDITIONS: S.B., No. 167.—Torchi, Vol. IV.—W. Weismann, 8 nos. in Edition Peters, 1931.

[43] ORAZIO VECCHI (b. c. 1550; d. Modena, 1605). His *L'Amfiparnasso* was presented in Modena in 1594, and published in 1597. It has been republished in Eitner's Publikationen, Vol. XXVI and Torchi, *L'Arte musicale*, Vol. IV.—See also S.B., No. 164.—See E. Dent, S. I. M. G. XII, 3, p. 330.

Monteverdi.[44]   The genius of the last-named at the same time also fructified the newly created opera.

Orazio Vecchi presented a strange precursor of the modern lyric music drama in his madrigal-comedy, *L'Amfiparnasso*. The text is a comedy, in part frolicsome, in part love-sick, composed altogether in the form of madrigals. In other words, both the speeches and the replies of the characters are all presented in choral form. The times were impelling toward something new. A desire for novelty was in the air. There was a longing for something complete in place of the many short pieces, for something dramatic in place of the incessant lyric. The opera ultimately appeared, but as an intermediary stage there was the madrigal-comedy, as Vecchi and several others beside him composed it.

The life of the Prince Gesualdo of Venosa exhibits, like his works, a romantic shimmer. He became a composer only after he had killed his faithless wife in a fit of jealousy. Hence it does not seem accidental that his passionate chromaticism, unheard of hitherto, reminds one of Wagner's *Tristan und Isolde*. The following short passage, which characterizes well Gesualdo's manner, is taken from a madrigal which Burney published in its entirety (*General History of Music*, III, 223):

Monteverdi is not less audacious. The chromatic alterations, the bold transitions, the unmediated juxtapositions of major and minor express passion with a force that it would be difficult to equal. Among his madrigals, almost all of which are beautiful, one should note especially the one entitled *M'e più dolce il penar per Amarilli*, which overflows with ideas that are always effective and never miss their point. At the beginning of the madrigal, which is to be found in the sixth book, and which appeared in the year 1614, one should observe the division of the voices into two groups: the two upper voices present in echo form lamentations which swell and increase little by little, while the three low voices unfold

[44] Madrigals of Monteverdi have been republished by Leichtentritt and Mendelssohn in the Edition Peters. A complete edition of his madrigals has been edited by Fr. Malipiero in the "Universal Edition," Vienna; cf. also the complete works. Asolo, 1926–32, 14 vols.— Cf. also E.B., No. 53; and S.B., Nos. 176–78.

the motifs of the laments in excited rhythms. At the words which evoke death, one feels in the music a desire for annihilation; then suddenly, the five voices combined celebrate, in full harmony, the nobility of the state of love. One should observe the accents which interpret the opposing adjectives *humile* and *gagliardo*. This simple fragment will reveal how wonderfully versatile Monteverdi is in his dramatic procedures:

Venice, edition of 1620.
(Paris, Bibl. nat).

Orlando di Lasso, as a composer of madrigals, must be placed between the classicists and the romanticists, though he is more closely related to the former. In taking from Ariosto the text of his madrigal *Sotto due negri e sottilissimi archi* (*Orlando furioso*, canto VII), he followed the example of the Italian composers who ransacked the classical literature of their country for their purposes. This original piece, which loses all its charm when merely played upon the piano, will be quite effective when sung in a manner which does justice to its vocal nature:

Works, ed. Haberl.

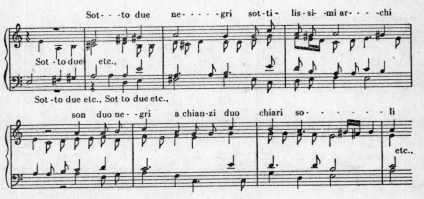

Elizabethan Music in England [45]

The Elizabethan age was not only the golden age of English literature, but of English music as well, as any reader of Shakespeare must surmise.

[45] BIBLIOGRAPHY: O. Becker, *Die englischen Madrigalisten, W. Byrd, Th. Morley, und J. Dowland* (Leipzig dissertation). L. Seidel, Leipzig, 1901.—E. H. Fellowes, *The English Madrigal*. O.U.P., London; by the same author, *English Madrigal Verse, 1585–1632.*

No poet has found finer words in praise of music than he, and his enthusiasm was well founded, for not only was England in its heyday with regard to both ecclesiastical and secular choral music, but the English virginal composers of the time were fashioning models of genuine keyboard music.

Byrd and Gibbons are the giants of English church music. The former [46] has been called "the English Palestrina." In the field of church music, he wrote Masses, Latin motets, psalms, anthems, and carols. His three Masses for three, four, and five voices, respectively, are the finest settings of the Mass produced in England. His five-part *Lullaby* has been called "one of the most exquisitely tender and delicate blossoms in all music." [47] His best work is characterized by a combination of ruggedness and tenderness. As examples of his finest anthems, may be cited the six-part *Sing Joyfully unto God* and the five-part *Sing We Merrily unto God Our Strength*.

Byrd remained in the Roman communion throughout his entire life; Gibbons [48] is really the father of pure Anglican music. In his sacred music he employed only his native tongue. Though he lacked the mysticism, the tenderness, and the sublimity of Byrd, he excelled him in variety. His service in F has been termed "Perhaps the most 'foursquare without blame' of all Anglican services; finely massive from start to finish, melodious and yet perfectly strong, technically polished and yet never dry." [49] Among his greatest anthems may be mentioned: *Hosanna*

Clarendon Press, Oxford, 1920; by the same author, *The English Madrigal Composers*. Clarendon Press, Oxford, 1921.—W. Nagel, *Geschichte der Musik in England*. K. J. Trübner, Strassburg, 1894–97.—P. Warlock (Ph. Heseltine) and P. Wilson, *The English Ayres, 1598–1612*. O.U.P., London, 1932. NEW EDITIONS: G. E. P. Arkwright, *The Old English Edition*. 25 vols., Joseph Williams, London, 1889–1902.—E. H. Fellowes, *The English Madrigal School*. 36 vols., Winthrop Rogers, London, 1913–24.—J. J. Maier, *Sammlung altenglischer Madrigale*. Peters, Leipzig, 1863.

[46] WILLIAM BYRD (b. Lincoln [?] 1543; d. Stondon in Essex, 1623) was a member of the Chapel Royal. BIBLIOGRAPHY: E. H. Fellowes, *Wm. Byrd; a Short Account of His Life and Work*. Clarendon Press, Oxford, 1923; 2d ed., 1929—W. H. Hadow, *William Byrd*. O.U.P., London, 1923.— Frank S. Howes, *William Byrd*. K. Paul Trench, Trubner, London, 1928. NEW EDITIONS: Cf. *List of the Music of William Byrd obtainable in modern editions*. Byrd Tercentenary Com., O.U.P., London, 1923.—E. H. Fellowes: see above.—S.B., No. 145.— For Byrd's Church Music, see *Tudor Church Music*, published for the Carnegie Trustees, O.U.P., London.

[47] ERNEST WALKER, *A History of Music in England*, p. 74.

[48] ORLANDO GIBBONS (b. Cambridge, 1583; d. Canterbury, 1625) was organist of the Chapel Royal in 1604, and of Westminster Abbey in 1623. See E. H. Fellowes, *Orlando Gibbons*. Clarendon Press, Oxford, 1925. NEW EDITIONS: E. H. Fellowes: see above.—*Tudor Church Music*, Vol. IV.

[49] Walker, *op. cit.*, p. 75.

to the Son of David; Lift up Your Heads; O Clap Your Hands; Behold,
Thou Hast Made My Days as It Were a Span Long.

Though primarily a secular composer, Thomas Morley [50] must also
be mentioned as the author of some of the finest religious music of the
period.

Nevertheless, splendid and important as is England's contribution to
the church music of the period, it is primarily the madrigal that one associates with the music of the Elizabethan age. It made its appearance in
England towards the close of the sixteenth century, and although its
glory lasted only some thirty years, it has been termed "perhaps on the
whole the greatest music treasure England possesses." [51] To be sure,
England is indebted for the madrigal to Italy, but she developed it in an
original and independent manner. At all times English music has distinguished itself by a tendency toward the popular, the folk song type.
It is fond of taking its departure from pithy melodies, such as live among
the rank and file. Even though these do not possess the vocal flight of
the Italian, they are nevertheless forceful and characteristic.

Two elements enter into the English madrigals, as into others, namely,
Netherlandish-Italian counterpoint and the Italian harmonic popular
song, such as the frottola. Both elements may generally be found in the
same composition. Hence it has been said: "The English madrigal is
an artistic compromise of astounding perfection and success." [52] A subsidiary form of madrigals is known as the ballet, or *fa la*, characterized
by strong rhythm and melodic swing. The madrigals were often played
as purely instrumental pieces. They were invariably published in
separate part books, for the most part unbarred. When used as songs,
they were sung by small groups of amateur soloists seated about a
table. Secular choral music made its advent in England only about the
time of Purcell. The amateur madrigal singers were allowed considerable
latitude in their interpretation and presentation. The poetry of the
madrigals is as a rule not on as high a lyrical plane as is that of the so-
called "ayres," though words may be found taken from Shakespeare,
Spenser, Marlowe, Jonson, Sidney, and Raleigh.

Wilbye's sixty-five madrigals, in three, four, five, and six parts, repre-

[50] THOMAS MORLEY (b. 1557; d. London, 1602) was a pupil of William Byrd, organist of
St. Paul's Cathedral, and a member of the Chapel Royal. NEW EDITIONS: E. H. Fellowes:
see above.—By the same editor, *The First Book of Ayres.* Winthrop Rogers, London, 1932.
[51] Walker, *op. cit.,* p. 58.
[52] *Op. cit.* p. 59.

issued in England was Morley's *A Plaine and Easie Introduction to Practicall Musicke*, which appeared in 1597. Dowland published a translation of the *Musicae activae micrologus* of Ornitoparchus in 1609. Ravenscroft edited *A Briefe Discourse* on mensurable music in 1611. The poet and musician Campion wrote *A New Way of Making Foure Parts in Counter-Point* in 1613.

In 1622, Henry Peacham, a pupil of Orazio Vecchi, wrote the *Complete Gentleman* which contains allusions to, and observations upon, contemporary musicians.

THE GERMAN MADRIGAL

In the second half of the sixteenth century, German choral music abandoned its tradition, which had taken its departure from the folk song, and entered upon the path of the Italian madrigal. Germany had not attained to a revival of its national literature through the influence of humanism and the Renaissance, like the Romance countries. In its literary ventures, as in its entire culture, it early came under foreign, especially Italian and French, influence. This was peculiarly true with regard to the song. In part, this was due to the many foreign musicians, Netherlanders and Italians, who sojourned in Germany and occupied foremost positions in the chapels. The outstanding example of this is the cosmopolite, Orlando di Lasso, in Munich. The deeper reason, however, for the change in musical styles doubtless lay in the fact that original German literary production ceased, and the poets took to imitating foreign forms.

In music, the change was brought about by the Italian, Antonio Scandello (1517–80), who labored in Dresden as master of the electoral chapel, and published different collections of songs from the year 1566 on, which domesticated the Italian madrigal in Germany. There followed, Jacob Regnart, the Prague Kapellmeister, a Netherlander (1540–c. 1600), with three-part *villanelle* in the German language; Leonhard Lechner, who arranged these *villanelle* of Regnart for five voices; the Rostock Kapellmeister, Daniel Friderici; and, finally, the distinguished Johann Eccard and Hans Leo Hassler. The last-named[57] wrote genuine Italian madrigals with Italian words, and also set Ger-

[57] BIBLIOGRAPHY: Rud. Schwartz, "Hans Leo Hassler unter dem Einfluss der italienischen Madrigalisten." Viertelj. f. MW. IX, 1893. NEW EDITIONS: *Lustgarten neuer teutscher Gesänge*, 1601. Publ. Eitner, Vol. XV.—For further reprints see D.T.B., V, 2, and XI, 2.—Songs and Madrigals for Practical Use, edited by A. Mendelssohn, Edition Peters.—Cf. S.B., No. 152.

man songs in madrigal form. The five-voiced *Ardo, si, ma non t'amo* [58] will serve as an illustration of the high art to which the madrigal attained, by utilizing all devices, declamation, counterpoint, polyphony, and the pictorial manner in which every line of the text finds expression.

Though Hassler, in his German compositions, employed the madrigal, he nevertheless strongly imbued it with German spirit and made the qualities of the true German Lied again supreme. That had to come about. Even foreigners brought hearty, pronouncedly German nuances, as did Scandello in his *Mit Lieb bin ich umfangen* [59] (With Love Am I Surrounded), especially in these heartfelt closing measures:

Quite the same is to be said of Orlando di Lasso, who is to be enrolled in the same group. His *Annelein* [60] (Little Anne), a piece full of tender charm, is a pearl among German songs. Hassler offers the most precious treasures in his *Lustgarten neuer teutscher Gesänge* (Pleasure-Garden of New German Songs, Nuremberg, 1601), wherein, as already mentioned, is to be found the secular original of the melody to "O Sacred Head Now Wounded." In general, he here again presents more compact, even strophically composed songs, in place of the madrigals with their division into sections. The Galliard *Mehr Lust und Freud' die Lieb mir geit* (More Joy and Bliss Love Gives to Me) is a dance, but a dance full of fervor and of spiritual depth:

Sag ich ohn' Scheu   Mich dünkt ich sei   Merk ich mit Fleiss

Im Pa - ra - - deis   Fa, la, la,   la, la, la,   fa, la, la, la.

In the choral song of the sixteenth century, there lives an abundance of imperishable poetry, for which one can only wish ardently a renaissance, both for the sake of the greater benefit to our choral organizations, and also for the inspiration of composers. Especially might such a revival regenerate our male-choruses which are still too much limited to a superficial "glee-clubism." The revival, however, is not such an easy matter. It is especially difficult to attain, in the delivery, the fresh charm and the spontaneity which this old art, so full of the joy of living, demands.

INSTRUMENTAL MUSIC IN THE MIDDLE AGES AND THE RENAISSANCE [61]

Wandering minstrels and town pipers.[62]—In the Middle Ages, the cultivation of instrumental music lay chiefly in the hands of the wandering minstrels. According to the pronouncements of the old books of law, the Saxon Mirror (*Sachsenspiegel*) and the Swabian Mirror (*Schwabenspiegel*), they were viewed as dishonorable. In order to elevate their position, they founded religious brotherhoods. The oldest is the Brotherhood of St. Nicholas (*Nicolaibrüderschaft*) in Vienna, of the year 1288. The Holy

[61] BIBLIOGRAPHY: M. Brenet, *Les Concerts en France sous l'ancien régime.* Fischbacher, Paris, 1900.—K. Nef, *Geschichte der Sinfonie und Suite* (Introduction). B. & H., Leipzig, 1921.—H. Quittard, "Musique Instrumentale," Enc. Lav., Parts 37–40.
[62] BIBLIOGRAPHY: P. Aubry, *Estampies et danses royales: les plus anciens textes de musique instrumentale au moyen âge.* Fischbacher, Paris, 1907.—Edward Buhle, *Die musikalischen Instrumente in den Miniaturen des frühen Mittelalters.* I: Die Blasinstrumente. B. & H., Leipzig, 1903 (with bibliography of the books concerning the instruments).—E. Faral, *Les Jongleurs en France.* H. Champion, Paris, 1910.—Hampe, *Die Fahrenden Leute.* E. Diederichs, Leipzig, 1905.—H. J. Moser, *Die Musikgenossenschaften im deutschen Mittelalter* Hinstorff, Rostock, 1910.—K. Nef, "Die Stadtpfeiferei in Basel;" also, "Die Musik in Basel," both articles in the S.I.M.G., Vol. X.—A. Schaer, *Die altdeutschen Fechter und Spielleute.* K. J. Trübner, Strassburg, 1901.—J. Wolf, "Die Tänze des Mittelalters," Arch. f. MW., I, 1918. For further literature, see under "The Orchestral Suite," p. 187.

Roman Empire possessed in 1355 a *Rex omnium histrionum*, **Hans der Fiedler** (John the Fiddler) appointed by the emperor Charles IV. Especially famous was the Strassburg Brotherhood of the Crowns (*Brüderschaft der Kronen*) in which the lords of Rappoltsstein named the King of the Pipers. In the territory of the Swiss confederacy such a right devolved upon the dukes of Kyburg, later upon their rightful successor, the city of Zurich, which created **Ulmann Meyer** of Bremgarten King of the Pipers in the year 1430.

In France, the corporation of musicians placed itself under the patronage of St. Julian. As early as 1295, Philipp the Fair had appointed Jean Charmillon *roy des menestriers* (King of the Minstrels). In 1321, twentynine musicians (*ménestrels*) and eight female jugglers (*jongleresses*) combined in Paris to establish for themselves statutes, which were sanctioned on the fourteenth of September of that year. They had a chapel (Saint Julien des Ménétriers) for their meetings, as well as a hospice for their aged members. Thus, the musicians, who had been isolated up to that time, placed themselves under the protection of the law. Nevertheless, unlike the German cities, which had begun in the fourteenth century to attach to themselves paid musicians, the cities of France did not possess such hired players at that early date. The city of Paris, in the fourteenth century, had only official trumpeters of the *châtelet* and of the palace, who transmitted signals and calls to the populace. The instrumental players lived with the princes and the lords, where they awaited the requests of the citizens, who came to ask their services at some wedding, baptism, or banquet. The Parisian who desired music at his home proceeded to choose his players in the *rue aux Jongleurs*, where the trumpeters, players on the tambourine, organists, flutists, players on the viol, harpists, lutenists, oboists, etc., congregated and were regularly inscribed in the confraternity.

The German cities, from Luzerne and St. Gall to Hamburg and Lübeck, possessed their *Stadtpfeifereien* (associations of municipal players of wind instruments) which consisted generally of four musicians, sometimes of a greater number. In Basel, the oath which the town pipers had to swear has been handed down. According to this, they had to play on summer evenings on the Rhine bridge; in the winter time, in the guild rooms. The council, accordingly, looked after the musical wants of the citizens—a practice that in recent times is only gradually again winning recognition.

The chief instruments of the town pipers were the trumpet, the trombone, and the cornett (*Zink*). The last-named, one of the favorite instruments of the Middle Ages, was a hybrid between wood-wind and brass instruments. From the latter, it received its mouthpiece and the method of tone production, i.e., it is sounded like a trumpet. On the other hand, it was made of wood, sometimes of ivory, and provided with holes like the flute. Its great advantage over the trumpet lay in the fact that it could produce the entire chromatic scale, whereas the trumpet was limited to the natural scale. This explains the great partiality for the cornet up to the appearance of the chromatic trumpet in the nineteenth century. The upper voices of the music played by the town pipers were supplied by the cornet, the lower by the trombones. For festival and martial music the trumpet assumed its natural rôle, played by a herald and escorted by a standard. Indeed, the trumpeters were considered as especially aristocratic officers of state. They were quite conscious of their position and developed their art to a high degree of virtuosity, of which we have ample proof in the trumpet parts of Bach and Handel.

In the German towns, the municipal musicians were, as a rule, clothed in the colors of their city. The well-known picture of Dürer *Der Pfeiferstuhl in Nürnberg* (The Pipers' Chair in Nuremberg) shows the composition of their orchestra. The town pipers existed in smaller towns in Germany into the nineteenth century, and continued the custom of blowing a chorale from the church spire both morning and evening—a beautiful custom which deserves a revival. The present-day municipal orchestras of Germany are, to a great extent, the immediate successors of the one-time town pipers.

The bowed instruments.[63]—A tremendous innovation in the field of instrumental music, an enrichment the like of which did not occur again, falls in the period of the Middle Ages, namely, the appearance of bowed instruments. Without them our music would be poor: indeed we

[63] BIBLIOGRAPHY: F. B. Emery, *The Violonist's Dictionary*. W. Reeves, London, 1925.—L. Grillet, *Les ancêtres du violon*. 2 vols., G. Schmid, Paris, 1901.—W. L. v. Lütgendorff, *Die Geigen-und Lautenmacher vom Mittelalter bis zur Gegenwart*. 5th & 6th rev. ed., Frankfurter Verlagsanstalt, Frankfurt ª/M., 1922.—Andreas Moser, *Geschichte des Violinspiels*. M. Hesse, Berlin, 1923.—K. Nef, *Geschichte unserer Musikinstrumente*. Quelle u. Meyer, Leipzig, 1926.—A. Vidal, *Les instruments à archet*. Impr. de J. Claye, Paris, 1876–78.—W. J. von Wasielewski, *Geschichte der Instrumentalmusik im 16. Jahrhundert*. J. Guttentag (D. Collin), Berlin, 1878; by the same author, *Die Violine im 17. Jahrhundert und die Anfänge der Violinkomposition*. M. Cohen u. Sohn, Bonn, 1874; new edition, 1905; with a booklet of musical examples.

cannot conceive of our present musical life without them. On account of their very great importance one would, of course, like to know where they arose, how they came to us, but their origin is shrouded in absolute darkness. It is possible, but not at all certain, indeed, not even especially probable, that we took them from the Arabians. They are mentioned for the first time in the ninth century, but were generally adopted only in the eleventh and twelfth centuries. The *rota* or *chrotta* is supposed to have been the oldest of the bowed instruments. Inasmuch, however, as this name is also frequently used to designate a plucked instrument, one must be cautious with conclusions based upon its early mention. We have already seen that the troubadours and minnesingers employed the *vielle* or *viole*, in German the *Fidel*, for the accompaniment of their songs. The *tromba marina* (*trompette marine*, *Trummscheit*), a narrow instrument, a man's stature in length, provided with only one string—now and then with two strings—was doubtless also an old form of bowed instrument. At a very early period the hurdy-gurdy (*campagnarde*, *Drehleier*), in which the strings are stroked by a revolving wheel, makes its appearance. The instrument was anciently called *symphonie* or *chifonie*. A famous old representation of this instrument is found among the sculptures of the Church of Saint Georges de Bocherville in Normandy.

The preëminence of the lute in the fifteenth and sixteenth centuries.[64]— In the fifteenth and sixteenth centuries, the lute once more outstripped the bowed instruments. The latter only gained their supremacy permanently in the seventeenth century. The lute, it has been definitely shown, comes from the Arabians, having come to Europe *via* Spain, and it was on the Iberian peninsula that lute playing and composition for the lute enjoyed their first brilliant period.

In the lute music of the sixteenth century we meet for the first time with independent instrumental music. Throughout the entire Middle

[64] BIBLIOGRAPHY: M. Brenet, "Notes sur l'histoire du luth en France," 1898, R.M.I.— Maria Rita Brondi, *Il liuto e la chitarra, ricerche storiche sulla loro origine.* Fratelli Bocca, Turin, 1926.—O. Chilesotti, article in Enc. Lav. (with the indication of the numerous works by this specialist).—A. Koczirz, "Oesterreichische Lautenmusik im 16. Jahrhundert," D.T. OE., XVIII, 2.—O. Körte, "Laute und Lautenmusik bis zur Mitte des 16. Jahrhunderts," supplement to the I.M.G., 1902.—L. de La Laurencie, *Les Luthistes.* Laurens, Paris, 1928.—Luis Milan, Compositions for the Lute, edited by L. Schrade. P.D.M., II.—Morphy, *Les Luthistes espagnols du XVIe siècle.* B. & H., Leipzig, 2 vols., 1902.—Joseph Zuth, *Handbuch der Laute und Gitarre.* A. Goll, Verlag der Zeitschrift für die Gitarre, Vienna, 1926–28.—Cf. the collection by E. H. Fellowes, *The English School of Lutenist Song-writers.* For examples of compositions for or with lute, see W.B., Nos. 32, 34.

Ages we find only now and then a piece intended especially and exclusively for instruments. We have already observed that vocal music was played on instruments also. The technique of the latter was not yet so highly developed that one needed special compositions for them. A genuine virtuosity, apart from the organ, was doubtless first developed on the lute, which invited the embellishments and mannerisms so essentially different from the vocal style, in other words, a virtuosity which created an instrumental style.

This instrumental style appears quite perfected in the works of the Spanish masters of the sixteenth century, the greatest of whom was doubtless Luis Milan. Following is the beginning of a pavane by that composer (1536):

Beside him, along with others, one may place Miguel de Fuenllana, whose *Fantasia sopra ut, re, mi, fa, sol, la* [65] exerts a charm even today because of its thematic skill, its melodious character, its utilization of the diverse registers of the lute, and its climactic close.

The whole of Europe in the sixteenth century was seized with a desire to play the lute. As today pianos are universal, so at that time lutes were everywhere to be found. Luther somewhere relates, to be sure as a droll incident, that on having to read Mass in a village, the sacristan appeared with a lute for the purpose of intoning the chant. The lute music offers much of interest from the point of view of the history of culture and customs, because many dances and songs have been preserved through it—pavans, galliards, sarabands. One of the most in-

[65] Cf. R.B., No. 41; S.B., No. 114.

teresting among the dances is the following galliard by the Netherlander, Emmanuel Adriansen (1584):

According to Wasielewski,

Instrumentalmusik im XVI. Jahrh.

Lute books, printed and in manuscript, have come down to us in great numbers. Among the famous German composers were Arnold Schlick, Hans Judenkunig, and Hans Gerle. Among Italians, suffice it to mention only Francesco Spinaccino,[67] whose compositions were already printed by Petrucci so early as 1507, and the distinguished Ambrosio Dalza, many of whose compositions should still find grateful listeners. That the instrumental style had to make its way slowly, is evident from the fact that the lute composers, instead of at once creating original compositions, occupied themselves, to a great extent, with the transcription of polyphonic choral compositions, attempts that were, obviously, successful only to a limited degree.

In Poland, where the royal court of the Jagellons at Cracow was one of the most musical in Europe, Valentin Bakfark (Greff) transcribed

---

[66] Cf. also a Pavan, a slow dance in four-part time, the "Muscadine-Song," in the arrangement of Hainhofer, in S.A., No. 33; also the "Padovan" by Johann Ghro in W.B., No. 55, and the "Paduane" by Isaac Posch, *loc. cit.*, No. 60.

[67] See S.B., No. 63, a and b.

for the lute songs and dances that were characteristically Polish. Somewhat later, under Stephen Bathory, Albert Dlugoray, also writing, as did all his contemporaries, villanelle and galliards, impregnated them with a character that was at once both vigorous and melancholic, which easily prevents them from being confused with similar pieces of French or Italian origin. One may observe this in the following villanella, taken from the book of H. Opienski on Polish music: [68]

Transcribed by Opienski
according to the tablature of Besard (1603).

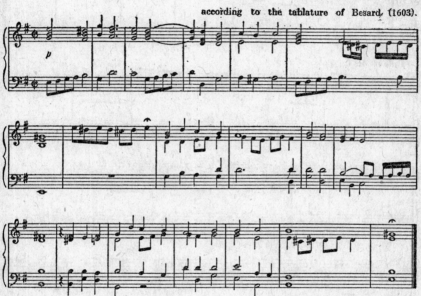

In France, lute music developed to a special degree of refinement. The first book of lute music was issued by the publisher Attaingnant in the year 1529 (*Dix-huit basses-dances*). One of the dances, transcribed from the tablature, is shown on page 136.

The *tourdion* is appended to the *basse danse* as the galliard is to the pavan. "The steps and movements of the pavan and of the *basse dance* are ponderous and slow," says Thoinot Arbeau in his *Orchésographie* of the year 1588; "those of the galliard and of the tourdion are light and jovial."

When one considers the venerable age of this piece, one cannot fail

[68] Paris, 1918. Cf., by the same author, the résumé, also entitled *La Musique polonaise*. Gebethner and Wolf, Paris, 1928.

La Magdalene, Basse Dance.   P.B.

Retour de la Basse Dance.

Tourdion

to admire the variety of its rhythms. The music of the lute developed rapidly in France under the lutenist of Francis I, Albert de Ripe, whose tablature was published after his death, in 1553. Guillaume Morlaye published about the same time his arrangements of the Psalms of Certon [69] for one voice with lute accompaniment, and the editor Adrien Le Roy published several books of Psalms and of airs of the court arranged for the lute.[70]

In the seventeenth century a new flight was achieved. The works of J. B. Besard (*Thesaurus harmonicus*), of Antoine Francisque (*Le Trésor d'Orphée*, Ballard, 1600), of Antoine Boësset, of Ch. Mouton, of Denis Gaultier,[71] of Le Sage de Richée, combine all the tonal and rhythmic effects of which the lute is capable.

In England, the best composers for the lute were, beside Dowland, Th. Morley, Ph. Rosseter, Fr. Pilkington, who wrote at the end of the sixteenth century a great number of songs with lute accompaniment and of transcriptions for the lute.[72]

Organ and Clavier Music in Germany, France, and Spain.[73]—About the middle of the fifteenth century, there labored in Nuremberg, at the Church of St. Sebaldus, the blind organist, Conrad Paumann. He was widely famed. Rosenpluet celebrates him in his verse on Nuremberg (1447), as the most remarkable man of the city. Later on he was called

---

[69] CERTON is also the author of Masses. Three of his Masses have been published by H. Expert in Vol. XIII of the *Monuments de la musique française au temps de la Renaissance.* Sénart, Paris, 1925.—A chanson for four voices by Certon will be found in E.B., No. 17.
[70] *Les Chansons au luth et airs de cours français du XVIᵉ siècle*, collections of the publishers Attaingnant, Phalèse, Le Roy and Ballard, have been published by A. Mairy, L. de la Laurencie, and G. Thibault (P.S.M.).
[71] *La Rhétorique des dieux* and other pieces for the lute by Denis Gaultier (c. 1652) have been published by André Tessier (P.S.M., 1931).—See G.M.B., No. 215, a and b.
[72] Cf. also the English works in the collection of Edmund H. Fellowes mentioned above (p. 125, note 54).
[73] BIBLIOGRAPHY: W. Merian, *Die Tabulaturen des Organisten Hans Kotter.* B. & H., Leipzig, 1916; by the same author, *Der Tanz in den deutschen Tabulaturbüchern.* B. & H., Leipzig, 1927.—H. J. Moser, *Paul Hofhaimer*, with a selection of his works. Cotta, Stuttgart, and Berlin, 1929.—André Pirro, "L'Art des organistes," Enc. Lav., Part 2, Vol. II, pp. 1181–1374; by the same author, *Les Clavecinistes.* Laurens, Paris, 1924.—Félix Raugel, *Les Organistes.* Laurens, Paris, 1923.—Aug. Gottf. Ritter, *Zur Geschichte des Orgelspiels im 14. bis 18. Jahrhundert* (with numerous musical examples). Max Hesse, Leipzig, 1884. A new edition of this work is in process of publication, under the editorship of G. Frotscher, by the original publishers.—Yvonne Rokseth, editor, *Deux Livres d'orgue parus chez P. Attaignant, 1531.* P.S.M., Paris, 1925; by the same author, *La Musique d'orgue au XVᵉ siècle et au début du XVIᵉ.* Droz, Paris, 1930.—Weitzmann-Seiffert, *Geschichte der Klaviermusik.* 3d ed., Vol. I, B. & H., Leipzig, 1899—a fundamental work for the period extending through Bach and Handel.

to Munich, where he died in the year 1473. Paumann left behind him a large work, dated 1452, with the title *Fundamentum organisandi*.[74] It is the oldest instruction book on instrumental composition, and contains, for organ or clavier, transcriptions of ecclesiastical songs, *Lieder*, and dances, and several preambles (*Praeambeln*) or preludes.

A large school of organists followed Paumann, especially in Austria, South Germany, and Switzerland. Its head, greatly celebrated by his contemporaries, was Paulus Hofhaimer (1459–1537), the court organist of Emperor Maximilian I, at St. Stephen's Cathedral in Vienna. We know of this school chiefly through another large Method or Foundation Book (*Fundamentbuch*), edited by Hans Buchner, a pupil of Hofhaimer, and organist at Constance from 1512 to 1526. The transcriptions of *Lieder*, which Hofhaimer wrote for the clavier, are found in the tablatures of Leonhard Kleber and of Hans Kotter, the work of the last named having been dedicated to the humanist, Bonifacius Amerbach of Basel. The compositions of Hofhaimer have been collected in the work of H. J. Moser, *Paul Hofhaimer* (1928).

In France, some anonymous contemporaries of Kleber and of Kotter transcribed for the organ or the spinet motets of disciples of Josquin: Brumel, Févin, Claudin de Sermisy, etc. These works, forming seven books of tablatures, were published in 1530–31 by P. Attaingnant. Four collections of religious compositions—verses of the Magnificat, Masses, transcriptions of motets—seem to have been intended for organists of the Church who were obliged to play these verses in alternation with the singing of the choir, whereas the three books of dances and of chansons were intended for secular usage. Some preludes, finally, reveal to us a most refined imagination on the part of the organists under Francis I.[75] The briefest among them unfolds a melody that is at the same time very pure and altogether instrumental,[76] as is shown on page 139.

The ordinary procedure which the French organists, as well as the German, followed was the art of embellishment. If they transcribed

[74] Facsimile edition by K. Ameln, *Lochheimer Liederbuch und fundamentum organisandi*. Wölbing Verlag, Berlin, 1925.—See G.M.B., Nos. 47, 48.
[75] NEW EDITIONS: four books of dances and chansons, in facsimile, by Ed. Bernoulli: *Chansons und Tänze*. C. Kuhn, Munich, 1914; three books of religious music by Yvonne Rokseth, *Deux livres d'orgue parus chez Pierre Attaingnant* (1531), P.S.M., 1925; and *Treize motets et un prélude pour orgue parus chez Pierre Attaingnant* (1531), P.S.M., 1930.—Cf. the bibliography of the new editions of ancient works for organ in the work by the same author entitled *La Musique d'orgue au XVe siècle* (p. 137, n. 73).
[76] *Treize motets et un prélude*, p. 1.

songs or dances for the clavier, what they primarily did was to surcharge
the melody with embroideries and trills. The process was called in
Germany *Kolorieren* (coloring) and the school was called the *Koloristen-
schule* (colorist school). These embellishments and ornaments impress
one as being still of a very superficial nature. They appear to have been
merely pasted on, as it were, rather than to be an organic growth. One
might compare the process with the festal decoration of a house, the
decoration not coalescing with the architecture, but being merely hung
upon the building. It is difficult for us to feel the fascination which such
compositions must have exerted in their day; but historical judgment
indicates that the correct road had at any rate been entered upon, the
road to the variation form, which is especially well adapted to the clavier
instruments.

In order to understand the procedures of this budding art one may
compare the fragment of the song *Adieu mes amours* of Josquin, cited
above (p. 46), with the beginning of the instrumental transcription
which Heinrich Isaak made, as is shown on page 140.

The treatises of Juan Bermudo and of Sancta Maria,[77] also the works

[77] The treatises have been analyzed by Otto Kinkeldey in his book *Orgel und Klavier in der
Musik des 16. Jahrhunderts.* B. & H., Leipzig, 1910.

of Antonio de Cabezon,[78] organist of Philip II, testify to the fact that the clavier art had reached a high degree of development in Spain.

D.T.Œ., XIV, 1.

Adiu mes amors.

English Virginal Music and the Development of the Variation Form.[79]— A special predilection for the virginal manifested itself in England at

---

[78] ANTONIO DE CABEZON (b. near Burgos, Spain, March 30, 1510; d. Madrid, May 26, 1566) blind from birth, has left *Obras de música para tecla* (clavier) *y arpa y vihuela* (lute) which were collected (Madrid, 1578) by his son, Hernando de Cabezon, himself a composer. Published by F. Pedrell, *Hispaniae Schola Musica sacra*, Vols. III, IV, VII, and VIII. See Kinkeldey, *Orgel und Klavier im 16. Jahrhundert.* B. & H., Leipzig, 1910.—For additional reprints, see G.M.B., No. 113.—Halbig, *Klaviertänze des 16. Jahrhunderts.* Cotta, Stuttgart and Berlin.—Riemann, *Notenschrift und Notendruck.* 1896.—Ritter, *Geschichte des Orgelspiels.*

[79] MODERN EDITIONS OF MUSIC FOR THE VIRGINAL: Hilda F. Andrews, *My Ladye Nevell's Book*, 1591. J. Curwen, London, 1926.—G. Bantock, *Album of Selected Pieces.* Novello, London; by the same editor, *Three Dances by Byrd.* Novello, London.—*Fitzwilliam Virginal Book* (the most important MS), new edition in 2 vols.; *Parthenia* (first printed collection); both collections published by Novello, London, and B. & H., Leipzig, 1894–99; the Parthe-

an early period. As early as 1502, so it is reported, twelve young virgins let themselves be heard on the virginal at a festival in Westminster Hall. The virginal is a small clavier instrument, oblong, rectangular in form, approaching the clavichord in timber, but resembling a clavicymbal in its method of tone production, i.e., the strings are plucked by small leather or metal quills. In the heyday of English music, in the time of Queen Elizabeth and of Shakespeare, when the madrigal was sending forth its precious blossoms, the composers cultivated a special literature for the virginal, that has a twofold historical and artistic significance: it presented for the first time genuine clavier music which takes cognizance of the peculiarities of the instrument, and it brought the variation form to artistic maturity. The rich chain of variations that extends through Bach and Beethoven to Brahms, C. Franck, and Reger had its beginnings in the English virginal pieces.

William Byrd's variations on *The Carman's Whistle* are justly famous examples. Typically English is the choice of a theme taken from the street. Taking as his point of departure the few notes which the carman can play on his modest whistle, Byrd gives the variation a new and significant richness. He does not content himself with clothing his theme with embellishments, but transforms its character at each repetition. The original melody, quite plebeian, makes way for episodes that are

nia collection was also published under the editorship of E. F. Rimbault, by the Musical Antiquarian Society, London, 1847.—Fuller-Maitland and Barclay Squire, editors, *Fourteen Pieces for Keyed Instruments by William Byrd*. Stainer & Bell, London, 1923; also, *Twenty-Five Pieces for Keyed Instruments from Benjamin Cosyn's Virginalbook*. J. & W. Chester, London, 1923.—Margaret H. Glyn, editor, *Elizabethan Virginal Music and Its Composers: John Bull*, Vol. I, and *Orlando Gibbons*, Vol. I. W. Reeves, London, 1924; by the same editor, a volume of easy pieces, Joseph Williams, London.—L. Köhler, *Les maitres du clavecin*. Litolff, Braunschweig, 187–?.—W. Niemann, *Alte Meister des Klavierspiels*. Edition Peters, Leipzig.—E. Pauer, *Old English Composers for the Virginals and Harpsichord*. Augener London; by the same editor, *Alte Klaviermusik*. Second series, Senff, Leipzig, 18–?. BIBLIOGRAPHY: H. Orsmond Anderton, *Early English Music*. Musical Opinion, London, 1920.—Ch. van den Borren, *Les Origines de la musique de clavier en Angleterre*. B. & H., Leipzig, 1914; Eng. tr., *The Sources of Keyboard Music in England*, by J. E. Matthew. Novello & Co., London, H. W. Gray Co., N. Y.—H. C. Colles, *The Growth of Music*. 2 vols., O.U.P., London, 1912–21.—Grattan Flood, *Early Tudor Composers*. O.U.P., London, 1925.—G. R. Hayes, *Musical Instruments and their Music (1500–1750)*: Vol. I, *The Treatment of Instrumental Music*. O.U.P., London, 1928.—E. W. Naylor, *An Elizabethan Virginal Book: a Critical Essay on the Contents of the Fitzwilliam Virginal Book*. J. M. Dent, London, E. P. Dutton, N. Y., 1905.—C. H. Parry, "The Music of the 17th Century." Vol. III of the *Oxford History of Music*.—J. Pulver, *A Biographical Dictionary of Old English Music and Musical Instruments*. E. P. Dutton, N. Y., Kegan Paul, London, 1927.—E. Walker, *A History of Music in England*. O.U.P., London, 1924.— H. E. Wooldridge, "The Polyphonic Period," *Oxford History of Music*, Vols. I & II. O.U.P., London.

now graceful, now capricious. Finally, the entire work is crowned with a stately conclusion that would not be unworthy of a Handel. Following is the theme, together with the beginnings of the fourth and the last variations:

Fitzwilliam Virginal Book ,Vol.I

Similar things might be said concerning the galliard *Mrs. Mary Brownlo* by the same composer, while the pavan *The Earl of Shaftesbury* reveals a proud dignity. Indeed, concerning the latter it has been said: "there is probably nothing more balanced and artistically complete in all the literature of virginal music." [80] The variations on a pavan in G major by John Bull, and on *The Queen's Command* by Orlando Gibbons are characterized by a special degree of virtuosity.

Such variations were based on a melody by some well-known composer, on some fragment of ecclesiastical plain song, on one of the secular, popular songs of the day, on a dance tune, or on a "ground." The outstanding names in the virginal field are Bull, Byrd, Gibbons, and Giles Farnaby. But while the choral music of Byrd and Gibbons is still sung on account of its intrinsic worth, the virginal compositions of the period are played, if at all, primarily because of their historical interest. For, as has been well said, beside some more serious work, there are "pages and pages of the merest 'passage-work,' which are obviously inspired by nothing else than the attractiveness of playing notes, no matter how artistically meaningless, at a quicker pace than voices could sing them. . . . Scale-playing, as such, had a fascination for these early instrumental composers that we find hard to realize; the mere succession of notes in fixed and persistent alphabetical order was a novelty to men whose ideas of music had been almost entirely gained from choral compositions, and when these successions were heard in extensions beyond the range of voices, and also at a brilliant speed, the fascination was complete, irrespectively of the artistic interest which listeners would have demanded when singing was in question." [81]

The English composers of that day were already fond of descriptive effects; they sought to imitate the storm, the chase, the ringing of bells,

[80] Ernest Walker, *A History of Music in England.* O.U.P., London, 1924, p. 108.
[81] *Loc. cit.*, p. 107. Cf. also the discussion in C. F. Pfatteicher, *The Organ Works of John Redford.* Bärenreiter Verlag, Kassel, 1934.

or a battle. John Bull's *The King's Hunting Jig* is a series of variations on the following fresh and piquant hunting-horn theme:

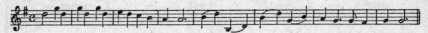

The entire chase is painted in the successive variations with their fanfares, their rapid runs, their morts, and their brilliant conclusion.

Venetian organ and orchestral music.—While the English virginalists establish the variation and the character piece for the clavier, the Venetian masters begin the series which leads to the fugue of J. S. Bach. It is the *ricercar* (ricercare) which these masters develop and which is to be viewed as the precursor of the fugue.[32] It does not as yet possess the unity of the later, more perfected form, inasmuch as, for the most part, it develops several themes, one after the other; but the fugal development is its underlying principle. The oldest creations of this kind known to us were published by Girolamo Cavazzoni in Venice in 1542. He understands better than do many of his successors how to treat this form of composition with expression, as is well illustrated by an elegiac *ricercar* for four voices, which will be found in its entirety in Torchi (*Arte musicale in Italia*, III), the beginning of which is as follows:

The conclusion, half melancholic, half ecstatic, is of a remarkable beauty, as is shown on page 145.

Beside the *ricercar*, Venice cultivated still other related forms, as the *canzone*, the *fantasia*, and the *toccata*. All of these are free creations, not dance forms, and are developed in a more or less contrapuntal-

[32] See J. Müller-Blattau, *Grundzüge einer Geschichte der Fuge*. Königsberger Studien zur Musikwissenschaft, 1923.

polyphonic manner. In this respect they represent a transference of the achievements of the Netherlanders from choral music to pure instrumental.

The first artists in this transformation, Willaert (b. c. 1480–90; d. 1562) and Jachet Buus (d. 1565) were, quite naturally, themselves Netherlanders. After them the Venetian school had as heads Andrea and Giovanni Gabrieli. Orazio Vecchi was, to be sure, born at Modena, but in his music he attached himself to Venice. A little later there followed Florentio Maschera (1540 or 1541–80 or –84), Annibale Padovano (1527–75), Girolamo Diruta (c. 1560–?), Adriano Banchieri (1565–1634).[84]

Giovanni Gabrieli especially brings a certain flow and a flight of virtuosity into the still somewhat stiff forms. Claudio Merulo (1533–1604) [85] must be mentioned as an especially interesting master, who achieved his best in the free *toccata*, going beyond Gabrieli in his demands upon virtuosity. He developed this bold improvisational form in a truly ingenious manner. (See four toccatas for organ in Torchi, *op. cit.*)

It has already been mentioned that Andrea and Giovanni Gabrieli created the free orchestral composition with their sonatas and *canzoni*. Their brilliant effects should again be emphasized. Compositions like the already mentioned *Sonata pian e forte* by G. Gabrieli were well fitted to accompany and enhance the splendor of the festivals of the proud Most Serene Republic of Venice. There is nothing similar in modern music, nothing that can be placed beside them. In their richness, and in the glow of their color, they are related to the works of the Venetian masters of painting, to the pictures of a Titian and a Palma Vecchio.

[83] An Easter hymn, transcribed by Cavazzoni for organ, will be found in S.B. at No. 103.
[84] Selections from the works of all these masters will be found in Torchi, *L'Arte musicale in Italia.*—See also E.B., Nos. 16, 20, 22; R.B., Nos. 40, 42, 49, 50, 52, 59, 60; S.B., Nos. 105, 151; and W.B., Nos. 27, 57.
[85] Cf. E.B., No. 23, and W.B., No. 43.

V

THE SEVENTEENTH CENTURY

THE BIRTH OF THE OPERA, THE ORATORIO, AND THE ACCOMPANIED SOLO SONG [1]

AT the turn from the sixteenth to the seventeenth century there arose in Italy those forms on which all modern music rests, the opera, the oratorio, and the accompanied solo song. The genuinely new feature was the accompaniment of songs by instruments in a chordal, harmonic manner. Even though the upper voice was given precedence in the first Netherlands school, and instruments were often added, the accompaniment was never a purely chordal one, and song and accompaniment were not separated so definitely and clearly as they have been since that time.

A new spirit entered, summoned by the study of classical antiquity. Even though the music of the Greeks does not have the same significance for us as their plastic art, nevertheless, invaluable suggestions for the tonal art did proceed from them.

In the eighties of the sixteenth century, friends of antiquity gathered in the house of Count Bardi, later in that of Jacopo Corsi. Inspired above all by Plato, calling themselves the Academy, they occupied themselves especially with conversations and investigations on the subject of music. They wanted to revive the tonal art of antiquity. Three old Greek hymns had been discovered. It was not yet possible to decipher them, but Vincenzo Galilei, the father of the famous astronomer, was inspired by them to undertake a first practical step. He set to music Count Ugolino's lament from Dante's "Divine Comedy" and sang the piece himself to the accompaniment of a viol. This first attempt was

[1] BIBLIOGRAPHY: Ambros, *Geschichte der Musik.* Vol. IV, 3d ed., edited by H. Leichtentritt, F. E. C. Leuckart, Leipzig, 1909.—Romain Rolland, *Histoire de l'opéra en Europe avant Lully et Scarlatti.* E. Thorin, Paris, 1895; 3d ed., E. de Boccard, Paris, 1931; by the same author, "L'Opéra au XVIIe siècle en Italie," in Enc. Lav.—Max Schneider, *Die Anfänge des Basso continuo.* B. & H., Leipzig, 1918.—Angelo Solerti, *Le origini del melodramma.* Fratelli Bocca, Turin, 1903. New editions of the Eurydice of Peri, published by Ricordi, Milan, in *L'Arte musicale in Italia*, 1907; and by Guidi, Florence; cf. also the transcribed score by Perinelli. Istituto editoriale italiano, Milan, 1919.—For a complete history of the practice of thorough-bass, see: F. T. Arnold, *The Art of Accompaniment from a Thorough-Bass.* O.U.P., Oxford, 1931.—Cf. also, Hermann Keller, *Schule des Generalbassspiels.* Bärenreiter Verlag, Kassel. 1931.

so well received that Galilei set a portion of the "Lamentations of Jeremiah" in the same style. Unfortunately they have not survived.

The movement attained large proportions when the poet Ottavio Rinuccini adapted the story of the battle of Apollo with the dragon Python in a dramatic poem *Dafne*, and the musician Jacopo Peri set it to music. The work was performed in the year 1594 in the house of Count Corsi in Florence. It was received with great acclaim, and was repeated during a period of three years in the carnival season. Unfortunately, only the text has been preserved; the music has been lost. Again Rinuccini and Peri united their efforts for a joint undertaking. They created a *Eurydice* which was presented in the year 1600 in connection with the marriage of Henry IV and Marie de Medicis in Florence, and was published at the same time.

With this work the history of the opera begins. The Florentines believed that they had revived the Greek tragedy; in reality they had created the new form of the opera. Their new creation is *toto coelo* removed from the spirit of antiquity. Indeed, it already shows all the advantages and disadvantages of the later music drama. No matter! With an admirable flight of phantasy, a living art species, in consonance with the modern time, was here founded, one which was destined to assume a leading rôle for centuries. Like the plastic artists of the Renaissance, the Florentine poets and musicians did not reconstruct antiquity, but created new art and new beauty.

This poem *Eurydice* has the character of a pastoral play. It presents great scenic pictures, broad situations, the prerequisites of a good operatic text. It is only to be regretted that the action issues happily, and that violence is therefore done the classical Orpheus legend. Because the piece was presented in connection with a royal wedding it could not end tragically. The oldest opera, therefore, issues a charter for reprehensible licenses, and subsequent times, unfortunately, made only too good use of them.

In a preface to *Eurydice*, Peri himself has discussed the nature and intention of his music. Elsewhere also, the renovators expressed themselves freely in dedications and separate writings. Taking their point of departure from the Greeks, their fundamental idea was that the poetry must be the mistress, and the music her servant. They condemned the old art of counterpoint, because in its case the music did violence to the poetry, and they passionately declared war against it. They would most gladly have extirpated it root and trunk. The new *stile recitativo* or *rappresentativo*, as it was called, adapted itself as closely as possible to the words, and was thus intended to accentuate and reënforce the expression of the poet. According to our present judgment, they succeeded in this endeavor only sparingly. Peri for the most part offered barren, declamatory song. Only occasionally do warmer, melodiously richer sounds penetrate it. But owing to the newness of the matter his contemporaries were deeply moved by the songs of his Orpheus.[2]

The accompaniment was performed, as a rule, on a harpsichord, at times also on a *chitarrone* (theorbo), lute, and lyre (bowed instrument). In the score, the method of notation known as thorough bass (*basso continuo*) made its appearance. The bass part only was recorded, supplied with figures which indicate the chords that were to be used with the given bass. This abbreviated method of notation, a kind of stenography, which left a certain freedom to the executant, came into general usage, and continued until the end of the eighteenth century.

Between the recitations of the solo songs, some short pieces for three flutes were interpolated in order to give an antique character to the whole, as the flute was considered the favorite instrument of the Greeks. Furthermore, there were a number of choruses and dances. These, however, take part in the action itself, and hence have nothing in common with the chorus of classical tragedy, but already correspond to the modern opera chorus.

In the same year, 1600, in which *Eurydice* was placed upon the stage in Florence, a work was performed in Rome which former historians viewed as the first oratorio,[3] but which, in fact, should rather be called a spiritual opera, the *Rappresentazione di anima e di corpo*,[4] the verse composed by Laura Guidiccioni, the music by Emilio de' Cavalieri (or del Cavaliere) (d. 1602). Textually it has affinity with the medieval

[2] A good example of that declamation is to be found in the Enc. Lav., I, 692, in the article by Romain Rolland on "L'Opéra en Italie au XVIIe siècle."—Cf. also R.B., No. 56, and S.B., No. 171, a, b, c.

[3] BIBLIOGRAPHY: Domenico Alaleona, *Studi sulla storia dell'oratorio musicale in Italia.* Fratelli Bocca, Turin, 1908.—Hermann Kretzschmar, *Führer durch den Konzertsaal,* Part 2, Vol. II. *Oratorien und weltliche Chorwerke,* 4th ed., 1920.—Guido Pasquetti, *L'oratorio musicale in Italia.* Successori Le Monnier, Florence, 1906.—Arnold Schering, *Geschichte des Oratoriums.* B. & H., Leipzig, 1911.

[4] New edition in facsimile by F. Mantica. Casa editrice Claudio Monteverdi, Rome, 1912. Published in transcription by Fr. Malipiero in *Raccolta nazionale delle musiche italiane.* Istituto editoriale italiano, Milan, 1919.—See S.B., No. 169.

mystery and the spiritual drama. The composition is in a recitative style, similar to the *Eurydice* of Peri, only perhaps still drier:

Duetto from *Anima e corpo.*

The performance took place in the prayer-meeting room of the Congregazione dell'oratorio of Philippo Neri. Here so-called *laudi spirituali* were formerly sung.[5] Out of these grew the oratorio. These *laudi* were originally simple hymns composed by Animuccia and Palestrina. Later they developed into mysteries in dialogue form, for three and four voices, which were a natural preparation for the oratorio.

The oratorio developed later in Italy into a form different from the thoroughly dramatic *rappresentazione*, which, as observed, was a kind of spiritual opera. The latter may, however, have been influential in the origin of the oratorio by showing that the new recitative style is effective also in spiritual music.

The attempts of Galilei in the composition of solo songs with accompaniment were continued with success by Giulio Caccini [6] who likewise

[5] Cf. W.B., No. 37.

[6] GIULIO CACCINI (b. Rome, 1550; d. Florence, 1618). In 1564 he came to Florence where he obtained a position as singer and lutenist at the court. From 1604 to 1605 he was in Paris on leave, at the request of the Queen, Maria de Medici. BIBLIOGRAPHY: A. Ehrichs, *Giulio Caccini.* Hesse & Becker, Leipzig, 1908.—Gandolfi, R.M.I., 1896.—Robert Marchal, "G. Caccini," R.M., 1925, Nos. 4, 10. NEW EDITIONS: *Le nuove musiche.* Vol. IX

belonged to the circle of Count Corsi. He created in great numbers "monodies," as they were called in those days, and published them under the proud title *Nuove musiche*. In fact it was a new music. Caccini is the earliest precursor of Schubert and Hugo Wolf.[7] In many places the Italian genius for song already manifested itself in his *Lieder*.[8] He did not remain alone in his attempts; a whole group of talented musicians vied with him. There at once developed in Italy a prosperous, although brief, period for the song. Strangely enough, there was no repetition later; the dramatic interest devoured all the others. The solo song was culti- vated, apart from the opera, only in the great form of the Cantata, which, of course, also tends more or less to dramatic expression. The *canzoni* and *villanelle* of this period are characterized by a primitive naturalness. They reveal a remarkable relationship with the modern *verismo*. Falconieri, Marini, Milanuzzi, Ottavio Durante, Cifra, Brunetti, Nighetti are the chief masters of this springtide of song, appearing like a brief dream in Italy's musical history.

Everywhere, from that time, only a *basso continuo* was noted beside the solo voice. Lodovico Grossi da Viadana carried over this system of thorough bass to the spiritual solo song in his *Cento concerti ecclesiastici*,[9] which appeared in the year 1602. They are important, because in a preface the composer developed the theory of thorough bass, and dis- cussed the application of the numerals. With the beginning of the seven- teenth century, the new art had established itself everywhere, and it is remarkable to observe how, in the shortest time, it swells into a flood that carries all before it, like a mountain stream with the melting snows of early spring.[10]

THE FLORENTINE AND THE ROMAN CHORUS OPERA [11]

Florence, which presented a great gift to the world with the creation of the opera, produced two further distinguished masters besides Peri: Giulio Caccini, who has already been mentioned as the originator of the

---

of "Prime fioriture del melodramma italiano," collection edited by Francesco Mantica. C. Monteverdi, Rome, 1930.—S.B., Nos. 172, 173; W.B., No. 49.

[7] See Hermann Kretzschmar, *Geschichte des neuen deutschen Liedes*. B. & H., Leipzig, 1911.

[8] The *Euridice* of Caccini may be found in the Publ. Eitner, Vol. XI.

[9] Cf. W.B., No. 52.

[10] NEW EDITIONS: Luigi Torchi, *Eleganti canzoni ed arie italiane del secolo XVII*. Ricordi, Milan, 1893.—See also Viadana's important preface to his *Centi Concerti* in Max Schneider, *Die Anfänge des Basso Continuo*. B. & H., Leipzig, 1918, p. 1 *et seq.*

[11] See Hugo Goldschmidt, *Studien zur Geschichte der italienischen Oper im 17. Jahrhundert*. 2 vols., B. & H., Leipzig, 1901 and 1904; with numerous musical examples. NEW EDITIONS:

solo song, and Marco da Gagliano. Later, strange to say, Florence completely receded from its former preëminence. Caccini composed the same text of "Eurydice" that Peri had composed, and at the first performance individual selections from his composition were presented. Gagliano wrote a *Dafne* for the court at Mantua in 1608 (according to the old revised text of Rinuccini),[12] and an allegorical wedding piece *Flora* (1628). In him, the Italian talent for song manifests itself, and he also understood how to develop his chorus effectively. Even these early operas were mounted with brilliant scenic and impressive mechanical effects. An ingeniously mechanized dragon makes its appearance in *Dafne*, as a worthy predecessor of the Wagnerian "Fafner." [13]

What has been said concerning Gagliano can also be said concerning the representatives of the Roman school who now assume the leadership. While a short time later Italian opera almost entirely abandoned the chorus, and even to the present day tends to neglect it, as though it were a stepchild, we find in these oldest Roman works remarkable dramatic choruses, which remind one of the best examples of modern Romantic opera. In *La catena d'Adone* by Domenico Mazzocchi (1626), shepherds and nymphs sing a delightful chorus of consolation, concluding with gentle melodic interlacings and undulations.[14] A hunting chorus from Michel Angelo Rossi's *Erminia sul Giordano* (1637), and a fishermen's chorus from Loreto Vittori's *La Galatea* (1639) are as fresh as nature, and abounding in atmosphere, genuine little genre pictures, such as are seldom to be found in Italian music. One cannot easily find anything more bewitching or enticing than the following slumber chorus from the *Orfeo* of Luigi Rossi (1598–1653): *Dormite, dormite begli occhi* (1647). It reminds one of the popular Barcarole from Offenbach's *Tales of Hoffman*, but Rossi's little piece is much more pure and chaste than that sultry song,[15] as is shown on page 152.

In the Roman opera, the comic element comes into its own for the first time. The roots of the later *opera buffa* are to be found here. Steffano Landi introduced it in his pastorale opera *La Morte d'Orfeo* (1619). Charon there sings a song *Drink, Drink the Precious Wave*, that is half weird, half amusing; certainly it is thoroughly original.[16] The legend-

---

Caccini, Gagliano, Monteverdi, Publ. Eitner, Vol. IX.—See also R.B., Nos. 57, 58, 66, 67, 69, 91, 92; also S.B., Nos. 176–178.
[12] Cf. E.B., No. 24.
[13] See S.B., No. 175.
[14] S.A., Nos. 44 ff.
[15] Cf. S.B., No. 199.
[16] S.A., No. 50.

Paris, Conservatoire, copie.

Chorus for three female voices.

Dor - mi - te begl,

Dor - mi - te begl' oc chi, dor - mi - - te,

Basso continuo:

oc - chi, dor - - mi - - te, dor mi - te begl' oc - chi, dor - mi - te, dor-

mi - - te, dor mi - te, dor - mi - te che se ben tant' im - pia -

- ga - te più dolce è'l mal che fa - te qual' - o - ra in pa - ce fe - ri -

- te. Dor - mi - te, Dor - mi - - te, begl' oc - chi, dor - mi - - te,

dor - mi - te, begl' oc - chi, dor - mi - te, Dor - mi - te, dor - mi - te.

opera *S. Alessio*, the chief work of Landi, dramatically important, also contains comic scenes.

CLAUDIO MONTEVERDI [17]

With surprising facility the Italians made themselves conversant with the newly-created art. In the very first years a genius arose who filled the new form with perennial content, Claudio Monteverdi. What the times were striving after, he expressed most perfectly, and that with a boldness that astounds us even today. The times were realistic. Never did a stronger urge toward directness prevail in music than in this period, not even in the period immediately before the World War. Certainly the modern *verismo* has brought forth no geniuses of the rank of a Claudio Monteverdi, who may be placed beside his contemporary Shakespeare. As the Briton in his dramas lets each one use plainly

[17] CLAUDIO MONTEVERDI (b. Cremona, 1567; d. Venice, 1643) was a pupil of Marc Antonio Ingegneri. In 1590 he was appointed singer and violinist at the court at Mantua; in 1601 he became master of the chapel there. In Mantua he wrote the operas *Orfeo*, 1607, and *Arianna*, 1608. In 1613 his fame called him to Venice as master of the chapel at St. Mark's. Here he wrote the dramatic scene *Il combattimento di Tancredi e Clorinda*, 1624, and the operas *Il ritorno d'Ulisse*, 1641, and *L'incoronazione di Poppea*, 1643. A few additional operas have been lost. Mention has already been made of his Italian madrigals. Significant also are his spiritual madrigals and his church works. BIBLIOGRAPHY: H. Kretzschmar, "Monteverdis Incoronazione di Poppea." Viertelj. f. MW., IX, 1894.— Malipiero, *Claudio Monteverdi*. Fratelli Treves, Milan, 1929.—H. Prunières, *Claudio Monteverdi*. Alcan, Paris, 1924; by the same author, *La Vie et l'œuvre de Claudio Monteverdi*. Editions musicales de la Librairie de France, Paris, 1926; 2d ed., 1931; Eng. tr., *Monteverdi, His Life and Works* by M. D. Mackie. J. M. Dent and Sons, Ltd., London and Toronto, 1926.—H. Redlich, *Claudio Monteverdi, ein formgeschichtlicher Versuch;* Vol. I: Das Madrigal. Edition Adler, Berlin, 1932.—Louis Schneider. *Claudio Monteverdi*. Perrin, Paris, 1921.—Emil Vogel, *Claudio Monteverdi*. Viertelj. f. MW., III, 1887.—A complete edition of his works is in course of publication under the editorship of Fr. Malipiero, *Tutte le opere di Claudio Monteverdi*. Asolo; to 1934, 14 vols. have appeared. NEW EDITIONS: *L'Orfeo:* facsimile of the first edition, ed. by Ad. Sandberger. Filser, Augsburg, 1927.—Complete reprint by Chester, London, 1924.—Selections from *Orfeo* and *L'incoronazione di Poppea*, under the editorship of V. d'Indy, in the editions of the Schola cantorum, Paris.—Selections also in Publ. Eitner, Vol. IX.—S. B., No. 176.—*Arianna:* the *Lamento d'Arianna* has been ed. by Gevaert (*Les Gloires de l'Italie;* Chefs-d'œuvre anciens et inédits de la musique vocale italienne aux XVIIe et XVIIIe siècles; Vol. II, No. 39b. Heugel, Paris, 1868); Parisotti (*Arie antiche*, 2 vols. Ricordi, Milan, 1885–90; *Anthology of Italian Song of the 17th and 18th Centuries*. G. Schirmer, N. Y., 1894); and Respighi (*Orpheus;* Iniziazione musicale, storia della musica; G. Barbera, Florence, 1925).—See also S.B., No. 177.—*Il ritorno d'Ulisse in patria:* R. Haas, in the D.T. OE., Vol. XXIX, 1.—*L'Incoronazione di Poppea:* Goldschmidt, *Studien zur italienischen Oper*, Vol. II.—S.B., No. 178.—Three volumes of selections of madrigals, edited by Leichtentritt and A. Mendelssohn, Peters, 192–?.—Five songs, Landshoff, *Alte Meister des Belcanto*. 5 vols., Peters, Leipzig, 1912–27.—Two madrigals, Torchi, Vol. IV.—A Mass and extracts from others, ed. by Tirabassi.—*Salve Regina*, Pineau, Sénart.—*O Quam Pulchra*, Vatielli.—A *Scherzo musicale* will be found in W.B., No. 53.

his own speech, so does the Italian in his operas. Demonic and raging passion are at his disposal as easily as grace and most tender fervor. One of
the most powerful pieces of Monteverdi is his "Lamentation of Ariadne,"
a torso that has alone survived from the lost opera *Arianna* (1608). In
a refrain the deserted Ariadne gives touching vent to her despair:

Monasth. f. M.G., 1877,

according to the MS of Florence.

Bibl. naz., Cl. XIX, No. 114.

We know the manner in which Monteverdi intended that long lamentation to be accompanied, because he himself transformed the lamentation, originally provided only with a figured bass, into a madrigal for
five voices which form a complete harmony:

Il sesto libro di madrigali, 1614,

according to the edition of Gardano, 1620.

(Paris, Bibl. nat.)

The elemental, changing rhythms, the harmonies thrown down like
massive blocks, the serrated dissonances, are the factors which especially
impress the listener. The freedom of the musical structure is unprecedented, especially in the treatment of the dissonance. But inasmuch as
the music expresses precisely what the composer wills, it is quite perfect,
despite its being so thoroughly exceptional.

Compare with this the arietta of Valletto from Monteverdi's last

opera *Poppea:* "Sent' un certo non so che." [18] Who does not think at
once of Mozart's Cherubin, with whom Valletto is not unworthy to be
compared. The aria of Nero [19] from the same opera is a fiery protestation
of love. Concerning this song, a commentator, Arnold Schering, says
appropriately and beautifully: "It belongs to that considerable number
of Venetian opera arias in which the composer has chosen the form of the
passacaglia in order to emphasize by external means also the unity of
the mood. This persistent, reiterated bass, working upon the hearer
unconsciously, becomes a symbol of the tenacious passion into which the
hero sings himself."

Monteverdi's activity attained further significance for the future
development of music in that he was the first one to employ instruments
for purposes of special characterization. In his just-mentioned opera
Orfeo he employed the following orchestra: 2 *gravicembali* (harpsichords),
2 *contrabassi da viola* (bass viols), 10 *viole da brazzo* (viols), 1 *arpa doppia*
(harp), 2 *violini piccoli alla francese* (violins), 2 *chitarroni* (large lutes),
2 *organi di legno* (small portable organs with flute stops), 1 *regal* (small
organ with reeds), 3 *bassi da gamba* (gambas), 4 *tromboni* (trombones),
2 *cornetti* (the old cornetts or zinkes; German *Zink*), 1 *flautino* (flute),
1 *clarino* (high trumpet), and 3 *trombe sordine* (trumpets with mute).

Characteristic of this orchestra are the many harmonic, chordal instruments—claviers, organs, lutes, and harps—which give forth a full, vibrant
tone. [20] These maintained their place in the orchestra until the second
half of the eighteenth century. It was only at the time of Haydn that
they were driven from the ensemble. Of course one must not imagine
that these instruments played continuously. On the contrary, they
interchanged according to the situation. For example, when Orpheus
descends into the lower world, a *Sinfonia* for four trombones is heard,
which creates quite perfectly the desired gloomy effect. The "moresca"
with which the *Orfeo* concludes unites both elegance and nobility with
tonal perfection, as is shown on page 156.

In the strange dramatic scene, *Il combattimento di Tancredi e Clorinda,*
which approaches the oratorio,—the text is taken from Tasso's *Jerusalem
Delivered*—Monteverdi for the first time employs the violin tremolo in
dramatic manner. Thus, he also has the distinction of having introduced
this requisite without which no later opera composer could get along.

[18] R. B., No. 92.   [19] R. B., No. 91.
[20] Cf. H. Quittard, "L'Orchestre de Monteverde," *Année musicale.* Alcan, Paris, 1908.

Publ. Eitner. Vol. XI.

Monteverdi wrote his first operas for the court of the Gonzagas in Mantua, where he was employed, *Orfeo* in 1607, *Arianna* in 1608. Mantua, for which also Gagliano wrote his *Dafne* in 1608, won for the time being high significance in the history of the opera.

The Venetian Opera; Cavalli and Cesti [21]

In the year 1637, in Venice, the first public opera house was opened in the Teatro Cassiano. Whereas formerly the music-drama was the private concern of the princes and the aristocracy, who enhanced the pomp of their festivals by its means, it now became a general, democratic institution in which everyone could share for the price of admission. The modern operatic system with its virtuoso singers, its impresarios, and its applauding public began. By this step, Venice gained, for a time, the foremost position in the musical world. The Venetian opera, with its characteristic style, spread through the whole of Italy and into Germany, where the supremacy of the Venetian school lasted until the end of the seventeenth century.

The new music-drama was regarded as a world wonder. German

[21] Bibliography: H. Kretzschmar, "Die venezianische Oper u. die Werke Cavallis und Cestis," Viertelj. f. MW., 1892.—Romain Rolland, "L'Opéra populaire à Venise," *Mercure musical.* Société du Mercure de France, Jan. and Feb., 1906.

princes retained theater-boxes for themselves in Venice, and kept themselves informed concerning new works. Beside the music, the scenery played a great rôle. Special surprise was evoked by the fact that the Venetians dared to play at night and with artificial illumination.

There was no lack of distinguished talent. Francesco Cavalli,[22] a pupil of Monteverdi, and Marc Antonio Cesti [23] took over the leadership. As formerly, so now also, subjects from antiquity formed the favorite bases for the plots; but they were interspersed with all kinds of love affairs, such as were doubtless in vogue in the society of that day, as well as with high plots of state. It lay in the nature of the case that the tone of the music should gradually become more popular; indeed, the composers larded their works with popular *canzoni*. The style becomes terse; short, easily grasped motifs are developed in pieces easily understood. The originally unrestricted, "infinite" melody is gradually divided into segments.

A good example of the pleasing and scintillating manner of the school is given by the aria of Arsetes "Non scherzi con amor" from Cesti's most popular opera *La Dori*, as is shown on page 158.

Even though the duet between Medea and Jason, "O mio bene! O

[22] FRANCESCO CAVALLI (b. Crema, 1602; d. Venice, 1676). His real name was Pier Francesco Caletti Bruni. On account of his musical talent he was taken to Venice by a Venetian nobleman, Federigo Cavalli, podesta in Crema, in order to complete his musical education. Bruni assumed the name of his patron. In 1617 he became a singer at St. Mark's; in 1628, second organist under Monteverdi; in 1665, first organist, and in 1668, master of the chapel. In celebration of the peace of the Pyrenees his opera *Serse* was produced in Paris in 1660, and in 1662 his opera *Ercole amante*, composed for the wedding of Louis XIV. Cavalli wrote forty-two operas. At his funeral, a requiem was performed which he had composed shortly before his death. His principal work, *Giasone*, was produced not only in Venice but also with the greatest success on other Italian stages. BIBLIOGRAPHY: H. Prunières, *E. Cavalli et l'opéra vénetien au XVIIᵉ siècle.* Rieder, Paris, 1931.—Egon Wellesz, "Cavalli und der Stil der venetianischen Oper von 1640–60," in the *Studien zur Musikwissenschaft*, ed. by G. Adler as supplements to the D.T. OE., 1913. REPRINTS: S.B., Nos. 200, 201.—Fragments from *Giasone* in Publ. Eitner, Vol. XII.—A cantata in Riemann's *Kantatenfrühling*. Siegel, Leipzig.—A canzona in Torchi, *Eleganti canzoni et arie del sec. XVII.* Ricordi, Milan, 1893.

[23] MARC ANTONIO CESTI (b. Arezzo, 1623; d. Florence, 1669) occupied positions in Volterra and in Innsbruck. He became a Franciscan monk of the order of San Spirito, and was a tenor singer in the papal chapel, 1659–62. In 1666 he came to Vienna as second master of the chapel of Leopold I, and wrote the opera *Il pomo d'oro* in 1667 for the wedding of the emperor. One of his chief works is *La Dori* which was produced in Florence in 1661, and in Venice in 1663. His *La magnanimità d'Alessandro* was produced in Innsbruck in 1662. He wrote more than a hundred operas. NEW EDITIONS: *Il pomo d'oro*, D.T. OE., III (2), IV (2).—S.B., Nos. 202, 203.—L. Landshoff, *Alle Meister des Bel canto*. Peters, 1912–27.— Fragments of *La Dori* in Publ. Eitner, Vol. XII.—Individual songs in Riemann's *Kantatenfrühling*. Siegel, Leipzig.—Torchi, *Canzone;* and in the collection Hettich, Paris, Vol. VII.

Publ. Eitner, Vol. XII.

Arsete.

Non scher--zi, non scher--zi, non scher-zi, con a-mor chi

non vuol pian------ge--re non scher-zi, con a--

-mor chi non vuol pian----ge--re etc,
etc.

mio ardore!," from the opera *Giasone* may not enable us to appreciate the full importance of Cavalli, it does at least enable us to recognize his dramatic, penetrating style:

O mio co-re, O mio amore, Ar-di　tu? S'io ar-do? S'io ar-do, oh Di--b!

Ar - di pur, o mio ben, che ardo anch' i - - o   ar - di pur, etc.

etc.

etc.

The *ritornelles* in the arias of Cesti indicate that the instruments took an active part in the execution. As a matter of fact, the Venetians continued along the paths staked out by Monteverdi. They took pleasure in allowing the orchestra to alternate with the singers in so-called *sinfonias*, little pieces of one movement, in which they delineate moods of nature, the sea, tempests, and similar things. The historian of the Venetian opera, Kretzschmar, has called attention to the fact that supernal spirits are indicated by high-lying violin chords. Sebastian Bach took over from the Venetians the beautiful means whereby, in the St. Matthew Passion, he surrounds the Christ, as it were, with an aureole.

Fanfares for an orchestra of trumpets were also popular. Monteverdi had already introduced his *Orfeo* with such an overture. Cavalli in his *Peleo e Teti*, presents a delightfully fresh soldiers' chorus.[24] Handel's well-known brilliant use of the trumpet clearly shows that he learned from his Venetian predecessors.

Besides Cavalli and Cesti, Giovanni Legrenzi (1626–90) should be especially mentioned, even though his significance lies more in the domain of church and instrumental music than in opera.[25]

THE ITALIAN OPERA IN GERMANY [26]

It was of great consequence that the Venetian opera reached Vienna. Austrian sovereigns themselves became distinguished composers, as Ferdinand III, Leopold I, and Josef I. Under the peace-loving Ferdinand III, who assisted in bringing about the conclusion of the Thirty

[24] S.A., No. 45.
[25] Cf. two examples from his opera *Eteocle e Polinice*, 1675, in R.B., No. 106.—S.B., No. 231.
[26] BIBLIOGRAPHY: Moritz Fürstenau, *Zur Geschichte der Musik und des Theaters am Hofe zu Dresden.* 2 vols., R. Kuntze, Dresden, 1861–62.—L. von Köchel, *Die kaiserliche Hofmusikkapelle zu Wien 1543–1867.* Beck'sche Universitätsbuchhandlung, Vienna, 1869.—M. Neuhaus, *A Draghi,* "Studien zur Musikwissenschaft," I. Beihefte der (supplements to the) D.T. OE., B. & H., Leipzig.—Fr. M. Rudhart, *Geschichte der Oper am Hofe zu München.* F. Datterer, Freising, 1865.—Josef Sittard, *Zur Geschichte der Musik und des Theaters am württembergischen Hofe.* 2 vols., W. Kohlhammer, Stuttgart, 1890, 1891.

Years' War, Cavalli's *Egisto* was presented in Vienna in the year 1642. Leopold I (1640–1705, known in general history through the Turkish wars) established a permanent Italian opera which vied with Venice in brilliancy, and brought out more than 400 new works in half a century. Cesti wrote for the imperial city, among other things, the festival opera *Il pomo d'oro* for the wedding festivities of the ruler in 1667. Those who wrote specifically for the Vienna opera were Antonio Bertali (1605–69) and Antonio Draghi (1635–1700). Their works present all the characteristics of the Venetian style.[27]

In Munich also, an Italian court opera was founded, in the year 1654. Among others, works by Cavalli were produced. In the year 1656 Johann Kaspar Kerl became kapellmeister here, and from the following year, he took a hand, as the first German to compose Italian opera. Unfortunately, his operas, composed on Italian texts, have not been preserved. We know him today only as an ingenious master of the organ, and as a creator of ecclesiastical music. Later, it is Italians who constitute the glory of the Munich opera: Ercole Bernabei (1620–87), and his son Antonio Bernabei; then, especially also, Agostino Steffani (1654–1728), whose activity reached into the eighteenth century, and who attained that formal clarity which was realized at the same time in southern Italy by Alessandro Scarlatti, the founder of the Neapolitan School. The aria of Rotrude in his opera *Tassilone* (1709) is a good example of his art; the melodic lines are both charming and restrained:[28]

D.T.B., XII, 2.

[27] Cf., as characteristic examples of the Venetian style, the two charming pieces given in R.B., Nos. 115, 116, from Antonio Draghi's *Psiche cercando amore* (1688): the arietta "Torn' o caro, Torna, si!," and the bravura aria, "Il giro snell' e rapido." See also S.B., No. 226.
[28] Cf. also R.B., No. 117. A French overture by Steffani will be found in E.B., No. 31.

Rotrude.

Pa - - dre Se col - pa in lui

Pa - - dre Se col - pa in

lui, La col - pa è sol di me, la col - pa è sol di

me, la col - - - pa, la col - - - - - pa è sol di me! etc.

Steffani's fame does not rest on his operas only; his chamber duets, for two voices and *basso continuo*, present a form of classic perfection. Even Handel took them as his models. These *duetti da camera* overflow with warm expression despite their formal structure.[29]

Dresden also received its Italian opera in the seventeenth century. Here, in the year 1662 was presented *Il Paride*, the text and the music by G. Andrea Bontempi (1624–1705); also, in the year 1671, a German *Liederspiel*, *Dafne*, by the same composer.[30] In the years 1664–67, an opera house was built, and Carlo Pallavicino was appointed kapellmeister and composer. His style also approaches the formal symmetry of the eighteenth century. There was apparently a contradiction between the impetuous and altogether Italian genius for expression which Pallavicino possessed and the perfect artistry with which he wrote his basses. His works possess a still greater charm when one perceives the manner in which the composer triumphed over that contradiction.[31]

ITALIAN ORATORIO; CARISSIMI, STRADELLA

From the simple *laudi* which were sung among the oratorians in Rome, there developed, as we have already seen (p. 149), dialogues, and from these in turn arose the oratorio. The *Teatro armonico spirituale* by G. Francesco Anerio, which appeared in Rome in 1619, contains dialogues which one can designate as oratorios, for the reason that narrative parts are combined with the dramatic dialogue. These narrative parts are characteristic of the Italian oratorio which now develops. A narrator appears in it, who plays a rôle similar to that played by the Evangelist in the "Passions" of Bach, to take a familiar example.

The oratorio which was composed on a free text was called in Italian, *oratorio volgare*. Beside this there developed also a second kind, the *oratorio Latino*, with Latin biblical text, which sprang from the ecclesiastical motet-dialogues of the sixteenth century. This *oratorio Latino* may be considered genuine church music, while the *oratorio volgare*, to which the entire later development attached itself, really stands removed from the true, ecclesiastical, liturgical music, even though its content is frequently of a religious nature.

Although the Latin oratorio enjoyed but a brief period of bloom, it nevertheless is important from the fact that a great master wrought

[29] See R.B., No. 118, and S.B., No. 242.
[30] See R.B., No. 105.
[31] See R.B., No. 120, and S.B., No. 224.

works of imperishable beauty in this form. This master was the Roman, Giacomo Carissimi,[32] who may be placed beside Monteverdi in significance. With the latter, he shares the realistic, expressive declamation. Younger than Monteverdi, he learned from him. He was one of the first who took over the form of the lamento, which Monteverdi had developed so brilliantly in his *Arianna*. In his oratorio *Jephta*, which has again become known at the present day through concert performances, the leading character, the unhappy father, sings a lamentation, which, like the lament of Ariadne, concludes with a most moving refrain:

Heu! heu mi - hi   fi - -li - a me - a,   heu, de - ce - pis - ti   me.

The care which Carissimi devoted to the treatment of the recitative can be observed also in a short example from the oratorio *Balthasar*, which shows how he occasionally wove descriptive strands into the recitative, e.g., in the case of the several-times-repeated word "Age," as is shown on page 164.

This kind of recitative, which paints in melodic imagery, was taken up by the German church composers, and was applied in manifold ways up to the time of J. S. Bach. It also occurs in the French operas, whereas it was cultivated only temporarily in the Italian.

[32] GIACOMO CARISSIMI (b. Marino in the States of the Church, c. 1604; d. Rome, 1674) was first organist of the Cathedral at Tivoli, 1624–27, and from 1628 master of the chapel at St. Apollinaris in Rome, and at the same time choirmaster at the Collegium Germanicum. He was respected highly as a teacher, among his personal pupils being Alessandro Scarlatti, J. K. Kerl, Chr. Bernhard, and M. A. Charpentier (composer of church oratorios in Paris). The following oratorios of Carissimi have been preserved: *Abraham and Isaac, Balthasar, Diluvium universale, Extremum Dei Judicium, Ezechias, Felicitas beatorum, Historia Divitis, Jephta, Job, Jonah, Judicium Salomonis, Lamentatio damnatorum, Lucifer, Martyres, Vis frugi et pater familias.*—BIBLIOGRAPHY: M. Brenet, "Les Oratoires de Carissimi." R.M.I., 1893.—A. Cametti, "Carissimi." R.M.I., 1917.—Fr. Chrysander, "Carissimi." Allg. MZ., 1876.—H. Quittard, "Giacomo Carissimi." *Tribune de Saint-Gervais*, Paris, 1900.—H. Riemann, "Carissimi." Hdb. d. MG., Vol. II, part 2, pp. 383 ff.— A. Schering, *Geschichte des Oratoriums*, pp. 70 ff.—E. Schmitz, *Beiträge zur Geschichte der italienischen Kammerkantate im 17. Jahrhundert* (Munich dissertation). B. & H., Leipzig, 1909; by the same author, *Geschichte der weltlichen Solokantate und des geistlichen Konzerts.* Kretzschmars Handbb., pp. 71 ff. B. & H., Leipzig, 1914; by the same author, *Zur Geschichte des italienischen Kammerduetts.* J.P., 1916.—E. Vogel, *Die Oratorientechnik G. Carissimis* (Prague dissertation), 1928. REPRINTS: "Jephta," "Judicium Salomonis," "Balthasar," "Jonah," in Chrysander's *Denkmäler der Tonkunst*, 1869.—*Jephta* also in a practical edition by Faisst. Rieter-Beidermann, Leipzig.—Individual numbers in *L'Arte musicale in Italia*, edited by Torchi, Vol. V, and in the cantata and aria collections by Landshoff, Riemann, and Torchi.—Some motets are contained in the *Première année de musique religieuse*, edited by H. Expert. Sénart, Paris, 1913.—A selection in *Histoires*

According to Paris, Bib. nat., MS Vm.[1] 1171, p. 229.

Au-di-vi de te Da-niel quod spi-ri-tum de-o — rum ha-be-as et multa va-le-as sa-pi-en-tia et doc-tri-na A- — ge, a-ge er-go, A- — ge, a-ge er-go scrip-tur-am hanc scrip-tur-am hanc per — le-ge et si mi-hi ve-ram e-jus in-ter-pre-ta-ti-o-nem ju-di-ca-ve-ris magna a me præ — mi a pro-me-re-be ris

Although it is true that Carissimi is related to Monteverdi in his fidelity to the text, he yet differs from him essentially, in so far as he rises above his realism. The great historical merit of Carissimi lies in the fact that he finally bridged the opposition between the old and the new art. The impetuous reformers in the style of Galilei quite unreasonably desired to forget completely the old choral art. However, they soon found themselves compelled to borrow from it, and a complete amalgamation took place in the case of Carissimi, who treated the chorus in his oratorios in

sacrées, by H. Quittard. Editions of the Schola Cantorum, Paris.—A scene from *Jephta* in S. B., No. 198.

as masterly a manner as he did the solo, and with consummate skill allowed them to relieve and supplement one another.

He stripped off the realistic elements which had long cleaved to the new music. In his compositions the new style confronts us in perfect clarity. Carissimi advanced to a classical purity, and he was fully conscious of this fact, for he had achieved it only through struggle. When anyone happened to speak of his facile style, he is reported to have answered: "O how difficult it is to be simple"!

Besides the oratorio, Carissimi especially cultivated the chamber cantata for solo voice. In this he established a type which subsequently became important, and in which the Italian composers developed an enormous fertility. In this period the solo-cantata was to the opera what today the string-quartet and the sonata are to the orchestral symphony. The aria "A morire, per servar giustizia e fede più non vaglion le corone" from the cantata on the death of Mary Queen of Scots, is typical of the symmetry and finesse which the style of Carissimi acquired:

Burney, *General History,* IV, 143.

The *oratorio volgare* does not possess the dignity of the Biblical oratorio. It developed rather into an edifying entertainment with pedagogical and moral purpose. In the second half of the seventeenth century the legendary stories and histories of the saints took their place beside the Biblical history, and very worldly scenes were woven into these. This was done as early as the Middle Ages, according to Schiller's recipe: *Wollt ihr zugleich den Kindern der Welt und den Frommen gefallen, malet die Wollust, nur malet den Teufel dazu.* ("Would you delight the children of this world and also the pious, Paint for them Lust then, but picture the Devil as well.")

In accordance with the Italian temperament, the texts more and more approached the purely dramatic, until finally the narrator (*il testo*) was dropped altogether. Pasquetti, the Italian historian of the Italian oratorio, points out the inner reason why the Italian oratorio could not attain the elevation of the German. The German oratorio is Christocentric, and this fact imparts to it its greatness. The Italian could not attain this standard, because occupation with the Bible itself, the reading of the Gospels, was denied to the layman.

The chief centers in which the oratorio was cultivated were Bologna, Modena, Rome, and Florence. It found scant soil in Venice, although belonging in style to the Venetian school.

As an especially famous work the *San Giovanni Battista* by Alessandro Stradella [33] may be mentioned, a work which, according to the well-known romantic story (cf. Flotow's opera), is supposed to have saved the composer from assassination. It is an important work. Stradella was a great artist, especially in the expression of passion. The beginning of Herod's "Thunder Aria," which Schering sketches in his *History of the Oratorio* will give an idea of Stradella's wide thematic sweep, as is shown on page 167. Stradella's art leads to the Neapolitan school. The founder of the latter, Alessandro Scarlatti, wrote a considerable number of oratorios.

Italian Church Music.—Church music adopted the new style in the

---

[33] ALESSANDRO STRADELLA (b. Naples, c. 1645, assassinated in Genoa, 1681). Nothing is known of his life except the love affair presented in Flotow's opera. Stradella had eloped with the beloved of a Venetian nobleman. The latter had him pursued, and on one occasion Stradella escaped death by means of his compositions. But the deceived one refused to rest until Stradella had been killed. The following oratorios of Stradella have been preserved: *San Giovanni Battista, Esther, S. Pelagio, S. Giovanni Crisostomo, Susanna, S. Edita.* BIBLIOGRAPHY: Chas. Burney, *A General History of Music.* Printed for the author, London, 1776–89.—E. J. Dent, *Alessandro Scarlatti, His Life and Works.* E. Arnold, London, 1905.— H. Hess, "Die Opern A. Stradellas." Supplement to the I.M.G., 2d series, No. 3. REPRINTS: S.B., No. 230.—H. Riemann, *Kantatenfrühling, 1633–1682.* Siegel, Leipzig, 1912.— L. Torchi, *Eleganti canzoni et arie del XVII. sec.* Ricordi, Milan, 1893.

seventeenth century, and faithfully participated in its transitions through the succeeding periods. Beside the already-mentioned Viadana (1564–1645), who took the very first step, Carissimi must be mentioned as the founder of the new species. Most of the operatic composers made contributions to church music, as Monteverdi and Cavalli. Legrenzi [34] achieved especial significance in this field.

Tuo-ne-rà — — — — — —

Tuo-ne-rà · · · · · · · · · · -tra mil · ·le tur · bi · ··ni.

However, the *a cappella* style did not disappear, but was still culti-vated by individual masters in the seventeenth and eighteenth centuries. Thus the gala style of the Venetians for numerous choirs was taken up in Rome and elsewhere. An especially famous composition of this kind is the fifty-three-voice Mass by Orazio Benevoli. The work is divided into seven choirs. It was produced in Salzburg in 1628.[35]

The Sistine Chapel in Rome, whose statutes excluded instruments, was a guardian of the old art, and this Chapel served as a model when the desire for *a cappella* music made itself felt anew in the nineteenth century.

French Church Music.—The grand master of the classical French motet, with soli, chorus, and orchestral accompaniment, is Lalande.[36] This

---

[34] GIOVANNI LEGRENZI (b. Clusone near Bergamo, c. 1625; d. Venice, 1690) began his activities as organist at Santa Maria Maggiore in Bergamo, later becoming director of the conservatory *dei Mendicanti* in Venice, and after 1685 also master of the chapel at St. Mark's. Here he enlarged the orchestra considerably, bringing it to 34 players: 8 violins, 11 small viols (*violettes*), 2 tenor viols, 3 viols da gamba and double basses, 4 theorbos, 2 cornets, 1 bassoon, and 3 trombones. He wrote 17 operas for Venice, 6 oratorios, chamber solo-cantatas, church sonatas, etc. Through his sonatas for several concerted stringed instruments, he has become one of the founders of modern chamber music. REPRINTS: R.B., Nos. 102, 106, 107.—S.B., No. 231.—J. W. Wasielewski, *Die Violine im 17. Jahrhundert* (Volume of Examples), three sonatas. M. Cohen u. Sohn, Bonn, 1874.

[35] New edition in *D.T.O.*, Vol. XX, 1903.

[36] MICHEL RICHARD DE LALANDE (LA LANDE) (b. Paris, 1657; d. Versailles, 1726) began his musical training as a chorister in the choir of Saint-Germain l'Auxerrois. In 1679 he became organist of Saint-Gervais, and in 1683 one of the four masters of music of the royal chapel and master of music to the sons of Mme. de Montespan. In 1689 he became director of the royal music, and in 1690 court composer. In 1709 he held almost all the important musical positions at the court. Louis XV raised him to the nobility in 1722. The great motets of Lalande were published after his death, by his widow and his favorite pupil, Collin de Blamont (Paris, 1729 and following years; 20 vols., containing 40 motets). A quantity of his works remains unedited. BIBLIOGRAPHY: Michel Brenet, *La Musique*

form had already had its birth before the middle of the seventeenth century at the hands of Nicolas Formé (1567–1638), master of the chapel of Louis XIII. Then Henri Dumont (1610–84), Pierre Robert, and Lully perfected it. But it was Lalande who filled it with a profound religious content, and who gave to it a true dramatic force. He also wrote a number of secular works, ballets and divertissements, intended for the court of Louis XIV; but his most distinguished works are the grand motets which were sung in the chapel of Versailles, and which were renowned during his life. After him an extensive and very fecund school cultivated the genre of the motet for a long time. Campra (1660–1744), Nicolas Bernier (1664–1734), J. F. Lallouëtte (1651–1728), Henry Desmarets (1662–1741), Sébastien de Brossard (1654–1730), Jean Gilles (1669–1705), and Ch. H. Gervais (1671–1744) were rivals or emulators of Lalande. Couperin also composed motets; so did Mondonville (1711–72) and Rameau, as well as Fr. Collin de Blamont (1690–1760), Esprit Blanchard (1696–1775), and others. One may consider the religious music of the Empire style, as represented especially by the important works of Le Sueur (1760–1837) and Cherubini, as the continuation of the school of Lalande.

German Church Music; Heinrich Schütz.—The Thuringian Heinrich Schütz [37] went to Venice in the year 1609 in order to study music with

sacrée sous Louis XIV. Tribune de Saint-Gervais, 1899.—H. Riemann, *Dictionnaire de musique*, 3d French edition (1931), article "La Lande," by André Tessier, who prepared a complete study of the work and life of this musician.—New edition of some fragments of the great motets by H. Expert and Ch. Pineau in the collection *Musique d'églises des xviie et xviiie siècles.* Sénart, Paris, 1913.

[37] HEINRICH SCHÜTZ (b. Köstritz near Gera, 1585; d. Dresden, 1672). In spite of his musical talent Schütz was compelled to study law, a fate which he shares with a number of composers, for example, Handel and Schumann. In his fourteenth year he entered the court chapel of the landgrave Moritz of Hesse-Kassel as a chorister, and this prince, through the bestowal of a scholarship, led him definitely to the study of music. In the year 1609 he went to Venice to study with Giovanni Gabrieli. After the latter's death, in 1612, he returned to Cassel. In 1615 the elector, Johann Georg I, summoned him to Dresden as master of the chapel; the landgrave Moritz, however, reclaimed him, as a subject, in the following year. From 1617 on, however, Schütz was again first master of the Dresden chapel, and retained this position throughout his life. In 1628 he again journeyed to Italy in order there to observe the progress of art. The disorders of the Thirty Years' War for a time brought about the almost complete dissolution of the Dresden chapel. In 1633 Schütz went to Copenhagen, where he acted as master of the chapel for some time. On his return he sojourned for a considerable period in Brunswick and Lüneburg. In 1645 it was again possible to establish the Dresden chapel, and Schütz remained its successful head until the end of his life. He was a man of noble character, without envy, bent upon developing the youthful talents entrusted to him, a veritable father to his chapel. BIBLIOGRAPHY: A. Einstein, *Heinrich Schütz.* Bärenreiter Verlag, Cassel, 1928.—R. Gerber, *Das Passionsrezitativ bei Heinrich Schütz.* C. Bertelsmann, Gütersloh, 1929.—E. H. Müller, *Heinrich Schütz.*

Giovanni Gabrieli, and he remained there until the time of Gabrieli's death in the year 1612. From his master he learned the whole great art of many-voiced choral music. The young genius, however, was not content to limit himself merely to sitting at the feet of the master, but he drank in everything that went on about him. These were the years when Italy was moved to amazement and tumult through the revolution in the musical style. From Florence came the news of the new music drama; in Mantua the star of Monteverdi was rising. Together with the old classical art, Schütz also appropriated these innovations. He possessed the power to combine both within himself. Upon his return to Germany he cultivated both the polyphony of the Venetians and the modern style of the Florentines. The latter thus entered the country to the north of the Alps without a struggle, and did not undertake to crowd out and destroy the good in the old.

Schütz even introduced the opera into Germany. No less a writer than Martin Opitz had translated Rinuccini's *Dafne* into German, and this work, with music by Schütz, was performed in the year 1627 by command of Johann Georg I, of Saxony, in the castle of Hartenfels in Torgau, on the occasion of the marriage of princess Sophie of Saxony with George II of Hesse-Darmstadt. Unfortunately the music has not been preserved. As a matter of fact, important as the event may be from a historical point of view, in the work of Schütz it is a mere episode, inasmuch as his remaining labors were directed almost exclusively to the Church.

The new cantata-like forms which Schütz cultivated in church music, after the manner of his Italian models, are especially the "Dialogue" and

B. & H., Leipzig, 1925.—J. M. Müller-Blattau, *Die Kompositionslehre Heinrich Schützens in der Fassung seines Schülers Christoph Bernhard.* B. & H., Leipzig, 1926.—André Pirro, *Heinrich Schütz.* Alcan, Paris, 1913; 2d enl. ed., 1923.—Willi Schuh, *Formprobleme bei Heinrich Schütz* (Bern dissertation). B. & H., Leipzig, 1928.—Fr. Spitta, *Die Passionen nach den vier Evangelisten, von Heinrich Schütz.* B. & H., Leipzig, 1886.—Ph. Spitta, Biography of Schütz in the *Allgemeine deutsche Biographie.* Duncker & Humbolt, Leipzig, 1875–1912; see also *Gesammelte Aufsätze, zur Geschichte der Musik.* Gebrüder Paetel, Berlin, 1892.—Critical edition of the *Complete Works:* ed. by Ph. Spitta. 16 vols., 1885–94, supplements in 1909 and 1927. B. & H., Leipzig. EDITIONS FOR PRACTICAL USE: B. & H., Leipzig, *The Passions according to St. John and St. Matthew; The Seven Last Words; The Christmas Oratorio; Three Biblical Scenes; 20 Psalms* for 4 voices; songs for solo voice with piano or organ accompaniment from the *Kleine geistliche Konzerte.*—Hug & Co., Basel, *Psalm 122,* for double chorus of 4 voices with piano; *Requiem for mixed chorus.*—Schweers, Bremen, *Geistliche Chorgesänge.*—Siegel edition, Leipzig, *Geistliche Chorgesänge:* "Wer Gottes Märtyr in Ehren hat," for 4 female voices.—Editions of the Schola Cantorum, Paris, selections from the *Kleine geistliche Konzerte,* with an introduction by A. Pirro.—A motet for solo voice will be found in E.B., No. 27; cf. also W.B., No. 65.

the "History." These led directly to the oratorio, to which latter form Schütz himself had already advanced. Here he showed the same realism, the same ingenuity and power of invention as Monteverdi. "The characters which appear in Schütz's Dialogues are copied from daily life, and always speak in the most natural language, but with an assurance which with the very first tones does justice to all the various emotions," says H. Kretzschmar correctly (*Fuehrer*, Part II, Vol. II, p. 87). He illustrates this with the following examples: "In the dialogue between the twelve-year-old Christ child and his parents in the temple, the youth does not answer the alarmed inquiries of his parents seriously and quietly, as one might expect, but in a surprised and ebullient manner, in quite jovial tones, not as the Son of God, but as an unusually lively child. In the Easter dialogue, *Weib, was weinest du?* (Woman, Why Weepest Thou?), Mary does not sing her words 'They have taken away my Lord' sadly and complainingly, but excitedly and confusedly." This dialogue also affords a good example of the bold application by Schütz of the chromatic element:

The history of the lamenting David, *Absalon, fili mi,* for solo voice with accompaniment, and the motet for three choruses, with accompaniment of wind instruments, *Saul, Saul, was verfolgst du mich?* (Saul, Saul, Why Persecutest Thou Me?), in which the heavenly voice gradually draws near and discharges itself mightily as in a thunder storm, are especially famous and realistic tone paintings of unsurpassed greatness. They have again become familiar through concert performances. The cantata-like pieces for one or more solo voices, as well as chorus, with instrumental accompaniment, were called *geistliche Konzerte* (Spiritual Concerts). Schütz wrote more than one hundred of these, as well as many motet-like choral works for numerous choirs in the brilliant style of the Venetians, especially Psalms, and also simple, more hymn-like choruses.

His *Passions* arouse especial interest. He wrote four church passions, according to the words of the four evangelists, the most important being the one according to St. Matthew. For the part of the evangelist he attempted a new and original method. He did not employ the recitation tone of the Gregorian choral, nor the modern, instrumentally accompanied recitative, but presented something between the two, *unaccompanied declamation*. This is dignified and churchly, but at the same time very expressive, and it accentuates principal passages in a piquant manner. It had for a long time been customary in the choral passion to compose the words of the *turba* in a concerted manner. Schütz followed this usage, but in accordance with his genius and his period, he presented them with an elemental, dramatic brevity and force, with an unsurpassed fidelity to life.

Not less significant is the oratorio-like work: *Die sieben Worte Jesu Christi am Kreuz* (The Seven Last Words of Christ upon the Cross). In the *Introitus,* or opening chorus, Schütz used the choral melody, *Da Jesus an dem Kreuze stund* (As Jesus Hung upon the Cross). He seldom used chorals, but this profound number clearly shows how thoroughly he also mastered this form of composition, derived from earlier times, how well he understood how to accentuate the impressive nuances of the *cantus firmus*, and to give them especial significance in the complex texture.

Finally, we have also a Christmas oratorio by Schütz, *Historia von der freuden- und gnadenreichen Geburt Jesu Christi* (History of the Joyful and Blessed Birth of Jesus Christ), which delights one with its precious folk-like features, and reveals the recitative style in a perfection not before attained in Germany. This Christmas History, of the year 1664, is to be viewed as the first genuine German oratorio.

The seventeenth century honored its three great S's. These are, besides Schütz, the Leipzig St. Thomas cantor Hermann Schein, and the Halle organist Samuel Scheidt. Historically, the last two are of especial significance as instrumental composers, but through their sacred and secular vocal compositions they also deserve great merit in connection with the introduction of the *nuove musiche* into Germany.

Schein's choral, *Komm heiliger Geist* (Come Holy Spirit), of the year 1628,[38] for soprano and orchestra, was doubtless written for a festival occasion, and is a composition which applies the modern style in an unusual manner. Like everything which Schein wrote, this composition

[38] See R.B., No. 79. Cf. also S.B., Nos. 187, 188.

also reveals a daring spirit directed toward great things. Andreas Hammerschmidt, in his *Dialogi oder Gespräche zwischen Gott und einer gläubigen Seele* (Dialogues or Conversations between God and a Believing Soul), from the year 1645, employs the modern style in a more modest manner, and one which appeals more to the general taste. He achieved a tremendous success and contributed much to the spread of the new style.[39] Finally, one must not fail to mention the distinguished theoretician and publisher of great collections, Michael Praetorius (1571–1621),[40] who accomplished much, both in the old, and in the new, style.

We must content ourselves with a mere enumeration of the names of the great line of distinguished German church musicians who, as co-

[39] Cf. also the dialogue: *Ich leide billig* (R.B., No. 97), which enjoyed an immense vogue, and thus assisted in the diffusion of the modern principles. See also S.B., No. 194.

[40] MICHAEL PRAETORIUS, Latinized for Schulz or Schulze, the actual name was Schultheiss (b. Kreuzburg in Thuringia, 1571; d. Wolfenbüttel, 1621) attended school at Torgau and the university at Frankfort on the Oder. During his university days he was organist at St. Mary's Church. In 1589, when eighteen years of age, he entered the service of Duke Heinrich Julius of Brunswick-Wolfenbüttel, remaining in Wolfenbüttel until his death, in the capacity of chamber-organist, court kapellmeister, privy chamber secretary, and also being honorary kapellmeister of the courts of Dresden and Halle. In 1619 he visited Dresden where he came into contact with the young Heinrich Schütz. Michael Praetorius was the most famous German musician of his time, celebrated as the "*Primarius,*" the "*Archimusicus*" by his colleagues. He was the highest authority in all musical questions, like Heinrich Schütz 30 years later. He was the greatest theoretician of his century. He carried the choral art of the sixteenth century into the seventeenth. Inspired by the Venetian multiple-chorus art, not unfamiliar with the concertizing style of Viadana, he cultivated the choral in all its forms. A new edition of the musical works of Praetorius is being published at present by Kallmeyer, Wolfenbüttel-Berlin, under the editorship of Friedrich Blume with the coöperation of Arnold Mendelssohn and Willibald Gurlitt. The magnitude of the work of Praetorius may be judged from the following titles: *Musae Sioniae,* 9 parts, 1605–11; between 1611 and 1613 there appeared, *Missodia, Hymnodia, Eulogodia, Megalynodia, Uranochorodia,* the *Large and Small Litany,* and a volume of *Motets and Psalms.* These two groups embrace settings of church hymns, Masses, magnificats, benedictuses, etc. The late work of the master consists of the *Polyhymnia Caduceatrix, Polyhymnia Exercitatrix,* and the *Puericinium.* This last group of three works appeared between 1619 and 1621. The group contains church-song compositions on a large scale, as well as solo compositions, etc. The only instrumental work published by Praetorius is the *Terpsichore,* 1612, containing more than three hundred dances for from four to five instruments. The chief of the theoretical works is the three-volume *Syntagma musicum,* 1619, a kind of summary presentation of the state of music c. 1600. Extensive prefaces serve as keys for the methods of execution of that day. The second part of the *Syntagma,* the *De organographia,* has been published as Vol. XIII of the P.G.M., and in facsimile, with a Postscript by W. Gurlitt, by the Bärenreiter Verlag, Cassel. The third volume of the *Syntagma* was published in a critical new edition by Kahnt, Leipzig, under the editorship of Bernoulli, 1916. BIBLIOGRAPHY: F. Blume, *Das monodische Prinzip in der protestantischen Kirchenmusik.* B. & H., Leipzig, 1925.—W. Gurlitt, *Leben und Werke des M. P. Creuzburgensis* (Leipzig dissertation), the first volume of a larger contemplated work. B. & H., Leipzig, 1914.—The organ works of Praetorius have been published by Kallmeyer, Wolfenbüttel-Berlin, with a preface by W. Gurlitt, 1930.—See S.B., Nos. 161, 162; and W.B., No. 59.

workers or followers of Schütz, mediated the transition between him and J. S. Bach. Those deserving of especial mention, among others, are the Lübeck musicians, Franz Tunder (1614–67) [41] and Dietrich Buxtehude (1637–1707); [42] the Hamburg musicians, Matthias Weckmann (1621–74) [43] and Johann Schop (d. c. 1665), the latter an especially famous violin player: the Berlin musician, Johann Crüger (1598–1662), [44] the composer of the chorale *Nun danket alle Gott* (Now Thank We All Our God); the Saxon, Johann Rosenmüller (d. 1684); [45] the Thuringian, Johann Rudolf Ahle (1625–73), organist in Mülhausen; and the Weissenfels kapellmeister, Johann Philipp Krieger (1649–1725). The Königsberg kapellmeister, Johann Sebastiani (1622–83) gained especial significance from the fact that he was the first to treat the "Passion" in the form of an oratorio, in 1672, in which form Bach later elevated it to undreamed of heights.

OPERA IN FRANCE; LULLY

At first the French assumed a hostile attitude toward the *nuove musiche* of the Italians. It was doubtless the strong intellectual individualism of the nation which rebelled against merely taking over and imitating the new and the strange. The realistic movement found no echo in a country which was approaching its national classical period. Germany is able to match Monteverde with a Schütz, but France produces no great master of the new style in the first half of the seventeenth century. The customary relation seems to have been reversed at that time. The French insisted that the Italians had no gift for beautiful song, which they themselves cultivated in the so-called *air de la cour*. Pater Mersenne pointed out clearly wherein the difference lay in his work *Harmonie universelle* (1636–37), a work which treats thoroughly of the music of his time. He says: "The Italians express the passions, the intellectual movements and the spiritual emotions as intensely as they are able, and with a strange vehemence, while our French content themselves with tickling the ear, and allowing a perpetual sweetness to dominate their songs."

The Italians did, however, find an influential friend in Paris in the person of the all-powerful minister, Mazarin. The latter had Italian singers come to Paris in the year 1643. Of the operas which they pre-

[41] See S.B., No. 211.
[42] See p. 202.
[43] See S.B., Nos. 212, 213 a.

[44] See S.B., No. 208.
[45] See p. 195.

sented, the most important was the *Orfeo* of Luigi Rossi (2d of March, 1647), a work which shows high development from the formal point of view and is rich also from the musical viewpoint.[46] Mention has already been made of its charming slumber-chorus *Dormite begli occhi*. Although the Sorbonne protested against the *Orfeo* on religious grounds, and parliament on account of the tremendous cost of production, nevertheless the performance had great success. It served as an incentive to the performance of plays with incidental music, like the *Andromède* of Corneille; and the sojourn of Luigi Rossi in Paris was helpful in developing French singers who were capable of dramatic performance.

The first attempts at a national opera in the French language were made by Abbé Pierre Perrin, who is represented as a phantastic adventurer and poet without talent, but nevertheless also as a man full of ideas. He joined forces with the musician Robert Cambert. The two together created a work called a *Pastorale*, the *Première Comédie française en musique, représentée en France*, as the program of the first performance in April, 1659, proudly points out. The score has been lost. Of still greater importance is the second work of the two, *Pomone*, a five-act pastorale, which was performed on the 3d of March, 1671.[47]

This performance at the same time marked the opening of the *Académie royale de musique*, that famous institution that still lives in Paris as the Grand Opera. Perrin had received from Louis XIV a patent for the presentation of operas, and thus became the founder of an institution that has been of permanent import for the musical life of France. The chauvinism which rebelled against the Italians under the patronage of Mazarin furthered the interests of the institution. *Pomone* had a huge success. It was given no fewer than 146 times.

Now that the project was prospering, the musician Jean-Baptiste Lully,[48] who had considerable influence at court, also suddenly interested

---

[46] A fragment of that work is contained in the supplement to the book by Romain Rolland, *Musiciens d'autrefois*. 4th ed., Hachette, Paris, 1914; Eng. tr., *Some Musicians of Former Days*, by Mary Blaiklock. K. Paul, Trench, Trubner, London, 1915.

[47] See S.B., No. 222.

[48] JEAN-BAPTISTE LULLY (b. Florence, 1632; d. Paris, 1687) came to Paris in his 14th year in the *entourage* of the Chevalier de Guise. He was at first kitchen boy, then music page in the service of the Mlle. de Montpensier, the Grande Mademoiselle. The Count de Nogent discovered his talent, and had him educated as a violinist. Because he composed a satirical piece upon his mistress, he was dismissed, came to the *Vingt-Quatre Violons du Roy*, and then rapidly made a place for himself through the favor of Louis XIV, who interested himself intensely in the opera. Lully possessed an intriguing and violent character, together

himself in the venture, although he had formerly declared that an opera in the French language was an impossibility. He bought the patent for the presentation of operatic performances from Perrin, who was confined in prison on account of debts, took over the leadership of the *Académie royale de musique*, and remodeled the institution according to his own ideas. Although a Florentine by birth, he became the founder of the national opera of the French, and according to the testimony of the French writers themselves, few composers are so thoroughly and genuinely French as he.

It is to be noted well, that before adopting the opera as a medium, Lully had already composed ballets, and also that among his later great dramatic works numerous so-called *comédies-ballets* are to be found. From olden times the French showed a special predilection and talent for the dance. No other nation has such a wealth of dances, dances that are original, rich, and of varied rhythms. The sense for the art of Terpsichore had already manifested itself in a brilliant way in the ballets which were instituted at court in the sixteenth century, in which the royal personages themselves joined. The ballet entitled *Le Ballet comique de la reine*, which was danced by King Henry III in the Louvre in the

---

with a biting wit. His death was due to an injury which he received from his baton while conducting.

Lully set to music the following opera texts written by Quinault: *Cadmus*, 1673; *Alceste*, 1674; *Thésée*, 1675; *Athys*, 1676; *Isis*, 1677; *Proserpine*, 1680; *Persée*, 1682; *Phaëton*, 1683; *Amadis*, 1684; *Roland*, 1685; *Armide*, 1686; and the texts by Fontenelle and Th. Corneille, *Psyché*, 1678, and *Bellérophon*, 1679. To these thirteen *tragédies* are to be added three pastorales and four ballets, as *Les Festes de l'amour et de Bacchus*, with which Lully began his operatic activities in 1672; *Le Carnaval*, 1675; *Le Triomphe de l'amour*, 1681; *L'Idylle sur la paix*, 1685; *L'Eglogue de Versailles*, 1685; and *Le Temple de la paix*, 1685.—These works were all engraved, and are to be found in original editions in various libraries. BIBLIOGRAPHY: Fr. Böttger, *Die Comédie-Ballets von Molière und Lully*. Graphisches Institut, P. Funk, Berlin, 1931.—Th. Gérold, *L'Art du chant en France au XVIIᵉ siècle*. Librarie Istra, Strasbourg 1921; Columbia University Press, N. Y., 1921.—L. de La Laurencie, *Histoire du goût musical en France*. A. Joanin, Paris, 1905; by the same author, *Lully*, Alcan, Paris, 1911; by the same author, *Les Créateurs de l'opéra française*. Alcan, Paris, 1921.—Henry Prunières, *Lully*. Laurens, Paris, 1910; by the same author, *L'Opéra italien en France avant Lully*. Champion, Paris, 1913; by the same author, *Le Ballet de cour en France avant Benserade et Lully*. Laurens, Paris, 1914; by the same author, *La Vie illustre et libertine de J. B. Lully*. Plon, Paris, 1929.—Romain Rolland, "L'Opéra en France au XVIIᵉ siècle," in the Enc. Lav., Sections 42–43; by the same author, *Musiciens d'autrefois*, 1908; Eng. tr., 1915. NEW EDITIONS: A complete edition of the works of Lully is in preparation under the editorship of Henry Prunières with the assistance of numerous collaborators. Paris, *Editions of the R.M.*—*Armide* has appeared as Vol. XIV of Publ. Eitner.—Numerous operas arranged for piano and voice have appeared in the collection *Les Chefs d'œuvre classiques de l'opéra français*. T. Michaelis, Paris, 1880 ff.; also B. & H., Leipzig.—See S. B., Nos. 233, 234.

year 1581, and in which the poets of the Pleiad and their musicians, Baïf, Mauduit, and Le Jeune, believed they had again revived the dance of antiquity, had already been conceived in a dramatic manner.

Historically, the court-ballet must be viewed as the foundation of the opera. Through all periods up to the present, the fondness for the dance is evident. Even the serious oratorio composer Lesueur occupied himself with it, both theoretically and practically. He believed he was able to resurrect the Greek ballet, and his pupil Berlioz had dreamed of a ballet "Faust" according to Goethe, as his first great work. It has doubtless been said correctly, that the failure of *Tannhäuser* in Paris in the year 1861 was due to the fact that Wagner was unwilling to accede to the demands for the traditional ballet. Even today, the ballet plays a rôle at the Grand Opera as nowhere else in the world. Immediately before the World War, Richard Strauss composed a ballet for the Grand Opera entitled *Die Josephslegende* (The Legend of Joseph), an undertaking which he would scarcely have entertained at that time for a German stage. Thus also Lully, with his most careful observation of the French taste, began with ballets, and opened a wide field for the dance in his operas.

Lully himself danced. Originally a violinist—and he must have been a good one, for in the letters of Madame de Sévigné she says literally *Jouer du violon comme Baptiste*—he early entered the famous band of musicians known as the *Vingt-Quatre violons du roi*. He established a second, smaller band, known as the *Seize petits violons*. In 1653 he became chamber composer, and in 1661, impresario of the royal music, and as such, the chief executant at the court ballets, as director, composer, player, and dancer. A friend of Molière, he composed the musical portion of his *comédie-ballets*, as, for example, of the *Mariage forcé* and the *Bourgeois gentilhomme*. Unfortunately, when later he had transferred his attention to opera, he completely suppressed the *comédie-ballet* which represented an unusually happy union of poetry and music in dramatic form.

Later on, in connection with his activity at the *Académie royale*, he substituted the *opéra-ballet* for the *comédie-ballet*. He wrote four such *opéra-ballets*, and called these great dramatic works not *opéras* but *tragédies;* with a certain justice, for the poet whom he chose and actually impressed into service, Quinault,[49] wrote genuine tragedies for him.

[49] See Et. Gros, *Philippe Quinault, sa vie et son œuvre*. Champion, Paris, 1926.

Quinault's libretti do not stand far below the masterpieces of Corneille and Racine in value. His contemporaries recognized this, and the critic Herder wrote, in *Früchte aus den sogenannten goldenen Zeiten des 18. Jahrhunderts* (Fruits from the So-Called Golden Times of the 18th Century):

" Quinault is in his field as great an organizer of the lyrical theater, as Corneille and Racine were of tragedy. Quinault has passages as strong and as tender as have those tragic poets in their branch, and he has achieved his success in a language which was less favorable to music than it was to tragic speech. In the recitatives as well as in the choruses he translated, as it were, the French ' sentiment ' into music. Clarity of exposition, order, logical sequence of scenes, decorum (*Anstand*) are to be found in his pieces, as they are in the works of those tragic poets."

In its poetic aspect, the French opera stands high above the Italian, and even if it is true that Lully followed the popular taste merely from policy, he yet deserves the credit of having pointed out a good way. He did everything in his power to give poetry its proper place. The recitative occupies the center of his works. He formulated the expression of this in exact accordance with the manner of declamation in the classical French theater. He is reported to have studied with diligence the delivery of the actors in the *Comédie française*, especially that of the famous Champmeslé, and to have copied it in his recitative. Because of his close confinement to the prosody of the classical Alexandrine, his long recitatives often become disconsolate, barren steppes. But there are also summits of most vivid word expression, and, above all, the French are given opportunity to hear what they want, namely, their own language.

In the second place, he gave them dances in abundance. His genius has fructified the music of all Europe with these. It is well-known that instrumental music drew for more than a hundred years on the dance forms of the French opera, the minuets, gavottes, *chaconnes, bourrées*. The aria-like song of Lully is also, to a great extent, a kind of dance song, and all the armies of Europe marched to the rhythm of his war marches.

Another medium, one which the Italians greatly neglected, he employed for great dramatic effects, namely, the chorus. By means of the chorus, mass scenes were enacted, which contributed greatly to the pomp of these operas which served to glorify the court of Louis XIV.

Festive prologues and epilogues served the same purpose. Preceding the whole, came the proud overture in the form created by Lully, which may be designated as truly regal, a slow, weighty opening, a fugal allegro, and a slow conclusion. It is not necessary to be endowed with great imagination to be able, on hearing the strains of the overture to *Roland*, to see the *Roi soleil*, as he appears in his *loge* surrounded by his court retinue:

According to the original edition of 1685,

Bibl. du Conservatoire, Paris.

ENGLISH OPERA; HENRY PURCELL [50]

The English national opera is associated with but a single name, that of Henry Purcell, whose light arose, brilliant as a meteor, and after whose demise it again became night. In the first half of the seventeenth century, the time of the unhappy Charles I and the wild struggles for and against the Commonwealth, music could not prosper. Nevertheless, two facts should be borne in mind: first, that the Commonwealth did not suppress music as completely as is sometimes imagined, for Oliver Cromwell himself gave state concerts at Whitehall; and second, that the Puritan suppression of church music actually gave an impetus to secular forms.[51] But new activity arose primarily when, with the Restora-

[50] HENRY PURCELL (b. Westminster, 1658 or 1659; d. London, 1695) was a son of a gentleman of the Chapel Royal, master of the choir at Westminster Abbey, and a member of the King's Band. Henry, Jr., received his musical training as choir boy in the Chapel Royal. His teachers were Cooke, Humphrey, and Blow. In 1680 he became organist of Westminster Abbey, in 1682, organist of the Chapel Royal, and in 1683, composer to the court. As such, he composed a cantata for the coronation of James II. His compositions include twenty-nine odes, music for fifty-four stage plays, anthems, services, miscellaneous vocal pieces with religious words, secular songs, duets, trios, catches, instrumental music, embracing theater overtures and airs, string sonatas, fantasias, organ pieces, and many works for the harpsichord. A complete edition of his works is being published by the Purcell Society (26 vols.); Vol. III, *Dido and Aeneas;* Vol. V, *Dioclesian;* Vol. XII, *The Fairy Queen.*— W. Barclay Squire has published the *Original Works for the Harpsichord* in 4 vols., Chester, London, 1913.—Among the masterpieces of Purcell's sacred music, mention should especially be made of the Psalm *Iehova, quam multi sunt,* for tenor and bass solos and five-part chorus. BIBLIOGRAPHY: G. E. P. Arkwright, "Purcell's Church Music" (Bibliography), in *Musical Antiquary,* July, 1910. H. Frowde, London and New York, 1909–1913.—Dennis Arundell, *Henry Purcell.* O.U.P., London, 1927 (in the series "The World's Manuals").— G. Azulay, *Purcell the Boy.* Boosey and Co., Ltd., London and New York, 1931.—W. H. Cummings, *Henry Purcell.* S. Law, London, 1881; 3d ed., 1911; popular ed., 1923 (in the series "Great Musicians"), Novello, London.—E. J. Dent, *Foundation of English Opera.* Cambridge University Press, Cambridge, 1928.—H. Dupré, *Purcell.* Alcan, Paris, 1927; Eng. tr. by C. A. Phillips and A. Bedford. Knopf, New York, 1928.—A. K. Holland, *Purcell.* G. Bell and Sons, Ltd., Liverpool and London, 1932 (popular).—Joh. Oettel, *Purcells Opern* (Leipzig dissertation—in preparation).—J. F. Runciman, *Purcell.* G. Bell and Sons, London, 1909.—W. Barclay Squire, "Purcell's Dramatic Music." S.I.M.G., V, 4, 1904.— P. F. Svanepol, *Das dramatische Schaffen Purcells* (Vienna dissertation), 1926. NEW EDITIONS: Cf. S.B., Nos. 246, 247, & 248 a.—Five sacred choruses in Blume's *Chorwerk,* Kallmeyer, 1932.—Cf. also, *Bonduca,* Chappell; *Dido and Aeneas,* O.U.P.; the masque from *Dioclesian,* Novello; *The Fairy Queen,* Novello. Modern editions of Purcell's chamber music: *3 Trio Sonatas,* ed. by G. Jensen, Augener, London; *1 Trio Sonata,* ed. by A. Egidi, Vieweg, Berlin; *1 Trio Sonata,* ed. by A. Moffat, Simrock, Berlin; *2 Trio Sonatas,* ed. by H. David, Schott, Mainz; *Sonata No. 9 (a 4),* called the *Golden Sonata* for two violins, keyboard and optional 'cello, ed. by G. Jensen, Augener, London; *Fantasias (a 3-5),* transcribed by P. Warlock (Ph. Heséltine), and ed. by André A. Mangeot, London, J. Curwen & Sons, 1927: contains 3 trios, 9 quartets, & 1 quintet; selection of the *Fantasias,* ed. by Just, Nagel, Hanover, No. 58; A *Pavan* and *Chaconne,* ed. by Just, Schott; and Pieces for Orchestra of Strings, ed. by Höckner, Kallmeyer, Berlin-Wolfenbüttel, 1932.
[51] See Percy A. Scholes, *The Puritans and Music.* O.U.P., London, 1934.

tion, Cambert came from Paris to London, in 1673, as master of the chapel to Charles II. Two of his operas seem to have been presented at court between 1672 and 1677. Various attempts, furthermore, had been made to combine the national drama with music, but Henry Purcell, perhaps the greatest genius among English composers, was the first one to crown them with success. Having been a choir boy in his youth, and after 1682 organist in the Chapel Royal, he first turned his attention to church music, and composed anthems and splendid compositions for the festival of St. Cecilia, which have been especially praised by his contemporaries.

The concerts in celebration of St. Cecilia's Day (November 22) are first heard of in 1683. They continued, with few exceptions, until 1703; and were under the supervision of "The Musical Society," which delegated a distinguished poet to write an ode in praise of music and commissioned a distinguished composer to set it. Among the poets whose services were enlisted were Dryden, Congreve, and Addison; among the musicians, Purcell, Blow,[52] and Jeremiah Clarke. Pope's famous "Ode" was written in 1708, but only set a long time afterwards. Handel, in 1736 and 1740, reset the Dryden odes written originally for the 1687 and 1697 festivals.

Purcell set his heart especially upon the establishment of a national music-drama. He devoted himself to the new task with colossal energy. He wrote no fewer than fifty-four dramatic works, chiefly music for plays, among which are Shakespeare's *Richard II* and *A Midsummer Night's Dream*, the latter under the title *The Fairy Queen*, although no line of the composed text is by Shakespeare; also many dramas of Dryden. Some of them rank as a kind of half-opera, like Dryden's *King Arthur*. Purcell is at his best in the incidental music to *The Prophetess;* or *The History of Dioclesian* (1690), *King Arthur* (1691), and *The Fairy Queen* (1692). The incidental music to *King Arthur* is commonly considered Purcell's masterpiece, although others would give preference to *The Fairy Queen*.

Purcell's only real opera is *Dido and Aeneas*, the libretto by Nahum

[52] JOHN BLOW (1649–1708), next after his pupil Purcell, was the greatest composer of the Restoration. His name is one of the most distinguished in English music. He was choir boy in the Chapel Royal under Henry Cooke, organist of Westminster Abbey, preceding, and again succeeding Purcell; organist of the Chapel Royal, Private Musician to the King, Master of the Choristers at St. Paul's, and Composer to the Chapel Royal. He wrote anthems, services, New Year songs, St. Cecilia Odes, and clavier suites. NEW EDITIONS: G. E. P. Arkwright, *The Old English Edition*, Vol. XXIII, 1900: *Songs;* Vol. XXV, 1902: *Venus and Adonis.*—See also W. H. Cummings, S.I.M.G., X, 3.

Tate. He based his work on that of the Venetians and Lully. His solo songs are especially influenced by the former. Like the Venetians and like Monteverdi, he was fond of employing a *basso ostinato,* called in English a "ground," a bass phrase that is repeated more or less throughout the entire composition. Even if the hearer is not fully conscious of the fact, a definite atmosphere is created thereby. Purcell achieved this end in a surprisingly beautiful manner in the death song of Dido, which is built upon a chromatically descending ground bass, a heroic piece of powerful directness of expression. The piquant rhythms which mingle strangely with the gloomy, groveling chromaticism seem to be descended from the old ballad song, as is shown on page 182.

A song in praise of music from *Oedipus* [53] and a gavotte from *Dido* [54] are developed in a similar *basso ostinato* manner. In both cases there is a great charm in the freedom with which the melody is superimposed upon the bass. The gavotte seems to have been influenced by Lully. Purcell surely learned from him his simple, effective treatment of the chorus. A festival chorus from *Oedipus* [55] is an example which baffles one by its very simplicity. Handel later seized upon and still further developed the characteristics of the English style of Purcell.

In the instrumental field also, Purcell is the outstanding genius of the period.

OPERA IN HAMBURG AND THE GERMAN LIED [56]

Schütz had introduced the opera into Germany. The Thirty Years' War, however, prevented a further development. The *Lied* alone prospered among the new secular forms. Heinrich Albert,[57] in Königsberg, a relative and pupil of Schütz, may be looked upon as the father of the modern *Lied* with clavier accompaniment. Simon Dach and the Königsberg circle of poets, among them Albert himself, furnished the poems.

---

[53] Cf. S.A., No. 40.   [54] Cf. R.B., No. 114.   [55] Cf. S.A., No. 41.

[56] See Romain Rolland, "Les Origines de l'opéra allemand," in Enc. Lav., Vol. I, 1912.

[57] HEINRICH ALBERT (b. Lobenstein in Reuss, 1604; d. Königsberg, 1651), studied law in Leipzig, went to Königsberg in 1626, and from there to Warsaw with a Dutch Embassage. In Warsaw he became a prisoner of the King of Sweden and endured all manner of hardships. But he also learned to know the Polish music, a fact that was not without influence upon his own composition. He returned to Königsberg in 1628, where he became organist of the cathedral in 1630.—New edition of the arias, by Ed. Bernoulli in the D.d.T., Vols. XII & XIII.—See also F. Dietrich, *Heinrich Albert, Lieder.* Bärenreiter Verlag, Kassel, 1932.—S.B., No. 193.—H. J. Moser, *Alte Meister des deutschen Liedes.* Peters, 1912; 2d ed. 1931.—M. Seiffert, *Organum.* Kistner & Siegel, Leipzig, 1923 ff.—*Staatliches Jugendliederbuch.* 4 vols., Peters, 1930.

Accompaniment of four strings.

Larghetto.

In his *Arias,* which appeared in eight parts, from 1638 to 1650, he cultivated the *Lied* in all its forms. He is most distinguished in the small
form. His *Vorjahrliedchen* (Little Song of Yester-Year), his *Anke von
Tharau* (Little Ann of Tharau) are the oldest pearls of the new art. From
his *Ich lobe, die allhier der Zeit in Froehlichkeit geniessen* (I Praise All
Those Who Here Enjoy the Time in Happiness) as well as from *O wie
gross ist doch der Mann, der durch hoher Weisheit Gaben* [58] one can discern
how Albert leaned upon and understood how to utilize the manifold
rhythms of the old German *Volkslied:*

[58] TRANSLATION:

O how great is he, the man
Who through gifts of highest wisdom
All can fathom, all can span,
What sea, earth and heav'n contain;
Who in all this life's conditions
Knows with wisdom to consort;
He receives in mirth or sadness
Ever-honored virtue's prize.

Through the favor which the *Arias* of Albert evoked, the new solo *Lied* with accompaniment was won for Germany. Among the numerous followers whom the Königsberg composer acquired, Adam Krieger,[59] in Dresden, must be considered the most important; indeed, one may call him the first classicist in this domain. He himself wrote the texts for his songs, which he published in 1657. In the time of the decay of German poetry, they are distinguished by their fresh naturalness. The Renaissance names and triflings, unavoidable in that day, are used sparingly. One feels that the serious and the jovial love songs, as well as the convivial drinking songs, are based upon personal experience. The musical form is highly developed, the melodic invention rich and manifold. The songs themselves are accompanied only by the *continuo*, but five-voice *ritornelles* are joined to these. We find a similar practice occasionally employed by Albert. These *ritornelles* are indicative of the great fondness of the Germans for concerted music, a fondness which shows itself in all the different periods. Besides Krieger, Wolfgang Franck[60] occupies a high place, especially as composer of spiritual songs. These songs of Franck, distinguished by their sweeping melodious line and their plastic form, have won a place in the modern concert hall.

Franck was also one of the first composers of opera in Hamburg. After 1678 the opera became a permanent institution here, so that Hamburg assumed the same rôle for Germany that Venice had played for Italy, and became for half a century a center of German musical life.[61]

[59] ADAM KRIEGER (b. Driesen in the March, 1634; d. Dresden, 1666) was organist at the court in Dresden at the same time that Heinrich Schütz was master of the chapel. His *Lieder* appeared in 1657. NEW EDITIONS: *Arien*, edited by A. Heuss in the D.d.T., Vol. XIX. A selection of the airs has been published under the editorship of H. Hoffmann, *Arien für eine Singstimme mit Generalbass und Orchesterritornellen*. Kallmeyer, Wolfenbüttel and Berlin, 1928.—See E.B., No. 59; S.B., No. 209 a & b; also, Seiffert, *Organum*.

[60] JOH. WOLFGANG FRANCK (b. Nuremberg, c. 1641; d. after 1695) was master of the chapel at the princely court of Ansbach, 1673–78. In 1679 he had to flee to Munich because, in a fit of jealousy, he had wounded his wife and had stabbed to death a musician of the chapel. Between 1679 and 1686 he wrote 14 operas for Hamburg. Between 1690 and 1695 he played a prominent rôle in the musical life of London. It is not known where or when he died. An unreliable report states that he went to Spain. The report that he was a physician rests upon an error. His *Geistliche Lieder* appeared in 1681 in Hamburg. BIBLIOGRAPHY: H. Kretzschmar, *Geschichte des neuen deutschen Liedes*, pp. 137 ff.—Barclay Squire, *Musical Antiquary*, July, 1912.—Arno Werner, S.I.M.G., XIV, pp. 208 ff. NEW EDITIONS: The spiritual *Lieder*, under the editorship of Kromolicki and Krabbe, D.d.T., Vol. XLV.— A selection from the *Lieder* by Karl Riedel.—Cf. also, W.B., Nos. 62, 63.

[61] Concerning the opera in Hamburg, see Fr. Chrysander, "Geschichte der Hamburger Oper," in Allg. MZ., 1878–79.—W. Kleefeld, "Das Orchester der Hamburger Oper." S.I.M.G., Vol. I.—Lindner, *Die erste stehende deutsche Oper*. Schlesinger, Berlin, 1855.

The Hamburg opera opened on January 2, 1678 with the Biblical *Adam und Eva* by Johann Theile. Numerous poets wrote for it with enthusiasm, e.g., L. von Bostel, Ch. H. Postel, Hunold (with the *nom de plume* "Menantes"), Barthold Feind, Ulrich Koenig, as well as less worthy scribes. The fact that the German opera could not sustain itself, but in the eighteenth century was completely driven from the field by the Italian opera, is due primarily to the poets, who were incapable of providing works of lasting quality. Indeed, the texts finally became degraded into filth, so that the disappearance of the opera, which institution had drawn upon itself the invectives of the clergy, was not to be regretted.

Germs for a comic, and especially a popular opera (*Volksoper*), were indeed present, but taste was too low to permit them to develop. The great spectacles which were in order at the time remind one of our vaudeville stage. Merry Andrew (*Der Hanswurst*) appeared with all kinds of animals, horses, donkeys, camels, and apes; decapitations took place before the eyes of the public, and colored water flowed as blood. Even when the subject matter was occasionally drawn from familiar and popular situations, this was done in too phantastic a manner. An opera which celebrates a famous captain of a robber band from the neighborhood of Hamburg *Der Stoertebecker*, by R. Keiser,[62] won great applause.

The opera was not lacking in musical talent. Able masters were devoting their efforts to it. Besides those noted, the following names should be mentioned: Nikolaus Adam Strungk, Christoph Graupner, J S. Kusser, the distinguished theoretician Joh. Mattheson,[63]

[62] REINHARD KEISER (b. Teuchern near Leipzig, 1674; d. Copenhagen, 1739) was a pupil at St. Thomas' School, Leipzig, in 1685. In 1692 he was in Brunswick where his great opera *Basilius* was performed in 1693. In the same year he went to Hamburg, the chief seat of his activities. Here he wrote not less than 126 operas. On a number of occasions he had to flee from Hamburg on account of debts. At such times he was active in Weissenfels, Copenhagen, and Ludwigslust near Stuttgart. For a time he was himself operatic impresario. In 1700 he established a series of winter concerts in Hamburg with a splendid orchestra and evening meals. His wife and his daughter were distinguished vocalists, the latter being engaged in Copenhagen. Besides his operas he wrote numerous church works and secular cantatas. BIBLIOGRAPHY: H. Leichtentritt, *Reinhard Keiser in seinen Opern* (to "Octavia," Berlin dissertation). Quelle & Meyer, Leipzig, 1930.—A. Schering, *Geschichte des Oratoriums*, pp. 340 ff.—L. Schiedermair, *Die deutsche Oper*. Druck der Tessarotypie-Actiengesellschaft, Berlin, 1901. NEW EDITIONS: "Der lächerliche Prinz Jodelet," 1726. Publ. Eitner, XX–XXII.—*Krösus* and a selection from *L'inganno felice*, in the D.d.T., Vols. XXXVII–XXXVIII.—*Ottavia*, as supplementary volume to the complete edition of the works of Handel.—G.M.B., Nos. 268, 269.

[63] JOHANN MATTHESON (b. Hamburg, 1681; d. there, 1764) was a composer and singer, but above all a theoretician of very great importance. His writings belong among the most

G. Phil. Telemann,[64] the most celebrated musician in Germany in his day, and, as is well known, also Handel, who was enticed to Hamburg by the glory of its opera in the first decade of the eighteenth century. He remained there from 1705 to 1708, and wrote four German operas. But all the wealth of music which these men offered was unable to furnish a permanent foundation for a further development of German opera on account of the lack of poetry. The comparison with the French opera, which arose in the same years, is instructive; this was able to endure because it possessed poems worthy of the name, and poems which expressed the sentiment of the nation.

The greatest genius of the Hamburg opera was Reinhard Keiser, one of those fortunate creatures who always have an inspiration, with whom everything turns into song. He might be compared with Mozart or Schubert, if his nature had been somewhat more profound. Depth is a

---

important sources for the knowledge of the music of that period. The most significant are: *Das neueröffnete Orchester*, 3 parts, 1713, 1717, 1721; *Der vollkommene Kapellmeister*, 1739; *Grundlagen einer Ehrenpforte*, 1740 (a collection of biographies and autobiographies, reprinted by M. Schneider in 1910); a large and a small *Generalbassschule*, etc. BIBLIOGRAPHY: F. X. Haberl, *Km. JB.*, Pustet, Regensburg, 1885.—L. Meinardus, "Mattheson und seine Verdienste um die deutsche Tonkunst," *Waldersee: Sammlung musikalischer Vorträge*. B. & H., Leipzig, 1879.—H. W. Riehl, *Musikalische Charakterköpfe*. 3 vols., Cotta, Stuttgart, 8th ed., 1899. See S.B., No. 267.

[64] GEORG PHILIPP TELEMANN (b. Magdeburg, 1681; d. Hamburg, 1767) entered the University of Leipzig in 1701 in order to study jurisprudence, but had already "imbibed too much note-poison" to become a jurist, as he once expressed himself, and he at once developed great musical activity. He wrote numerous operas for the Leipzig theater, and founded a *collegium musicum* that quickly attained importance. In 1708 he became concert master, and later court kapellmeister in Eisenach. Here too he formed a friendship with J. S. Bach. In 1712 he took over the position of a master of the chapel at the Carmelite Church in Frankfort on the Main. In 1721 he went to Hamburg as municipal music director, and he remained here until his death. In 1722 Telemann was offered the position of cantor at St. Thomas', Leipzig. It was only after his declination that Bach, who had applied for the position, was chosen. The fecundity of Telemann surpasses even that of Handel and Bach, and borders on the fabulous. A summary of his works may be found in Riemann's *Musiklexikon*. He wrote 12 complete cycles of cantatas, 44 passions, an indefinite number of occasional pieces, French overtures, oratorios, sonatas and suites for various instruments, concertos and operas; among the last-named, 40 were written for the opera at Hamburg. BIBLIOGRAPHY: Autobiography in Mattheson's *Ehrenpforte;* new ed. by Max Schneider. Kommissionsverlag von Leo Liepmannssohn, Antiquariat, Berlin, 1910.—Kurt Ottzenn, *Telemann als Opernkomponist*, with music supplements. E. Eberling, Berlin, 1902.—Romain Rolland, "L'Autobiographie d'un illustre oublié," in *Voyage musical au pays du passé*. Hachette, Paris, 1920; Eng. tr. by Bernard Miall. H. Holt, New York, 1922. NEW EDITIONS: A concerto in the D.d.T., Vol. XXIX.—G.M.B., Nos. 266, 299.—*Singe, Spiel- und Generalbass Übungen* (Hamburg, 1733–34), ed. by M. Seiffert. L. Liepmannssohn, Berlin, 1914.—The *Tafelmusik*, ed. by M. Seiffert in the D.d.T., Vols. LXI and LXII. *Tag des Gerichts*, and *Ino*, ed. by M. Schneider in the D.d.T., Vol. XXVIII. *Trio Sonata in E flat Major*, in Riemann's "Collegium Musicum." B. & H.

quality which is always lacking in Keiser. He delights, flatters, pleases, but scarcely ever is one really moved by his music. He understood his trade, and his forms are artistic. These are characteristics of his time, the end of the seventeenth century and the beginning of the eighteenth. The principle of *thorough bass*, as it developed during the course of the seventeenth century, has something stiff and coldly formal about it, with the uninterrupted continuation of a fundamental bass; but it drove the composers to a formal richness, and thus a new artistic counterpoint developed which reached its climax in the Neapolitan school, and in the works of Rameau, Handel, and Bach.

The creations of even a light talent such as Keiser are of solid structure. The characteristics of his art may be observed in the aria "Ich weiss es wohl, ihr falschen Sterne" (I Know It Well, Ye Treach'rous Stars) from the opera *L'inganno felice*, which already reveals the *da capo* form of the Neapolitan school, and is artistically united with an oboe solo, as is shown on page 188.

His winning, flattering charm is reflected in the pastorale, "Beblümte Felder, ihr grünen Wälder vergnügt die Brust" (Ye Flowered Meadows, Ye Forests Green, Rejoice the Breast), from his cantata collection *Von dem, Landleben* (Life in the Country).[65] It is characteristic that here, in the second part, the "Setze dich" (Seat Thyself) is composed, as it were, in a pictorial manner. This method, which sometimes impresses us as rather amusing, is quite common to the German composers of the seventeenth century, who were constantly concerned with painting the individual word in the music. The method prevailed, not only in the secular field, but also in the sacred. As is well known, even J. S. Bach did not hesitate to do obeisance to it.[66]

Keiser and his associates belong to the eighteenth century, and they represent in their department the climax of the development which is represented in another by the masters Scarlatti, Rameau, Handel, and Bach.

THE ORCHESTRAL SUITE [67]

It was believed for a long time that it is impossible to recover the music which the instrumentalists played in the Middle Ages. In our day

[65] Cf. S.A., No. 97.
[66] Cf. André Pirro, *L'Esthétique de J. S. Bach*. Fischbacher, Paris, 1907.
[67] BIBLIOGRAPHY: F. Blume, *Studien zur Vorgeschichte der Orchestersuite im 15. und 16. Jahrhundert*. Kistner & Siegel, Leipzig, 1925.—F. M. Böhme, *Geschichte des Tanzes in*

D.T.D., XXXVIII. 256.

Aria with Oboe Solo.

Ich weiss es wohl, ich weiss es wohl, ihr fals--chen Ster---ne!

dass ihr mir zu-wi-der seid, dass ihr mir

zu-wi-der seid, ich weiss es wohl, etc.

it is almost certain that the instrumental repertoire is not distinguished from that of the singers. The works of the fourteenth and fifteenth centuries which have come down to us, and which were hitherto regarded as purely vocal, were executed by the contemporaries on groups of instruments which the circumstances offered. Frequently one of the parts was sung and bore words which were accompanied by the instrumental parts: viol and lute, flute and harp, portative organ, ensemble of viols, etc.

Moreover, a small number of pieces have come down to us from the thirteenth and fourteenth centuries, that were especially composed for instruments. The majority are monodic; some are polyphonic; all are strictly defined in form and are divided into strongly marked periods. Some bear the marks of the dance, as the *dance royale* in France, the *saltarello* and the *trotto* in Italy. The *estampie* (*estampida, istampita*), more highly developed, already reminds one of the French clavecin music. The following is the beginning of a two-part dance from the thirteenth century: [68]

From the beginning of the fifteenth century, there come *basses-dances*, preserved especially in a collection which belonged to the princess

Deutschland. B. & H., Leipzig, 1886.—E. Closson, *Basses-Danses de Marguerite d'Autriche* (facsimile). Société des bibliophiles et iconophiles de Belgique, Lamertin, Brussels, 1913.—K. Nef, *Geschichte der Sinfonie und Suite.* B. & H., Leipzig, 1921.—T. Norlind, "Zur Geschichte der Suite," S.I.M.G., Vol. VII.—H. Riemann, "Zur Geschichte der Suite," S.I.M.G., Vol. VI; also Vol. XIV; by the same author, "Tänze des 16. Jahrhunderts *a double emploi*" (Attaingnant 1529 and 1530), *Die Musik*, Vol. XXI, ed. by Bernhard Schuster. Max Hesse, Berlin.—J. Wolf, "Die Tänze des Mittelalters," Arch. f. MW., I. NEW EDITIONS: H. Riemann, *Reigen und Tänze aus Kaiser Matthias' Zeit.* Arrangements for piano, two hands. Kistner, Leipzig, and Augener, London.
[68] According to Joh. Wolf, *Handbuch der Notationskunde*, I, 225. B. & H., Leipzig, 1913. Reprinted with the permission of the publishers.

Margaret of Austria, the little daughter of the Burgundian, Charles the Bold. In the sixteenth century, several large collections of orchestral dances were published by Attaingnant, in Paris, from 1529 on (*Basses-dances, Livres de danceries*, etc.); in Brussels, by Phalèse. In Breslau, in 1555, the town musicians, Paul and Bartholomäus Hesse, published a book of "Spanish, Italian, English, and French Compositions and Dances," more than three hundred in number, besides a book of German and Polish dances. These orchestral compositions add new color to the already variegated picture of the sixteenth century, a subject which has received little attention heretofore.[69],[70]

In the sixteenth century we are primarily confronted with genuine dances. At the beginning of the seventeenth, there blossoms forth in Germany a form of wide compass, in which the dance develops into the character piece, several of which are then combined in cyclical form into a suite. The suites appear in print, in especially fertile years as many as ten. The Thirty Years' War caused a lull in the publication, but after this, the suite arose anew, and remained a favorite form of composition until far into the eighteenth century.

At the beginning of the seventeenth century, the two most important dances are the pavan (or paduan) [71] and the galliard. The latter corresponds to the saltarello in Italy. In Germany the two are often briefly designated as dance and after-dance (*Tanz und Nachtanz*, or *Hupfauf*). Their combination was the result of the prevalent method of dancing. In the sixteenth century, the dance regularly consisted of two parts, the first in a sedate walking style, the second in a lively dancing or skipping style. The pavan in four-part time corresponded to the first; the saltarello, the *Hupfauf* (Leap), or the galliard, in three-part time, to the second. Somewhat later we find the allemande and the courante standing in the same relation to one another. Frequently, originally even regularly, the same music lay at the basis of both, i.e., the second dance has the same music, melodically, as well as harmonically, as the first. It is merely changed from four-part to three-part time.

[69] An example from Attaingnant may be found in R.B., p. 58, and an example by Isaak, *loc. cit.*, p. 31.

[70] One cannot count among the antecedents of the orchestral suite the fantasies for instruments by Claude Le Jeune and Eustache du Caurroy (1549–1609), because the style of these works compels one to classify them under the ancient forms of vocal counterpoint. One will, nevertheless, read with interest the trios and quartets for strings or wind instruments, which H. Expert has published (Senart, Paris).

[71] The name *Paduane* comes from that of the city of Padua.

The dance here led the art of composition to the variation form. Later on, the principle was expanded still further by several composers, and was applied not only to two, but to several, dances, indeed to an entire suite; thus, e.g., by the Styrian organist, Paul Bäwerl (Peurl, 1611),[72] and the well-known Hermann Schein (1617).

The pavan is an especially serious, majestic dance, a proud witness to a former gravity, aristocracy and dignity, which we have completely lost. One can observe these in the first dances for clavier instruments published by Attaingnant, c. 1530. The following is a series consisting of a pavan and a galliard, taken from the book entitled: *Quatorze gaillardes, neuf pavannes*, of the year 1531:[73]

Pavan.

Galliard.

In his *Orchésographie* (1588), Th. Arbeau says a pavan was played when one led an aristocratic bride to the altar, or as an accompaniment for distinguished fraternal organizations, or in the case of masquerades for the triumphal chariots with their gods and goddesses, emperors and

[72] Cf. E.B., No. 26.
[73] Published in facsimile by Ed. Bernoulli. C. Kuhn, Munich, 1914. (Cf. p. 138, note 75.)

kings. Bartholomäus Praetorius, the Berlin town musician, wrote unusually splendid pavans.[74] One can also observe in these the solid character of this old orchestral music which, written chiefly in five parts,
combines artistic polyphony with the dance form.

The intrada, which was played in connection with festal processions
and the like, is related to the pavan. Hans Leo Hassler, already frequently mentioned, wrote magnificent pieces of this kind. They occur in
the same work, the *Lustgarten* (Pleasure Garden) of 1601, which also
contains the melody of "O Haupt voll Blut und Wunden" (O Sacred
Head Now Wounded). In their vigor and diversity they hold their own
beside everything which German instrumental music later brought
forth. They should therefore be reinstated in the repertoire of our wind
orchestras. The following is an example of these intradas:

Publ. Eitner, Vol. XV.

[74] Cf. R.B., Nos. 82, 84.

The folk tone which permeates the old orchestral suite is especially delicious, and gives it the privilege of assuming its place directly beside the old German *Volkslied*. It resounds delightfully from the dances of Melchior Franck [75] and Erasmus Widmann,[76] as one can observe from the following allemande:

Deutsche weltliche Gesäng and Tänze, 1604,

D.d.T., Vol. XVI.

The folk tone sounds forth still more clearly from the pavans and allemandes of Hermann Schein.[78] His pavan for four *Krummhörner* (cromornes, a kind of oboe, or English horn) impresses one as being almost as heartfelt and romantic as Eichendorff, as is shown on page 194. Moreover, the suites of Schein also reveal a bold, daring, modern character, that reminds one of his contemporary, Monteverdi.

[75] MELCHIOR FRANCK (b. Zittau, c. 1573; d. Coburg, 1639) was master of the chapel to the Duke of Coburg from 1603; he was an unusually fecund composer. NEW EDITIONS: Instrumental works edited by Bölsche in D.d.T., Vol. XVI; in the same volume, the Suites of Hausmann.—Cf. also, E. Mauersberger, Bärenreiter; also, Schöberlein, *Schatz des liturgischen Chor- und Gemeindegesangs;* also, W.B., Nos. 54, 62, 63.

[76] ERASMUS WIDMANN (b. Hall, Württemberg, 1572; d. Rotenburg on the Tauber, 1634) was cantor at the principal church of Rotenburg. See R.B. No. 85; also S.B., No. 106.

[77] Cf. R.B., Nos. 63, 82; S.A., No. 27.

[78] JOHANN HERMANN SCHEIN (b. Grünhain in Saxony, 1586; d. Leipzig, 1630) came to Dresden in 1599 as soprano in the princely chapel. In 1603 he was a pupil at Schulpforta; in 1607 he was matriculated as a student of law at Leipzig. In 1615 he became kapellmeister at the court of Weimar, and in 1616 cantor at St. Thomas' School at Leipzig. Schein is one of the greatest of the predecessors of Bach in this office. Complete edition, ed. by Arthur Prüfer, since 1902, 8 vols., B. & H., Leipzig. Vol. I contains the collection of suites entitled "Banchetto musicale," 1617.—See A. Prüfer, *J. H. Schein und das weltliche deutsche Lied des 17. Jahrhunderts, mit einem Anhange: Scheins Stellung zur Instrumentalmusik.* Supplement, I.M.G., II, 7. B. & H., Leipzig, 1908; by the same author, *Scheins Cymbalum Sionium, Lilieneronfestschrift.* B. & H., Leipzig, 1910.

Works, I, 201.

The second of the great S's of the seventeenth century, Samuel Scheidt,[79] is also very significant in orchestral composition. The German genius for harmony shows itself in him; one is reminded of Brahms. In

[79] SAMUEL SCHEIDT (b. Halle, 1587; d. there, 1654) was a pupil of Sweelinck at Amsterdam. He became organist at the Moritzkirche (St. Maurice) in Halle in 1609, and remained in that position during his life. He was also kapellmeister of the administrators of the city. NEW EDITIONS: *Tabulatura nova* for organ, D.d.T., Vol. I, ed. by M. Seiffert.—A complete edition has been undertaken by Gottlieb Harms. Ugrino Verlag, Hamburg-Klecken; 4 vols. have appeared, 1923–33.—Cf. G.M.B., No. 185.—See Ch. Mahrenholz, *Samuel Scheidt, sein Leben und sein Werk.* B. & H., Leipzig, 1925.

a *Courante* by him, published by Riemann [80] even our modern ear, deadened by so many forms of tonal stimuli, is fascinated by the color play of the conclusion.

The orchestral suite of the first half of the seventeenth century is a specifically German manifestation. But foreigners laboring in Germany also cultivated it in an original manner, e.g., English composers who had crossed the channel with the comedians, such as Simpson and Brade; also Italians, such as the violin virtuoso, Biagio Marini,[81] who labored for a time at the ducal court of the Palatinate in Neuburg and Düsseldorf.

In the second half of the seventeenth century, the German composers began to interlard the dances of the suite with free compositions called *sinfonie* or sonatas. Johann Rosenmüller [82] was both ingenious and influential in this new departure. His *sinfonie*, with which he opened his *Sonate da camera* (1667), point in their lively expressiveness to the great, German instrumental music of the future.

Toward the end of the seventeenth century, the German orchestral suite enters upon still a new phase of its development. Lully, in Paris, had established a new manner and method of dance in his operas and ballets. He soon exerted a great influence. German composers, such as Gottlieb Muffat (d. 1704), Johann Sigismund Kusser (d. 1727), and others went to Paris, studied with him, and transferred his style to the German suite. Others imitated their example, e.g., J. C. F. Fischer (1650–1746), Ph. Erlebach (1657–1714), and J. A. Schmierer. The result was the kind of suite which Bach and Handel cultivated, which developed much rhythmical piquancy, and added new dances, as the minuet, sarabande, gavotte, *bourrée*, etc. The overture, as Lully had

---

[80] Cf. R.B., No. 86.

[81] Cf. D. Rittmeyer-Iselin, *B. Marini. Leben und Instrumentalwerke* (Basel dissertation). F. W. Gadow, Hildburghausen, 1930.

[82] JOHANN ROSENMÜLLER (b. Oelsnitz, c. 1620; d. Wolfenbüttel, 1684) studied in Leipzig in 1640, became collaborator at St. Thomas' in 1642, organist at St. Nicholas' and deputy to the cantor at St. Thomas' in 1651. In 1655 he was imprisoned on account of immorality, escaped to Hamburg and later went to Italy. In 1674 he was called from Venice to become master of the chapel at the court at Wolfenbüttel. BIBLIOGRAPHY: Horneffer, *Johann Rosenmüller* (Berlin dissertation). Buchdr. "Gutenberg," Charlottenburg, 1898.—K. Nef, "Zur Geschichte der deutschen Instrumentalmusik in der zweiten Hälfte des 17. Jahrhunderts." Supplement to the I.M.G., 1st series, No. 5. New edition of the suites of J. C. F. Fischer and Schmierer in Vol. X, D.d.T.—Cf. also, E.B., No. 35. NEW EDITIONS: *Sonate da camera*, edited by Nef, Vol. XVIII, D.d.T.—A *Sonata* for several instruments (without dances), a form cultivated by Rosenmüller in the last creative period of his life, may be found in R.B., p. 203.—Cf. also, S.B., No. 220.

developed it, attained especial significance. This was used, not only as an introduction to the suite, but especially also for the opening of oratorios. A well-known example is, of course, the overture to Handel's *Messiah*. The Lully, or French overture, as already remarked, begins with a solemn, dignified *grave*, which is followed by a fugal movement, usually *allegro*, and concludes with the resumption of the serious, slow tempo. Sometimes this third part is omitted, in which case we have merely the slow introduction followed by a concluding *allegro*, i.e., the form which later was generally adopted for the overture. The overture to *Iphigenia in Aulis*, by Gluck, is a classical example. This scheme was still employed by Cherubini, Beethoven, C. M. von Weber, and numerous later composers.

THE ORIGIN OF THE SONATA AND THE CONCERTO [83]

After the great upheaval at the turn from the sixteenth to the seventeenth century, which had created the new forms of the opera and the oratorio, new life stirred on all sides, including the domain of instrumental music. Its free forms, as we have observed, were created by the Venetians. In consonance with the proud character of the school, these were at first many-voice sonatas and canzonas. Now these forms began to be cultivated within more modest bounds also, i.e., for four or three instruments, or for a solo instrument with *continuo*. At an early time the so-called trio was developed as a normal ensemble, consisting of two violins and *continuo*. As a rule the *continuo* was played by two instruments, a clavier instrument and a string bass, a gamba, or something similar. This trio remained the chief form of chamber music, beside the solo sonata, until the second half of the eighteenth century. Only then was it dispelled by the string quartet of Haydn and the classical piano trio with only one violin, a cello, and the piano treated in an obligato manner.

It is a variegated assemblage which at first meets us in these sonatas and canzonas. There is no definite formal scheme. They are developed freely; so freely that they often appear to us as flighty and uncertain in expression.[84]

[83] BIBLIOGRAPHY: L. de la Laurencie, *L'École française de violon de Lulli à Viotti*. Delagrave, Paris, 1922—L. Villanis, "La Musique instrumentale italienne au XVIIᵉ siècle," in Enc. Lav., I.—Wasielewski, *Die Violine und ihre Meister;* 3 vols., revised and supplemented by Waldemar von Wasielewski. B. & H., Leipzig, 1927.

[84] Examples from B. Marini, Sal. Rossi, Tarquinio Merula, Massimiliano Neri, Nikolas à Kempis, Giov. Legrenzi, will be found in R.B., Nos. 81, 88, 90, 98, 99, 102; also S.B., Nos. 182, 183.

The formal genius of the Italians finally succeeded in finding a scheme that was esthetically satisfactory, and that furnished numerous masters with a method of presenting their thoughts in an orderly and effective manner. The free forms were created without exception by the Romance peoples; the Germans adopted them, and filled them with profound content.

Arcangelo Corelli [85] was the first to create a definite sonata form. This form rests upon the principle of contrast. It begins with a slow, dignified tempo, which is followed by an *allegro*, often fugal in form; this is again followed by a slow tempo, which in turn is followed by a second *allegro*, the latter now for the most part approaching the dance form. Put briefly, it is the form, slow-fast-slow-fast, which lies at the basis of this older sonata form, and which prevailed until the middle of the eighteenth century, and was also regularly applied by Bach and Handel. In the second half of the eighteenth century it was supplanted by the

[85] ARCANGELO CORELLI (b. Fusignano, near Imola, 1653; d. Rome, 1713) was violinist in Rome after 1671. It is doubtful whether he visited Germany (Munich, Hannover, Heidelberg) between 1679 and 1681, as has been reported, though the Count of the Palatinate appointed him *Marchese di Ladenburg* (near Heidelberg). After 1682 he was in the service of Queen Christina of Sweden in Rome and of the Duke of Modena; after 1690 in that of the Roman Cardinals Panfili and Ottoboni (Pope Alexander VIII). A modest, lovable man, he became a prey to melancholia, suffering from an inferiority complex. At the court of Cardinal Ottoboni he conducted great orchestral concerts and met traveling musical celebrities, among them N. A. Strungk and Handel. Corelli was a distinguished violinist who cultivated a melodious, expressive playing, a noble classicality, rather than mere virtuosity. BIBLIOGRAPHY: H. Engel, "Das Instrumentalkonzert" in Kretzschmar's *Führer*, Part 1, Vol. III, 1932, pp. 17 ff.—W. Krüger, *Das Concerto Grosso* (Berlin dissertation). Kallmeyer, Wolfenbüttel & Berlin, 1932, pp. 20 ff.—A. Moser, "Arcangelo Corelli und Antonio Lotti, Zwei künstlerische Ehrenrettungen." Z. f. MW., III, April, 1921, pp. 415–25; by the same author, "Corellis Ornamentik." Z. f. MW., I; by the same author, *Geschichte des Violinspiels*. Max Hesse, 1923, pp. 69 ff.; by the same author, "Zur Folie d'Espagne und Die Violin Skordatur," Arch. f. MW., I.—Fr. Vatielli, "Corelli e i maestri bolognesi del suo tempo," R.M.I., 1916. NEW EDITIONS: Complete works, op. 1–6, edited by Chrysander (not by Joachim, as on the title-page), in Chrysander's *Denkmäler der Tonkunst.—12 Sonate da camera a tre* (op. 2, 1685), by Schäffler, Vieweg; 6 of them, by A. Moffat, Simrock; one in G.M.B., No. 240.—*12 sonate da chiesa a tre* (op. 3, 1689): one in Seiffert's *Organum.—12 sonate da camera a tre* (op. 4, 1694): the first six by G. Jensen, Augener; six others by Sitt, Peters.—*12 Solo Violin Sonatas* (op. 5, 1700): individual ones by F.David, D. Alard, M. Seiffert (*Organum*), Riemann (*Collegium Musicum*).—*12 concerti grossi* (op. 6, 1712): score by Pepusch, Walsh, London; No. 1, in editions Nagel and Eulenburg; three in Schering's *Perlen alter Kammermusik*, Kahnt, among them the Christmas Concerto; No. 8, Durand, Paris.—The series of variations *Follia d'Espagne*: best modern ed. by H. Léonard; also ed. by D. Alard and F. David; the same collection by David—*Die Hohe Schule des Violinspiels* (B. & H., Leipzig, 1870)—that contains the *Follia d'Espagne* also contains sonatas of Porpora, Vivaldi, Veracini, etc.—Alard's collection is entitled *Les Maîtres classiques du violon*. Schott, Mainz, 1863.—Cf. also, F. David, *Vorstudien zur hohen Schule des Violinspiels*. B. & H., 1868–73: No. 7, Corelli, 3 Suites; No. 10, Corelli, 2 Suites. Some trio sonatas in the popular French ed., Senart, Paris.

newer threefold scheme, fast-slow-fast. Corelli himself not only determined the form, but in his solo sonatas and trio sonatas also created works of art of significant content, which, especially on account of their genuine violin character, will remain models for all time.[86] The following is a fragment of a sonata which reveals a sure art of melodic construction:

Sonate II. op. 5.

Original Edition, Paris, Bibl. nat.,

As distinguished German masters of violin composition, one must mention the Thuringian, Johann Jakob Walther (b. 1650),[87] and Heinrich Biber (1644–1704),[88] master of the court chapel at Salzburg. The Germans developed an especial virtuosity in double stopping.[88a]

[86] Trio sonata in B minor, from op. 2 by Corelli will be found in R.B., No. 121.—A fragment from the *Follia d'Espagne*, in S.A., No. 62.
[87] See S.B., No. 239.
[88] See S.B., No. 238 and D.T. OE. V, 2 and XII, 2.
[88a] See G. Beckmann, *Das Violinspiel in Deutschland vor 1700.* 1918.

While Italy invented sonatas for the chamber and for the Church (*sonata da camera* and *da chiesa*), while Germany wrote suites and sonatas for violin in abundance, in France, in the words of L. de la Laurencie,[89] the violin seemed "limited to subordinate functions, to the needs of the dance and of merry-making." The two bands of violins of Louis XIV, nevertheless, played the overtures and ballets of theatrical pieces besides dance suites. The first sonatas in France are merely suits of dances, introduced by a prelude. François Couperin was the first to write sonatas for the violin. Among his works one must especially mention *Les Nations* (1726), sonatas for two treble violins and bass. The bass is executed by the clavecin and a string bass. F. Couperin was followed by Sébastien de Brossard (c. 1654–1730), J. F. Rebel (1661–1747), Fr. Duval and Elizabeth Jacquet de la Guerre (1659–1729); a little later by J. Marchand, J. B. Senaillé (1687–1730), Jacques Aubert (1678–1753), François and Louis Francœur (1698–1787, 1738–1804).

The second half of the seventeenth century created a new species which soon became the delight of all friends of music, and was viewed as a wonder—the concerto.[90] The pleasing effect of the interchange between *tutti* and *soli* was discovered. In the earliest days, the concerto was chiefly *concerto grosso*, as the Italians called it; not only one, but several soloists were opposed to the *tutti*. Lully had introduced the custom of employing strings in great numbers, and had already contrasted with these, for solo effect, in his famous trio passages, either two violins and viola, or two oboes and bassoon. The founders of the concerto in Italy were Stradella, Alessandro Scarlatti, G. Torelli. Corelli again stands forth as the first classical composer in this field.

Music for Keyboard Instruments [91]

Venice had established the free forms of organ music. The Roman organ master Girolamo Frescobaldi [92] continued the work of the Venetian

---

[89] *L'École française du violon*, I, 15. Delagrave, Paris, 1922.

[90] Cf. A. Schering, *Geschichte des Instrumentalkonzertes*. 2d ed., B. & H., Leipzig, 1927.

[91] Bibliography: André Pirro, "L'Art des organistes," Enc. Lav., Part 2, Vol. II; by the same author, *Les Clavecinistes*. Laurens, Paris, 1924.—Félix Raugel, *Les Organistes*. Laurens, Paris, 1923.

[92] Girolamo Frescobaldi (b. Ferrara, 1583; d. Rome, 1643) was an infant prodigy. He was conducted about the cities of Italy and celebrated as an angel by the enthusiastic Italians. As a young man he seems to have sojourned in the Netherlands. In 1608 he was elected organist at St. Peter's in Rome, a position which he held until shortly before his death. On leave from 1628 to 1633 he sojourned in Florence, as organist of the duke. The plague and the rigors of war doubtless again drove him thence. He had the reputation of

masters, and crowned it with success. Frescobaldi has been called the
Italian Bach. Properly so, inasmuch as he is a master of counterpoint.
But one must remember that Frescobaldi belongs to the seventeenth
century, Bach to the eighteenth century, and that the one was the great
precursor of, and path-finder for, the other. Frescobaldi wrote *canzonas*,
caprices, fantasias, toccatas for his instrument. A *canzona* on the following theme, as simple as it is strong, will serve to characterize his plastic
style: [93]

He, too, was seized by the desire for new harmonies, which had en-
thralled the madrigalists by their spell. Of especial interest are pieces
like the *Toccata di durezze* with its chromaticism and its surprising
nuances, as one can judge from its final measures:

being a veritable wizard on the organ: report had it that he played better with his hands
inverted than did others with hands in normal position. BIBLIOGRAPHY: L. Ronga, *Girolamo Frescobaldi*. Bocca, Turin, 1930.—Weitzmann-Seiffert, *Geschichte der Klaviermusik*,
pp. 126–46. B. & H., Leipzig, 1899; Eng. tr., from the 2d ed., *A History of Pianoforte
Playing and Pianoforte Literature*, by Th. Baker. G. Schirmer, New York, 1893, 1894.—
Haberl, Monograph in the Km. JB., 1887. NEW EDITIONS: F. Boghen, *Sei madrigali a
cinque voci* (Six Madrigals for Five Voices). Casa editrice musicale italiana, Florence,
1920; by the same editor, sixteen ricercari and fifteen capriccios. Senart, Paris, 1922.—
Joseph Bonnet, *Fiori musicali*, 1635. Senart, Paris, 1922.—G.M.B., No. 196.—Haberl,
Collectio musices organicae, 68 organ numbers. B. & H., Leipzig.—E. Pauer, *Alte Meister*,
12 toccatas. B. & H., Leipzig, 1912.—Torchi, *L'arte musicale in Italia*. Vol. III.
[93] Cf. S.A.. No. 56.

A direct line leads from such pieces to Bach's *Chromatic Fantasy and Fugue*. The *Fiori musicali* (1635), the last work which Frescobaldi published, are of a transfigured heavenly purity.

A great figure in the north, that one can juxtapose with the Italian Frescobaldi, is the Amsterdam organist, Jan Pieters Sweelinck.[94] He studied in Venice with Zarlino, but also had associations with English music, and transmitted the two forms, counterpoint and the variation, to Germany. He was called "the German organist maker," because numerous Germans were his pupils, and because the line descends from him which leads directly to Bach. He is outstanding in the art of fugal composition, and indeed is surpassed therein only by Bach himself. That romantic imagination, by means of which the north-German organists created such characteristic works, is already living in him. A toccata in G minor,[95] especially in its virtuoso second part, will convey at least a slight realization of this.[96]

Samuel Scheidt, the pupil of Sweelinck, was chiefly a master of the art of variation. In a delightfully charming manner he converts, in a series of variations, secular folk songs into profound Protestant chorales. (Cf. especially the choral fantasia " Ich ruf' zu dir Herr Jesu Christ " in Straube's *Alte Meister des Orgelspiels*, Peters.)

A bold phantasy that anticipates Schumann and Liszt, with the difference, however, that it moves in the powerful and strict domain of the organ, is met in the ingenious J. J. Froberger,[97] as well as in two

[94] JAN PIETERS SWEELINCK (b. Deventer or Amsterdam, 1562; d. Amsterdam, 1621) was a pupil of Zarlino in Venice, and became successor to his father as organist of the Old Church in Amsterdam as early as 1580. Complete edition, edited by Max Seiffert, 1895–1903. B. & H., Leipzig. See M. Seiffert "Jan Pieters Sweelinck und seine direkten Schüler," Viertelj. f. MW., 1891. The study of old organ music has received an impetus through the "Praetorius Organ," erected at the University of Freiburg under the supervision of Professor W. Gurlitt, according to specifications proposed by Michael Praetorius in 1618. Cf. the report on the congress devoted to German organ art, held in Freiburg in 1926: *Bericht über die Freiburger Tagung für deutsche Orgelkunst*, ed. by Wilibald Gurlitt. Bärenreiter Verlag, Augsburg, 1926.

[95] Cf. R.B., No. 78 and S.B., No. 158.

[96] As a further example of harmonic discoverers, mention should also be made of Jean Titelouze of Rouen. Titelouze (b. St. Omer, 1553; d. Rouen, 1633) was organist of the Rouen Cathedral. His organ works (*Hymnes de l'eglise* and *Magnificat*) have been published in the *Archives des mattres de l'orgue*, 9 vols. by A. Guilmant, with a historical introduction by A. Pirro. Durand, Paris, 1898–1909. The same collection contains the works of the organists Nicolas de Grigny (1671–1703)—see G.M.B., No. 263; Nicolas Gigault (c. 1624–c. 1707): *Livre de musique pour l'orgue*, 1685; André Raison: *Livre d'orgue*, 1687; Louis Marchand (1669–1732), and Clérambault (1676–1749, organist of the Jacobins of the Rue St. Jacques and of St. Sulpice): *Premier livre d'orgue*, 1710.

[97] JOHANN JAKOB FROBERGER (b. Stuttgart, 1616; d. Héricourt near Montbéliard [Mömpel-

younger musicians, Dietrich Buxtehude,[98] who labored in Lübeck, and, in milder form, in Johann Pachelbel [99] of Nuremberg.

gart], 1667) became court organist in Vienna in 1637, but immediately proceeded to Rome to Frescobaldi, with whom he remained until 1641. Until 1645 he again occupied his court position at Vienna. After a second Italian sojourn, he occupied his Vienna position for a third time in 1649. In 1650 he concertized in Brussels, Paris, and London; from 1653–1657 he was again in Vienna. His remaining years he spent as chamber virtuoso of the countess Sibylla of Württemberg, his friend and admirer. He died at her home. BIBLIOGRAPHY: Kurt Seidler, *Untersuchungen über Biographie und Klavierstil Johann Jakob Frobergers* (Königsberg dissertation). E. Rautenberg, Königsberg, 1930.—A. Tessier, "Une pièce inédite de Froberger," in the *Adler-Festschrift*. Universal Edition, Vienna, 1930.—Weitzmann-Seiffert, *Geschichte der Klaviermusik*, pp. 169–80. NEW EDITIONS: Complete edition of his clavier and organ works in the D.T. OE., Vols. IV, 1; VI, 2; and X, 2, under the editorship of Guido Adler.—Numbers also in the *Meisterwerke*, B. & H., which give selections from the *Denkmäler*.—G.M.B., No. 205.—Organ Works by Karl Matthaei, Bärenreiter Verlag, Kassel, 1931.—Selections under the editorship of W. Niemann, *Frobergeriana*, Senff, Leipzig.—Ten organ numbers in Seiffert's "Organum." —Cf. also Harold Bauer, *Great Composers of the Past*. Boston Music Co., 1918.

[98] DIETRICH BUXTEHUDE (b. Helsingborg, 1637; d. Lübeck, 1707) was organist of St. Mary's Church in Lübeck from 1668, having become the son-in-law of his predecessor, Tunder. In 1673 he instituted the famous Lübeck "Abendmusiken" (evening musicales), great church concerts. The young J. S. Bach wandered to Lübeck on foot in 1705 in order to hear Buxtehude and to learn from him. Complete edition of his works in preparation under the editorship of W. Gurlitt, Ugrino Verlag, Klecken, near Hamburg: Vols. I and II, 1915 and 1926, contain solo cantatas; Vol. III, 1930, terzetto cantatas; Vol. IV, 1931, choral works.—Complete edition of the organ works, under the editorship of Ph. Spitta, 1876–78, 2 vols., B. & H., Leipzig.—Selections from the church cantatas in the D.d.T., Vol. XIV, 1903.—The *Trio Sonatas*, in the D.d.T., Vol. XI, 1903; two of these trio sonatas are presented in Seiffert's *Organum* collection, one in Riemann's *Collegium musicum* collection.—*Missa brevis*, ed. by W. Gurlitt, Bärenreiter, 1928.—Additional vocal works, under the editorship of Br. Grusnick, Bärenreiter.—Cantatas and evening musicales, in the D.T.B., Vol. XIV.—G.M.B., No. 249, a prelude and fugue. BIBLIOGRAPHY: Max Hagen, *Dietrich Buxtehude*. Copenhagen, 1920.—Andre Pirro, *Dietrich Buxtehude*. Fischbacher, Paris, 1913.—Max Seiffert, *Buxtehude, Händel, Bach*. J.P., 1902.— Wilhelm Stahl, *Franz Tunder und Dietrich Buxtehude*. Kistner & Siegel, Leipzig, 1926.— Since 1931 a Buxtehude Society exists in Lübeck.

[99] JOHANN PACHELBEL (b. Nuremberg, 1653; d. there, 1706) became second organist (under J. K. Kerll) at St. Stephen's Cathedral in Vienna in 1674, in 1677 organist at the court of Eisenach, in 1678 organist of the *Predigerkirche* at Erfurt. Here he lost his young wife and his child through the pestilence. The artistic repercussions of this sad experience are his *Musikalische Sterbensgedanken*, 1683 (Musical Thoughts on Death), variations on *Alle Menschen müssen sterben* (All Men Must Die) and other choral preludes. In 1690 he became court organist in Stuttgart; in 1692 in Gotha; and in 1695, at the Sebalduskirche in Nuremberg. In honor of his native city he wrote his variations on the *Aria Sebaldina*. BIBLIOGRAPHY: G. Beckmann, A. f. MW., I.—Albert Schweitzer, *J. S. Bach*. Paris, 1905 (1915); Leipzig, 1908 (1913); Eng. tr., 1912.—Ph. Spitta, *J. S. Bach*. B. & H., Leipzig, 1873–80; Eng. tr., Novello and Co., London, 1899. NEW EDITIONS: 94 Magnificat Fugues for organ in the D.T. OE., Vol. VIII, 2, published under the editorship of Botsiber and Seiffert.—Numerous clavier and organ works in the D.T.B., Vols. II, 1, IV, 1.—Some organ works in the collections of Commer.—Cf. also Straube's *Alte Meister*, 1st & 2d series. Peters.—A Practical Edition of *Pachelbel's Organ Works*, ed. by Karl Matthaei. 2 vols., Bärenreiter Verlag, Kassel, 1928.—Cf. also E.B., No. 36 and S.B., No. 243.

Froberger, a pupil of Frescobaldi, is great, not only as master of the organ, but also as a composer of suites for the clavier. Here he allowed himself to be influenced by the French.

In order that the further development of instrumental music may be the better understood, a glance must be cast, at this point, at the new appearances in France.

The suite for clavier arose at the time of Lully. One may consider as its founder the first clavecinist of Louis XIV, Jacques Champion de Chambonnières.[100] He introduced the four-movement sequence: allemande, courante, saraband, gigue, which four parts still form the foundation-stones in the suites of Bach. Beside him labored the various Couperins,[101] who formed a family of organists in France, similar to the Bachs in Thuringia. Louis,[102] the uncle of the great and famous François, deserves especial mention. The French clavier suite, inspired by the ballet of the opera, resembles it in its scintillating rhythm and a striking art of characterization. Furthermore, it fits the clavecin as the glove the hand. With that talent for color, which is a special gift, the French know how to evoke the charms which are peculiar to the silver tones of the clavecin. After the English virginal music, we here again find, for the first time, pronounced and genuine clavier music.

Froberger, a musician full of happy *Wanderlust*, and an international musician, as Orlando di Lasso was in his day, sojourned in Paris from 1652 to 1653, and was greatly fêted, though it is reported that even in that day there were chauvinists who begrudged such honors to the *piffre allemand*. Here, doubtless, he came to know the art of Chambonnières. He has left behind him a great number of suites, mostly in four divisions. He adds German inwardness to French elegance, and his inspiration is inexhaustible. He is the first genius of clavier music, and

[100] JACQUES CHAMPION DE CHAMBONNIÈRES (c. 1602–1672) became clavecinist to Louis XIV in 1643. He published two books of *Pièces de Clavessin*. BIBLIOGRAPHY: Article by Quittard in Enc. Lav., III, 1239.—Quittard, "Jacques Champion de Chambonnières," *Tribune de Saint-Gervais*. Paris, 1901; by the same author, "Les Origines de la suite de clavecin," *Courrier musical*, Nov. & Dec., Paris, 1911.—Weitzmann-Seiffert, *Geschichte der Klaviermusik*, pp. 153 ff.—See also the article by L. de la Laurencie on chamber music in France in the xvii and xviii centuries in the same work, p. 1491. New edition of the complete works, under the editorship of Paul Brunold and André Tessier. Senart, Paris, 1925.—Cf. G.M.B., No. 218.
[101] On the Couperin family, see Ch. Bouvet, *Une Dynastie des musiciens français, les Couperins*. Delagrave, Paris, 1919.—A. Tessier, *Couperins*. Laurens, Paris, 1926.—J. Tiersot, *Les Couperins*. Alcan, Paris, 1926.—The articles by André Pirro, R.M., 1920–1921.
[102] Modern editions of the works of Louis Couperin: *Carillons*, for organ; 2 *Symphonies* for Viols; 3 *Fantaisies* for viol and *basso continuo*, all published by Demets, Paris.

his works still deserve to adorn the desk of every pianist. His versatility is astounding. On one hand, the organ toccatas and fantasies of overwhelming boldness; on the other, the finely chiseled, translucent cembalo suites. Froberger was a specialist. He wrote only organ and clavier works, as later Field or Chopin wrote only for the piano. But he is more universal than these in his special sphere.

Still one more clavier master of the period at the turn from the seventeenth to the eighteenth century must be mentioned on account of the important historical position which he occupies, namely, Johann Kuhnau,[103] the immediate predecessor of J. S. Bach, as cantor of St. Thomas', at Leipzig; one might call him the Berlioz of his time. Like Berlioz, he was highly educated, of scintillating mind, was an author, and composed program music. His *Biblische Sonaten* (Biblical Sonatas) for clavier are more than curiosities. His *Saul* and his *David und Goliath* present fascinating pictures of external events and inner experiences. They may well serve to enlighten those who either do not know, or do not wish to know, how fundamentally, after all, music is related to the external world. The second of his biblical sonatas portrays the melancholy Saul by means of the following descriptive music:

[103] JOHANN KUHNAU (b. Geising in Saxony, 1660; d. Leipzig, 1722) was a pupil at the Gymnasium in Dresden and at the same time singer of the municipal council. He studied law and philosophy at the University of Leipzig. In 1664 he became organist at St. Thomas' Church in that city, and in 1701, cantor at St. Thomas' and director of the music of the university. Up to the time of his appointment as cantor, he was also an attorney. He translated from both the Greek and the Hebrew. His humorous romance *Der musikalische Quacksalber* (The Musical Charlatan), 1700, is a satirical stigmatization of the overestimation of everything Italian in the music of his day. The work is historically instructive and still entertaining (new edition by Kurt Benndorf, Bock, Berlin, 1900). Cf. Romain Rolland, "Le Roman comique d'un musicien au xviie siècle," in *Voyage musical au pays*

The rapid darts, the broken chords, a fugue on a violent subject, portray the anger of the king, when suddenly the sound of David's harp comes to refresh him (*la Canzone refrigerativa dell'arpa di Davide*):

The last part of the sonata, based entirely on a joyful rhythm, finally reveals the tranquil and contented soul of Saul.

An act of Kuhnau's, historically more important, was his transference of the sonata, as it had long existed for stringed instruments, to the clavier. To his *Neue Klavierübung* (New Clavier-Practice), which appeared in the year 1672 and consisted otherwise of suites, he for the first time appended a sonata. The success was so encouraging that in 1696 he followed it by *Frische Klavierfrüchte oder sieben Sonaten von guter Invention* (Fresh Clavier-Fruits or Seven Sonatas of Good Invention) which went through not less than five editions. Up to this time clavier music had consisted of pieces that were primarily of a dance nature. With his sonatas Kuhnau opened a new path, which in the following century led to Haydn, Mozart, and Beethoven.

du passé. Hachette, Paris, 1920; Eng. tr. by B. Miall. H. Holt, N. Y., 1922. BIBLIOGRAPHY: W. Danckert, *Geschichte der Gigue*. Kistner & Siegel, Leipzig, 1924.—J. Martin, *Die Kirchenkantaten Kuhnaus* (Berlin dissertation). R. Noske, Borna, Leipzig, 1928.—R. Münnich, "J. Kuhnaus Leben," S.I.M.G., III, pp. 473 ff.—A. Schering, *Bachjahrbuch*. B. & H., Leipzig, 1912.—Ph. Spitta, *J. S. Bach*, Vol. I, 236, 243 ff.—On the cantatas of Kuhnau, see the Enc. Lav., II, p. 963, the article by André Pirro on German religious music. NEW EDITIONS: S.B., No. 244.—Päsler, Works for the harpsichord, in the D.d.T., Vol. IV.—Shedlock, *Biblical Sonatas*. Novello, London, 1895.

VI

THE EIGHTEENTH CENTURY

SCARLATTI, RAMEAU, HANDEL, AND BACH

IN the first half of the eighteenth century, musical development reaches a climax. The new forms which had entered into life at the beginning of the seventeenth century, and which all rest upon the principle of thorough bass, reach their highest development. This is signalized by four masters who labored in four different countries: Alessandro Scarlatti in Italy, Jean Philippe Rameau in France, George Frederick Handel in England, and Johann Sebastian Bach in Germany.

The esthetic judgment concerning these may vary according to disposition and taste, but historically they fulfilled the same mission, and occupy, each one, the same position in his particular field. Two are of German nationality; the Netherlands, Spain, and England are eliminated; the supremacy tends toward Germany. Externally, to be sure, it still lies in the hands of the Italians; indeed, it was never so undisputedly and so brilliantly theirs, as in the first half of the eighteenth century. We have observed that already in the seventeenth century the German princes began to maintain Italian opera. In the following century they did so to a much greater extent, and the expense and ostentation which were lavished upon this surpassed everything that had gone before. Italian musicians are to be found everywhere, and hold the foremost positions, not only in Germany, but also in England, in Poland, and in Russia. France alone doggedly resists the Italian operatic use and abuse, in spite of various attacks.

At this time the Italian musical terms spread throughout the entire musical world. They still hold their own after repeated invective and defense, whether just or unjust.

NEAPOLITAN OPERA; ALESSANDRO SCARLATTI AND HIS SUCCESSORS [1]

At the beginning of the eighteenth century, Naples supplanted Venice in leadership in the operatic field. The southern city, which up to this

[1] BIBLIOGRAPHY: Francesco Florimo, *La scuola musicale di Napoli.* 4 vols., Stabilimento tip. V. Morano, Naples, 1880–84. NEW EDITIONS: A. Parisotti, *Arie antiche.* 3 vols., Ricordi, Milan, 1885, c. 1898; also Parisotti, *Anthology of Italian Songs of the 17th & 18th centuries;* Eng. tr. by Theo. Baker. 2 vols., Schirmer, N. Y., 1894.—H. Riemann, *Kantatenfrühling* (1633–82), and selected chamber cantatas from about 1700. Siegel, Leipzig.

time had made itself little known, owes its preëminence especially to Alessandro Scarlatti,[2] whose works became world-famous and created a definite school. To be sure, Scarlatti did not invent a new species or new forms, but he carried them to victory by the force of his genius. The new style had already been adopted by such masters as Steffani and Pallavicino. The Neapolitan-born Alessandro Stradella was a great power tending in the same direction. Before Scarlatti, Francesco Provenzale labored in Naples as operatic composer. But only the mighty work of Alessandro Scarlatti could bring the Neapolitan school to world mastery.

The predecessor of Scarlatti in Naples itself, Provenzale, was director of the Conservatory "della Pietà de' Turchini," and this gives occasion to recall the conservatories which now became highly significant for the musical life of Italy. Originally they were children's orphanages—hence the name *Conservatorio*—the inmates of which were educated to be singers and musicians. In Naples, there were no fewer than four such conservatories; in Venice, an equal number.

At the center of the Neapolitan operas stands the *aria;* indeed the operas are veritable series of arias, linked together by means of recitatives. The aria evolved as a formal, strictly organic whole from the originally free effusion of realistic musical declamation in the oldest operas. Of course, this evolution did not take place with one bound, but gradually. Alessandro Scarlatti brought it to a conclusion.

The aria is strictly organized. It consists of three parts according to the scheme *a b a*, the so-called *da capo aria*. Its form, as already observed, seems to be original to music. It became generally prevalent in the eighteenth century. Every friend of music is familiar with it from the works of Handel and Bach, as well as those of Gluck and Mozart.

The sense for form, which ruled the entire eighteenth century, reveals

---

[2] ALESSANDRO SCARLATTI (b. Palermo, 1659; d. Naples, 1725) was a pupil of Carissimi, became master of the chapel to the queen of Sweden in Rome in 1680, and master of the chapel in Naples in 1694. From 1703–8 he was master of the chapel at Santa Maria Maggiore in Rome, later again in Naples. Scarlatti wrote 115 operas, 200 Masses, c. 700 cantatas, numerous oratorios, etc. BIBLIOGRAPHY: Ch. van den Borren, *Alessandro Scarlatti, et l'esthétique de l'opéra napolitain.* La Renaissance d'Occident, Paris & Brussels, 1921.—Ed. Dent, "The Operas of Alessandro Scarlatti," S.I.M.G., IV, 1902, pp.143–156; by the same author, *Alessandro Scarlatti, His Life and Work.* Arnold, London, 1905.—A. Lorenz, *Alessandro Scarlatti, Jugendoper.* Filser, Augsburg, 1927.—Ulisse Prota-Giurleo, *Alessandro Scarlatti, il Palermitano.* L'autore, Naples, 1926. NEW EDITIONS: The opera *La Rosaura* (c. 1690), in Publ. Eitner, Vol. XIV.—G.M.B., Nos. 258–260.—Some church music in the collections of Proske, Commer, etc.

itself with especial clarity in this *da capo aria*. Not realism, or truthfulness to life, is the prime object sought after, but a harmoniously rounded form that is in itself esthetically effective.

This does not imply that these arias no longer expressed genuine feeling; quite to the contrary, the arias of the great masters are fine and frequently sublime soul pictures. Those of Scarlatti have, for the most part, remained in manuscript form, and are disseminated throughout the libraries of Europe. The following is one of the arias contained in a collection attributed to Scarlatti, and one which presents the best characteristics of his style:

Collection of Airs in MS.
Paris, Bibl nat., Vm^7 16.

ques-te   ca - - -te-ne   non   non son ser - - -te

Scarlatti himself still moves within narrow limits.[3] Later on, the arias assume great architectonic proportions. They always afford the singing voice opportunity to develop its individual powers to the highest degree. The Neapolitan school brought the vocal solo to its highest perfection. The composers understood how to treat the human voice, how to utilize its capabilities and charms to the best advantage, an art with which the instrumentally-minded moderns are no longer conversant.

Compositions for solo song stood on the highest pinnacle that they ever attained. A renaissance of the art of singing might be achieved by resurrecting these. As the interest of the present day centers in instruments and in instrumental virtuosity, so at that time the whole interest was centered in the song. The public possessed a fine ear; it knew how to evaluate the accomplishments not only of the singers, but those of the composers as well. Every finesse of vocal expression was noted and rewarded with praise. A witness to this thorough comprehension may be found in Heinse's novel *Hildegard von Hohenthal* (1795–96). Beyle (Stendhal) [4] also reveals himself in his writings relating to music as an example of this far-reaching vocal knowledge on the part of the friends of music.

Even if one knew nothing further about it, one could see from the scores themselves that the singers possessed the highest virtuosity. Even a creative gift was required of them, for in the *da capo aria* they were expected to introduce embellishments into the repetition of the first part. The virtuoso was judged according to his ability to introduce these

[3] For further examples of Scarlatti's style, cf. the aria from *Rosaura* in R.B., No. 119, and the aria from *Il prigionero fortunato* in S.A., p. 74.

[4] *Vie de Rossini;* new ed. by H. Prunières. Champion, Paris, 1922; Eng. tr., *Life of Rossini*, by H. S. Edwards, Hurst & Blackett, London, O. Ditson & Co., Boston, 1869; condensed in "Great Musicians," 1881.—*Vies de Haydn, Mozart, et Métastase;* new ed. by D. Müller, with an introduction by R. Rolland. Champion, Paris, 1914; also Le Divan, Paris, 1928.

in conformity with the spirit of the composition and to heighten its effect. In order to understand the *da capo aria* properly, one must bear this fact in mind. The tediousness of the repetition was mitigated by these free embellishments. When at the present day the *da capo* is performed without these embellishments, which are intended to heighten the effect, justice is not done such arias. There is no doubt that in the best period there were singers who were capable of heightening the effect of a work of art by their ingenious improvisation.

To be sure, there also lay a danger in the freedom which was accorded the singer. Indeed, in time this freedom became a veritable menace. In place of expression, the singers substituted bravura; and more and more a superficial virtuosity gained the upper hand. Unfortunately, the composers also flattered this virtuosity. The ultimate result was decay, superficiality, those senseless and endless coloraturas of which the modern music lover has an inkling from certain pieces of Mozart.

The vicious practice of castration contributed greatly to the rapidly developing unnaturalness. Boys with beautiful voices were emasculated in early youth in order to preserve their boyish voices. But since as adults they possessed a man's chest and a man's lungs, they were masters over vocal organs of a power unattainable by women. Trained from early youth for their profession, these castrates attained the highest virtuosity. Some of them must have been quite exceptional artists, as Farinelli, Senesino, Bernacchi, Manzuoli, etc. But of course the criminal act, performed purely for the sake of a beautiful voice, remained an affront against nature, and it must be reckoned to the credit of the French that they rejected the practice of castration; whereas in Germany and in England, as well as in Italy itself, Italian castrates were extensively employed. As these had no interests other than their singing it is natural that with them the conceit of the virtuoso reached its culmination and allowed itself the most audacious feats.

Scarlatti himself was still far removed from the weaknesses with which the later Neapolitan opera was justly charged. His style is more fluent and more vocal, as well as more charming, than that of J. S. Bach; at the same time it is scarcely less solid. He was a master of form and of counterpoint, and at the same time a fine portrayer of character. His works will remain models for all time.

The *siciliana* must be mentioned as a particular species of aria which the Neapolitans developed. Originally a dance in 12/8 time, this pleasingly flowing movement became the frequent means of lyrical expression, the veritable symbol of lyricism. Sicilianas were written by the

thousands; and Bach and Handel poured their most vocal, their most winsome arias into this mold, as one will realize on recalling the "He Shall Feed His Flock" from *The Messiah*, and the alto solo *Erbarme dich mein* (Have Mercy upon Me) from the *St. Matthew Passion*. A refined model, a jewel of singability, charm, and fine organization, from an early period, may be found in the aria *Ahi, che la pena mia mi guida a morte* by Leonardo Leo (1694–1744), shown on page 211.

Between the arias stands the recitative, originally the *recitativo secco*, accompanied only by the cembalo, later also the *recitativo accompagnato*, in which the orchestra takes over the accompaniment. Leonardo da Vinci (1690–1730), a descendant of the family of the great master, won distinction in the development of the latter form. In the later Neapolitan opera, it was employed by composers like Jomelli and Traetta, and in the grandest manner by Gluck, as a means for exalted dramatic expression that was intended to regenerate an opera that had grown insipid. The action takes place in the recitative, the arias represent the points of pause for lyrical reflection. On account of the superabundance of arias, the Neapolitan opera has been called a "concert opera," in most cases unjustly, because in the recitative a quite lively action commonly takes place, and the scenic effect and stage machinery also play an important rôle.

As poet, Metastasio, whose real name was Pietro Trapassi,[5] has the same significance for the Neapolitan opera that Quinault had for the older French opera. Apostolo Zeno[6] had prepared the way for him. The poets themselves had already arranged the scheme of the opera as we have described it, with the interchange of arias and recitatives. Metastasio possessed in high degree the ability to adapt his poetry to musical expression. His arias contain, not only euphonious words, but not infrequently also pregnant thought. He also understands how to arrange his scenes in a climactic manner, as the music demands. In order to understand fully his significance as an operatic librettist, one should read Stendhal's fine appreciation in his book, *Vies de Haydn, Mozart et Métastase* (1817).[7]

[5] Cf. Romain Rolland, *Voyage musical au pays du passé:* "Métastase précurseur de Gluck." Hachette, Paris, 1920.
[6] See Max Fehr, *Apostolo Zeno, 1668–1750, und seine Reform des Operntextes* (Zurich dissertation). A. Tschopp, Zurich, 1912. A Wotquenne, *Alphabetisches Verzeichnis der Stücke in Versen aus den dramatischen Werken von Zeno, Metastasio und Goldoni.* B. & H., Leipzig, 1905.
[7] See p. 209, note 4.

Alessandro Scarlatti has also won a distinguished place in the history of instrumental music through the development of a special type of overture, or *sinfonia*, as the Italians call the orchestral introduction to an opera. His overture—which was later called the Italian overture or symphony, in contradistinction to the French,—consists of three movements, an allegro, an adagio or an andante, and again an allegro, the last generally in uneven time and approaching the dance form. H. Kretzschmar properly calls this form an example of renaissance art at its best, inasmuch as the three movements, through the simple, clear contrast between rest and motion, form an esthetic, completely satisfying whole. The form has therefore survived. It became the chief scheme for all instrumental music in general. The sonata and the concerto adopted it. The symphony was detached from the opera, and formed the basis for the great development which culminated in Beethoven.

Among names of the first rank, besides those already given, must also be mentioned that of Giov. Battista Pergolesi,[8] who attained special significance as founder of the comic opera and as church composer; and also that of Francesco Durante,[9] the latter, however, exclusively as church composer.

Retrogression began with da Vinci. More serious natures recognized this decline and struggled against it even before the time of Gluck,

[8] GIOVANNI BATTISTA PERGOLESI (b. Jesi, 1710; d. Pozzuoli, near Naples, 1736) was a pupil of Greco, Durante, and Feo at the Conservatory *dei poveri* in Naples. As the result of the composition of a Mass, which he dedicated to the patron saint of Naples on the occasion of an earthquake, he became a celebrated master. Besides the *Serva padrona*, his most celebrated work is the *Stabat Mater* for soprano, alto, chorus, and orchestra, composed for a convent shortly before the end of his brief life. BIBLIOGRAPHY: Radiciotti, *Giovanni Battista Pergolesi.* Edizione "Musica," Rome, 1910; 2d ed., 1931. NEW EDITIONS: *Serva padrona*, ed. by H. Abert. Munich, Wunderhorn-Verlag, 1911.—The *Stabat Mater*, ed. by G. Schreck. B. & H.; also ed. by A. Einstein, according to the autograph MS in the monastery of Monte Cassino. Eulenburg, Leipzig, 1927; also published by Durand, Paris; an aria in G.M.B., No. 275.—Two Trio-Sonatas, in Riemann's *Collegium Musicum;* three others, published by Liepmannssohn, Berlin.—Some arias in the collection Hettich, Vol. II.—The opera, *Il Maestro di Musica* (Der getreue Musikmeister) ed. by A. Schering. C. F. Kahnt, Leipzig, 1928.—The Intermezzo, *La finta polacca* (= Livietta e Tracollo = La contadina astuta), edited by S. Radiciotti. Senart, Paris, 1914.—A violin concerto, in *Wunderhorn Verlag*, Munich.—E.B., No. 37.

[9] FRANCESCO DURANTE (b. Fratta Maggiore, near Naples, 1684; d. Naples, 1755) became director of music at the conservatory of Sant' Onofrio, Naples, in 1718, and director at that of Santa Maria di Loreto in 1742. NEW EDITIONS: *Magnificat*, numerous editions for piano and voice.—*Duetti da camera*. B. & H.—Individual numbers in the collections of Commer: also of Hettich. Leduc, Paris.—Clavier pieces, by H. M. Schletterer, in *Studien u. Divertissements*. Rieter-Biedermann, Leipzig, c. 1860.—An instrumental aria, by Franz Ries, in *Album-Blätter*. Sulzer, Bielefeld, 1871, 1873.

so especially Nicolò Jomelli [10] and Tommaso Traetta.[11] Both used the accompanied recitative and the chorus. Traetta, whose newly published *Sofonisba* sufficiently confuted the view of the concert opera, achieved striking dramatic effects. He not only presented a moving soul drama, but also gripping external effects, like the unexpected entrance of the soldiers' chorus in the parting scene at the close of the opera. One is almost reminded of Verdi.

The power of the Neapolitan school was so compelling, that German composers, in a manner absolutely unprecedented, not only came under its spell, but actually composed in a manner identical with that of the Italians. The most famous among these, Johann Adolf Hasse [12] was

[10] NICOLÒ JOMELLI (b. Aversa, near Naples, 1714; d. Naples, 1774) was a pupil of Durante, Leo, and Feo, then, in his maturity, of Padre Martini in Bologna. From 1741 to 1747 he was director of the conservatory *degli Incurabili* in Venice; in 1749 he became second master of the chapel at St. Peter's in Rome (in conjunction with Bencini); in the same year he was called to Vienna; in 1753 he became master of the court chapel in Stuttgart, where German music exerted a strong influence upon him. In 1769 he returned to Naples, but had become too serious—*troppo tedesco*—for the Italians, and no longer achieved his former successes, a fact which is said to have hastened his death. Fifty-three of his eighty-two operas have been preserved. Shortly before his death he wrote his famous *Miserere* for 2 sopranos and orchestra. A Requiem and a Magnificat are likewise masterpieces. BIBLIOGRAPHY: H. Abert, *Nicolò Jommelli als Opernkomponist*. Niemeyer, Halle a. S., 1908. New edition of the opera *Fetonte* under the editorship of H. Abert in the D.d.T., Vols. XXXII & XXXIII.

[11] TOMMASO TRAETTA (b. Bitonto, near Naples, 1727; d. Venice, 1779) was a pupil of Durante, became master of the chapel at the court at Parma in 1758; in 1765 director of the Ospedaletto S. Giovanni e Paolo in Venice; in 1768 court composer to Catherine II at St. Petersburg. In 1774 he went to London, whence he again returned to Italy. Forty-two operas in addition to church music have been preserved. BIBLIOGRAPHY: A. Damerini, *Tommaso Traetta*. Boll. bibliografico musicale, anno 2, no. 7, pp. 1–13. Parma and Milan, 1927. NEW EDITIONS: Selections from various operas and *Sofonisba* (almost complete) in the D.T.B., Vols. XIV & XVII, under the editorship of H. Goldschmidt.

[12] JOHANN ADOLF HASSE (b. Bergedorf, near Hamburg, 1699; d. Venice, 1783) began his career as operatic singer (tenor) in Hamburg and Brunswick, and studied in Naples with Porpora and Alessandro Scarlatti. He became famous in Italy through his operas, and was known there as *Il Sassone*. In 1727 he became master of the chapel of the *Conservatorio degli Incurabili* in Venice. In 1730 he married the famous singer Faustina Bordoni in Venice. In 1731 he became master of the court chapel in Dresden. From then on he divided his time between Dresden and Italy, with the exception of a journey to London, where for a brief time he joined in the competition against Handel. Everywhere he was acclaimed as composer, his wife as singer. BIBLIOGRAPHY: H. Abert, *Mozart*, A new ed. of Otto Jahn's work, I, 232 ff., 286, 299 ff. B. & H., Leipzig, 6th ed., 1923–24.—R. Gerber, *Der Operntypus Hasses und seine textlichen Grundlagen*. Kistner & Siegel, Leipzig, 1925.—O. Mennicke, *Hasse und die Gebrüder Graun als Sinfoniker* (Leipzig dissertation). B. & H., Leipzig, 1906.—W. Müller, *J. A. Hasse als Kirchenkomponist* (Leipzig dissertation). B. & H., Leipzig, 1911.—L. Kamieński, *Die Oratorien von J. A. Hasse* (Berlin dissertation). B. & H., Leipzig, 1912. NEW EDITIONS: S.B., No. 310.—Of the eighty operas, *Arminio* is being ed. by R. Gerber for the D.d.T.—Ten selected orchestral compositions, ed. by G. Goehler. C. A. Klemm, Leipzig, 1904.—*Die Pilger am heiligen Grabe*, piano

even regarded as the leader of the school in Italy itself, where he was celebrated as "il Sassone." Handel composed a great number of operas in the style of the Neapolitans; so also Gluck, before he entered upon his work of reform. Haydn, too, wrote Italian operas, and Mozart also was grounded in the Neapolitan school. Further well-known composers who have adopted their forms are J. Gottlieb Naumann at Dresden and the master of the chapel of Frederick the Great, Karl Heinrich Graun.

In Vienna, there labored as composer of Italian operas Johann Joseph Fux,[13] original as an instrumental composer, famous as a theoretician, and in general a "character." During the Neapolitan period, numerous Italians were also active there. Among these, the serious, profound Caldara is worthy of mention.

THE FRENCH OPERA; JEAN PHILIPPE RAMEAU

Lully's work of founding the French national opera was continued by musicians who had received their training from him, especially by Pascal Colasse (1649–1709), Lully's own sons, Louis and Jean, and H. Desmarets (1659–1741). Marin Marais (1656–1728), and especially André Campra,[14] emancipated themselves from that tutelage, the former enriching the orchestra of the opera, the latter making the vocal melody more mellifluent. Finally, Destouches (1672 or 1673–1749), by the boldness of his harmonies, prepared the way for and announced Rameau.

score by C. Grau, 1929.—*Five Arias*, by Haböck and Farinelli. Universal Edition, Vienna. —*Clavier sonatas*, by E. Pauer, *Alte Klaviermusik;* also by R. Engländer. Kistner & Siegel, Leipzig, 1930. The oratorio *La conversione de Sant' Agostino*, ed. by Schering in the D.d.T., Vol. XX.—A flute concerto (flute, two violins, and bass), Schering, D.d.T., Vols. XXIX and XXX.—Selected vocal numbers in *Musik am sächsischen Hofe*, by O. Schmid.

[13] JOHANN JOSEPH FUX (b. Hirtenfeld, Styria, 1660; d. Vienna, 1741) became organist of the Scotch Foundation in Vienna, in 1696, court composer to the emperor in 1698, 2d master of the chapel at St. Stephen's Cathedral in 1705, and first master of the chapel at the court in 1715. BIBLIOGRAPHY: Fr. Benn, *Die Messkomposition des Johann Joseph Fux* (Vienna dissertation), 1931.—L. von Koechel, *Johann Joseph Fux*. Hölder, Vienna, 1872. NEW EDITIONS: The opera *Costanza e Fortezza*, under the editorship of E. Wellesz, in the D.T. OE., Vol. XVII.—Masses and church music, *loc. cit.*, Vols. I, 1, and II, 1.—Instrumental works, *loc. cit.*, Vols. IX, 2, and XXIII, 2.—S.B., Nos. 271, 272.

[14] ANDRÉ CAMPRA (b. Aix-en-Provence, 1660; d. Versailles, 1744) was ordained priest in 1678, then became master of the chapel at Saint-Trophime at Arles (1681) and at Saint-Etienne at Toulouse (1683). In 1694 he was called to Notre-Dame at Paris. In 1722 he became master of the royal chapel. Soon after his arrival in Paris, he directed his attention to the opera. His principal works in that category are: *l'Europe Galante, les Fêtes vénitiennes* and *Tancrède*. They have been published in the *Chefs-d'œuvres de l'opéra français*. T. Michaelis, Paris, 1880 ff.—G.M.B., No. 261. BIBLIOGRAPHY: K. Dulle, *André Cardinal Destouches* (Leipzig dissertation). 1909.—J. Ecorcheville, *De Lully à Rameau, l'esthétique musicale*. Impressions. L. M. Fortin & cie., Paris, 1906.—L. de la Laurencie, "Notes sur la jeunesse d'André Campra," S.I.M.G., X, 1909; and *L'année musicale*, III, 1913; also Enc. Lav., Vol. II, pp. 1372–1379.

Jean Philippe Rameau [15] began his activities as organist, church musician, and theoretician. It was only in his fifty-first year, in 1733, that he appeared before the public with the opera *Hippolyte et Aricie*. Rameau is thoroughly original and typically French. There is no other instance of a musician who is equally great as composer and theoretician, although it is characteristically French to combine the *raisonnement* with the practice. The French history of music is especially instructive, inasmuch as the French artists and devotees were always striving to account for the effects of the music. The many literary feuds concerning controversial musical questions are well known; much acumen was displayed, and in spite of not a little superfluous work, much of lasting value was also accomplished. France, which refined questions of morals most minutely, played the rôle of ethical judge in music also. Rameau entered into his art profoundly; in his *Traité de l'harmonie* (1722) he established the modern theory of harmony.

[15] JEAN PHILIPPE RAMEAU (b. Dijon, 1683; d. Paris, 1764) was an eccentric character, who himself intentionally shrouded the circumstances of his life in mystery. He was the son of an organist, attended the college of the Jesuits for four years in his native city of Dijon, and subsequently devoted himself entirely to music. In 1701 his father sent him to Italy, but, fortunately for his own development and for French music, the Italian music did not please him. In 1702 already he returned to France as a violinist in a theatrical troupe where, after substituting for a short time for the organist of Notre Dame at Avignon, he became cathedral organist at Clermont in the Auvergne. In 1706 he went to Paris, where he occupied modest organ positions. For a time he again sojourned in Dijon and Lyons. In 1722 he was organist in Clermont for a brief time. In 1723 he settled in Paris definitely (the same year in which Bach entered upon his position as cantor at St. Thomas in Leipzig). Rameau's *Traité de l'harmonie* had appeared in print in 1722. Having become known through this, he found a patron in the wealthy farmer-general of revenues La Pouplinière, who created him his music-master, gave him and his wife lodgings in his palace, and directed him along the path leading to dramatic composition and Grand Opera. To be sure, the first opera of Rameau, *Samson*, on a text by Voltaire, was rejected because its biblical subject was displeasing. But in 1733 *Hippolyte et Aricie* was performed, and aroused—quite typically for France—a literary feud. Rameau became the man of the hour. Louis XV soon appointed him his *Compositeur de cabinet*. There followed the operas *les Indes Galantes*, 1735; *Castor et Pollux*, 1737; *Les Fêtes d'Hébé*, 1739; *Dardanus*, 1739; and 25 others up to 1760. COMPLETE EDITION: edited by Saint Saëns, Malherbe, Emmanuel Teneo, etc., published by Durand, Paris; 18 vols. from 1895 to 1924.—A number of operas transcribed for piano and voice in the *Chefs-d'œuvre de l'opéra français*.—Clavier-works, ed. by H. Riemann, published by Steingräber, Leipzig.—G.M.B., Nos. 296, 297.—The standard edition of Rameau's Harpsichord Music is that edited by Saint Saëns and published by Durand, Paris, 1894 ff.—Cf. also, Pauer, *Selected Pieces*, Augener, London. BIBLIOGRAPHY: Michel Brenet, "La jeunesse de Rameau." R.M.I., 1903.—G. Graf, *J. Ph. Rameau in seiner Oper "Hippolyte et Aricie"* (Basel dissertation). Villiger and Co., Wädenswil, 1927.—Louis Laloy, *Rameau*. Alcan, Paris, 1908.—L. de la Laurencie, "La Musique française de Lully à Gluck," 1687–1789, in Enc. Lav., Vol. II, pp. 1362 ff.—P. M. Masson, *L'Opéra de Rameau*. Laurens, Paris, 1930; by the same author, *Rameau et Beethoven*. Congressional report of the first congress of the International Society of Musicol-

It is also characteristic for the Frenchman that he finally arrives at the stage. The theater is the center of intellectual life in France; everything proceeds from it, everything returns to it. The same is true in equal or still higher degree of the opera, and here again of the ballet. All French concert music, even domestic music, remains in contact with this, from the suites of Couperin to the symphonies and oratorios of Berlioz, and the piano and orchestral compositions of Debussy.

In the operas of Rameau also, the ballets form a valuable part. He reveals himself in these as a great characterizer of unlimited wealth of imagination. To be sure, being thoroughly of the eighteenth century he clung firmly to form. He wrote minuets, gavottes, rigadoons, bourrées, and marches, which are distinguished by an unusual finesse in formal gradation. Each piece is a sharply defined character-sketch. Can one picture Zephyr playing with flowers more daintily than in the following figure (*Indes Galantes*, III, Entrée):

Petite flute a l'8va.

Or the comic fury of savages more vividly than with this one (l. c., Nouvelle Entrée):

The following "Rondeau tendre" from *Dardanus* is a pleasing dream picture:

The march from *Castor and Pollux* is genuinely heroic:

ogy, held at Liège, 1930, No. 1, pp. 174–81; the report published by the Plainsong and Mediaeval Music Society, Nashdom Abbey, Burnham, Bucks.—M. Shirlaw, *The Theory of Harmony*. Novello, London; presents an account of Rameau's views on harmony.— G. Migot, *Rameau et le génie de la musique française*. Delagrave, Paris, 1930.

A rigadoon from *Les Indes galantes* reveals the natural grace of the master:

Rigaudon en rondeau.

etc.

The general impression is frequently strengthened by a rich and bold harmony. In this domain Rameau belongs to the most original discoverers of all times. He treated the recitative, like Lully, in strictly French manner, and, like him, but with much greater skill, he drew upon the chorus for dramatic purposes. In his own manner, Rameau created a well-rounded work of art, which combines in unified manner poetry, action, solo, chorus, and orchestra, an accomplishment that is to be reckoned among the greatest achievements in the field of musico-dramatic art.

HANDEL AND THE ORATORIO [16]

Like the opera, so also the Italian oratorio received a new form through the Neapolitan school. *Da capo aria*, as well as recitative, became regnant in oratorio, as it did in opera, but the chorus received a more important position in the oratorio as contrasted with the opera. Metastasio

[16] GEORG FRIEDRICH HANDEL (b. Halle, 1685; d. London, 1759) was the son of a barber-surgeon. The father was determined to make a lawyer of his son, and Handel was actually matriculated as a student of law at the university Halle in 1702, even though his father had already died in 1697. Handel's teacher was Fr. W. Zachau, organist of the chief church in Halle. Visits in Weissenfels and Berlin (the latter in 1696) exerted a great influence on the development of Handel's talent. The duke of Weissenfels persuaded the unwilling father to allow his son to receive a musical education. In Berlin the composers Bononcini and Ariosti labored under Frederick William I, and Handel thus became acquainted with Italian opera. In 1702, at the time of his immatriculation, Handel became organist of the Reformed Schlosskirche. In 1703 he went to Hamburg where he plunged into the operatic life. In 1707 he went to Italy. His opera *Rodrigo* was performed in Florence, his *Agrippina* in Venice, with Handel's friend, the singer Tesi, in the cast. In Rome, Handel became acquainted with Lotti, the two Scarlattis and Corelli, and himself played a brilliant part in the musical life of the day. In 1710 Agostino Steffani attracted him to Hannover. Twice he went to London, the second time, in 1712, to remain there perma-

has the same importance as poet for the oratorio that he has as librettist for the opera. His oratorio books, which are regularly divided into two parts, in contradistinction to his three-act opera libretti, present, preferably, idyllic scenes from the biblical history. The times especially demanded detailed expression of feeling. Metastasio presented this in his numerous arias with sentimental text. Hundreds of oratorios which were written in this manner have long disappeared from the scene. One can, however, easily gain an idea of these from Joseph Haydn's *Il ritorno di Tobia* (The Return of Tobias), the poem by G. G. Boccherini, which is

---

nently. In 1719 he founded an Academy for Opera for which he engaged famous Italian singers on the continent. Bononcini, however, instituted a rival undertaking, and in 1728, after the accession of George II, Handel's opera became bankrupt. The *Beggar's Opera* by Gay and Pepusch, which ridiculed the unpopular Italian opera, had contributed its share to Handel's failure. For the first Academy, Handel wrote the following operas: *Numitore, Muzio Scevola, Floridante, Ottone, Flavio, Giulio Cesare, Tamerlano, Rodelinda, Scipione, Alessandro, Admeto, Riccardo I, Siroe, Tolommeo;* for the second, *Lotario, Partenope, Poro, Ezio, Sosarme, Terpsichore, Ariodante, Alcina, Atalanta, Giustino, Arminio,* and *Berenice.* With the Zurich impresario, Heidegger, Handel established a new opera in 1729. Again a rival undertaking was established, this time under the direction of Porpora and Hasse, in 1733. Handel, even though deserted by Heidegger, maintained himself with the greatest energy. Nevertheless, the difficulties became too great. In 1736 he suffered a stroke of apoplexy, and he became partially lamed, spiritually dejected, and financially ruined. By means of a vigorous cure in Aachen and an indomitable spirit his health was again restored. Handel now directed his efforts completely to the oratorio. He had already composed a number, as *Acis and Galathea* and *Esther* (revised) in 1732, *Deborah* and *Athaliah* in 1733. There followed *Alexander's Feast or The Power of Music,* 1736; *Saul,* 1738; *Israel in Egypt,* 1739; *l'Allegro, il Pensieroso ed il Moderato,* 1740; *The Messiah,* 1742 (first performance on April 13th in Dublin): *Samson,* 1743; *Judas Maccabaeus,* 1746; *Joshua,* 1748; *Susanna, Solomon, Theodora* and *Jephthah,* 1748–51. Handel won over the English populace especially with his *Messiah.* The great oratorio performances became veritable triumphs for him. He became blind while composing *Jephthah,* but nevertheless participated in the performances at the organ. He died on April 14th, 1759, between Good-Friday and Easter, and was interred in Westminster Abbey. A monument by Roubillac was erected over the vault in his memory. Complete edition of Handel's works in 100 vols., under the editorship of Friedrich Chrysander. B. & H., Leipzig.—S.B., Nos. 278–280. BIBLIOGRAPHY: E. C. Bairstow, *Handel's Oratorio "The Messiah."* O.U.P., London, 1928.—Michel Brenet, *Haendel.* Laurens, Paris, 1903.—F. Chrysander, *Georg Friedrich Händel.* 3 vols., B. & H., Leipzig, 1919 (unfortunately extends only to 1740).—W. H. Cummings, *Handel.* Bell, London, 1904.—F. Ehrlinger, *Händels Orgelkonzerte* (Erlangen dissertation in preparation).—W. N. Flower, *George Frederic Handel, His Personality and His Times.* Cassell and Co., Ltd., London and New York, 1922.—J. A. Fuller-Maitland, "The Age of Bach and Handel." Vol. IV of the *Oxford History of Music.*—H. Leichentritt, *Händel.* Deutsche Verlaganstalt, Stuttgart, Berlin, 1924.—J. Müller-Blattau, *Händel.* Athenaion, Potsdam, 1933.—Percy Robinson, *Handel and His Orbit.* Sherratt and Hughes, London, 1908.— Rockstro, *Life of George Frederick Handel.* Macmillan and Co., London, 1883.—Romain Rolland, *Haendel.* Alcan, Paris, 1910; by the same author, *Voyage au pays du passé.* Chapter III. Hachette, Paris, 1920.—Streatfeild, *Handel.* J. Lane Co., New York, 1909; Methuen, London.—Sedley Taylor, *The Indebtedness of Handel to Works of Other Composers.* Cambridge University Press, 1906.—Fritz Volbach, *Georg Friedrich Händel.* Schlesisch Verlagsanstalt, Berlin, 1898; 3d ed., 1914.

easily accessible in piano score in the Universal Edition, Vienna. The work consists of touching family scenes, psychological portrayals of emotions, as they reveal themselves in the most intimate circle.

Handel placed the oratorio on an entirely different basis. His biographer, F. Chrysander, once showed in a lecture how Handel's oratorios, taken in their totality, relate the history of the Jewish people. As a matter of fact, he presents national dramas. Handel made use, as did no other composer, of the advantage which music possesses over the spoken word of being able to present the masses, to make real their feelings and their actions.

Handel had passed through the Neapolitan school; he wrote numerous operas in the Neapolitan style. To be sure, they contain many beautiful passages, but they do not present Handel in his entirety. He could not present his best and most original self in a foreign form. Like Gluck and Mozart at a later time, he too had to wrestle his way through to his inmost self.

England, with its choral system organized from early times on a grand scale, offered him his opportunity. The collapse of his London operatic undertakings was a personal misfortune for him, but it was a fortunate thing for art, because it opened Handel's eyes, and pointed out his better path.

Of course he was filled with a devotion to opera. In his oratorios, too, he originally wanted to present music dramas, and the very fact that he disposed these into three acts indicates that he intended to attach himself to the opera and not to the oratorio. He had his first oratorio, *Esther*, presented in scenic form (1731). It was only the objection of the Bishop of London, who was unwilling to allow theatrical presentations of biblical history, that caused all later performances to take place in concert form. The texts of most of Handel's oratorios are purely dramatic, have no narrator, and could be presented on the stage. Their character is also dramatic, yet not theatrical. Superb dramatic effects are to be found in them; and yet the rich musical nature of Handel expends itself in them in an epic grandeur which would be disadvantageous, indeed impossible in a stage drama. The stage demands concentration, as it is found in the case of Gluck, in contrast to Handel. For the latter, the oratorio was the native form.

Handel places the chorus in the center of his works; with this he attains monumental effects and the ability to bring national events and national sentiments to expression. In all this he succeeded in the highest degree, as when, e.g., in his *Belshazzar*, the Jews, the Babylonians, and the Persians are juxtaposed in most colorful and dramatic manner. *Judas Maccabaeus*, as is well known, is a truly national oratorio of liberty. But the sufferings and struggles of the entire nation are most superbly expressed in *Israel in Egypt*. So far as poetic form is concerned, this oratorio, like *The Messiah*, is an exception; it is not constructed dramatically, but epically. But here also one perceives the nation as a dramatic hero, with whom one feels and suffers. The famous lamentation choruses remain unexcelled from the point of view of the art of characterization in the exalted style.

By nature Handel was disposed toward the simple and the monumental, but he had not passed through the Neapolitan school in vain. Here he had learned to express himself simply, beautifully, and vocally; and his special significance lies in his ability to unite perfect artistry with the element of popularity, depth with sensuous beauty. The "Hallelujah Chorus" from *The Messiah* is an imperishable monument of this, his own peculiar gift. The chorus "See the Conq'ring Hero Comes" from *Judas Maccabaeus*, the *Messiah* aria "I Know That My Redeemer Liveth," and many another piece have become common property.

The excellent qualities of Handel show themselves in his arias no less than in his choruses. Some from otherwise forgotten operas have also maintained themselves in our treasury of music, as the "Lascia ch'io pianga" from *Rinaldo*, or the world famous "Largo" from *Xerxes*.

The wealth of invention in Handel's arias is inexhaustible, as is also his ability to characterize accurately with the simplest means, and at the same time in the most beautifully sensuous form. Suffice it to recall just two examples. In the oratorio *Samson*, Micha bewails his son deprived of his sight in the following phrase:

He surely could not express his grief in a more genuine or profound manner. The following well-known tenor melody from *Alexander's Feast* requires no special explanation:

Yet another characteristic of Handel must be especially emphasized, a trait which distinguishes him from the Italians, namely, his love of nature. The appreciation of nature can be traced through German music like a golden thread, from the minnesingers and the *Volkslied* to Richard Wagner and Anton Bruckner, and beyond. It appears in Handel in the most winsome manner. A work that is especially redolent with impressions from nature is the secular oratorio, on the text by Milton, *L'allegro, il pensieroso ed il moderato*, in which the most varied sounds of nature are presented, as well as dusk and moonlight; even quite modern romanticism appears, as in the bass aria with horn obligato:

Bach and Religious Music

The modern musician generally considers Bach [17] the beginning of music, whereas, as a matter of fact, he really represents the conclusion

[17] JOHANN SEBASTIAN BACH (b. Eisenach, 1685; d. Leipzig, 1750) was a son of the municipal musician (Ratsmusikant) Ambrosius Bach in Eisenach. He became orphaned in his tenth year, and went to live with his brother Johann Christoph, organist in Ohrdruf. It was a matter of course that Johann Sebastian devoted himself to music, for the Bach family had provided all Thuringia with organists and pipers since the seventeenth century. A great number of distinguished artists blossomed forth on this family tree; indeed the musicians in general, in the Thuringia of that time, were simply called "*the Bachs*." In the year 1700, when Bach was 15 years of age, he became a soprano singer in the pupils' choir of the Michaeligymnasium, St. Michael's school, in Lüneburg. Without doubt, the organist at St. John's Church in Lüneburg, the distinguished composer, Georg Böhm, exercised a considerable influence upon him at that time. Endowed both with a thirst for knowledge and a Wanderlust, Bach made a pilgrimage to Hamburg in order to hear the organist Reinken, and to Celle, where the court chapel or orchestra had been formed after the Parisian model of Lully. He obtained his first position in 1703 as a violinist in the private orchestra of Prince Johann Ernst of Saxony in Weimar, but in the same year he moved to Arnstadt where he was engaged as organist. In 1705–06 he journeyed from here to Lübeck in order to become acquainted with the organist Buxtehude, and to hear the famous Evening Musicales which Buxtehude had instituted in Lübeck. He outstayed his leave, much to the displeasure of the congregation at Arnstadt. The latter, however, avoided an actual rupture with the young genius. In 1707 Bach became organist at Mühlhausen in Thuringia, and there wedded his cousin Maria Barbara Bach. In 1708 he came to Weimar as court organist and chamber-musician, and in 1714 became court concert-master there. In 1717 he went to Cöthen as court Kapellmeister to Prince Leopold of Anhalt. Here he had neither organ nor choir at his disposal, and hence directed his attention chiefly to orchestral composition. The Brandeburg Concertos were written here. His wife died in 1720. In 1721 he married Anna Magdalena Wülken, a singer of talent. Chiefly for the sake of the further education of his children, he applied for the position of cantor at St. Thomas' in Leipzig. He entered upon his position there in 1723, and continued in this capacity until his death. The musical forces over which Bach presided in Leipzig were very modest, a very small choir and a limited orchestra. The more marvellous is the power of his works. Among his sons four gained distinction as composers: WILHELM FRIEDEMANN (b. Weimar, 1710;

of a great development. His works are like a dome which spans a mighty structure. To be sure, in a certain sense the modern musician is correct;

---

d. Berlin, 1784) was endowed with genius, but given to a dissolute life. He was at first organist in Dresden, 1733–47, then in Halle until 1764, later living a more or less migratory existence. CARL PHILIPP EMANUEL (b. Weimar, 1714; d. Hamburg, 1788) was called the "Berlin" or "Hamburg" Bach. He studied law in Frankfurt on the Oder, became chamber-harpsichordist to Frederick the Great in Berlin in 1740, and Director of Church Music in Hamburg, as successor to Telemann, in 1767. JOHANN CHRISTOPH FRIEDRICH (b. Leipzig, 1732; d. Bückeburg, 1795), called the "Bückeburg" Bach, at first studied law, but in 1756 became master of the chapel of the count of Lippe. JOHANN CHRISTIAN (b. Leipzig, 1735; d. London, 1782), called the "Milan" or "London" Bach, was a pupil of his brother Phil. Emanuel. He tended toward a lighter manner of composition, and became a chief representative of the so-called "galant" style. In 1754 he went to Milan, and became organist of the cathedral there in 1760, after having embraced the Roman Catholic faith. In 1762 he came to London, becoming music-master to the queen in 1763, and conducting with Abel the famous subscription concerts after 1764. His chief works are operas and symphonies. He exerted a strong influence upon Mozart. BIBLIOGRAPHY: The first biography of Bach, that of Forkel (*Über J. S. Bachs Leben, Kunst, und Kunstwerke*, 1802) has been edited by J. M. Müller-Blattau. Bärenreiter Verlag, Augsburg, 1925; Eng. tr. and Appendices by C. S. Terry. Constable and Co., Ltd., London, 1920.—R. Boughton, *Bach*. Lane, London, 1907.—Th. Gérold, *J. S. Bach*. Laurens, Paris, 1925.—J. A. Fuller-Maitland, *Bach's "48."* O.U.P., London, 1925; by the same author, *The Age of Bach and Handel*. O.U.P., 1902; 2d ed., 1931; by the same author, *The Keyboard Suites of J. S. Bach*. O.U.P., London, 1925.—Harvey Grace, *The Organ Works of Bach*. Novello & Co., Ltd., London, H. W. Gray & Co., New York, 1922.—A. Heuss, *J. S. Bachs Matthäuspassion*. B. & H., Leipzig, 1909.—F. Iliffe, *The 48 Preludes and Fugues of J. S. B., Analyzed for the Use of Students*. Novello, London, 1896; 1902; Novello, Ewer & Co., N. Y., 1906.—E. Kurth, *Grundlagen des linearen Kontrapunkts, Einführung in Stil und Technik von Bachs melodischer Polyphonie*. Max Hesse, Berlin, 1917; 2d ed., 1922.—C. H. H. Parry, *J. S. Bach: The Story of the Development of a Great Personality*. G. P. Putnam's Sons, New York and London, 1909.—André Pirro, *L'Orgue de J. S. Bach*. Fischbacher, Paris, 1895; Eng. tr. by Wallace Goodrich, G. Schirmer, New York, 1902; by the same author, *J. S. Bach*. Alcan, Paris, 1906; 5th ed. 1919; German tr. by Engelke, Schuster & Loeffler, Berlin, 1910; by the same author, *L Esthétique de J. S. Bach*. Fischbacher, Paris, 1907.—E. Prout, *Analyses of Bach's "48."* Ashdown, London; by the same author, *Some Notes on Bach's Church Cantatas*. B. & H., Leipzig, 1907. Max Schneider, full bibliography: *Bach Jahrbuch*, 1905, pp. 76 ff., and 1910, pp. 133 ff.; also in C. S. Terry's edition of Forkel, pp. 287 ff.—Albert Schweitzer, *J. S. Bach, le musicien poète*. B. & H., Leipzig, 1905; Ger. tr. enlarged, B. & H., Leipzig, 1908; Eng. tr. by Ernest Newman, 2 vols., B. & H., Leipzig, 1911, A. & C. Black, Ltd., London, 1923.—Ph. Spitta, *J. S. Bach*. 2 vols., B. & H., Leipzig, 3d ed., 1921; Eng. tr. by Clara Bell and J. A. Fuller-Maitland. 3 vols., Novello and Co., London, Novello, Ewer, & Co., New York, 1899.— C. S. Terry. *Bach's Chorals*. 3 vols., Cambridge University Press, Cambridge, 1915–21; by the same author, *B Minor Mass*. O.U.P., London, 1924; by the same author, *Bach's Cantato Texts*. Constable, London, 1926; by the same author, *Bach's Cantatas and Oratorios* O.U.P., London, 1925; by the same author, *Bach's Passions*. 2 Parts, O.U.P., London, 1925; by the same author, *Bach's Orchestra*. O.U.P., London, 1932; by the same author, *J. S. Bach, a Biography*. O.U.P., London, 1928; by the same author, *The Music of Bach, an Introduction*. O.U.P., London, 1933; by the same author, *The Origins of the Family of Bach Musicians*. O.U.P., London, 1929.—W. G. Whittaker, *Fugitive Notes on certain Cantatas and the Motets of J. S. Bach*. O.U.P., London, 1925.—C. F. Abdy Williams, *Bach* in "Master Musicians." Dent. London, 1934.—Ph. Wolfrum, *J. S. Bach*. 2 vols., B. & H.. Leipzig, revised ed., 1910.—The *St. Matthew Passion*, the *B Minor Mass*,

only in the nineteenth century did Bach come fully into his own; in a sense, he is the beginning of modern music.

He did not have the good fortune to get to Italy, but for this very reason he preserved a rugged Teutonism in his works. The great music world of his day, under the spell of the mellifluent tones of the Neapolitan school, neither regarded nor understood the genius of Bach. His compositions were regarded as bombastic; indeed, he was compared with Lohenstein, the representative of bombast in literature. Apart from his small North-German circle of organ pupils, he exerted no influence upon his time. Very few of his works were printed, the large ones were for the most part performed by him only, and all of them, with the exception of the *Well-Tempered Clavichord* and the motets, were forgotten after his death. It was Mendelssohn who first awoke them from their slumber through his epoch-making performance of the St. Matthew Passion in the year 1829. From then on, but only from then on, all composers became pupils of Bach. Wagner, Brahms, and Reger are his disciples even more than Mendelssohn and Schumann.

In his own day, Bach was properly esteemed only as an organ virtuoso. His marvellous art and skill in this field could not remain unrecognized. The organ is also the center of his creative activity. All his works are more or less dominated by the organ style. For vocal style, Bach is not an example worthy of emulation. Here Palestrina remains the eternally valid classic. Bach writes instrumental counterpoint for the voices also. To be sure, it is not necessary to mention the power with which he makes this subservient to his wishes.

Every consideration of Bach must take its departure from the chorales. They, too, stand under the influence of his organ style. But what perfect works of art they are in their own class! In these, Bach unites his highest technical mastery and unlimited genius for profound expression with the most simple and naïve form. More genuine content in fewer measures

the *Brandenburg Concertos*, and a number of the Cantatas can be obtained as miniature full scores (Goodwin & Tabb). Concerning the sons of Bach, cf. K. H. Bitter, *Carl Ph. Emanuel Bach und Wilhelm Friedemann Bach und deren Brüder*. 2 vols. W. Müller, Berlin, 1868.—Martin Falk, *Wilhelm Friedemann Bach* (Leipzig dissertation). C. F. Kahnt Nachfolger, Leipzig, 1913.—H. P. Schökel, *J. Christian Bach und die Instrumentalmusik seiner Zeit*. G. Kallmeyer, Wolfenbüttel, 1926.—Charles Sanford Terry, *John Chr. Bach, A Biography*. O.U.P., London, 1929.—Fr. Tutenberg, *Die Sinfonik Johann Christian Bachs*. Kallmeyer, Wolfenbüttel, 1928.—Ten Sonatas by Joh. Chr. Bach have been published under the editorship of L. Landshoff. Peters, 1925.—Complete edition of Bach's works, published by the Bachgesellschaft, 1815–1900, in 56 vols., B. & H., Leipzig.— E.B., No. 34.—R.B., Nos. 130 and 131.—S.A., No. 59 a.—S.B., Nos. 283–286.

can nowhere be found than in these polyphonic, four-part settings of simple church hymns.

As the Gregorian choral was for Palestrina the framework of his labors, so for Bach was the Protestant church hymn. It fulfilled the high mission of bridging over the gulf between Bach's complicated creations and the emotional life of the masses, and thus making these accessible to the great generality of listeners.

If one wishes to understand Bach, one must first comprehend him, as one does Palestrina, as a church musician. A large part of his work serves the purposes of the liturgy. What the Mass is for Palestrina, that the church cantata is for Bach. The Catholic Palestrina had the advantage in having at his disposal a universally recognized Latin text of eternal content, whereas the Protestant Bach had to set the insipid versifications of his contemporaries. A tragic lot befell German music in the eighteenth century that Handel, Gluck, and Mozart were compelled to compose to foreign languages, and that Bach had only shallow German poems at his command.

The church cantata is adapted in its content to the particular significance of each Sunday and festival of the church year; in other words, it is altogether liturgical. Every Sunday in Leipzig in Bach's day a cantata was performed in the service—as is still customary. Bach wrote five complete sets of cantatas for the church year, but only two hundred have survived. In these works he pursued all the paths suggested by his inexhaustible invention. He attempted everything that seemed to his genius worth attempting, vocal, instrumental, and harmonic. The cantatas are a musical cosmos, and it has been said that there is nothing in modern music which is not already contained in the cantatas of Bach. However, one must never lose sight of the fact that the cantatas will have their full effect only in the service; their composer did not write them for the concert hall.

Beside the cantatas stand the motets, which do not have an independent orchestral accompaniment. In pure choral effects, they belong to the most sublime works of art in existence, and they almost strike terror with their mighty pulsations reminding one of storm-wind and moaning sea.

In a wider sense, the Passions must also be reckoned as church music. They were intended for the minor services during Holy Week. They have contributed most to the glory of Bach, and have again become universally familiar. A contributory factor has doubtless been the circumstance that, in part at least, they are based upon the dignified scriptural text, and also that in their case, at any rate in the *St. Matthew Passion*, the contemporary poetic addition by Picander is comparatively good. In themselves, of course, they represent heights which are attained only seldom in a century; and in addition to this, Bach has won the historical merit of having conducted the Passion back into the Church, whence it came, and where alone it belongs.

We have seen how the Passion arose in the Middle Ages as an especial form of recitative in the Gregorian choral. In the great choral period the strange custom arose of composing the biblical Passion text throughout in the form of motets, everything being in concerted form, even the speeches of the individual persons. It has already been observed how Schütz developed the Passion in a characteristic manner. In his day the oratorio-Passion also arose, which treats the Passion story as an oratorio, with soli, chorus, and orchestra. This is the form which Bach uses. At that time it prospered in Hamburg, but under the influence of the Hamburg opera, it had received a strongly worldly, theatrical quality. Bach again restored its churchly character.

The chorales, which represent, as it were, the Christian congregation, again occupy a central position. As Bach had combined in the 371 chorales individually, on a small scale, highest art with perfect popularity, so he does the same in the Passions on a great scale, especially in the *Passion according to St. Matthew*. He avoids such forms as fugue and canon, which might create the impression of being present or employed merely on account of their artistic treatment. But that does not prevent him from using his highest skill, as in the architectonically monumental creation of the very opening number of the *St. Matthew Passion*, with its dramatic double choir and double orchestra, and its choral superimposed above them. A fine representation of the sublimity of the Kingdom of God in which each one has his place!

The Passions represent a remarkable combination of epic and drama. They are neither, but are church music. The believing Christian here follows the Lenten story with a passionate participation as an artist— as an ingenious and imaginative artist, as Bach was—he immerses himself in its individual moments, now with dramatic, now with lyrical, emotion, or he follows the external situations presented with epic breadth and vividness, but he always does so from the stand-point of a marveling and grateful devotion. Only with such a conception, will one arrive at a genuine understanding, but never if one applies and sets up purely esthetic principles and dramatic demands. That would be as erroneous as to judge the ceremonies of the Catholic ritual from the point of view of a theatrical performance.

Between the Passions and the colossal *B Minor Mass*, the charming *Magnificat* takes its place, a Protestant homage to Mary. Bach composed his Mass for the Roman Catholic court at Dresden. While the Passions are still "occasional" music, in the highest sense of the term, in the Mass Bach did obeisance to the principle *L'art pour l'art*, at least according to his own conception of this principle, inasmuch as he subjected himself to no limitations in this work. Whether the work is adapted to use in the Church, whether its execution may present difficulties or not, whether it will appeal to the public, about all this Bach did not inquire. He simply immersed himself in the text, and interpreted it with all the colossal art which was his. Of course this does not imply that it has in any way become an artificial work. Bach was a son of the people, and even if he could not introduce any church hymns, the fresh notes of the song of the people nevertheless resound more than once from the richly woven fugues. Is there a melody of greater naturalness than that of the Gloria:

Beside such melodies there are, of course, themes of the most refined power of expression, as the well-known Kyrie Eleison:

The entire work, in its limitless yet wonderfully ordered richness, is one of the most exalted temples ever constructed by the hand of man to the glory of God.

CHURCH MUSIC IN ITALY

At the head of the church music of the Neapolitan school stands its leader, Alessandro Scarlatti himself, of great significance in this field also. Following is the beginning of a cantata which depicts the anguish of the Virgin in accents that cannot fail to move:

Violins:

Bass:

Voice: Il mio fi - -glio ov' è   che fa   do-ve sta la mi-a gio   a

il mi-o te - - - -sor   ov' è che fa,   Fi-glio   che fa, do-ve sta?

The specialist in church music, Francesco Durante (1684–1755), wrote Masses, Psalms, motets, antiphones, hymns, lamentations, *duetti da camera*,[18] etc. Important works are the two entitled *Stabat Mater*, the one by E. d'Astorga,[19] the other by Pergolesi, both of which combine sweetness and exquisite beauty of melodic line with tender and heartfelt expression.[20] The Psalm compositions of Benedetto Marcello [21] still stand high in general favor. Antonio Lotti [22] is another master who has

[18] A chamber duet by Durante will be found in R.B., No. 136; 3 vols. of chamber duets have been published by B. & H.

[19] EMANUELE D'ASTORGA (b. Augusta, Sicily, 1680; d. Spain, 1757). BIBLIOGRAPHY: H. Volkmann, *Emmanuele d'Astorga*. 2 vols., B. & H., Leipzig, 1911 and 1919. NEW EDITIONS: *Stabat Mater*, published by Leuckart and by B. & H., Leipzig.

[20] Cf. R.B., Nos. 135, 137; and S.A., Nos. 69, 70; and S.B., No. 275.

[21] BENEDETTO MARCELLO (b. Venice, 1686; d. Brescia, 1739), was, like d'Astorga, an able dilettant, one of that distinguished kind that has made the appellation dilettant a title of glory in Italy. There are numerous editions of his famous Psalm compositions of the Italian paraphrases by G. A. Giustiniani, the most recent, with Italian and French text, under the editorship of Mirecki, published by Carli in Paris (piano and voice), c. 1820.— A new edition of the satirical work *Il teatro alla moda*, 1722, in Italian, under the editorship of E. Fondi, Lauciano, R. Carabba, 1913; in German, *Das Theater nach der Mode*, under the editorship of A. Einstein in the *Perlen älterer romanischer Prosa*, Vol. XXIV. G. Müller, Munich & Berlin, 1917; French by E. David, *Le Théatre a la mode*. Fischbacher, Paris, 1890.—A cantata and an arietta of Marcello are to be found in the collection Hettich. Leduc, Paris, Vol. XI.—Violoncello sonatas by Salmon, Ricordi; also arranged for violin.

[22] ANTONIO LOTTI (b. Venice, 1667; d. there, 1740), was a pupil of Legrenzi, and rose through various positions as organist to that of master of the chapel at St. Mark's in 1736. From 1717 to 1719 he sojourned in Dresden, where he wrote numerous operas, as he had

survived the centuries as a church composer. His reputation is based especially upon his dramatic *Crucifixus* for six voices, concerning which Kretzschmar says, that as a plastic tone picture it is a bull's-eye of the first class, but as a part of a *Credo*, as fitting as a pistol shot from the pulpit.[23] This, of course, intimates that the church music of the day, under the influence of the opera, frequently deserted its churchly character. Nevertheless, there still exists, beside these divagations, churchly art; and Lotti himself wrote *a cappella* Masses which are serious and worthy of their great exemplars.[24]

Important representatives of the stricter tendency are G. Pitoni, master of the papal chapel in Rome, Pater Martini in Bologna, Antonio Caldara[25] and J. J. Fux in Vienna. The high and serious art of the last two especially deserves a general renaissance. The *Stabat Mater* of Caldara, less well-known than that of Pergolese, is scarcely less beautiful. A fragment of the piece *Sancta Mater*, written for four voices and instruments, is shown on page 230.

In his *Gradus ad Parnassum* (Latin, 1725, German, 1742), Fux laid down in classical manner the old doctrine of vocal counterpoint.

In the second half of the eighteenth century, church music became more and more secularized. The church compositions of Hasse and related German masters, of which this must be said, as well as those of the Italian composers, are to be reckoned to the Neapolitan school. In a certain sense those of Haydn and Mozart must also extensively submit to the charge of being unchurchly. To be sure there are exceptions, a very great one being the famous *Requiem* by Mozart.

previously done for Venice. His chief importance lies in the sphere of church music. New editions of individual works may be found in the collections of Rochlitz, Proske, and Commer.—A volume of Masses, ed. by Herm. Müller, D.d.T., Vol. LX.—An aria from the opera *Alessandro severo* will be found in S.B., No. 270.

[23] Kretzschmar, *Führer*, II, 1, 4th ed., p. 181. The allusion is to the title of the novel *Der Schuss von der Kanzel* by Conrad Ferdinand Meyer. Vol. III, Sämmtliche Werke, Taschenausgabe, H. Haessel, Leipzig, 1922–31; 3d ed., 1882, ed. by M. H. Haertel, Ginn and Co., Boston and New York, 1905.

[24] A *Kyrie* of a Mass in G minor for four voices will be found in R.B., No. 128.

[25] ANTONIO CALDARA (b. Venice, 1670; d. Vienna, 1736) was a pupil of Legrenzi, sojourned for some time in Venice, Rome, and Madrid, and finally settled in Vienna where he was assistant master of the chapel to Fux. He wrote 87 operas and 31 oratorios. His strength lies especially in his church and instrumental music. BIBLIOGRAPHY: The operas are discussed by A. Gmeyner (Vienna dissertation), 1927.—The oratorios are discussed by A. Schering, *Geschichte des Oratoriums*, pp. 205 ff. NEW EDITIONS: A "Trio Sonata" in Riemann's *Collegium musicum*.—Church works in the D.T.OE., Vol. XIII, 1, under the editorship of Mandyczewski.—For a *Crucifixus* by Caldara, cf. S.A., No. 55.—The beginning of the *Stabat Mater* for chorus and orchestra, in S.B., No. 273.

D.T.Œ., Vol. XIII.

Instrumental Music in the First Half of the Eighteenth Century [26]

The transition from the seventeenth to the eighteenth century does not show any gap; there are no changes and novelties in the development of instrumental music, but on the contrary, there is a quiet growth toward efflorescence. This appears in all fields. All the forms of the seventeenth century reached the highest degree of development in the first half of the eighteenth. The fruits became ripe, and the period succeeding this culmination had to enter with an entirely new development.

[26] BIBLIOGRAPHY: Michel Brenet, *Les Concerts en France sous l'ancien régime*. Fischbacher, Paris, 1900.—G. Cucuel, *La Pouplinière et la musique de chambre au XVIIIe siècle*. Fischbacher, Paris, 1913.—L. de la Laurencie, "La Musique instrumentale en France," in Enc. Lav., II, pp. 1491–1535.—By the same author, *Études sur un orchestre du XVIIIe siècle*. Fischbacher. Paris. 1913.

An entire line of masters marks this efflorescence, and among them a single one, *J. S. Bach*, achieved the highest in all forms. With him the unusual genius of the Germans for instrumental music announces itself for the first time and in an astounding manner.

In his four orchestral suites Bach created classical examples of this old German form. One of the two magnificent ones in D major has become popular; its well-known "Air," arranged for almost all instruments, has become a universal favorite. On hearing its overture in French form, Goethe imagined he saw a procession of groomed people majestically descending a great staircase, and with this picture he characterized poetically not only this piece in particular, but the French overture in general. Just as Bach employed here the brilliant style, he used the rococo in equally masterly manner in the B minor suite with solo flute.

The Viennese, J. J. Fux, approaches Bach in wealth of invention and solidity of form in the orchestral suites of his *Concentus musico-instrumentalis* (1701). A certain Austrian flavor combined with all sorts of instrumental effects produce charming results. In lighter vein is the *Musique de table*, by G. Ph. Telemann, the most famous and most popular composer of Bach's day. It is always amusing, and reminds one of the tone of the present-day café music. Handel, on the other hand, is genuinely great; but his suites, the *Water Music* and the *Fire Music*, with their endless numbers, intended not for concert but for open-air performance, are cumbersome. Yet they are of great interest on account of the variety of their instrumentation, and one could and should, by careful selection, show in public performances how great a palette the eighteenth century employed.

In the domain of the *concerto grosso*, Bach in his *Brandenburg Concertos*, and Handel in his *concerti grossi* for stringed instruments, are equally distinguished, both with regard to the wealth of their ideas, and the manifoldness of their forms, which are related to those of the suite. Bach, moreover, offers a variegated instrumentation. The noble, high-minded F. dall' Abaco,[27] who is to be numbered among the classics of

[27] FELICE DALL' ABACO (b. Verona, 1675; d. Munich, 1742) was an important composer who had long been forgotten. He came to Munich as chamber-musician (cellist) in 1704, sojourned for a time, with the court, in Brussels, later was chamber-concert-master in Munich. NEW EDITIONS: A large selection of his instrumental works (with a biographical study by Sandberger) in the D.T.B., Vols. I & IX, 1.—Three Trio Sonatas in the *Collegium musicum* of Riemann, B. & H.; a third published by Augener, London.—Three violin sonatas published by Ricordi. one by Simrock, one by Schott.—See S.B., No. 277.

the *concerto grosso*, employs a more reposeful style, and prefers the now commonly prevalent tripartite division. The same is to be said concerning Antonio Vivaldi,[28] who also has the distinction of being preëminent in the field of the solo violin concerto. To his name in this field must be added that of Giuseppe Tartini [29] and others. To the Italians is due the credit of having developed the art of violin playing, and for having first created the fine-nerved, expressive, instrumental melody. They did this especially in their solo and trio sonatas, in the old fourfold form, chief composers of which, besides those already mentioned, were Benedetto Marcello, G. B. Pergolesi, F. M. Veracini, G. Pugnani, P. Nardini, and P. Locatelli.[30]

Bach, who learned from the Italians in his use of the instruments, takes his place on an equal footing with these Italian masters in all these fields. It is a well-known fact that he transcribed a number of Vivaldi's violin concertos as clavier concertos. What he achieved in such arrangements, as well as in original concertos for one, two, three, and four claviers, is unique both as to quantity and quality. Handel distinguished himself through his organ concertos and his sonatas for different instruments, compositions very worthy of his name.

In the domain of the organ, Bach stands unexcelled. Nothing can be compared with his fugues and toccatas, which belong to the most sublime masterpieces in the world of music. His choral preludes are

---

[28] ANTONIO VIVALDI (b. Venice, c. 1680; d. there, 1734) was a composer highly valued by J. S. Bach. He was active as violinist at St. Mark's after 1714, and also director of the Ospedale della Pietà, a conservatory for girls. BIBLIOGRAPHY: M. Pincherle, "Antonio Vivaldi," R.M. 1930. NEW EDITIONS: Various concertos and sonatas in the publications of Breitkopf, Kistner, Wernthal, Cranz, Simrock, Augener, and Eulenburg; also in Schering, *Perlen alter Kammermusik deutscher und italienischer Meister*, Kahnt, Leipzig.— S.B., No. 276.

[29] GIUSEPPE TARTINI (b. Pirano, Istria, 1692; d. Padua, 1770). After an agitated youth, with romantic incidents, Tartini, strongly influenced by the violinist Veracini, developed into the most celebrated and greatest master of the violin of his day, and established in Padua, that had become his second home, an excellent school from which proceeded such violinists as Nardini, Gottlieb Graun, Naumann, and many others. His method of bowing became the model for the entire future development. Tartini discovered the resultant or partial tones, and thus also occupies a place in the history of physics. BIBLIOGRAPHY: H. Engel, "Das Instrumentalkonzert," in Kretzschmars *Führer durch den Konzertsaal*, Part I, Vol. III. B. & H., Leipzig, 1932. A. Moser, *Geschichte des Violinspiels*, p. 250 ff. Max Hesse, Berlin, 1923.—W. von Wasielewski, *Die Violine und ihre Meister*.—New editions of his solo and trio sonatas, also of his quartets, in the publications of B. & H., Benjamin, Beyer, André, Leuckart, Peters, Schmidl, Schott, Rieter, and the Società Tipografica, Turin; see also S.B., No. 295.

[30] On French violin music *vide:* L. de la Laurencie, *l'École française de violon*. 3 vols., Delagrave, Paris, 1922; also M. Pincherle, *Les Violonistes*. Laurens, Paris, 1922.

jewels that cannot be found elsewhere in the entire world. Just as little can one find a second *Well-Tempered Clavichord*. On the other hand, so far as the suite is concerned, Handel, the classic representative of the clavier suite, can be placed beside Bach; and the same is true of the Austrian, Gottlieb Muffat, whose *Componimenti musicali* are perfect in form.

The Germans borrowed the dances of their suites from the French, and they also followed these in their general treatment of them; nevertheless there is a great difference between the creations of Bach and Handel, and those of Rameau and Couperin. These two, as is well known, represent the high-water mark of French clavier music; indeed their work belongs to the finest expressions of French spirit in the art of music.

François Couperin [31] deserves particular mention as a specializing genius of the clavier, like Froberger or Chopin. His characteristic observation *J'avoueray de bonne foy, que j'aime beaucoup mieux ce qui me touche, que ce qui me surprend* (I confess openly that I love that which stimulates me much more than that which overwhelms me) is familiar. One must not look for overwhelming passion in his music; but in his four books *Pièces de clavecin*, which appeared in 1713, 1716, 1722, and 1730, a veritable world picture book, an *orbis pictus*, he has presented with a delightful charm and sureness, with an amazing precision, everything that can in any way be expressed in tone. As a color genius, he draws forth every tonal charm that slumbers in the clavecin.

[31] FRANÇOIS COUPERIN LE GRAND (b. Paris, 1668; d. there, 1733) sprang from a musical family which provided France with organists in a manner similar to, though not as extensively as, the Bachs in Thuringia. In 1693 he became court-harpsichordist and teacher of the princes; in 1698, the successor of his uncle Louis as organist at Saint-Gervais. BIBLIOGRAPHY: Cf. the books and articles cited on p. 203, note 101.—M. Roberts, English editor, *L'Art de toucher le clavecin* (The art of playing the harpsichord) *1717*. B. & H., Leipzig, 1933. NEW EDITIONS: *Complete Works.* 12 vols., Edition de l'Oiseau-Lyre, Paris, 1933.— An edition of the complete works has also been undertaken by the house of Durand, Paris, 1932 ff. So far there have appeared: 4 vols. of *Pièces de clavecin*, concertos for violin and clavecin, trio sonatas, concertos and symphonies for 2 violins and violoncello, etc.—Brahms and Chrysander, editors, *Pièces de clavecin*, in the *Denkmäler der Tonkunst of Chrysander*, Vol. IV. Bergedorf near Hamburg, Expedition der Denkmäler, and Rieter-Biedermann, Leipzig, 1869–71; 4 books, by these editors, have been published by Augener, London.— Vocal works have been published by Demets, Paris.—See also J. Bouvet, editor, "Anthologie des maîtres anciens du violon:" *Pièces pour violon et piano.* Janin, Lyon, 1925.—G.M.B., No. 264 a, b.—M. Pauer, *Alte Meister des Klavierspiels.*—K. H. Pillney, *Altfranzösische Meister.* Cotta, Stuttgart & Berlin.—Roloff, a small volume of popular numbers, published by Augener, London.

Besides Couperin, one can cite among the French authors of works for the harpsichord in the eighteenth century, Louis Marchand (1669–1732), L. N. Clerambault (1676–1749), Elisabeth Jacquet de la Guerre, Gaspard Le Roux, Dagincour, and Rameau.[32]

Domenico Scarlatti [33] obtains similar results, but in a different manner, with Italian *brio*. His clavecin pieces form a special class. They are generally called sonatas, but he himself called them *Essercizi*. Today one would call them concert *études*, because for the first time they bring pianistic virtuosity into its own, with their runs and arpeggios, that belong specifically to the piano. He also applied special devices, such as the crossing of hands. A technical-tonal problem serves as the point of departure in every one of the *Essercizi*. They do not attempt to be profound, but effective and brilliant. At the same time this does not mean that they are superficial; they are always elegant and scintillating.

Formally, they limit themselves to one movement. They may, accordingly, be viewed as the last representatives of the old canzonas and capriccios. In their division into two parts, with a repetition of each part, they already anticipate the modern first sonata movement. As in Germany through Kuhnau, so in Italy through Bernardo Pasquini (1637–1710), the old form of the sonata for stringed instruments was transferred to the clavier. In certain respects the *Essercizi* of Domenico Scarlatti point to the coming sonata, in the development of which the Italians still coöperated, but which, in the time of its maturity, they altogether abandoned to the Germans. In this field also, Bach, who literally stands in the vanguard of the whole musical development, takes a hand, especially with his *Italian Concerto* which, written for piano only, without orchestral accompaniment, anticipates in a remarkable manner the later classical sonata with its tripartite division. It is as though Bach

---

[32] Cf. André Pirro, *Les Clavecinistes*. Laurens, Paris, 1924.—See also S.B., No. 296 c.
[33] DOMENICO SCARLATTI (b. Naples, 1685; d. there, 1757) was the son of Alessandro Scarlatti and wrote operas, like his father, but was especially celebrated as a master of the harpsichord. As such he was even victorious over Handel in a contest in Rome. In 1719 he went to London, 1721 to Lisbon as teacher of the princesses at the Portuguese court. In 1725 he is again in Naples, 1729 in Madrid, whither he had been drawn by his former pupil, the princess Magdalena Teresa, who was married to the crown-prince of Spain, the subsequent Ferdinand VI. In 1754 he again returned to Naples. NEW EDITIONS: A critical complete edition of the clavier works, under the editorship of Longo, has been published by Ricordi, Milan.—Czerny, 200 pieces, published by Schlesinger.—Sixty pieces published by B. & H., Leipzig,—Thomas Dunhill has edited 29 Sonatas. Augener, London; cf. also. *Fifty Harpsichord Lessons*, Augener, London.—See S.B., No. 282[1,2].

had a presentiment of what was about to appear. Like Moses, he viewed the promised land without actually setting foot upon it.

OPERA BUFFA AND OPÉRA COMIQUE [34]

The comic opera made its appearance as the earliest reaction against the all-dominating formalism of the beginning of the eighteenth century. In France and in England it first appears in modest form as a parody of the great opera. In Paris there existed at the end of the seventeenth century the *théâtre de la foire* in which both the serious drama and the opera were parodied, the latter primarily by means of folk melodies. By 1712, it had assumed the proud title *opéra comique*, and under the ingenious poets Lesage and Favart produced genuine operettas.

In London, the poet John Gay and the musician J. Ch. Pepusch collaborated in the production of the *Beggar's Opera*, 1728, which also limiting itself primarily to popular airs, derided the Italian opera, and had such great success that it contributed greatly to the fall of Handel's operatic ventures.

Fertile beginnings, which led to the formation of an independent comic opera, arose in the dominant home of opera, in Naples itself. Here, in the third decade of the eighteenth century, lively intermezzi began to be interpolated between the acts of the serious operas. Originally, these were in the Neapolitan dialect. One of these, written, however, not in dialect, *La serva padrona* (The Servant as Mistress), by Giovanni Battista Pergolesi (1710–36), produced in Naples for the first time in the year 1733, won the greatest success, and may be designated as the actual beginning of comic opera. The simple plot of *La serva padrona* deals with the servant's notifying her master of her leaving, whereupon the master, foreseeing all kinds of inconveniences and pressed by her intrigues, finally resolves to marry her, which, of course, was her original object. There are only three characters in the play, one of whom is silent. But the little play is so lively in its music, so telling in its characterization, so full of jests and humor, that it has

---

[34] BIBLIOGRAPHY: Nicola d'Arienzo, *Origini dell' opera comica*. Rivista Musicale Italiana, VII: 1, 1900; printed separately by Fratelli Bocca, Turin; German translation, *Die Entstehung der komischen Oper*, by F. Lugscheider. H. Seemann Nachfolger, Leipzig, 1902.— G. E. Bonnet, *Philidor et l'évolution de la musique française au XVIIIᵉ siècle*. Delagrave, Paris, 1921.—G. Cucuel, *Les Createurs de l'opéra-comique français*. Alcan, Paris, 1914.— L. de la Laurencie, "L'Opéra-comique en France au XVIIIᵉ siècle" in Enc. Lav., II, pp. 1457 ff.

continued as a masterpiece of the first rank until the present day. It is the oldest opera that still maintains its place in the operatic repertoire.

In the year 1752, an Italian opera troupe brought *La serva padrona* to Paris. The jovial piece went off like a rocket. The devotees of music immediately divided into two camps, the buffonists and the antibuffonists, the latter sensing a danger for the holy tradition of grand opera in the new free-spirited creation. Jean Jacques Rousseau [35] came to the defense of *La serva padrona;* naturally, because in the new genre he perceived the accomplishment of that which he preached, a return to nature. In order to appreciate the effect which the jovial doings of the Italian buffonists must have created, one must remember that the female singers of the grand opera always appeared in corsets and hoop skirts, and that everyone was presented in the style of the day, whether god, hero, or peasant. The Italians restored actual life to the theater. This must have affected spirits like those of Jean Jacques Rousseau as a veritable liberation.

The always glowingly enthusiastic Genevan philosopher himself also immediately took a practical hand in the matter. He wrote a little French operetta in the style of the Italian *intermezzi*, entitled *Le Devin du village* (The Village Soothsayer) which he had performed in the year 1752. It had a tremendous success. Even Louis XV sang—as falsely as enthusiastically—the favorite arietta "J'ai perdu mon serviteur—J'ai perdu tout mon bonheur."

Even though Rousseau was no great musician, his operetta nevertheless became the model for the French comic opera. This was taken up anew and soon blossomed forth, its chief representatives being E. R. Duni (1709–75), F. A. Danican Philidor (1726–95),[36] P. Alex. Mon-

---

[35] JEAN JACQUES ROUSSEAU (b. Geneva, 1712; d. Ermenonville, near Paris, 1778). Not only Rousseau's opera-comique, but his melodrama *Pygmalion* as well, which latter work was the first of its kind, gave strong impetus to the lighter operatic movement. BIBLIOGRAPHY: Edgar Istel, *J. J. Rousseau als Komponist seiner lyrischen Szene Pygmalion.* B. & H., Leipzig, 1901.—A. Jansen, *J. J. Rousseau als Musiker.* G. Reimer, Berlin, 1884.—Julien Tiersot, *J. J. Rousseau.* Alcan, 2d ed., revised, 1920. New edition of the *Devin du village*, piano and voice, Geneva, Henn, 1924.

[36] FRANÇOIS ANDRÉ DANICAN PHILIDOR (b. Dreux, 1726; d. London, 1795) was famous as a traveling chess player, as well as a composer. He wrote both comic and serious operas. His *Tom Jones* (1765) employs for the first time in operatic history an *a cappella* quartet. (Cf. the quintet in the *Meistersinger.*) BIBLIOGRAPHY: G. Allen, *The Life of Philidor.* E. H. Butler & Co., Philadelphia, 1863.—G. E. Bonnet, *Philidor et l'évolution de la musique française au XVIIIe siècle.* Delagrave, Paris, 1921.

signy (1729–1817),[37] and F. J. Gossec (1734–1829).[38] Its classic representative is André Ernest Modeste Grétry.[39]

The high literary culture which characterizes France stood the comic opera in good stead, as it had done in the case of the grand opera. Under the influence of the *bourgeois* drama, introduced by Diderot, poets like Favart, Sedaine, and Marmontel created worthwhile libretti. A characteristic piece of this class is the *Deserteur*, by Sedaine-Monsigny, a somewhat sentimental narrative of the eleventh-hour rescue of a deserter who is in love. The piece also became a favorite in Germany; it was repeated everywhere over and over again, and even Heinrich Heine enjoyed its sweet innocence and the fragrance of its forest flowers. That the music is not devoid of subtle charm is made clear by the duet "Serait-il vrai?" with its carefully chosen harmony and rhythm:

[37] Monsigny did not at first devote himself to music exclusively, although he finally became an inspector at the Conservatory and a member of the Academy. Cf. the biography by A. Pougin. Fischbacher, Paris, 1908.

[38] Gossec, a pupil of Rameau, revived from 1773–77 the *Concerts Spirituels*, was second conductor at the Grand Opera, became head of the *École royale de chant* in 1784, and after its expansion into the National Conservatory in 1795, one of the five inspectors, finally also becoming a member of the Academy. He wrote seven comic, and eleven grand, operas BIBLIOGRAPHY: L. Dufrane, *Gossec*. Fischbacher, Paris, 1927.—Fr. Hellouin, *Gossec et la musique française à la fin du XVIIIe siècle*. A. Charles, Paris, 1903. A string-quartet has been reprinted by W. Höckner, Zwickau, 1932.

[39] ANDRÉ ERNEST MODESTE GRÉTRY (b. Liége, 1742; d. Montmorency near Paris, 1813), received his first instruction as a choir boy in his native city. In 1759 he went to Rome, without however devoting himself to serious contrapuntal studies, inasmuch as he had his own definite ideas concerning composition. He devoted himself entirely to the opera, and went to Geneva in order to obtain a libretto from Voltaire. Although he was unsuccessful in this attempt, he composed for Geneva, with good success, an already existing libretto *Isabelle et Gertrude*. Upon the advice of Voltaire, he went to Paris, where, however, he had to surmount great difficulties. But his second opera *Le Huron*, 1768, found favor, while *Le Tableau Parlant*, 1769, was a pronounced success and won him great popularity. He now developed a great fertility. Among his numerous operas may be mentioned: *les Deux*

Grétry, like Lully, took as his point of departure the declamation of the French language, and arrived from this, even more than Lully, at original melodies. Through the introduction of old melodies and the spirit of the old French folk song, he also frequently comes upon peculiar harmonies. He is distinguished in the art of characterization; the opera *Les Deux Avares* will afford good illustrations.

In his chief work, *Richard Cœur de Lion*, the romanza "Une fièvre brûlante" is utilized as a basis for the whole, almost like a *Leitmotiv*. The troubadour poetry had been rediscovered at that time, and the composition of romanzas blossomed forth in, naïve imitation of this. These became principal numbers of the opera also, and laid the seed for that romanticism in music which developed so fully in the nineteenth century.

Beside the French comic opera or the operetta, an independent *opera buffa* developed in the Neapolitan school. It presented not only a new musical spirit, but new musical forms as well, above all the "finale" at the conclusion of the acts. The sole supremacy of the aria was abandoned. By the "finale" was meant, as is well known, the ensemble numbers, in which the united personnel join, both for concerted singing and for dramatic interchange. Such finales had already been employed by Logroscino, a contemporary of Pergolesi in Naples. Logroscino really shares with Pergolesi the honor of having founded the *opera buffa*. The *opera buffa* retains the jovial character of the *intermezzi*. Its fascination

Avares, 1770; *Aucassin et Nicolette*, 1779; *La Caravane du Caire, Richard Cœur de Lion*, 1784; *Raoul Barbe-Bleue*, 1789; his last work, *Ménage* was written in 1803. As happily did many musicians, Grétry also wrote his Memoires. They are characterized by original points of view, the development of esthetic principles, and are written in a captivating style. The *Mémoires ou Essais sur la musique* appeared in 1789 in one volume, and in 1795 in 3 vols. BIBLIOGRAPHY: Michel Brenet (Marie Bobillier), *Grétry*. Gauthier-Villars, Paris, 1884.—J. E. Bruyr, *Grétry*. Rieder, Paris, 1931.—E. Closson, *Grétry*. Établissements Brepols, Turnhout, 1920.—G. Cucuel, *Les Créateurs de l'Opéra-comique française*. Alcan, Paris, 1914.—H. de Curzon, *Grétry*. Laurens, Paris, 1907.—Ch. Gheude, *Grétry*. 1906.—P. Long des Clavières, *La Jeunesse de Grétry et ses débuts à Paris*. Jacques et Demontrond, Besançon, 1921.—H. Quittard, "A propos d'Isabelle et Gertrude." R.M., 1908.—G. O. Sonneck, in the festival book for Scheurleer, pp. 321–326. M. Nijhoff, 's-Gravenhage, 1925.—Heinz Wichmann, *Grétry und das musikalische Theater in Frankreich* (Berlin dissertation). Niemeyer, Halle, 1929.—Those literary works of Grétry, published, like his music, by the authority of the Belgian government, which have already appeared, are: *Mémoires ou Essais sur la musique*. 3 vols., Lamberty, Brussels, 1924–25.—*Réflexions d'un solitaire*. 4 vols., G. van Oestet cie, Brussels & Paris, 1919–21.—*Voyages, études et travaux*. Delagrave, Paris, 1889.—A complete edition of Grétry's works has been undertaken under the authority of the Belgian government. Up to the present time 45 vols. have appeared. B. & H.—A piano score of *Richard Cœur de Lion* has been published by Litolff; of the *Deux Avares* by Senff.

lies in the light, jocular horseplay, in the liveliness of the action, which is only possible in the musical drama in connection with the liquid Italian language. As a special enticement for the public, these *opera buffa* composers interspersed their works with popular, charming melodies, "hits," as one would call them at the present day. Some of these still live, owing to the fact that the Vienna classic composers employed them as themes for instrumental variations. A famous example of this kind is the "Nel cor più" from Paisiello's [40] *La molinara*, an air on which Beethoven wrote a series of variations. The opera is popular in Germany as well as in Italy. Paisiello also composed a *Barber of Seville*, to the same text which Rossini used later. Mozart was probably moved by the same libretto to write his *Marriage of Figaro*.

One of the most famous works which is produced from time to time at the present day is Domenico Cimarosa's [41] *Il matrimonio segreto* (The secret marriage). A classical composer of this species is Nicola Piccinni,[42] the rival of Gluck. Among the most fertile, one must mention

[40] GIOVANNI PAISIELLO or PAËSIELLO (b. Tarentum, 1740; d. Naples, 1816) was already one of the most popular *opera buffa* composers when still a young man in the early twenties. In 1776 the Empress Catherine II called him to St. Petersburg where he remained until 1784, when he returned to Naples as composer to the court. In 1802 Napoleon, who was especially fond of his music, called him to Paris, but Paisiello did not remain there long; he returned to his home in the following year. He wrote more than 100 operas. He exerted a great influence upon his friend, Mozart. BIBLIOGRAPHY: H. Abert, "Paisiellos Verhältniss zu Mozart," A. f. MW., I, 402 ff.; see also by the same author, *Gesammelte Schriften und Vorträge*, ed. by F. Blume. Niemeyer, Halle, 1929. New editions of the *Barber of Seville* (piano and voice), Ricordi, Milan; and of *La molinara*, Senff, Leipzig (with German text).
[41] DOMENICO CIMAROSA (b. Aversa, near Naples, 1749; d. Venice, 1801) became famous when still a young man. In 1789 he was summoned to St. Petersburg as Paisiello's successor under most flattering conditions. He returned in 1792 by way of Vienna where he wrote his famous *Il matrimonio segreto*. In 1798 he participated in the Neapolitan insurrection, was arrested and condemned to death, but was pardoned by King Ferdinand. Fifty-four stage works have been recorded. NEW EDITION: *Il matrimonio segreto*, piano score, Edition Peters.—His 32 harpsichord sonatas have been published under the editorship of Boghen by Eschig, Paris, 1926.
[42] NICOLA PICCINNI (b. Bari, 1728; d. Passy, near Paris, 1800) had a stirring life on account of his having been called to Paris by Marie Antoinette and made the rival of Gluck against his will, and also because later he had to experience bitterly the vicissitudes of the revolution, having to abandon his professorship at the *École royale de chant et de déclamation*, the later Conservatory. After a sojourn at the court of Naples, he became sixth inspector at the Conservatory in Paris. He became famous through the comic opera, *La Cecchina* (*La buona figliuola*) which was given in Rome in 1760 with unparalleled success. Piccinni was one of the most fecund operatic composers of all times, having written 127 stage works, for the most part successful. BIBLIOGRAPHY: H. Abert, "Piccinni als Buffokomponist." J.P., Leipzig, 1913; by the same author, *Gesammelte Schriften und Vorträge*, pp. 346 ff. Niemeyer, Halle, 1929.—Alb. Cametti, "Saggio cronologico delle opere teatrali di N. Piccinni," R.M.I., 1901.—New edition of the opera "Roland" in the *Chefs d'œuvre.*—Cf. E.B., No. 32.

the somewhat older Baldassare Galluppi (1706–85). Joseph Haydn also wrote Italian *buffa* operas. His *Lo speziale* (The Apothecary) has again been successfully reproduced in recent years, though to be sure, in greatly abbreviated form. Mozart's masterpieces, *Figaro* and *Don Juan*, are grounded on the Italian comic opera. He still used its forms, but we shall see that so far as the spirit is concerned he created something new.

REFORM OF THE OPERA BY GLUCK [43]

Gluck, in his great work of reform, which affected the future development profoundly, set out from the Neapolitan opera, but concluded his

[43] CHRISTOPH WILLIBALD GLUCK (b. Erasbach, in the Upper Palatinate, 1714; d. Vienna, 1787) was the son of a forester, and received his first musical education as choir boy at the Jesuit Church in Komotau, 1726–32. Later he went to Prague where Pater Czernohorsky became his teacher. By means of his violoncello, Gluck made his way to Vienna. Here he found a patron in the person of the prince Melzi who brought him to Milan to Sammartini. Soon Gluck's career as Italian opera composer began, at first in Italy itself, then, in 1745–46, in London, where he became acquainted with Handel's oratorios. These, as well as the operas of Rameau, some of which he must have seen on his journey through Paris, surely had a great influence upon his artistic development. They afforded suggestions or points of departure for his later operatic reforms. With the traveling operatic troupe of Mingotti, Gluck visited Dresden, Prague, Hamburg, and Copenhagen. In 1750 he was in Vienna; 1754–64, master of the chapel at the court of Maria Theresa. While visiting Rome in 1756 he was made a papal knight of the Order of the Golden Spur. His call to Paris in 1772, where Marie Antoinette became his powerful patroness, was of determining influence upon him. He began his reform in 1762 with *Orpheus*. The following are the memorable dates connected with that reform: *Alceste*, Vienna, 1767; *Paride ed Elena*, Vienna, 1769; *Iphigénie en Aulide*, Paris, 1774; and in the same year, *Orpheus* and *Alceste* in French versions; *Armide*, 1777; *Iphigénie en Tauride*, 1779; *Echo et Narcisse*, 1779. Monteverdi, Gluck, and Wagner are the three greatest dramatic composers in operatic history. BIBLIOGRAPHY: M. Arend, *Gluck, eine Biographie.* Schuster & Loeffler, Berlin, 1921.—H. Berlioz, *Gluck and His Operas;* Eng. tr. by Ed. Evans, sr. L. Reeves, London, 1915.—*Gluck-Jahrbuch der Gluckgesellschaft* (since 1914). B. & H., Leipzig.—G. M. Leblond, *Mémoires pour servir à l'histoire de la révolution opérée dans la musique par M. le Chevalier Gluck.* Bailly, Naples and Paris, 1781; Ger. tr. by J. G. Siegmeyer, *Über den Ritter von Gluck und seine Werke. Briefe von ihm und andern berühmten Männern seiner Zeit.* Voss, Berlin, 1837.— B. Marx, *Gluck und die Oper.* Janke, Berlin, 1863.—E. Newman, *Gluck and the Opera.* B. Dobell, London, 1895.—Numerous letters of Gluck in the *Écrits de musiciens* of J. G. Prod'homme. Mercure de France, Paris, 1912.—A. Reissmann, *W. Gluck, sein Leben und seine Werke.* J. Guttentag (D. Collin), Berlin, 1882.—Romain Rolland, *Musiciens d'autrefois.* 4th ed., Hachette & cie., Paris, 1914; Eng. tr., *Some Musicians of Former Days,* by M. Blaiklock. H. Holt, N. Y., Kegan Paul, London, 1915.—Anton Schmid, *C. W. Ritter von Gluck.* Fleischer, Leipzig, 1854.—Julien Tiersot, *Gluck.* Alcan, Paris, 1910.—Jean d'Udine (Albert Cozanet), *Gluck.* Laurens, Paris, 1906.—Heinrich Welti, *Gluck.* Reclam, Leipzig, 1890.—Cf. also E. T. A. Hoffman, *Ritter Gluck* (a novel; a good portraiture). M. Hesse, Leipzig, 1900. NEW EDITIONS: *Edition de luxe* of the six principle operas—the two *Iphigénie, Alceste, Armide, Orpheus,* and *Echo et Narcisse*—at the instigation of Berlioz and under the patronage of Mlle. Pelletan, ed. by Damcke, Saint Saëns, and Tiersot, French, German, & Italian words. B. & H., Leipzig, 1873–96.—*Alceste,* piano score with German tr., ed. by H. Abert. B. & H.; by the same editor, introduction to Cornelius' translation of *Iphigénie en Tauride.* Eulenburg, Leipzig, 1928; by the same

reformation on the basis of the French. He had already written more than two dozen completely Italian operas. It became of importance for his later work that in Vienna, from 1758 to 1764, he found occasion to write French comic operas. The new species of *Opéra bouffon*, as it was originally called, had just arisen in the footsteps of the Italian *intermezzi*. It had resulted from the same desire which subsequently drove Gluck to his work of reform, the desire for a return to naturalness, or "to nature," as it was expressed at the time.

The shortcomings of the Neapolitan opera, which consisted not only in its undue stress upon virtuosity and in the vicious custom of employing castrates, but also in the over variegated plots with their superfluity of love intrigues, had long been recognized by thoughtful men, and much propaganda and sarcasm had been directed against them. Even as early as the beginning of the second decade of the century, Benedetto Marcello had published his biting satire *Il teatro alla moda*. In his *Saggio sopra l'opera in musica* (Critical Essay on the Opera), of the year 1755, which appeared under the title "Essai sur l'opéra" in the French *Mercure* in 1757, Count Algarotti laid down principles quite similar to those which Gluck later on made his own.

The chief moment, however, as always in art, was not the theory, but the practice, which Gluck initiated. He was stimulated and supported in his undertaking by the Italian poet Calsabigi who was living in Vienna. The latter had translated the works of Metastasio into French, and had become conscious of how much of arbitrariness and artificiality they contained. He was of the opinion that music required a simple, concentrated action, filled with genuine passion. From this point of view he wrote the text of *Orpheus and Eurydice*. The opera, the music by Gluck, was produced in Vienna in the year 1762. With this work the path of reform was opened. In his *Orpheus* Gluck had set up a new ideal, and had created a work of imperishable beauty.

---

editor, *Le nozze d'Ercole e d'Ebe*, D.T.B., XIV, 2; by the same editor, the Italian *Orfeo*, D.T. OE., 2d series, No. 1.—*L'Arbre enchanté*, comic opera, piano score under the title "Der Zauberbaum," ed. by M. Arend. G. D. W. Callwey, Munich, 1911; by the same editor, the comic opera *La Rencontre imprévue*, under the title "Die Pilger von Mekka," Vol. I, Gluck Gesellschaft, 1910. B. & H., Leipzig, c. 1928.—G.M.B., No. 313.—The Ballet *Don Juan*, ed. by R. Haas, D.T. OE., XXX, 2.—*Echo et Narcisse*, ed. by M. Merz, Hamburg, 1913.—Seven orchestral trios, in Riemanns' *Collegium musicum*.—A Gluck Society (Gluck Gemeinde) was founded by M. Arend in 1913.— The New Gluck Society (Neue Gluck Gesellschaft), founded by H. Abert, has published since 1914 four numbers (Jahrgänge) of a valuable Gluck annual.

First of all, the work is characterized by a simple plot, which, without any intrigues and interludes, even without any minor or subsidiary characters—the unfortunate *deus ex machina*, *Amor*, is the only concession to the old operatic method—presents the old myth as a purely human experience. The chorus and the ballet are not merely superimposed, but are organically interwoven in the plot. The famous "No!" which the subterranean spirits thunder forth in reply to the pleas of Orpheus is one of the greatest dramatic effects the theater has ever brought forth, and there is nothing more touching than the rounds and dances of the spirits in the fields of the blessed.

Gluck's *Orpheus* is composed for an Italian text, the title rôle written for an alto castrate; but the music has abandoned Italian virtuosity in favor of pure dramatic expression. The Italians, too much accustomed to dulcet sing-song, did not comprehend it, and Gluck, who continued along the new path with his *Alceste* and *Paris and Helen*, found himself confronted with opposition.

He turned his eyes toward Paris; quite naturally, because Lully and Rameau had cherished the dramatic principle. Here the German master might hope for an appreciation of his ideas and, in spite of preliminary hostility, he finally gained complete success on the French stage. He found an enthusiastic poet for his art in Le Blanc du Roullet, who worked over Racine's *Iphigénie en Aulide* as an opera libretto according to Gluck's ideas. The work was produced at the Grand Opera in the year 1774. In 1777 *Armide* followed, the libretto being the old text by Quinault, which Lully had set; in 1779 *Iphigénie en Tauride*, with text by Guillard, followed. *Orpheus*, with a revision of the title rôle for tenor, and *Alceste* were also repeated, in French garb.

Through the appearance of Gluck intellectual Paris was now set in commotion, as it had been by the buffonists. Two parties, one *pro*, one *con*, were formed, and a lively war of pens took place. Rousseau, who had formerly declared that the French language was not adapted to the music drama, became an ardent supporter of Gluck. Converted by the beauty of Gluck's operas, the former Saul became a Paul. The opponents set up the Italian Piccinni in opposition to the German master. Although the former's *Roland*, produced in 1778, according to the old textbook by Quinault, was successful, Gluck nevertheless finally remained victor. It must, however, be said that the two masters, pitted against one another by the two parties, respected one another highly, and Hanslick justly ᴌᴇsents the fact that Piccinni has been made the scape-goat of music history.[44]

The crown of Gluck's creations is his last, highly dramatic work *Iphigénie en Tauride*. The overture, which pictures the storm which cast Orestes and Pylades ashore, stands in closest union with the drama. Iphigenia's narration of her dream, as a matter of fact all of her narratives, as well as those of Orestes and Pylades, are classical models of a musical recitation which follows every minute emotion. Formally, the most important part of Gluck's reform lies in the emphasis which he placed upon the recitative. The latter is the axis upon which all dramatic action turns. This was recognized and emphasized not only by the founders of the opera, but also by its later reformer, Richard Wagner. If the recitative is treated superficially or episodically, subordinately or incidentally, the entire work disintegrates, however ingenious the individual parts may be.

The characters are sharply delineated, the exalted priestess Iphigenia, the Greek Orestes, noble also in his despair, and over against him, the clumsily impetuous king, Thoas! These are set off by the choruses of the priestesses, characterized by their religious fervor, and by the wild scenes of the Scythians with their dances. Everywhere the wisest restraint is observed; the instrumentation also, applied with elemental effect, adds essentially to the characterization. Among individual scenes, one may mention the one in which Orestes is pursued by the Eumenides. The scene in the underworld in *Orpheus* is the only one that can be compared with this. There are few scenes in all literature of similarly great tragic effect.

Gluck created a school; through him, Paris became a European center for opera, and it maintained this position to the days of Meyerbeer. J. Ch. Vogel (1756–88), who died in early life was still under the personal influence of Gluck (*La Toison d'or*, 1786; *Démophon*, 1789). A. M. G. Sacchini (1734–86), who occupies a distinguished place in Italian opera, followed, in his latest works in Paris, in the footsteps of Gluck (*Dardanus*, 1784; *Oedipe à Colone*, 1786). There are two important composers both of whom maintain a classical restraint and also deserve to be called Gluck's followers: Cherubini,[45] with his chief works *Lodoiska*

---

[44] Cf. Desnoiresterres, *La Musique française au XVIIIᵉ siècle, Gluck et Piccinni, 1774–1800.* 2d ed., Perrin, Paris, 1875.
[45] LUIGI CHERUBINI (b. Florence, 1760; d. Paris, 1842) was inducted into the style of

(1791), *Médée* (1797), and *Les Deux Journées* (1800), and Méhul [46] with his biblical opera *Joseph et ses frères* (1807), an opera in which there is no love plot, and indeed not even a female rôle. Spontini [47] once more brought the classical opera to special brilliance. He was the composer of the Empire, the epoch of Napoleon I, steeped in its external and military glory (*La Vestale*, 1807; *Ferdinand Cortez*, 1809). After him came romanticism which cleared away the classical ideals and the classical subject matter to which the opera had clung during the first two hundred years of its existence.

Palestrina by Sarti in Venice, devoted himself at first to church music, and then entered upon a successful career as Italian opera composer. In 1788 he settled permanently in Paris. Here he wrote his chief works, the French operas. When the Conservatory was founded in 1795, he became one of the four inspectors. In 1805 he went to Vienna for the production of his opera *Lodoiska*. For Vienna he also wrote the weak opera *Faniska*. Haydn and Beethoven admired both works. Later he again turned successfully to the composition of church music. In 1822 he became director of the Paris Conservatory and gave a new *éclat* to that illustrious institution. BIBLIOGRAPHY: Edward Bellasis, *Cherubini: Memorials Illustrative of His Life*. Burns & Oates, London, 1874; new ed., 1912.—Crowest, *Cherubini*. S. Low, Marston, Searle, & Rington, Ltd., London and New York, 1890.—M. Quatrelles l'Epine, *Cherubini*. Lefebvre-Ducrocq, Lille, 1913.—R. Hohenemser, *L. Cherubini, sein Leben und seine Werke*. B. & H., Leipzig, 1913.—H. Kretzschmar, "Über die Bedeutung von Cherubinis Ouvertüren und Hauptopern für die Gegenwart." J.P., 1906.—L. Schemann, *L. Cherubini*. Deutsche Verlagsanstalt, Stuttgart, 1925. NEW EDITIONS: Cherubini's chief work, *Les Deux Journées*, ed. by Egon Bloch under the title "Der Wasserträger." Beck, Leipzig, 1932.—*Médée*, ed. by H. Strobel. Neue Musikzeitung, Vol. 46, No. 13, Erfurt, April, 1925.—*Lo sposo di tre*, ed. by H. Tessmer, under the title "Don Pistacchio." Dresden, 1926.—The *Theory of Counterpoint and of Fugue* has been reëdited in German by G. Jensen. H. von Ende, Cologne & Leipzig, 1896; and by R. Heuberger. F. E. C. Leuckart, Leipzig, 1911.

[46] ÉTIENNE NICOLAS MÉHUL (b. Givet, in the Ardennes, 1763; d. Paris, 1817). His early discovered talent was developed in his home. He came to Paris in 1778, was encouraged by Gluck to turn his efforts toward dramatic composition, and wrote a large number of operas here. Upon the founding of the conservatory he was made one of the four inspectors. BIBLIOGRAPHY: René Brancour, *Méhul*. Laurens, Paris, 1912.—A. Pougin, *Méhul, sa vie, son génie, son caractère*. Fischbacher, Paris, 2d ed., 1893.—Heinrich Strobel, "Die Opern von Étienne Nicolas Méhul," Z. f. MW., VI, pp. 362 ff.

[47] GASPARO SPONTINI (b. Majolati in the States of the Church, 1774; d. there, 1851), entered the Conservatory *della Pietà* in Naples in 1791. After his first success in opera, he won the patronage of Piccinni. In 1803 he went to Paris. At first he was unsuccessful in his operatic ventures, but collaboration with the poet Jouy brought him the great triumph of his *Vestale*. This was repeated in the case of *Ferdinand Cortez*. Spontini was music-master to the Empress Josephine, later *chef d'orchestre* of the Italian opera, and still later court composer to Louis XVIII. In 1820 Frederick William III summoned him to Berlin as director of music at the court opera. Here the third of his famous operas, *Olympie*, was produced in the German version of E. T. A. Hoffmann. Subsequently Spontini made himself unpopular in Berlin through autocracy and self-conceit; in 1841 public demonstrations forced him to retire. BIBLIOGRAPHY: W. Altmann, "Spontini an der Berliner Oper," S.I.M.G., 1903.—Ph. Spitta, "Spontini in Berlin," *Zur Musik*, 1892.—Richard Wagner, "Erinnerungen an Spontini," in the *Collected Works*, Vol. V.

THE BIRTH OF THE SYMPHONY [48]

About the middle of the eighteenth century, the Italian operatic symphony, in its three-movement, Scarlatti form, passed from the theater into the concert hall. It at once became the avowed favorite of the public, took over the leadership in concert music, soon banished the suite completely, and influenced all instrumental forms in such a manner that they all conform to it more or less. The *concerto grosso*, which formerly stood in first place, and had occupied the position of the symphony, was pushed aside. Only the solo concerto with orchestral accompaniment remained, and this also assumed the three fold form of the symphony. As is well known, it has retained this form until most recent times. The clavier sonata also assumed the three-movement form, after the model of the symphony, and took over the leadership in its domain. The clavier suite disappeared, as well as the fugue after the manner of the *Well-Tempered Clavichord.*

Simultaneously with this change in form, a change in style also took place. The homophonic setting supplanted the contrapuntal. The *basso continuo*, the continuous support by a thorough bass, was abandoned, a more flexible movement was striven after and attained. The upper voice received the chief emphasis. Whereas formerly short motifs and frequent cadences were extensively employed, the attempt was now made to construct symmetrical periods of many measures, which form an architectonic structure. The climax of this development was reached in Beethoven, whose great thematic structure is well known.

At first, before it reached its higher development, the new style appeared more empty, more tenuous than the old, but it was more mobile, and could follow all the flights and movements of phantasy much more freely. We feel it to be more natural and more direct. Its origin is closely connected with the great spiritual and intellectual changes during the eighteenth century. The same causes called it forth which brought forth the comic opera. The spokesman of the latter was Jean Jacques Rousseau. The mention of this, the most modern of the philosophers of the eighteenth century, suffices to indicate and make clear the spiritual relationship.

[48] BIBLIOGRAPHY: Michel Brenet, *Histoire de la symphonie à orchestre.* Gauthier-Villars, Paris, 1882.—Karl Nef, *Geschichte der Sinfonie und Suite.* B. & H., Leipzig, 1921.—L. de la Laurencie and G. de Saint-Foix, "Contribution à l'histoire de la symphonie française vers 1750," *Année musicale,* 1911.—L. de la Laurencie, article in Enc. Lav., Vol. II, pp. 1535 ff.

After the theater symphony had been transferred to the concert hall, the musical world was seized by a veritable mania to play symphonies. The composers never published less than half a dozen at a time. Many of them wrote a hundred and more, the sum total mounted to many thousands. Under these circumstances it would be idle to attempt to discover the man who founded the new style. Numerous composers collaborated in the new movement, in the earliest period Italians, Frenchmen, and Germans.

Among the Italians, G. B. Sammartini, in Milan (1701–75), the teacher of Gluck, assumes an important place. To be sure, J. Haydn repudiated with indignation the thought of having learned anything from this "smearer," but nevertheless, the light, sometimes frivolous manner in which Sammartini employed the instrumental style must be reckoned to his credit by musical history. He broke radically with the ponderousness of the old style, and recent Italian historians even give him the honorary title of one of the oldest impressionists.

The Mannheim School.—Karl Theodore, who ruled as elector of the Palatinate in Mannheim from 1743 to 1777, maintained, as did most of the princes of his day, an orchestra. According to the musical travel journal of the Englishman, Burney, it was a "Band of generals," according to Schubart, the best in Europe. He says in his *Ideen zu einer Aesthetik der Tonkunst* (Ideas toward an Aesthetic of Music): "No orchestra of the world has ever surpassed the Mannheim orchestra in execution. Its forte is a thunder, its crescendo a cataract, its diminuendo a crystal stream babbling along in the distance, its piano a breath of spring." The characterization is significant, inasmuch as it indicates that in Mannheim music was performed in the modern manner. The old style distinguished between forte and piano, but the transitions, the crescendi and diminuendi, appear either seldom or not at all, whereas, with the Mannheimers, they play the chief rôle. The Mannheim concert master, Johann Stamitz,[49] the leader

[49] JOHANN ANTON STAMITZ (b. Deutsch-Brod, Bohemia, 1717; d. Mannheim, 1757) aroused attention as a violin virtuoso at Frankfurt in 1742 on the occasion of the coronation of Emperor Charles VII, with the result that the Elector-Palatine, Karl Theodore, engaged him as chamber-musician, advancing him in 1745 to the position of concert-master and director of chamber-music. Stamitz had long been known as a virtuoso of the violin, and as the founder of the later German violin technique, but it was only H. Riemann who again called attention to his significance as a composer. As such he had been esteemed in Paris, where symphonies by him were played as early as 1751, and where he sojourned in 1755. Numerous works, both by himself and his school, were printed in Paris as well as in London. BIBLIOGRAPHY: Michel Brenet, *Les Concerts en France sous l'ancien régime.*

among the composers of the school, employed them regularly in his
symphonies and orchestral trios as an especial characteristic of his
compositions, and indeed, in general contributed much of significance
toward the development of the new style.

His first movements already approached the classical structure of the
sonata form: first and second theme, development, and reprise. His slow
movements are charming in their expression of tender sentiment, and
frequently they are already scored in that flexible, mobile manner, which
is a characteristic of the newer orchestral music. An example may be
found in the following fragment [for strings] from one of the symphonies:

D.T.B.. Vol. VII².

Fischbacher, Paris, 1900.—Romain Rolland, *Voyage musicale au pays du passé*, chap.
VII, 2.—Fr. Walter, *Geschichte der Musik und des Theaters am kurpfälzischen Hofe.* B. & H.,
Leipzig, 1898. NEW EDITIONS: Symphonies, orchestral trios, and chamber music by
Stamitz and other masters of the Mannheim School (including a monograph concerning
the same) under the editorship of H. Riemann in the D.T.B., III, 1; VII, 2; XV, and
XVI; also in Riemann's *Collegium musicum.*—Cf. also S.B., No. 305, and R.B., No. 144.

Stamitz also regularly inserted the minuet in the symphony. In this, he anticipated J. Haydn.

The significance of Stamitz, finally, also appears in the fact that he created a following. A whole circle of composers grouped themselves about him: the violinists Franz Xaver Richter (1709–89), and Carlo Guiseppe Toëschi (1724–88), the cellist Anton Filtz (c. 1730–60), the master of the chapel Christian Cannabich (1731–98). Though Richter still belongs to the old school more than do the others, he is nevertheless the most distinguished. Riemann in his *Beispiele* (p. 304) gives the first movement of the E flat major symphony, opus 4, which, after all, contains not a few indications of the Mannheim style: pronounced antitheses, crescendi, decrescendi, and chromatic transitions; only the periodic structure was as yet little developed.[50]

Carl Philipp Emanuel Bach and the North German School.[51]— C. P. E. Bach, the second oldest son of Joh. Sebastian, is the founder of the modern clavier sonata, and thereby historically of great significance. He was intended for the law, was highly educated, and took a deep interest in the great intellectual fermentation of his day. He is the musical representative of the "storm and stress" period and of the "epoch of the genius." With a sureness he laid hold upon the new form of the clavier sonata, in which he was anxious to present something quite unusual. He is the founder of the personal style, which Beethoven finally brought to consummation. One may well say that what C. P. E. Bach strove after, Beethoven accomplished. Though Bach's compositions still interest us greatly, they seldom satisfy us with their bold runs, their harmonic and rhythmic surprises, and their sudden pianissimos and fortissimos. C. P. E. Bach, like most of his contemporaries, appears most genuine and profound when he surrenders himself to sentimentality (*Empfindsamkeit*). An illustration of this will be found in the *cantabile e mesto* from a clavier sonata in D minor, 1781, in which bold harmony and expression mingle strangely with rococo figuration.[52] The style of C. P. E., expressive in every detail, requires either the gentle clavichord, the favorite instrument of the sentimentalists, the enthusiasts of the day in Germany, or the modern pianoforte, which began its victorious career at that time.

[50] Some symphonies of Richter will be found in the D.T.B., III, 1, and VII, 2. He has written at least 69.—See also R.B., No. 143.

[51] See Max Flüeler, *Die norddeutsche Sinfonie zur Zeit Friedrich des Grossen* (Berlin dissertation), 1901. E. Ebering, Berlin, 1908.   [52] R.B., No. 147.

Carl Philipp Emanuel Bach also contributed to the development of the modern style in his, in many respects, strange symphonies. Beside him, one must mention as representatives of the North German school, his brother Wilhelm Friedemann Bach, who in his symphonies sometimes approached the depth of his father, and the two brothers Karl Heinrich (1701–59), and Johann Gottlieb Graun (1698–1771), both in the service of Frederick the Great, the former as master of the chapel, the latter as concert master. As a further member of the family, not as a representative of the North German school, one might also mention Johann Christian Bach (1735–82), the so-called London Bach, who as a chief representative of the so-called "galant" (style) advanced the new form more after the manner of, and as successor to Sammartini. He is also of importance on account of the strong influence which he exerted on the youthful Mozart.

JOSEPH HAYDN AND THE REFORM OF THE SYMPHONY [53]

Austria also contributed its share to the early development of the symphony. The most interesting master at the time of the Mannheimers is Georg Matthias Monn (1717–50), but the symphony first attained its preëminent position through Joseph Haydn.[54] His reform of the sym-

---

[53] Cf. Michel Brenet, the article entitled "Les Grands Classiques" in Enc. Lav., Vol. II.

[54] JOSEPH HAYDN (b. Rohrau on the Leitha, 1732; d. Vienna, 1809). Even though Haydn's father was no musician, but merely a simple wheelwright, the son nevertheless received an important musical heritage from his parents. The father played the harp, and the mother sang to it. In this way, Haydn was led in early youth to the fountain of folk music, from which he later frequently drew his themes, and as the result of which he has become one of the most popular of the great masters. As was the case with Bach, Haydn was denied the privilege of a journey to Italy for musical study, a fact which, however, was probably one of good fortune for German music and the symphony in general. Haydn received his musical training as a choir boy in St. Stephen's Cathedral in Vienna, where he had been accepted on account of his good soprano voice. In his 13th year, after his voice changed, he was turned out on the street, and for ten years had to eke out a livelihood by giving lessons and playing in public. The popular character of his music which especially delights us was doubtless still further nurtured during that period. At that time, a friend and patron, K. von Fürnberg, counseled him to write string quartets. The first one, in B♭ Major, appeared in 1755. Altogether he wrote eighty-three quartets. His lot became improved when in 1759 he became master of the chapel of Count Morzin in Lukavetz, near Pilsen, and still more so when he entered upon his life position as master of the chapel of Prince Esterhazy in Eisenstadt. He remained there until 1790, but he bore the title of *Kapellmeister* to Prince Esterhazy until the end of his life, and also drew a pension, although he was absolutely at liberty after 1790, and resided in Vienna. His journeys to England occurred in the years 1790–92 and 1794–95. His services had been engaged under most flattering terms for the Salomon concerts in London. For these concerts he wrote his famous 12 London symphonies. In England Haydn became acquainted with Handel's oratorios. The fruits of this acquaintance were his two master works, written in his old age, "*The Creation*," 1798, and "*The Seasons*," 1801. Haydn's position with Count Morzin and

phony must be counted one of the greatest achievements in the history of art. Through his achievement, the symphony was first elevated to the level of the great works of art. Like Handel and Gluck, Haydn wrestled his way through to his great deed only after a long development, in mature life. In the symphonies which he wrote for Paris in

Prince Esterhazy recalls the numerous orchestras which were maintained by the nobility of Austria, Bohemia, and Hungary in the eighteenth century, and which contributed immensely to the great development of music. In winter the aristocracy came to Vienna with their orchestras, and developed a private musical life the brilliancy of which can scarcely be conceived. Even Beethoven wrote several of his symphonies for such private orchestras. Haydn composed his first symphony for the orchestra of Count Morzin in 1759. Further symphonies were composed for Prince Esterhazy. In 1779 he received a commission to write six symphonies for the *Concert Spirituel* of Paris. While the youthful symphonies delight because of their diversity and their spontaneity, the style of the Paris symphonies becomes more profound. There is also program music, such as *Le Matin, Le Midi, Le Soir, La Chasse* and *Les Adieux* (Farewell Symphony). Among the quartets are *The Bird Quartet* and *The Nightingale Quartet.* Haydn wrote 120 symphonies, according to Sandberger's reckoning. A complete edition is appearing through B. & H. since 1908 under the editorship of E. von Mandyczewski. Up to the present there have appeared: 3 vols. of symphonies; 3 vols. of piano sonatas; the two oratorios; songs and vocal solos. The complete edition will extend to c. 80 vols. BIBLIOGRAPHY: Michel Brenet (Marie Bobillier), *Haydn.* Alcan, Paris, 1909; Eng. tr. by C. L. Leese, with a commentary by W. H. Hadow. O.U.P., London, 1926.—D. G. A. Fox, *Joseph Haydn: An Introduction,* in "The Musical Pilgrim Series." O.U.P., London, 1929.—K. Geiringer, *Joseph Haydn* (in Bücken's "Grosse Meister"). Athenaion, Potsdam, 1932.— W. H. Hadow, *Haydn: a Croatian Composer.* Seeley, Service & Co., 1897; reprinted in Hadow's *Collected Essays.* O.U.P., London, 1929; by the same author, *Haydn.* Dent. London.—K. Kobald, *Joseph Haydn.* Verlag Dr. Epstein, Vienna, 1932.—C. F. Pohl, *Joseph Haydn.* 2 vols., A. Sacco Nachfolger, Berlin, 1875–82; 2d ed., 1928; incomplete, extending only to 1760; a third volume published by H. Botisber. B. & H., Leipzig, 1927; also by C. F. Pohl, *Mozart und Haydn in London.* C. Gerold's Sohn, Vienna, 1867.—J. Runciman, *Haydn.* Bell, London, 1908.—A. Sandberger, *Zur Geschichte des Haydnschen Streichquartetts.* Altbayrische Monatsschrift, 1899, published by the historischer Verein von Oberbayern, 1899–1926.—Leopold Schmidt, *Joseph Haydn.* "Harmonie," Berlin, 1898; 2d ed., 1907.—A. Schnerich, *Der Messentypus von Haydn bis Schubert.* Selbstverlag, Vienna, 1892; by the same author, *Joseph Haydn und seine Sendung,* with list of Haydn's works, bibliography, iconography, etc. Amalthea-Bücherei, Vol. XXII, Amalthea-Verlag, Zurich, 2d ed., 1926.—R. Tenschert, *Haydn,* in "Klassiker der Musik." Max Hesse, Berlin-Schöneberg, 1932.—L. Wendschuh, *Über Joseph Haydns Opern* (Rostock dissertation). C. A. Kaemmerer, Halle, 1896. NEW EDITIONS: String quartets; complete edition by Jokisch; selections by A. Moser; also by H. Dechert, Peters.—Piano sonatas: selections by C. Prohaska, Cotta, Stuttgart, 1926; Zilcher, B. & H., Leipzig, 1932.—Twelve German dances, ed. by O. E. Deutsch in Moser's *Musikkränzlein.* Kistner & Siegel, Leipzig, 1932.—Fourteen minuets—*Menuetti ballabili*—for small orchestra, ed. by Th. W. Werner. B. & H., Leipzig, 1933.—Eight-voice *Field Partitas* (Feldpartita)—Divertimenti—ed. by K. Geiringer. F. Schuberth, Leipzig, c. 1932.—Echo, for orchestra of stringed instruments. Universal Edition.—Two piano concertos, ed. by K. Schubert. Nagel, Hannover, 1932.— *Il ritorno di Tobia,* German by Glossner. Universal Edition, 1909.—Of the 24 operas: *Lo Speziale* (The Apothecary), edited by R. Hirschfeld. A. J. Gutman, Vienna & Leipzig, G. Schirmer, New York, 1895.—*Orlando Paladino,* edited by E. Latzko. Max Beck, Hamburg and Leipzig, 1932.—*Il mondo della luna* (The World on the Moon), M. Lothar. Adler, Berlin, 1932.—The English Canzonettas have been ed. by Landshoff, Peters.—Cf. E.B., No. 39.

the 1780's, the new, profounder style broke through for the first time. It reached its maturity in the London symphonies of the 1790's.

The symphony is a child of the Italian theater. In the concert hall, also, it at first paraded about in high buskin. A superficial Italian pathos still clung to it. Haydn removed this by forgetting tradition and, following the dictates of his heart, by using popular themes as a basis. Thus he gave the symphony a German character. More important still than the new element in the invention, is the emphasis which Haydn laid upon the development. He made this the chief thing, and introduced the so-called thematic development, a procedure which, to be sure, had already been applied in isolated instances, especially in the concerto, e.g., in the Brandenburg Concertos of Bach, but which now won an entirely new significance in the symphony. Haydn did not carry through or develop the entire themes, but he preferred to select apparently insignificant, small motifs from these, and by means of their transmutation, he succeeded in forming great periods and presenting dramatic developments. As a rule he took a cheerful theme as his point of departure, but with his ingenious art, surpassed by no one, he was capable of transporting us in flight, as it were, to all the regions of the spirit. One finds oneself in the domain of the passionate, of the tragic, even of the demonic, one knows not how. The classical example which may be quoted here, also because it is taken from the most familiar of the Haydn symphonies, is afforded by the theme of the London D Major Symphony (Breitkopf Edition, No. 2), in which the motif indicated by the bracket, apparently quite subsidiary, furnished Haydn the opportunity for a superb development:

The developments, of course, proceed rapidly. One must follow with alert attention, if one would understand. Haydn was a son of his time, which demanded that art present even the lofty and the profound in agreeable form, and despised all one-sidedness. His symphonies are perfect reflections of the culture of the eighteenth century. Hermann Kretzschmar has demonstrated this convincingly in his *Führer* (Guide). Whoever wishes to understand Haydn should read the passage there (1. Division, *Sinfonie und Suite*, 6th edition, 1921, p. 129).

The thematic development occurs chiefly in the first and in the concluding movements, the latter frequently being in rondo form. Haydn also gave a new form to the slow, middle movement by adopting the variation form, which formerly, except for the old German orchestral suite, had been employed largely only in the clavier and chamber music. The most beautiful slow movements are variations, as is also the case in Beethoven and Brahms. This indicates sufficiently the significance of the introduction of this form. Haydn, furthermore, enriched the symphony by prefacing a slow introduction, which had perhaps been suggested to him by Monn, who had already introduced his symphonies by short, though profound, slow movements. They have their origin in the French *ouverture*, from which accordingly a valuable element was derived for the structure of the symphony, just as the minuet, as well as the popular spirit in general, was derived from the suite.

The thorough bass disappears in the later Haydn symphonies. They are written in a flexible style which applies that modern orchestration that constantly changes, leaping from one instrument to another, as birds flit from branch to branch.

In chamber music also, Haydn effected the end of the *continuo*. He is the founder of the string quartet. The clavier instrument that was formerly considered indispensable is excluded, while in the new clavier trio, it takes the place of the thorough bass, but is treated as an obligato instrument.

Mozart.[55]—Haydn wrote his London master symphonies when Mozart was already dead. In his string quartets, the young Mozart gratefully

[55] WOLFGANG AMADEUS MOZART (b. Salzburg, 1756; d. Vienna, 1791) had an admirable teacher in his father Leopold, the renowned violin pedagogue. The latter recognized the genius of his son, and devoted his life to its cultivation. The chief dates in Mozart's life are briefly the following: in 1762 he journeyed as a wonder child, with the likewise highly gifted sister Maria Anna (Nannerl), to Munich and Vienna; 1763–66, to Brussels, Paris, London, Amsterdam, and Zurich; 1769–71 (with his father only), to Milan and as far as Naples—in Rome he was made a papal knight of the golden spur, like Gluck and Spontini; in Bologna he was instructed by Padre Martini, and elected a member of the Accademia dei Filarmonici; the fall of 1771, he made a second journey to Milan; in 1772, a third journey thither. For the Carnival in Munich in 1775 he composed *La finta giardiniera;* for Salzburg in the same year, *Il re pastore.* During 1777–78 he journeyed to Mannheim and Paris with his mother, who died in the latter city in 1778. Matured, Mozart returned to Salzburg; and in 1779 he became court organist; in 1781 he composed *Idomeneo* in Munich. Up to this time Mozart had been in the service of the Archbishop of Salzburg. Exasperated by the ill treatment which he received at the hands of this ecclesiastic, he severed the relation and went to Vienna; here, 1782, the *Entführung aus dem Serail* (Abduction from the Seraglio) was composed, and he married Konstanze Weber. He composed in 1786, *Figaro;* in 1787, *Don Juan,* in Prague; in 1788, the three great symphonies in E flat major, G minor, and C major (Jupiter). In 1789 he went to

acknowledged that he had learned from Haydn, and had striven to follow his example. In the symphony, on the other hand, Haydn was

Berlin. In 1790 he composed *Cosi fan tutte* (So Do They All); in 1791, *Titus, Zauberflöte* (Magic Flute) and the *Requiem*. Although almost deified in his youth, Mozart had to struggle against adversity in his maturity, caused, to be sure, in no small measure by the fact that both he and his wife were poor managers. BIBLIOGRAPHY: M. M. Bozman, *Letters of W. A. Mozart*, translated from the German ed. of H. Mersmann. J. M. Dent, London and Toronto, E. P. Dutton, N. Y., 1928.—E. J. Breakspeare, *Mozart*. J. M. Dent, London, E. P. Dutton, N. Y., 1902.—H. de Curzon, *Mozart*. Alcan, Paris, 1914; by the same author, *Lettres de W. A. Mozart* (complete translation of the letters of Mozart). Plon, Paris, 1928.—A. E. F. Dickinson, *A Study of Mozart's Last Three Symphonies*. O.U.P., London, 1927.—E. J. Dent, *Mozart's Operas, a Critical Study*. Chatto & Windus, London, McBride, Nast & Co., N. Y., 1913.—T. F. Dunhill, *Mozart's String Quartets*. O.U.P., London, 1927.—F. Gehring, *Mozart*. S. Low, Marston, Searle, and Rivington, London, Scribner, N. Y., 1883; new ed., 1911.—E. Holmes, *The Life and Correspondence of Mozart*. Chapman & Hall, London, 1845; Harper Bros., N. Y., 1860; Novello, Ewer, & Co., London, 1878; new ed. by Eb. Prout; reprinted in "Everyman's Library." J. M. Dent, London & Toronto, E. P. Dutton, N. Y., 1921.—Otto Jahn, *W. A. Mozart*. 4 vols., B. & H., Leipzig, 2d ed., 1867; in 2 vols. by Deiters. B. & H., Leipzig, 1905–07; Eng. tr. in 3 vols. by P. D. Townsend. Novello, Ewer, & Co., London, 1882, 1891; new ed. by H. Abert. B. & H., Leipzig, 6th ed., 1923–24.—Fr. Kerst, *Mozart-Brevier*. Schuster & Loeffler, Leipzig and Berlin, 2d ed., 1905; Eng. tr. by H. E. Krehbiel. B. W. Huebsch, N. Y., 1905.—L. von Köchel, *Chronol. Thematisches Verzeichniss sämmtlicher Tonwerke Mozarts* (Chronological-Thematic Index of the Complete Musical Works of Mozart). B. & H., Leipzig, 1862; supplement, 1889; 2d ed., 1905.—A. Leitzmann, *Mozarts Briefe*. Insel-Verlag, Leipzig, 1910.—F. H. Marks, *Questions on Mozarts Piano Sonatas*. William Reeves, London, 1929; by the same author, *The Sonata, Its Form and Meaning as Exemplified in the Piano Sonatas by Mozart*. W. Reeves, London, 1921.—L. Nohl, *Mozarts Leben*. E. G. Günther, Leipzig, 1863; 3d ed., by P. Sakolowski. Harmonie, Berlin, 1906; Eng. tr., *The Life of Mozart* by Lady Wallace. Longmans, Green, London, 1877; Eng. tr. also by J. J. Lalor. Jansen, McClurg and Co., Chicago, 1880; 8th ed., McClurg, Chicago, 1908; also by L. Nohl, *Mozarts Briefe*. B. & H., Leipzig, 1877; Eng. tr., *The Letters of W. A. Mozart* by Lady Wallace. 2 vols., Longmans, Green, London, 1865; Hurd, N. Y., 1866.—J. G. Prod'homme, *Mozart raconté par ceux qui l'ont vu (1756–91)*. Stock, Paris, 1928.—E. Prout, *Mozart*. G. Bell and Sons, London, 1903 and 1907.—G. de Saint-Foix, *Les Sinfonies de Mozart*. Mellottée, Paris, 1932.—L. Schiedermayer, *Mozart*. C. H. Beck, Munich, 1922; by the same author, *Die Briefe W. A. Mozarts und seiner Familie* (complete critical edition of the letters of Mozart and his family). G. Müller, Munich & Leipzig, 1914.—L. Schmidt, *Mozart*. Schlesische Verlagsanstalt, Berlin, 1912.—A. Schurig, *W. A. Mozart, Sein Leben und Sein Werk*. 2 vols., Inselverlag, Leipzig, 2d ed., 1923; French adaptation by J. G. Prod'homme. Delagrave, Paris, 1925.— Stendahl (Beyle), *Vies de Haydn, Mozart, et Metastase;* Eng. tr. by R. Brewin. J. Murray, London, 1818; latest Fr. ed., Le Divan, Paris, 1928; cf. also the Fr. ed. with text annotated by Dan. Muller and a Preface by R. Rolland. Champion, Paris, 1914.—V. Wilder, *Mozart: l'homme et l'artiste*. Heugel, Paris, 1880; 4th ed. Charpentier et cie., Paris, 1889; Eng. tr. *Mozart, the story of his life as man and artist* by L. Liebich. 2 vols., Scribner, N. Y., 1906.— T. de Wyzewa and G. de Saint-Foix, *W. A. Mozart, sa vie musicale et son œuvre de l'enfance à la pleine maturité, 1756–77*. Perrin, Paris, 1912.—Cf. also G. Gugitz, "Mozarts Schädel und Dr. Gall." Z. f. MW., XVI, pp. 32 ff.—Since 1923 a Mozart-Jahrbuch has been published, originally under the editorship of H. Abert. Drei Masken Verlag, Munich.—A selection of the works of Leopold Mozart will be found in the D.T.B., Vol. XIX, 2.— Complete edition of Mozart's works by B. & H.—To this the following must be added: the 7th violin concerto, ed. by Kopfermann. B. & H., Leipzig, 1907; 6 deutsche Tänze (Ger aan

the pupil of Mozart. Haydn would never have written the wonderful second theme of the symphony in D major already cited—Haydn's last symphony—if there had been no Mozart:

It contains what one commonly calls the Mozartean songfulness, or *cantabile*. In other words, it is an allegro theme that is filled with a song-like, adagio spirit; and to have introduced this songful quality into the rapid passages of the symphony is Mozart's merit in the history of the symphony. For this reason, indeed, that patron of song, Hans Georg Nägeli of Zurich, although a thorough musician, called Mozart an "impure instrumental composer" (*ein unreiner Instrumentalkomponist*) and a "mixer of styles" (*Stilvermischer*). But all progress occurs through a mixture, a mingling of styles, as we have just observed in the case of Haydn's reform. As a matter of fact, by carrying a special *cantabile* element into the symphony, Mozart really made the symphony more profound. We cited the above theme, because it accrues to the high honor of Haydn that he recognized the new and the significant in Mozart, and did not hesitate to learn from him, although much older than Mozart. The passage at the same time shows how Haydn, in the setting up of two contrasting themes, prepared the way for Beethoven.

What is meant by, or understood under, the Mozartean *cantabile*,

---

dances), ed. by Soldan. Peters, 1932; 15 Kontertänze (contra-dances). Vieweg, Berlin; the Ballet discovered in Gratz in 1932, *Die Rekrutierung*, or *Die Liebesprobe*, or Chun-yang, ed. by R. von Mojsisovics. F. Schuberth, Leipzig, 1930; from the same work, little Ballet-Suite, arranged by A. Pagel for small orchestra. F. Schuberth, Leipzig, 1931; 5 *Lieder*. Ed. Nagel, Hannover, No. 66; 3 new tercets for 3 voices and 3 basset horns.—In 1928 Mozart's oratorio *Isacco* was discovered in Bologna (cf. Felice Boghen, "Mozart's 'Isacco,'" in *Musik*, Stuttgart, 1923, pp. 491–494).—An 8th violin concerto, in D major (*Adelaide concerto*), dedicated to a daughter of Louis XV, was recently discovered in Paris, edited by M. Casadesus. Mainz & Leipzig, B. Schott, 1933.—The *Requiem*, completed by Mozart's pupil, F. X. Süssmayr, edited in the complete edition by Brahms, has been published in facsimile under the editorship of Schnerich. Gesellschaft für graphische Industrie, Vienna, 1913; Keussler has suggested a version "without Süssmayr," Deutsches Musikjahrbuch, Vol. I, pp. 210–216. O. Schlinghoff, Rheinischer Musikverlag, Essen, c. 1923.—Mozart wrote 40 symphonies, 31 serenades, cassations, etc.; an organ number for a mechanical instrument will be found in Bonnet's *Historical Organist*. Schirmer, N. Y.—Cf. also, E.B., No. 38.

can perhaps best be perceived from the following familiar theme from the symphony in E flat major:

It is allegro throughout, but it is also songful throughout, in a manner that was not characteristic of the older allegro. In this way an elegiac element enters into the rapid movements, that is frequently heightened in Mozart's case by his fondness for short chromatic transitional passages. Kretzschmar indicates the deeper root of this characteristic, which, thanks to the universal nature of Mozart, is sufficiently held in check by counter-balances, in the following pertinent words. "On Haydn's side, the nobility and a dying race; on Mozart's, the young aspiring middle class, the leaders in literature, works of art like *Clavigo, Die Räuber, Kabale und Liebe* (Schiller), like Hogarth's picture cycles. In the longing for a more just and more perfect world, the pessimism of the Illumination came into contact with devout Christianity, Mozart—without knowing it—with Voltaire whom he hated."

Mozart and the German Opera

In the year 1752 a version of an English play in the succession of *The Beggars' Opera* (p. 235) was presented in Leipzig by the Koch troupe under the title *Der Teufel ist los, oder die verwandelten Weiber* (The Devil to Pay, or, The Wives Metamorphosed). The German text was by Chr. Felix Weisse, the music by the violinist of the troupe, J. C. Standfuss. This must be viewed as the first German *Singspiel* or operetta, which gave the impetus to the movement out of which grew the Mozartean *Singspiel* and the German opera in general. Weisse later studied in Paris. Inspired by the French comic opera, he again resumed his attempts in Leipzig, now with the composer Joh. Adam Hiller (1728–1804). The latter at first again composed the libretto *The Devil to Pay*. This was presented in Leipzig in 1766; there followed in 1767 *Lottchen am Hofe* (Lotta at Court); *Die Liebe auf dem Lande* (Love in the Country); *Der Dorfbarbier* (The Village Barber), and a whole series of further pieces, the most famous among them being *Die Jagd* (The Chase) of the year 1770. This contains the song *Als ich auf meiner Bleiche ein Stückchen*

Garn begoss (When I upon my Bleaching-Ground a Piece of Yarn Did Sprinkle), which continued as one of the most popular songs throughout an entire century.

It was the songs, above all else, that won a tremendous success for the Hiller *Singspiele*. They succeeded in striking the popular vein that many composers sought after. In the 50's a movement had arisen in Berlin, which set up as its object the creation of popular songs, which even the German people, in other periods so richly blessed with songs, then lacked. The Moses who was to bring the desired water from the rock was not found at once. It was only with the coming of the *Singspiel* that the ideal was realized. Later, to be sure, the proper talents appeared, and the German song bloomed more beautifully than ever. Remarkable is the rococo character of the Hiller songs. Such pretty and variegated, embellished rhythms as occur in the *Als ich auf meiner Bleiche*, already mentioned, or in the other *Ohne Lieb' und ohne Wein* (Without Love and without Wine), which latter still lives in the schools, with a moralizing text, could only have been produced in that day. The taste of the populace at large is also subject to change.

Contemporaneously with these beginnings of the *Singspiel*, first attempts at the creation of a great German opera manifest themselves. Wieland wrote *Alceste;* Anton Schweitzer wrote music for it in 1773. The poet Klein wrote *Günther von Schwarzburg* in 1776, for which the Mannheimer kapellmeister, Ignaz Holzbauer, wrote the music. But these productions remained attempts, without further significance and influence.

More important in its results was the establishment of a "National Singspiel" in Vienna by Joseph II, in the year 1778. Heretofore Vienna had possessed virtually only an Italian opera. The new venture opened with Umlauf's *Bergknappen* (The Miners). Others followed: on the 12th of July, 1782, *Die Entführung aus dem Serail* (The Abduction from the Seraglio) by Wolfgang Mozart. This work was epoch making in the history of German opera. Goethe, who himself became an eager protagonist of the *Singspiel*, wrote: "The 'Abduction' carried everything before it." Everything fell short of the model which Mozart had set up, even that which Goethe had attempted on poetic lines. The way for German opera was now marked. This can be taken quite literally, inasmuch as later works, even in their external arrangement, imitated the *Entführung*, written by Bretzner, and revised by Stephani the younger. As in the

Entführung, so, e.g., we also always find in Lortzing the aristocratic, ideal pair of lovers, the naïve servant, and the comic figure. Even in Wagner's *Meistersinger* the scheme can still be detected. The really great features of the *Entführung* are to be found in the truly original character of the Turk, Osmin, in the perfect manner in which certain songs of Belmonte and Constanze express youthful love and the pangs of love, and in a quartet which already presents the model for a dramatic ensemble. One can also observe in the colorful Romanza of Pedrillo an early adumbration of the later romanticism.

In his last year Mozart wrote the *Zauberflöte* (The Magic Flute), which also still rests on the *Singspiel,* in particular on the motley, popular magic opera, but which offers such a wealth of characterization and expression, in the simplest forms comprehensible by all, that it itself appears like an inconceivable work of magic. It is a "Song of Songs" on love, which is presented in all its forms. Through the interweaving of mysticism, the music approaches the highest themes that can move the soul of man. The individual lines of Schikaneder's text are frequently silly, but Mozart read a deep meaning into the whole, as did also Goethe, who did not hesitate to follow in the footsteps of Schikaneder by at least beginning a second part to the *Zauberflöte.* The *Zauberflöte* fulfills in an ideal way the demand of the period of the Illumination for a union of profundity and popularity. It became the point of departure for the German opera, for Beethoven's *Fidelio* and Weber's *Freischütz.*

The remaining chief works of Mozart are written in the Italian language. They must be classified as *opere serie* and *opere buffe.* To the former, in addition to two youthful works, belong *Idomeneo* and *Titus,* works whose significance is, to be sure, recognized, but which are no longer capable of revival. Although post-Gluck, they are afflicted with the weaknesses of the old *opera seria.* Mozart did not follow Gluck's ideal of a libretto with a simple but great action. In the *Idomeneo,* and still more in *Titus,* one finds the old intrigues with their complicated love entanglements, that are unable to arouse a lasting interest, and are quite undigestible at the present day. In the storm and temple scenes of *Idomeneo,* and in the scene of the burning of the capitol in *Titus,* one does, to be sure, recognize Gluck's influence. These are great dramatic pictures with chorus, and they, as well as some of the classical arias of Ilia in *Idomeneo,* arouse our highest interest. But it is only such fragments that satisfy, not the works in their entirety.

It was in the field of the *opera buffa* that Mozart wrought imperishable works. He did not merely accept the Italian form as he found it, but he modeled it according to his own genius. It was sufficiently flexible to permit of modification. The Italians conceived the comic opera as a frolicsome, colorful bit of delusion or horseplay, in which charm and jovial humor, seductive sensuality and intoxicating wit, are the chief elements. They vaulted gracefully over the exaggerations and improbabilities of burlesque texts, and created in their lightly flowing *opere buffe* something that is not to be found elsewhere in this species. Mozart attempted something similar in a youthful work, the *Finta giardiniera* (The Pseudo Garden-Woman). But the unscrupulous frivolity of the Italians was denied him. Where he attempts to be as over-exuberant as the southerners, his music lacks spice. The *Finta giardiniera* becomes significant only when the music penetrates more deeply and undertakes genuine characterization.

Mozart's greatness rests upon his representation of characters. Herein his art is imperishable. His *Nozze di Figaro* (Marriage of Figaro), based on the comedy of Beaumarchais, a text that would have been impossible for every Italian, because the actual *buffo* scenes in it are quite episodic, became his masterpiece. Here he created the figures of Figaro and Susanne, of the page Cherubin, of the count and the countess, which will live forever. They preserve their personalities even in the incomparable ensembles, while the orchestral accompaniment adds depth and background.

Mozart's librettist, da Ponte, had recognized that Mozart required great and sharply delineated figures, and therefore suggested to him the counterpart of the German Faust, "Don Juan," who had existed on the stage for centuries and offered a great dramatic problem. It is well known how Mozart solved this. Here he presented also the demonic in human nature with the power of a Shakespeare, and as an artist piercing the most recondite depths, came to grips with the supersensual. Moreover, he again created characters which are unmatched in the whole literature of the world, e.g., the heroic and at the same time genuinely womanly, Donna Anna, adorned with the noblest virtues.

From the highest point of mastery, Mozart once more turned in his *Cosi fan tutte* (So Do They All)—written at the command of the Emperor—to a text which, like the *Finta giardiniera* presents primarily a gay exuberant horseplay, without a semblance of probability. Here he devoted himself almost exclusively to profound characterization, and wrote a purely playful music, adorned with all the charms of form and euphony which he alone commanded. *Cosi fan tutte* has been called the master's "Midsummer Night's Dream," and this designation indicates well the spirit in which this music should be enjoyed. If despite this, it is difficult to overlook completely the weaknesses of the text, this may have its cause in the fact that it is almost impossible for German singers to strip off the shackles of earth in as complete a manner as is here required.

VII

THE NINETEENTH CENTURY

BEETHOVEN [1]

THE first important work of Beethoven is his cantata on the death of Emperor Joseph II in the year 1790. As a young man he took lessons in Vienna from the Italian, Salieri, in vocal composition, and he is supposed to have learned from him especially the proper declamation. Thus he is still related to the old Italian school. However, when he entered upon his career as a composer in Vienna, he turned with all his energy to instru-

---

[1] LUDWIG VAN BEETHOVEN (b. Bonn, 1770; d. Vienna, 1827) belonged to a family of musicians that originally came from Antwerp. His grandfather was master of the chapel in Bonn, his father tenor singer there. The father was of a frivolous character and addicted to drink, the education of the youth, very desultory. The teacher who exerted the greatest influence upon him was Chr. Gottlieb Neefe, a composer of *Lieder* and of comic operas, and since 1781 vice-chapel-master in Bonn. Neefe made the young Beethoven acquainted with Bach's *Well-Tempered Clavichord*, and also published early compositions by his young pupil. Neefe was highly educated and of lively spirit, and doubtless aroused his pupil's desire for culture. Beethoven read with eagerness the Greek and Roman classics and Shakespeare (in translations), Klopstock, Goethe, Schiller, and others. In 1787 he sojourned in Vienna, where he was to have become a pupil of Mozart. He settled there permanently in 1792. At first he devoted himself to renewed study, appeared as pianist, finally devoting himself to composition entirely. Beethoven never occupied a definite position. He was doubtless primarily prevented from doing so by his deafness, which distressed him from the year 1801. This suffering placed a tragic seal upon his life; in his last years he was completely deaf. Several love affairs also ended unhappily, leaving their indelible impressions behind. As is well known, he was never married. The relationship of the aging Beethoven to his nephew, Karl, was also a source of great annoyance to him. Beethoven had taken the youth from a frivolous mother, and had adopted him. Unfortunately, the latter had inherited his mother's characteristics, and indeed even attempted to commit suicide in 1826. In his independent situation as a free composer, which Beethoven energetically affirmed in the face of the great world, Beethoven represents the modern artist in contrast to Haydn and Mozart, who, employed in the *entourage* of small rulers, were treated more or less as servants. The stations in Beethoven's life are indicated by the following dates of his principal works: 1800, First Symphony, in C major; 1802, Second Symphony, in D major; 1804, Third Symphony (*Eroica*), in E flat major; 1805, the opera, *Fidelio* (Leonore); 1806, the Fourth Symphony, in B flat major; 1807, the Fifth Symphony, in C minor; 1808, the Sixth Symphony (*Pastorale*), in F major; 1812, the Seventh Symphony, in A major, and the Eighth Symphony, in F major; 1814, the third version of *Fidelio;* 1818, sonata for "hammer-piano," op. 106 (dedicated to the Archduke Rudolph); from 1818 to 1823, *Missa solemnis*, in D major; 1823, the Ninth Symphony, in D minor; 1824–26, the last quartets. The complete works are published by B. & H. BIBLIOGRAPHY: G. Becking, *Studien zu Beethovens Personalstil. Das Scherzothema.* Mit einem bisher unveröffentlichten Scherzo Beethovens. B. & H., Leipzig, 1921.—Behrend, *Beethoven's Pianoforte Sonatas;* the Eng. tr. by I. Lund. Dent, London, E. P. Dutton, N. Y., 1927.—Paul Bekker, *Beethoven.* Schuster & Loeffler, Berlin & Leipzig, 1911; Eng. tr. by M. M. Bozman. Dent, London, E. P. Dutton, N. Y., 1925.—H. Berlioz, *A Critical Study of Beethovens Nine Symphonies;* the Eng.

mental music, which it was his destiny to raise to an undreamed-of elevation. One can already detect the pupil of Haydn and Mozart in the works which he published in 1795, the piano trios, published as *opus 1*, and the three piano sonatas as *opus 2*. He consistently took up and

tr. by Edwin Evans, Sr. C. Scribner's, N. Y., W. Reeves, London, 1923.—Jean Chanta-voine, *Beethoven*. Alcan, Paris, 13th ed., 1929; by the same author, *Correspondance de Beethoven*. Calman-Lévy, Paris, 1904; by the same author, *Les Symphonies de Beethoven*. Mellottée, Paris, 1932.—Th. v. Frimmel, *Beethoven und Goethe*. C. Gerold's Sohn, Vienna, 1883; by the same author, *Neue Beethoveniana*. C. Gerold's Sohn, Vienna, 1890; by the same author, *Beethoven-Studien*. G. Müller, Munich & Leipzig, 1905–06; by the same author, *L. v. Beethoven*. Schlesische Verlagsanstalt, Berlin, 5th ed. 1919; by the same author, *Beethoven im zeitgenössischen Bildnis*. W. König, Vienna, 1923; by the same author, *Beethoven-Handbuch*. B. & H., Leipzig, 1926.—H. Grace, *Ludwig van Beethoven*. Kegan Paul, London, 1927.—George Grove, *Beethoven and His 9 Symphonies*. Novello & Co., London, Novello, Ewer & Co., N. Y., 1906.—W. H. Hadow, *Beethoven's Op. 18 Quartets*. O.U.P., London, 1926.—Th. Helm, *Beethovens Streichquartette*. Siegel, Leipzig, 2d ed., 1910.—E. Herriot, *La Vie de Beethoven*. Libr. Gallimard, Paris, 1929.—A. de Hevesy, *Beethoven the Man;* the Eng. tr. by F. S. Flint. Faber & Gwyer, London, 1927.—V. d'Indy, *Beethoven*. Laurens, Paris, 1911; Eng. tr. by Th. Baker, Boston Music Co., Boston, G. Schirmer, N. Y., 1913.—A. Kalischer, *Beethoven und seine Zeitgenossen*. 4 vols., Schuster & Loeffler, Leipzig, 1910; by the same author, complete edition of the correspondence, *Beethovens Sämmtliche Briefe*. 5 vols., Schuster & Loeffler, Berlin and Leipzig, 1906–8; 2d ed. by Th. v. Frimmel.—F. Kerst, *Beethoven im eignen Wort*. Schuster & Loeffler, Berlin and Leipzig, 1904; Eng. tr., *Beethoven, the Man and the Artist as Revealed in His Own Words*, by H. E. Krehbiel. Huebsch, New York, 1905, Gay & Bird, London, 1906; also by F. Kerst, *Die Erinnerungen an Beethoven*. J. Hoffmann, Stuttgart, 2d ed. 1925.—W. von Lenz, *Beethoven: eine Kunststudie*. 2 vols., E. Balde, Cassell, 1855–60; I, *Das Leben des Meisters*, new edition by A. Kalischer. Schuster & Loeffler, Berlin, 1908; II, *Der Stil in Beethoven; Die Mit- und Nachwelt Beethovens; Der Beethoven Status quo in Russland.*—C. E. Lowe, *Beethoven's Pianoforte Sonatas: Hints on Their Rendering, Form, etc.* Novello, London, 1923.—J. de Marliave, *Beethoven's Quartets;* Eng. tr. by H. Andrews. O.U.P., London, 1928.—A. B. Marx, *Ludwig van Beethovens Leben und Schaffen*. O. Janke, Berlin, 1859; 6th ed. by Behncke. 2 vols., O. Janke, Berlin, 1911.—P. Mies, *Die Bedeutung der Skizzen Beethovens zur Erkenntuis seines Stiles*. B. & H., Leipzig, 1925; Eng. tr., *Beethoven's Sketches; an Analysis of His Style Based on a Study of His Sketch-Books*, by D. L. Mackin-non. O.U.P., London, 1929.—Milne, *Beethoven: the Pianoforte Sonatas*. O.U.P., London.— W. Nagel, *Beethoven und seine Klaviersonaten*. 2 vols., H. Beyer & Söhne (Beyer & Mann), Langensalza, 1903 and 1923–24.—K. Nef, *Die neun Sinfonien Beethovens*. B. & H., Leipzig, 1928.—E. Newman, *The Unconscious Beethoven: an Essay in Musical Psychology*. A. A. Knopf, N. Y., Parsons, London, 1927.—L. Nohl, *Beethovens Leben*. 3 vols., new ed., Schlesische Verlagsanstalt, Berlin, 1912–13; Eng. tr. by J. J. Lalor. W. Reeves, London, 1880, Jansen, McClurg & Co., Chicago, 1881; also by L. Nohl, *Beethoven nach den Schil-derungen seiner Zeitgenossen*. Cotta, Stuttgart, 1877; Eng. tr., *Beethoven Depicted by His Contemporaries*, by E. Hill. W. Reeves, London, 1880.—Nottebohm, *Beethoveniana*. Rieter-Biedermann, Leipzig & Winterthur, 1872; by the same author, *Neue Beethoveniana*. Rieter-Biedermann, Leipzig, 1887; by the same author, *Thematic Catalogue of the Works of Beethoven*. B. & H., Leipzig, 2d ed., 1868.—New edition of Nottebohm's, *Zwei Skizzen-bücher von Beethoven*, by P. Mies. B. & H., Leipzig, 1925.—F. Prelinger, Complete Corre-spondence, *Beethovens Sämmtliche Briefe*. 5 vols., C. W. Stern, Vienna & Leipzig, 1907–11.— J. G. Prod'homme, *Les Symphonies de Beethoven*. Delagrave, Paris, 1906; by the same au-thor, *La Jeunesse de Beethoven*. Payot, Paris, 1921.—H. Riemann, *Beethovens sämmtliche Klavier-Solosonaten*. 3 vols., Hesse, Berlin, 1919–20; by the same author, *Beethovens*

developed the achievements of his predecessors, the thematic development of Haydn and the songfulness of Mozart. More yet than in the case of Haydn, the first movement rests upon the two themes which, as contrasts, generally conjure up the entire development in dramatic manner. The development is built up on a larger scale, the entire movement is carried out with a view to thematic unity without free episodes. Short thematic developments already occur in the exposition and in the reprise. Frequently a long coda is attached, and it is only with the appearance of this, that the knot of the dramatic development is finally unraveled.

Streichquartette erläutert ("Meisterführer" No. 12). Schlesinger (R. Lienau), Berlin, 1910.—Romain Rolland, *Beethoven.* 4th ed., Hachette, Paris, 1910; Eng. tr. by B. C. Hull, with a brief analysis of the sonatas, the symphonies and the quartets by A. E. Hull. H. Holt, N. Y., 1917, Kegan Paul, London, 5th ed., 1924; by the same author, *Beethoven, les grandes époques créatrices:* I (1928), *de l'Héroïque à l'Appassionata.* Editions du Sablier, Paris; Eng. tr., *The Great Creative Epochs,* by Ernest Newman. Harper & Bros., N. Y., 1929, V. Gollancz, Ltd., London, 1929.—M. Rosenmann, *Studie zum Gestaltungsproblem der letzten fünf Streichquartette L. v. Beethovens.* (Vienna dissertation), 1930.—Ad. Sandberger, *Neues Beethoven Jahrbuch.* Vols. I–V, 1925 ff. Benno Filser, Augsburg.—L. Schiedermair, *Der junge Beethoven.* Quelle & Meyer, Leipzig, 1925; by the same author, *Beethoven; Beiträge zum Leben und Schaffen.* Quelle & Meyer, Leipzig, 1930.—A. Schindler, *Biographie von Ludwig van Beethoven.* Aschendorff, Münster, 1840; new ed. by F. Volbach. Aschendorff, Münster, 1927; Eng. tr., *The Life of Beethoven, Including His Correspondence with His Friends,* by Ignace Moscheles. H. Colburn, London, 1841, Oliver Ditson, Boston, c. 1870.—A. Schmitz, *Beethovens "zwei Principe."* F. Dümmler, Berlin, 1923; by the same author, *Beethoven.* Buchgemeinde, Bonn, 1927.—J. S. Shedlock, *Beethoven's Letters.* 2 vols., translated from the German edition of Kalischer. J. M. Dent, London, E. P. Dutton, N. Y., 1909; abridged ed., ed. by A. Eaglefield Hull. G. Bell & Sons, London, 1926; by the same author, *Beethoven.* G. Bell, London, 1903; Lane, London, 1905; by the same author, *Beethoven's Pianoforte Sonatas.* Augener, London, 1918.—O. Sonneck, *Beethoven: Impressions of Contemporaries.* O.U.P., London, 1926; by the same author, *Beethoven Letters in America,* Beethoven Association, N. Y., 1927; also, *The Riddle of the Immortal Beloved.* G. Schirmer, N. Y., 1927.—J. W. N. Sullivan, *Beethoven: His Spiritual Development.* A. A. Knopf, N. Y., 1927.—A. W. Thayer, *Ludwig van Beethovens Leben.* New ed. in 5 vols.; (vols. 4–5 edited by H. Riemann). B. & H., Leipzig, 1901–11; ed. by Deiters. B. & H., 1917; Eng. original, edited by H. E. Krehbiel. Beethoven Association, N. Y., 1925, Novello, London.—D. F. Tovey, *Beethoven's Ninth Symphony.* O.U.P., London, 2d ed., 1928.—W. J. Turner, *Beethoven: the Search for Realty.* Benn, London, 1927.—Richard Wagner, *Beethoven.* E. W. Fritzsch, Leipzig, 1870; Eng. tr. by A. R. Parsons. G. Schirmer, N. Y., 3d ed., 1883; published as, *Schriften über Beethoven,* in one volume. Engelhorn, Stuttgart, 1923; by the same author, *A Pilgrimage to Beethoven* (a novel); Eng. tr. by O. W. Meyer. Open Court Publ. Co., Chicago, 1897.—Ernest Walker, *Beethoven.* 3d ed., J. Lane, London, 1920 ("Music of the Masters").—J. W. von Wasielewski, *Ludwig van Beethoven.* 2 vols., Brachvogel & Ranft, Berlin, 1888.—F. G. Wegeler and Ferd. Ries, *Biographische Notizen über Ludwig van Beethoven.* K. Bädeker, Koblenz, 1838; new ed. by A. Kalischer. Schuster & Loeffler, Berlin & Leipzig, 1906. We possess about forty sketch-books of Beethoven, partially published by G. Nottebohm (*Ein Skizzenbuch von Beethoven aus dem Jahre 1803.* B. & H., Leipzig, 1865, 1880; *Beethoveniana,* 1872, 1887) and by K. L. Mikulicz (*Ein Notierungsbuch von Beethoven.* B. & H., Leipzig, 1927.)

Beethoven brought the new homophonic instrumental style to its perfection. There is always a chief dominating melody. Harmony, accompaniment, and subsidiary voices are inseparably and organically united with it, and strengthen its meaning and expression. The theme itself is often constructed so broadly that it engages various instruments, indeed even the entire orchestra. The theme of the First Symphony, in which the new method already revealed itself, will explain the situation better than words. Strings and wood-winds equally share in its formation:

All music lovers will remember how the allegro theme of the Second Symphony, in D Major, ascends from the basses to the upper registers, and how here too the entire orchestra participates in its presentation. The sweep of the periodic structure in the above-cited example is already grandiose. Beethoven carries this structure to almost superhuman power in the works of his last creative period, e.g., in the theme of the adagio of the Ninth Symphony, as is shown on page 264.

The thematic development is carried through in the most imposing manner in the first movement of the Fifth Symphony, in C minor. Beethoven here reveals with the highest ingenuity what overpowering dramatic development can be conjured forth from a small motif. The first movement of the Seventh Symphony, in A major, shows a similar ingenuity, expended this time upon a cheerful theme. Beethoven abandons himself most freely in the Fourth Symphony, in B flat major, where a large number of themes relieve one another in romantic fashion. This symphony was also the favorite of Mendelssohn and became the point of departure for the romantic symphony. In the *Eroica* the situation is unique. Here apparently a multitude of themes are proposed, but on closer investigation, one discovers that they hang together thematically very strictly, and that the entire work is perfectly unified. This work, written in honor of Napoleon, shows most clearly how Beethoven conceived the task of the symphonist. It presents a picture of the hero drawn with dramatic lifelikeness. Beethoven saw in him the founder of freedom; when he discovered that he was mistaken, the work had been completed, and he experienced bitter disappointment.

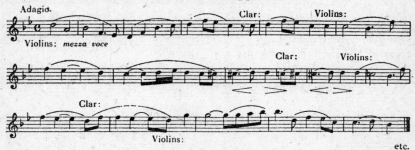

"No one can love nature more than I," Beethoven is reported to have said. An ideal witness to this is the *Pastoral Symphony*, which copied its style of short, and even very short, motifs from nature herself. In the Eighth Symphony, in F major, Beethoven returned to old forms of the eighteenth century, which represented for him the good old times, and which he treats with genial good humor.

Humor, which the Italians do not know, and which was introduced into instrumental music through Haydn, is one of the great factors in Beethoven's art. He created a special form for it in the *scherzo*, developed from the transformed minuet. The first trio of *opus* 1 already contained a *scherzo*, and we find it present in the symphonies from the second one on. Beethoven's humor finds its most vigorous expression in the *scherzo* of the Ninth Symphony. In this exceptional work, in which Faustian brooding wrestles its way through to a revelry of joy which bursts all bounds, Beethoven also bursts the form of the symphony itself by converting the last movement into a cantata with soli and chorus. From the notes which he left behind at his death, it is evident that he entertained still further plans for the combination of symphony and cantata; unfortunately they remained unfulfilled. Perhaps he would have created the model sought after, as he hardly did in the Ninth, with its rather arbitrary combination of instrumental music and song. It stimulated numerous composers to imitation, but up to the present time no well-rounded, completely satisfying form has been discovered.

Every Beethoven symphony is a completely rounded, logically developed character sketch. Each differs completely from the others. The piano pieces, though following the momentary inspiration of phantasy more freely, are no less logical. Their mention suggests a word concerning the Beethoven adagio, which draws its content from the spirit of the German Lied. In the slow movements of Mozart one is often reminded of the aria, a native of Italy; Haydn favors the rhythmically piquant French romanza tone; the Beethoven adagio is filled with that simple and deep spiritual tone which especially characterizes the German Lied of the best periods. Esthetes may deplore the fact, but it is no mere accident that the adagio of the *Apassionata* has become a favorite male chorus. The fact reveals a deep connection.

As in the symphony and the sonata, in the string quartet also, Beethoven enhanced expressiveness to the highest degree. Indeed, in this field he sometimes approached the very limit, and even transgressed the bounds of good style. He was for the time being a finality; no school could follow directly in his footsteps. And yet his conception was new after all, different from that of the eighteenth century; this art so rich indeed, that the later composers drew thousandfold inspiration from him.

The attempt has been made to divide Beethoven's life work into three stylistic periods. It is difficult to define definitely the boundary between the first two, but the third can easily be set off. In the creations of the last, the third period, Beethoven renewed the old contrapuntal-polyphonic style by combining his rich, great themes in contrapuntal-polyphonic manner, while the thematic development recedes somewhat. So in the Ninth Symphony, so in the last sonatas and quartets. With these characteristics of the last period he unites a tendency to create an impression of improvisation, whereby his last works receive quite a special physiognomy.

If, in conclusion, we endeavor to enumerate the roots of new developments which lie in Beethoven's instrumental works, the following may be said: Berlioz and Liszt have taken their point of departure from the *Pastoral Symphony;* Liszt and his school also from the improvisational manner of the last works; Mendelssohn and Schumann from the romantic colorfulness of the Fourth Symphony; Brahms took over the great period structure and the consistency of Beethoven's work; Richard Wagner transferred Beethoven's orchestra to the opera.

Although it is true that Beethoven's significance rests primarily on his instrumental compositions, in his opera *Fidelio* and his *Missa solemnis*, he established the style of modern vocal music. Here, too, he is both powerful consummator and fecund originator.

The Italian Opera

"Beethoven and Rossini" is the title which Kiesewetter gave the last chapter of his *Geschichte der europäisch-abendländischen Musik* (History of European-Occidental Music), which appeared in the year 1834. He was persuaded that beside Beethoven, Rossini [2] was the most distinguished representative of the epoch. At least he was the most successful. C. H. Riehl, in his well-known *Musikalische Charakterköpfe* (Musical Character-Heads) gives a good explanation of his colossal success in the following words:

"Rossini's world-fame originated in the days of the Congress of Vienna, in the sultry, retrogressive decade after the wars of liberation. The weary nations needed slumber-songs for sleep and dreams, and the Italians offered them the most charming, voluptuous songs of this nature. On the stage, as well as in life, men were satiated with the pompous tragic pathos of the Neapolitan school. They wanted to drink sweet self-forgetfulness at the fountain of entertaining art, and where was art more entertaining than in the opera of Rossini?"

As a matter of fact, Rossini possessed an effervescent ease of invention, that can scarcely be equaled. With greatest rapidity he threw a mass of pleasing melodies on paper, and our opera and operetta com-

[2] Gioacchino Rossini (b. Pesaro, 1792; d. Passy, near Paris, 1868). Bibliography: H. Beyle (Stendhal), *Vie de Rossini*. Boulland & cie., Paris, 1824; Ger. tr. by A. Wendt. L. Voss, Leipzig, 1824; reprinted 1892; Eng. tr. by H. S. Edwards. Hurst & Blackett, London, O. Ditson & Co., Boston, 1869; condensed in "Great Musicians," 1881; new French ed. by H. Prunières. 2 vols., Champion, Paris, 1923.—H. de Curzon, *Rossini*. Alcan, Paris, 1920.—Guido M. Gatti, *Le Barbier de Seville*. Mellottée, Paris, 1926.—E. Istel, "Rossiniana," *Musik*. B. Schuster, Berlin, 1911.—G. Radiciotti, *Rossini*. 3 vols., Arti grafiche Majella di A. Chicca, Tivoli, 1927–29.—Francesco Vatielli, *Rossini a Bologna*. Corp. Tip. Azzoguidi, Bologna, 1917.

posers could still find inspiration for their phantasy in the works of Rossini. His serious operas are properly forgotten today on account of their very lack of seriousness. His best works in this category are *L'Italiana in Algeri* (The Italian at Algiers) and *Semiramis*. On the other hand, his masterpiece, in the style of the *opera buffa*, *Il Barbiere di Seviglia* (The Barber of Seville), first performed in Rome in 1816, is still as fresh as youth, and always delights anew by its scintillating, vivacious melodies. With his *Guillaume Tell* (William Tell) Rossini added a significant work to French grand opera.

The romanticist of the Italian opera, on account of his somewhat sentimental melodies a kind of Mendelssohn, is Vincenzo Bellini (1801–35). He rose to actual greatness in his *Norma* (1831), a work that made a strong impression on the youthful Richard Wagner through the masterful performance of Schroeder-Devrient in the title rôle. Bellini's works are not devoid of the great weaknesses of the Italian virtuoso opera, but they also contain genuinely poetic passages. More sure of producing effects, excellent in their stagecraft, are the operas of Gaetano Donizetti (1797–1848), whose *La Fille du Régiment* (Daughter of the Regiment), 1840, is indestructible. A pleasing aftergrowth of the old *opera buffa* is *Don Pasquale*, which was again successfully produced in recent years.

Giuseppe Verdi [3] raised the Italian opera to new glory. He was a personality, one of those shining examples that ought to be held up as models for the younger generation. His early works are nationally tinged. His *Nabucco*, his *Lombardi*, his *Giovanna d'Arco* stirred up patriotism and glorified the national uprising. With his Italian melodies, full of temperament, Verdi, in his *Rigoletto* (1851), *Trovatore* (1853), and *Traviata* (1853), mingled somewhat of the international tone which proceeded from Paris and from Meyerbeer. As a result of this, he attained an international success which continues to the present day. All the brutality which these works contain is compensated for by their genuine, dramatic effectiveness, and some parts are artistic and on a high plane, e.g., the

[3] GIUSEPPE VERDI (b. Roncolo, Parma, 1813; d. Milan, 1901). BIBLIOGRAPHY: M. Bonaventura, *Verdi*. Alcan, Paris, new ed., 1930.—F. Bonavia, *Verdi*. O.U.P., London, 1930.—G. Cesari and A. Luzio, editors, *I copialettere di G. Verdi* (Correspondence). Tip. Stucchi Ceretti and Co., Milan, 1913; Ger. tr. ed. by Werfel, tr. by Paul Stefan. P. Zsolnay, Berlin, 1926.—H. Kretzschmar, "G. Verdi," J.P., 1913.—A. C. Mackenzie, *Verdi*. T. C. & E. C. Jack, London, F. A. Stokes, N. Y., 1913.—C. Perinelli, *G. Verdi*. "Harmonie," Berlin, 1900 (Reimann's "Berühmte Musiker").—A. C. Visetti. *Verdi*. Bell, London, 1905.

entire characterization and the death scene of *Traviata*, or the quartet from *Rigoletto*.

Verdi's character shows itself in the fact that, stimulated by Richard Wagner, but not an imitator, he sought a higher dramatic ideal at a ripe age, and realized this in his *Aïda*, a pure and genuinely Italian work of art. This was followed by *Othello*, less full of imagination, but nevertheless rich in poetic features, and finally by *Falstaff*, a model of a comic opera in sparkling *parlando* style, in which both harmonization and orchestration unite as interpreters.

In the year 1890, a work by an utterly unknown composer, written in a competition for a prize offered by the publisher, Sonzogno, struck like a bombshell. It was the *Cavalleria rusticana* by Pietro Mascagni. The hot-blooded, one-act piece founded the modern *verismo* in opera. To be sure, this had been prepared by Bizet's *Carmen*, but the realistic method of expression is still more concise and more pointed in the case of Mascagni. Leoncavallo's *I pagliacci* (1892) took its place, as a pendant of unbridled passion, beside *Cavalleria*. The most distinguished representative of the *verismo* is Giacomo Puccini. His finest work is *La Bohème* in which the "veristic" style, with its avoidance of all strictly measured forms, and its fondness for interweaving the sounds of nature, appears pleasingly combined with genuinely Italian melos. In his *Madame Butterfly* the style is combined with exotic sounds. In *Tosca*, Puccini unfortunately chose one of those dubiously sentimental cinema subjects that were popular before the World War. His last work, *Turandot*, not quite completed at the time of his death—Puccini died in 1924—again turns to fairyland and romanticism.

The most youthful Italian masters are far removed from the principles of the veristic school. The most distinguished of these operatic composers are: R. Zandonai (*Francesca da Rimini*), Ildebrando Pizzetti (*Fedra, Debora e Jaele*), and Franco Alfano (*La Leggenda di Sakúntala*, 1920).

THE FRENCH OPERA

The first germs of the latter romanticism are to be found in the romanza of the French comic opera of the end of the eighteenth century, especially that type which was called *genre troubadour*. When this romanticism became the dominant spiritual tendency in Europe, in the second decade of the nineteenth century, the French operetta succumbed to its influence. F. Adrien Boïeldieu [4] is a typical romanticist. His

[4] FRANÇOIS ADRIEN BOÏELDIEU (b. Rouen, 1775; d. Jarcy, near Paris, 1834). CHIEF WORKS:

Dame blanche (1825) is a pleasing counterpart to the German *Freischütz*. As is already the case with Grétry's *Richard Cœur-de-Lion*, the entire opera has been composed around a single romanza, but the tone of the opera, even though harmless, is in consonance with the time of Victor Hugo, containing all kinds of horrors and gruesomeness.

The comic opera retained its romantic plots for a long time, but— just as in the case of the grand opera—they soon became a mere pretext for motley stage pictures and all kinds of scenic effects. Even if this admixture, in the seriously intended music drama, seems unbearable to us at the present day, and even if it be true that Scribe wrote veritable monstrosities of opera books for Meyerbeer, one must nevertheless concede that in the operetta his French *esprit* produced very entertaining and humorous libretti. The delightful *Fra Diavolo* still bears witness to this truth. It was composed by D. F. E. Auber,[5] the most famous successor of Boïeldieu, who had sufficient versatility and wit at his disposal in his music—he could also assume a romantic tone—to convert the jolly potpourri into proper sound. His chief works of the species of the romantically-colored *Lustspiel*, or conversational opera, are *Le Maçon* (The Mason, 1825), and *La Part du diable* (The Devil's Share), 1843.

Auber is not only the master of the refined *genre* of the comic opera, but is also the founder of the romantic tendency in grand opera. His *La Muette de Portici* (The Mute Maid of Portici) shows the influence of the crass neo-romanticism of Victor Hugo, with its predilection for the gruesome and the horrible. It represents the complete break with the classical tradition of the Lully-Rameau-Gluck opera. It was produced in 1828, and, as is well known, helped to ignite the July revolution of 1830 in Belgium. Richard Wagner characterizes the work well, when he says in his recollections of Auber: "Of stiffness, shallow pathos, high-

Le Calife de Bagdad, 1800; *Jean de Paris*, 1812; *Le Petit Chaperon rouge*, 1818; *La Dame blanche*, 1825. BIBLIOGRAPHY: Lucien Augé de Lassus, *Boïeldieu*. Laurens, Paris, 1908 ("Les Musiciens célèbres").—A. Pougin, *Boïeldieu, sa vie et ses œuvres*. Charpentier, Paris, 1875.

[5] DANIEL FRANÇOIS ÉSPRIT AUBER (b. Caen, Normandy, 1782; d. Paris, 1871) passed his entire life in Paris for which he composed more than forty operas, the majority of which were more or less successful. His most celebrated works are: *Le Maçon*, 1825; *La Muette de Portici*, 1828; *Fra Diavolo*, 1830; *Le Domino noir*, 1837; *Les Diamants de la Couronne*, 1841; *La Part du diable*, 1843; *Haydée*, 1847. BIBLIOGRAPHY: A. Kohut, *Auber*. Reclam, Leipzig, 1895.—Ch. Malherbe, *Auber* (in "Musiciens célèbres"). Laurens, Paris.—A. Pougin, *Auber*. Pottier de Lalaine, Paris, 1873; by the same author, in "Musiciens du XIXe siècle." Fischbacher, Paris, 1911.

priestly dignity, and all the classical rummage, not a trace; hot as fire, entertaining to the last degree."

Although this work was actually born out of the spiritual atmosphere of the times, romanticism soon after became a mere pretext, as above remarked, for the piling up of all kinds of effects. The most unheard of were accomplished by J. Meyerbeer,[6] who as a foreigner—like Lully, Gluck, Cherubini, and others—took a hand in the development of French opera. In the first of his "spectacle operas" (*opéra de spectacle*), as they have been properly called, in *Robert le Diable*, which was produced at the Grand Opera in 1831, nuns arise from their graves in a convent cemetery, cast aside their garbs, and dance a ballet. We mention this merely to show to what extent the passion for effect was carried. In 1836 Meyerbeer's *chef-d'œuvre* appeared: *Les Huguenots;* in 1849, *Le Prophète;* in 1859, at the Opéra Comique, *Le Pardon de Ploërmel;* after his death, *L'Africaine*, in 1865. Much as the errors in taste on the part of Meyerbeer are to be regretted, nevertheless, one dare not deny his great dramatic talent. The consecration of the swords in the Huguenots, and the duet which follows and which reaches a tremendous dramatic climax even beyond the choral scene, are among the greatest achievements in the domain of the opera. Meyerbeer is also successful in the most manifold characterization, and in addition—he was educated in Italy—he developed a rich treasure of melodic beauty. In no less degree did he understand how to satisfy the French demands for ballet music.

In Auber's species of grand opera, Rossini wrote his already-mentioned *Guillaume Tell*, and Halévy his *Juive*.

Externally, the distinction still exists in Paris between "grand opera" and "opera comique." Originally, the latter was interspersed with

---

[6] GIACOMO MEYERBEER, the name was originally Beer (b. Berlin, 1791; d. Paris, 1864), was the son of a banker, and received a careful musical education through Lauska, Clementi, Zelter, Anselm Weber, and the Abbé Vogler with whom he studied in Darmstadt, 1810–12, at the same time at which C. M. von Weber and Gänsbacher were pupils. At first he attempted German operas; then he went to Italy in 1815 and wrote a number of Italian operas in the style of Rossini. In 1826 he went to Paris where he achieved his great success. Besides the works mentioned in the text above, the following should also be enumerated: the opera *Das Feldlager in Schlesien* (1844 in Berlin, with Jenny Lind; 1854 under the title *L'Étoile du Nord* at the Opéra comique); also the music to the drama of his brother Michael, *Struensee*, Berlin, 1846. BIBLIOGRAPHY: W. Altmann, "Meyerbeer-Forschungen," S.I.M.G., IV.—H. de Curzon, *Meyerbeer*. Laurens, Paris, 1910 ("Musiciens célèbres").—L. Dauriac, *Meyerbeer*. Alcan, Paris, 1913 ("Les Maîtres de la musique"); new ed., 1930.—A. Hervey, *Giacomo Meyerbeer*. T. C. and E. C. Jack, London, F. A. Stokes, New York, 1913.— E. Istel, in *Musical Quarterly*. G. Schirmer, N. Y., 1926.—A. Kohut, "Meyerbeer," in Reclam's *Universalbibliothek*, Leipzig, 1890.—A. Pougin, *Meyerbeer*. J. Tresse, Paris, 1864.

spoken dialogue, while the libretto of the grand opera was composed throughout. However, the species became intermingled, and no sharp line of distinction can be drawn between them any longer.

Charles Gounod,[7] with his formally beautiful and very melodious *Faust* (1859) and *Roméo et Juliette*, and Ambroise Thomas (1811–96) with his *Mignon*, follow in the footsteps of a modified romanticism. After Madame de Stael had acquainted the French with German literature, the French romanticists began especially to admire Goethe. This by no means bad taste also took possession of the opera librettists who took a special pleasure in bowdlerizing Goethe's poems. Thus we possess *Werther* from the decidedly nationalistic Jules Massenet.[8] Massenet's characteristics, which consist in the taste and sureness with which he handles his forms, have scarcely ever been properly understood by the Germans. His works are almost impossible in German translation. His chief work is *Manon* (1884), a picture of Parisian grace and elegance, and of a delicate sensuality with all its *raffinement*.

Saint-Saëns [9] approaches more the solemn manner of the old Grand

[7] CHARLES GOUNOD (b. Paris, 1818; d. there, 1893) studied at first with his mother, then at the Conservatoire with Halévy and Lesueur. He obtained the Prix de Rome in 1839. In his youth he thought of becoming a priest. His first important work was a *Messe solennelle*. Abandoning his original intention he turned to the music of the theater, and presented, notably, *Faust* in 1859; *La Reine de Saba* (The Queen of Sheba) in 1862; *Mireille* in 1864; *Roméo et Juliette* in 1867. After 1870 he wrote the funeral cantata *Gallia*. His religious works, oratorios, Masses, cantatas, etc., have also contributed to his reputation. He produced various fragmentary writings, in particular the *Mémoires d'un artiste* (up to 1859). BIBLIOGRAPHY: *Autobiographie de Chas. Gounod*. W. Reeves, London, 1875; a biographical record to 1859 only, edited by Georgina Weldon; published by Mrs. Weldon, Tavistock House, Tavistock Square, London, 1875.—*Mémoires d'un artiste*. Calman Levy, Paris, 1896 and 1909 (5th ed.); Eng. tr., *Chas. Gounod, Autobiographical Reminiscences*, edited by W. H. Hutchinson. Heinemann, London, 1896; also Eng. tr. by Annette E. Crocker. Rand, McNally, and Co., Chicago and New York, 1895.—Camille Bellaigue, *Gounod*. Alcan, Paris, 3d ed., 1911.—M. A. Bovet, *Ch. Gounod, His Life and His Works*. S. Low, Marston, Searle and Rivington, Ltd., London, 1891.—Hillemacher, *Gounod*. Laurens, Paris, 1914.— J. G. Prod'homme and Dandelot, *Gounod*. 2 vols., Delagrave, Paris, 1911.—Soubies and H. de Curzon, *Documents inédits sur le Faust de Gounod*. Fischbacher, Paris, 1912.— H. Tolhurst, *Gounod*. G. Bell and Sons, London, 1905.

[8] JULES MASSENET (b. 1842, near Saint-Étienne; d. Paris, 1912) received the Prix de Rome in 1863. He at first gained a reputation by his biblical works: *Marie Madeleine, Eve, La Vierge*. The most celebrated of his Grand Operas are: *Le Roi de Lahore*, 1877; *Hérodiade*, 1881; *Thaïs*, 1894; his opéras-comiques (besides *Manon*) are: *Werther*, 1886; *Grisélidis*, 1901; *Le Jongleur de Notre-Dame*, 1902, etc. Massenet has also written numerous orchestral compositions, songs, etc. BIBLIOGRAPHY: Ch. Bouvet, *Massenet*. Laurens, Paris, 1929.— R. Brancour, *Massenet*. Alcan, Paris, 1922.—H. T. Finck, *Massenet and His Operas*. Lane, London, 1910.—A. Pougin, *Massenet*. Fischbacher, Paris, 1914.—L. Schneider, *Jules Massenet*. L. Carteret, Paris, 1908.

[9] CAMILLE SAINT-SAËNS (b. Paris, 1835; d. Algiers, 1921) was organist, pianist, and com-

Opera in his *Samson et Dalila* (Weimar, 1877). So also do the works, slightly influenced by Wagner, of Ernest Reyer (1823–1909): *Sigurd* (Brussels, 1884) and *Salammbô* (1900). In 1881, a last echo of romanticism was heard in the *Contes d'Hoffmann* of Jacques Offenbach (1819–80). As is well known, by far the greatest number of Offenbach's works are in another sphere. With his *Belle Hélène* and his *Orphée aux enfers* (Orpheus in Hell), he is the creator of the modern French operetta. Hervé (1825–95) followed him in that field in which the best contemporary musicians are Charles Lecocq (1832–1918), André Messager (1853–1929), and Claude Terrasse (1867–1923).

Berlioz's operas did not achieve any lasting success in the nineteenth century. This seems to have been reserved for them until recent times, especially for his *Béatrice et Bénédict* and his *Les Troyens*. On the other hand, the *Carmen* (1875) of Georges Bizet [10] was epoch making. Besides the works of Wagner, it is the most popular opera on the European stage. At the time of naturalism in literature, Bizet transplanted, if not a naturalism, at least a musical realism to the opera. We have already observed that his work formed the point of departure for the Italian *verismo*. This realism, happily, proceeds from popular art, from popular dances and tunes, and Bizet's work has, like the works of Massenet, a national infusion, only in an entirely different manner. Not only the opera, but all music acquired a national impress in the second half of the nineteenth century. Charpentier's *Louise* (1900) is a realistic and

poser. His four symphonic poems, his three symphonies, among which the third, in C minor, with organ, 1886, must especially be emphasized, his suites for orchestra, his concertos, his numerous fantasias for diverse instruments, his cantatas, his religious pieces, have contributed more to his celebrity than his operas. The most important works in the last-named category are (besides *Samson*): *Henry VIII*, 1883; and *Ascanio*, 1890. BIBLIOGRAPHY: A. Hervey, *Saint-Saëns*. Lane, London, 1921.—Augé de Lassus, *Saint-Saëns*. Delagrave, Paris, 1914.—W. Lyle, *Camille Saint-Saëns—His Life and Art*. E. P. Dutton, N. Y., Kegan Paul, London, 1923; 1926.—Saint-Saëns, *Outspoken Essays on Music;* the Eng. tr. by F. Rothwell. Kegan Paul, London, 1922.—Saint-Saëns, *Musical Memories;* the Eng. tr. by R. Murray, London, 1921.—G. Servières, *Saint-Saëns*. Alcan, Paris, 1923.

[10] GEORGES BIZET (b. Paris, 1838; d. Bougival, 1875). His master in composition was Halévy. His first two operas, *Les Pêcheurs de perles*, 1863, and *La Jolie Fille de Perth*, 1867, did not meet with success. *L'Arlésienne* was better received, but the failure of *Carmen*, 1875, probably caused his death. Among his operas there is also a one-act work of charming, oriental inspiration, *Djamilé*, 1872. Important orchestral suites (besides *L'Arlésienne*) are *Roma*, and *Jeux d'enfants*. BIBLIOGRAPHY: C. Bellaigue, *Bizet*. Delagrave, Paris, 1890.—M. Delmas, *Bizet*. P. Bossuet, Paris, 1930.—H. Gauthier-Villars, *Bizet*. Laurens, Paris, 1912 ("Les Musiciens célèbres").—P. Landormy, *Bizet*. Alcan, Paris, 1924 ("Les Maîtres de la musique").—Paul Voss, *Bizet*. Reclam, Leipzig, 1899.—Ad. Weissmann, *Bizet*. Marquardt & Co., Berlin, 1907.

locally Parisian work. The works of Alfred Bruneau endeavor to interpret lyrically the novels of Zola. The opera *Les Armaillis* (Paris, 1906) by the Lausanne composer, G. Doret, breathes the atmosphere of the Swiss mountains.

In the twentieth century, a new turn took place: "impressionism" announced its appearance in the *Pelléas et Mélisande* (1902) of Claude Debussy. It may be said that the work shows Wagner's influence in so far as it also possesses a distinguished libretto. The French libretti are, for the most part, good. Complete blunders in judgment and taste, such as frequently appear in Germany, occur comparatively seldom, even if the libretti do not always possess an independent literary value. But Maeterlinck's *Pelléas et Mélisande* is a work of genuine value. Debussy's work, therefore, has a great advantage to begin with; and although the music makes no great pretenses, it nevertheless accentuates and deepens the effect of the poem by its close and characteristic union with the word, so that the total result is a modern work of genuine significance.

Ariane et Barbe-Bleue by Paul Dukas (b. Paris, 1865), the first performance of which was given in 1907, attaches itself more to symphonic than to dramatic music, and applies a science of counterpoint which fully comes into its own in the composer's works of pure music.

One must also mention, as producers of operas in comparatively recent times: Léo Delibes [11] (*Lakmé*, 1883); Edouard Lalo (1823–92; *Le Roi d'Ys*, 1888), Sylvio Lazzari, Gabriel Fauré (*Pénélope*, 1913), Henri Rabaud (*Marouf*, 1914). A work, original in form, which participates in the lyric drama and the oratorio with recitative and chorus, and which is called a "sacred drama," is the *Légende de Saint-Christophe* of Vincent d'Indy,[12] performed in 1920. The same musician had presented before, in a style influenced by Wagner, *Fervaal* (1897) and *L'Etranger* (1903).

[11] Cf. H. de Curzon, *Léo Delibes*. Legouix, Paris, 1926.
[12] VINCENT D'INDY (b. Paris, 1851; d. there, 1931) was a pupil of César Franck. With Ch. Bordes and A. Guilmant he founded the *Schola cantorum* in Paris, at which institution he taught composition from 1897 until his death.—His chief works, besides the operas cited, are: *Wallenstein*, trilogy for orchestra; *Symphonie sur un thème montagnard*, with piano, 1886; *Istar*, symphonic variations, 1896; 2d symphony in B flat, 1902–03; 3d symphony, *De bello gallico*, 1919; 2 quartets for strings, 1 quintet, 1925; songs, piano music, etc. BIBLIOGRAPHY: L. Borgex, *Vincent d'Indy*. A. Durand et fils, Paris, 1913.—A. Hervey, *French Music in the 19th Century*. G. Richards, London, E. P. Dutton, New York, 1903.— V. d'Indy, *La Schola cantorum: s. histoire depuis s. fondation jusque en 1925*. Blond & Gay, Paris, 1927.—A. Sérieyx, *Vincent d'Indy*. Société de trente, A. Messin, Paris, 1914.

Mention should finally be made, as being among the most distinguished of modern operas, of *Padmâvati* by Albert Roussel (1923).

THE GERMAN OPERA

Beethoven loved especially the *Magic Flute*, and declared it to be Mozart's greatest work. This indicates his standpoint. In his *Fidelio* (1805), he placed the opera completely on German ground, and pursued the path which had been entered upon by Mozart. The text compiled by Sonnleithner, according to an older French libretto by Bouilly, later reworked by Treitschke, necessarily appealed to Beethoven. As with Schiller also, Beethoven's phantasy demanded the stimulation of a lofty moral act—Beethoven is reported to have said that he could never have composed *The Marriage of Figaro*. *Fidelio* exalts the power of love, and wherever this phase of the subject dominates, wherever Leonore steps into action, the music is profound and significant, whereas the subsidiary figures do not reach the same heights. The style of *Fidelio* is to a great extent instrumental, and on this account the work had difficulty in making its way, despite its many beauties. Moreover, the music is so pronouncedly German that its effect chiefly remained limited to German territory.

German opera was definitely established by Beethoven's work, but its further development proceeded slowly. It was only with the *Freischütz* of Weber,[13] which was received by the Berlin public in 1821 with

[13] CARL MARIA VON WEBER (b. Eutin, Oldenburg, 1786; d. London, 1826) in his youth accompanied his father (a theatrical impresario) throughout Germany, and received instruction from various teachers: Heuschkel in Hildburghausen; Michael Haydn in Salzburg; the Abbé Vogler in Vienna. The last-named exerted the greatest influence upon his musical education; among other things Vogler called his pupil's attention to the beauty of folk melodies. Weber's first dramatic work of significance was *Silvana* (Frankfurt, 1810, Berlin, 1812). In 1813 he became *Kapellmeister* at the theater in Prague, where he began his exemplary activity as operatic conductor, presenting also Beethoven's *Fidelio*. In 1814 appeared his *Lieder* to words taken from Körner's *Leyer und Schwert*. In 1816 he was called to Dresden by the king of Saxony, in order to organize and conduct the new German opera about to be established. Weber continued in this position, conducting to the time of his death. However, his great works were not produced in Dresden; two of them, *Preziosa* (music to the drama of P. A. Wolff) and *Freischütz*, 1821, in Berlin; *Euryanthe*, 1823 in *Vienna*; and *Oberon*, 1826, in London. BIBLIOGRAPHY: Sir J. Benedict, *Weber*. S. Low, Marston, Searle, and Rivington, London, Scribner & Welford, N. Y., 1881; 2d ed., 1913; 5th ed., ed. by F. Hueffer. S. Low, Marston, & Co., London, 1899 ("Great Musicians").—André Coeuroy, *Weber*. Alcan, Paris, 1925.—M. Degen. *Die Lieder von Carl Maria von Weber*. Herder & Co., Freiburg im Breisgau, 1924.—W. Georgii, *Weber als Klavierkomponist*. B. & H., Leipzig, 1914.—F. W. Jähns, *Carl Maria von Weber in seinen Werken*, complete chronological-thematic index, with esthetic and historical notes. Schlesinger (R. Lienau), Berlin, 1871; by the same author, *Carl Maria von Weber, eine Lebensskizze*. F. W. Grunow, Leipzig, 1873.—G. Kaiser, complete

thunderous applause, that a work of lasting value again appeared. Moreover, Weber's *Freischütz* created a school. A constant development begins, and German opera takes its legitimate place besides the Italian and the French. The Romantic school had, in general, brought the national consciousness to the fore in Germany, as over against the internationalism of the Illumination, and thus the ground was also prepared for a national opera. *Freischütz* and romanticism are equivalent terms. The piece is based on folklore, popular songs occupy the central position, the music presents the local atmosphere of the German forest and pictures the eeriness of phantastic powers of nature. That is the new and characteristic thing which Weber presented. Over against the universally human figures in Mozart, Weber offers German romantic figures with local atmosphere, such as the opera of the eighteenth century had not known.

Weber did not pass beyond this romanticism in his later works, although he strove to realize a higher dramatic ideal. His last opera *Oberon*, written for London in 1826, is thoroughly romantic. The eeriness of nature powers again plays a chief rôle here, but now it is in the more friendly form of elves and mermaids. The German heroes are placed in an oriental, fairy-like atmosphere, but the work as a whole is not satisfactory on account of the weak text.

Unfortunately, Weber's *Euryanthe*, with which he had hoped to realize his higher dramatic ideal, also suffered shipwreck, on account of the shortcomings of the libretto written by Wilhelmine von Chezy. To be sure, he here placed the chief element of this ideal, the dramatic declamation, in the foreground. By dissolving the smaller forms into larger connected ones, he brought movement into the whole. The orchestra is also used extensively for the purposes of characterization. Weber expressed his intentions clearly in a writing to the Akademischer Konzertverein in Breslau which wanted to present *Euryanthe* in concert form. He says: "Euryanthe is a purely dramatic attempt, anticipating its effectiveness solely through the union of all the sister arts, surely without effect when deprived of this coöperation." Weber already anticipated

writings of Carl Maria von Weber, critical edition. Schuster & Loeffler, Berlin & Leipzig, 1908; by the same author, *Beiträge zu einer Charakteristik Carl Maria von Webers.* Schuster & Loeffler, Berlin and Leipzig, 1910.—Max Maria von Weber, *Carl Maria von Weber, ein Lebensbild.* E. Keil, Leipzig, 1864–66, 3 vols., the third volume containing the writings of Weber; Eng. tr. in 2 vols. by J. P. Simpson. Chapman & Hall, London, 1865–68, Ditson & Co., Boston, 1865; new Ger. ed., by Rud. Pechel. G. Grote, Berlin, 1912.

the complete art work which Wagner realized. External relationships with *Lohengrin* also point prophetically to the coming great master of the music drama.

Heinrich Marschner [14] was a pupil of Weber, especially strong in the expression of the gruesome and the demonic. The very title of one of his chief works, *Der Vampyr* (1828), already indicates this side of his phantasy. But in true romantic manner, he moves in contrasts. He is also a master of the grossly comic, and has written the best drinking songs, e.g., *Im Frühling muss man trinken* (In Springtime One Must Drink), etc. His best work is *Hans Heiling* (1833), which in some respects anticipates the *Flying Dutchman*.

Louis Spohr [15] represents the sentimental side in opera. Passing by Beethoven, he proceeds from Mozart, develops further the latter's elegiac, fanciful vein, adopts his chromaticism, which, with the constant chromatic transitions in the middle voices, becomes a veritable mannerism with him. In his *Faust* (not according to Goethe) there are characteristic, romantic choral scenes. His chief work is *Jessonda* (1823). The latter's gentle, fanciful figure was doubtless not without influence in the creation of "Elsa" in Wagner's *Lohengrin*. The lyrical direction of the romantic opera, finally, is represented by Konradin Kreutzer and his *Nachtlager von Granada* (1834).

A German counterpart of the French operettas of Auber are the only partially romantic works of Albert Lortzing. [16] He was his own librettist.

---

[14] HEINRICH MARSCHNER (b. Zittau, Saxony, 1795; d. Hannover, 1861) was director of the opera at Dresden from 1824 to 1826 with Weber. From 1831 on he was court kapellmeister in Hannover. For Leipzig he wrote *Der Vampyr*, 1828; *Der Templer und die Jüdin* (The Knight-Templar and the Jewess), 1829; *Hans Heiling* had its première in Berlin in 1833. BIBLIOGRAPHY: H. Gaartz, *Die Opern H. Marschners*. B. & H., Leipzig, 1912.—G. Münzer, *H. Marschner*. "Harmonie," Berlin, 1901.

[15] LOUIS SPOHR (b. Brunswick, 1784; d. Kassel, 1859) was the founder of the modern German violin school, and a distinguished composer for and virtuoso upon his special instrument. After a varied career as virtuoso, he became court kapellmeister in Kassel in 1822. Among his works should be mentioned: 9 symphonies, 12 violin concertos (the eighth, in A major, in the form of a vocal scene); the operas *Faust*, 1816, in Prague; and *Jessonda*, 1823, in Kassel. BIBLIOGRAPHY: *Selbstbiographie* (Autobiography). 2 vols. G. H. Wigand, Cassel & Göttingen, 1860–61; Eng. tr., Reeves & Turner, London, 1878.—R. Wassermann, *L. Spohr als Opernkomponist* (Rostock dissertation). Huber, Munich, 1909.

[16] GUSTAV ALBERT LORTZING (b. Berlin, 1801; d. there, 1851) was actor and buffo-tenor at the municipal theater in Leipzig from 1833, where the following works were produced: *Die beiden Schützen* (The Two Riflemen), 1835; *Zar und Zimmerman* (Zar and Carpenter), 1837; *Der Wildschütz* (The Poacher), 1842. From 1845 on, Lortzing led an unsettled life, acting as guest singer and kapellmeister, constantly troubled with material cares, although he achieved further successes with the operas *Undine*, Magdeburg and Hamburg, 1845, and *Der Waffenschmied* (The Armorer), Vienna, 1846. BIBLIOGRAPHY: G. R. Kruse, *A. Lor-*

They present cozy and humorous pictures of conditions among the narrow *bourgeoisie*. They are often trivial, but always scenically effective and well rounded. The old German *Singspiel* found a continuation in Lortzing's works. As in those, so in these also the popular songs are the best. The German people still cling to them with a stubborn devotion, despite their sentimental character of a by-gone day. Lortzing's *Zar und Zimmerman* (Czar and Carpenter), 1837, was always considered his chief work, but his *Waffenschmied* (Armorer), 1846, seems to continue longest in the public favor, probably because it presents German artisanry, from which Lortzing himself sprang, in a pleasing and straightforward manner. Lortzing's father had exchanged the saddler's trade with the vocation of an actor. *Der Wildschütz* (The Poacher), finally, happily approaches the lively *genre* of the conversational opera.

Further successful German works of a related kind are the imperishable *Martha* (1847) by Friedrich Flotow (1812–83), and *Die lustigen Weiber von Windsor* (The Merry Wives of Windsor) by Otto Nicolai (1810–49). To a later period belong *Der Widerspenstigen Zähmung* (The Taming of the Shrew) by Hermann Götz (1840–76), and *Der Barbier von Bagdad* (The Barber of Bagdad) by Peter Cornelius (1824–74). This last work has been mildly influenced by Richard Wagner, and contains the seeds for a modern *Lustspiel* opera.

Stimulated by the example which Offenbach had set in Paris, the German operetta arose in Vienna. Here Joseph Lanner (1801–43) and Johann Strauss (1825–99), the father of the operetta composer, had brought the waltz to the highest degree of development. It plays a distinguished rôle in art music also, since the days of Franz Schubert and C. M. von Weber, just as the minuet did in the eighteenth century. There is no composer who did not make obeisance to the lightly-flowing, three-quarter movement. But it indulges in veritable orgies in the Vienna operetta by Johann Strauss, *Die Fledermaus* (The Bat), 1874, and his numerous contemporaries and successors. The operettas of Franz Suppé (1819–95), e.g., *Boccaccio*, 1879, are less one-sided in their devotion to the dance, and are musically richer.

The great reform of the opera through Richard Wagner [17] occurred

---

tzing. "Harmonie," Berlin, 1899.—Helm. Laue, *Die Operndichtung L's.*, (Bonn dissertation). L. Röhrscheid, Bonn, 1932.

[17] RICHARD WAGNER (b. Leipzig, 1813; d. Venice, 1883). His stepfather, Ludwig Geyer, was an actor and a writer of librettos for comic operas in Dresden. Wagner grew up, as it were, on the stage. In Leipzig he studied philosophy at the university and counterpoint

toward the end of the romantic period. It started from a new emphasis upon the text. Wagner's librettos, written by himself, are poems of genuine worth, and represent a tremendous advance when compared with those of Meyerbeer. They have as their subjects romantic materials

with Weinlig, the cantor at St. Thomas'. In 1834 he set out upon his migratory life as theater-conductor in Magdeburg, Königsberg, Riga, having written an opera *Die Feen* in 1833. From 1839 to 1842 he experienced a period of great hardship in Paris, in 1842 *Rienzi* was produced in Dresden, and Wagner was appointed court-conductor. Having participated in the Revolution of 1848, he arrived in Zürich as a political refugee in 1849. This city became his haven of refuge for ten years. In 1864 he experienced the favor of King Ludwig II of Bavaria. This, together with the assistance of numerous musical friends, made it possible for him to realize his plan for a festival theater, which was built in Bayreuth and opened in 1876 with the performance of the Ring of the Nibelung. The following dates will supplement the preceding outline: 1843, Dresden, *Der Fliegende Holländer;* 1847, *Lohengrin* written (produced, 1850, under the direction of Liszt in Weimar); 1859, *Tristan* completed (produced, 1865, under the direction of von Bülow in Munich); 1868, *Die Meistersinger*, in Munich; after the *Ring* in Bayreuth in 1876, *Parsifal* was produced there in 1882. BIBLIOGRAPHY: Autobiography, *Mein Leben*. F. Bruckmann, Munich, 1911; cheap popular ed., 1914. B. & H., Leipzig, 1928; Eng. tr., *My Life*. Dodd, Mead Co., New York, Constable & Co., London, 1911; also Dodd, Mead & Co., New York, 1924.—G. Adler, *Richard Wagner* (lectures). B. & H., Leipzig, 1904; 2d ed., Drei Masken Verlag, Munich, 1923; French tr. by L. Laloy. Fischbacher, Paris, 1910.—Supplementary vols. published by B. & H.—Mrs. M. (neé Banks) Burrell, *Richard Wagner, His Life and Works from 1813 to 1834*. Allan Wyon, London, 1898.—Houston S. Chamberlain, *Wagner*. F. Bruckmann, Munich, 1894; new ed., illustrated, 1911; Eng. tr. by G. A. Hight. J. M. Dent & Co., London, J. B. Lippincott Co., Philadelphia, 1897; French tr., Perrin & Cie., Paris, 1899.—Cleather and Crump, *The Ring of the Nibelung*. Methuen, London; by the same authors, *Lohengrin and Parsifal*. Methuen, London; by the same authors, *Tristan and Isolda*. Methuen, London; by the same authors, *Tannhäuser and the Mastersingers of Nuremberg*. Methuen, London.—A. E. F. Dickinson, *The Musical Design of the Ring*. O.U.P., London, 1926.—W. A. Ellis, *Life of Richard Wagner*. 6 vols., K. Paul, Trench, Trübner & Co., Ltd., London, 1900–08; Vols. I–III, a translation (with extensive additions) of the 1st ed. of Glasenapp, the remaining vols. original.—E. Evans, *Wagner, Opera and Drama*. 2 vols., Reeves, London, 1913.—H. T. Finck, *Wagner and His Works*. 2 vols., C. Scribner's Sons, N. Y., 1911.—First complete edition of his writings, published by Fritzsch, Leipzig, 1871–83.—A. George, *Tristan et Isolde de R. Wagner, étude historique et critique*. Mellottée, Paris, 1929.—K. F. Glasenapp, *Richard Wagners Leben und Wirken*. 6 vols., B. & H., Leipzig, 1876–1912; Eng. tr., see above under W. A. Ellis.—J. C. Hadden, *The Operas of Wagner*. T. C. & E. C. Jack, London, 1908.—W. J. Henderson, *Richard Wagner, His Life and His Dramas*. G. P. Putnam's Sons, N. Y. & London, 2d ed., 1923.—A. Heintz, *Die Meistersinger von Nürnberg;* Eng. tr., *The Master-Singers of Nuremberg*, by J. H. Cornell. G. Schirmer, N. Y., 1890; Novello, London, & Novello, Ewer, & Co., N. Y., 1892.—A. Heintz, Eng. tr. by C. Bache, *Parsifal, by Richard Wagner, Its Origin in the Old Legends and Its Musical Motives Explained*. Novello, London.—G. A. Hight, *Richard Wagner—A Critical Biography*. 2 vols., Arrowsmith, London, 1925.—O. Huckel, *Wagner, the Man and His Work*. T. Y. Crowell Co., N. Y., 1914.—F. Hueffer, *Richard Wagner*. S. Low, Marston, Searle & Rivington, London, 3d ed., 1890; new ed., 1912.—A. Jullien, *Richard Wagner, sa vie et ses œuvres*. J. Rouam, Paris, 1886; Eng. tr. by F. P. Hall. J. B. Millet Co., Boston, 1892; reprinted, Th. Presser Co., Philadelphia, 1910.—Kobbé, *Wagner's Music-Dramas Analysed—With the Leading Motives*. Schirmer, N. Y., 1904; by the same author, *How to Understand Wagner's Ring of the Nibelung*. Reeves, London.—M. Koch, *Richard Wagner*. 3 vols., E. Hoffmann, Berlin, 1907–18; by the same author, *Richard Wagners*

drawn from the elemental, Germanic hero sagas. Wagner molds them with classical simplicity and monumentality. His dramas form great connected pictures, such as are required by music. He broke completely with the complex entanglements of the old opera. He treated chiefly of the idea of redemption, the power of sacrificial love. Antiquity, Schopenhauer, and nature, which last he learned to know from its overpowering side in Switzerland, are the influences which determined his creative activity.

The chief musical means of reform was the introduction of the musical declamation—*Sprechgesang*—as Wagner himself called it, or to use the familiar term, the reëstablishment of the recitative. This becomes the center of the opera, to be sure in an expressive and often melodious form, and as Weber had already anticipated in his *Euryanthe*, the individual forms, such as the aria, etc., are sacrificed in the interest of the uninterrupted dramatic development. In the earlier works, *The Flying Dutchman*, *Tannhäuser*, and *Lohengrin*, there are still at least intimations of them present. Later they disappear entirely. It is absolutely unique how Wagner understood in those earlier works how to combine the demands of the drama and of the music in perfect manner. The history of the opera is an incessant battle between the drama and the music. The former demands rapid action, the music requires time and hinders the rapid development. There are few works in all literature in which the compromise is so well solved as in those named. *Tannhäuser* and *Lohengrin* are thrilling theater dramas, which at once grip even the naïve theatergoer, and at the same time, the music receives its due, and attains its full development.

Geschichtliche Völkische Sendung. H. Beyer & Söhne, Langensalza, 1927.—H. Lichtenberger, *Wagner*. Alcan, Paris, 6th ed., 1925.—C. A. Lidgey, *Wagner*. J. M. Dent & Co., London, E. P. Dutton & Co., N. Y., 2d ed., 1904.—E. Newman, *Wagner*. J. Lane, London, 1922; by the same author, *Wagner as Man and Artist*. J. M. Dent & Sons, Ltd., London, 1914 & 1926; A. A. Knopf, N. Y., 1924; by the same author, *The Life of Richard Wagner* (Vol. I only, to 1848). Cassell, London, 1933.—Élie Poirée, *Richard Wagner, L'Homme, le Poète, le Musicien*. Laurens, Paris, 1922.—J. G. Prod'homme, F. Holl, Fr. Caillé, and L. van Vassenhove, translators, *Prose Works*. 13 vols., Delagrave, Paris, 1908–25; Eng. tr. of the *Prose Works*, by W. A. Ellis. 8 vols., K. Paul, Trench, Trübner, London, 1892–99.— J. F. Runciman, *Richard Wagner, Composer of Operas*. G. Bell & Sons, Ltd., London, 1913; by the same author, *Old Scores and New Readings*. Unicorn Press, London, 2d ed., 1901.— W. Wallace, *Richard Wagner as He Lived*. Kegan Paul, London, Harper & Bros., N. Y. 1925; 1933.—H. Thompson, *Wagner and Wagenseil—A Source of Wagner's Opera "Die Meistersinger."* O.U.P., London. 1927.—C. Winn. *The Master-Singers of Nuremberg*. O.U.P., London, 1925.—For a list of translations of the Wagner libretti, both metrical and prose, see Percy A. Scholes, *The Listener's History of Music*. Vol. II, pp. 223–24, O.U.P., 1930.

Wagner employs the *Leitmotiv* as an effective dramatic means. Indications of this already appear in the French operettas of Grétry and his circle. Berlioz was the first to elevate it to the rank of a principle in his symphonies. C. M. von Weber already utilizes it in individual instances as a reminiscent motif (*Erinnerungsmotiv*), e.g., the motif of the chorus of derision in the *Freischütz*. In Wagner's case it is also primarily a motif of reminiscence, and every music lover knows how extremely effectively he utilized this in *Lohengrin:* "Nie sollst du mich befragen" (Ne'er shalt thou ask the question). In the second act of this opera, however, he utilized it in a symphonic manner, as a theme for larger developments.

Finally, he employed the principle of the *Leitmotiv* symphonically on a grand scale in his later dramas, *Tristan, Nibelungen, Meistersinger,* and *Parsifal.* He transferred, as it were, the symphony to the opera. The leitmotifs are the themes upon which the entire work is constructed. In the *Ring des Nibelungen* Wagner even combines four extensive dramas by means of the same dramatic material, and thereby gained a unity of overpowering magnitude. The orchestra becomes a chief factor. It characterizes the situations, and gives expression to the emotions of the actors. Wagner employed to this end the Haydn-Beethoven thematic development, as well as the Bach counterpoint and polyphony, and thus reveals himself as the heir of Bach and Beethoven alike. He molds ingeniously the tone of his orchestra, which he enriches by a number of additional instruments.

It is evident that the really dramatic element necessarily suffered somewhat as the result of this strong utilization of the orchestra. The hearer must willingly follow the diffuse excursuses of the orchestra, and must be willing to dispense with the continuous tension, the uninterrupted development of the action which the drama should offer. Although it is true that Wagner's last works are not to be viewed as perfect models from the purely dramatic point of view, it is none the less true that they are colossal creations of a giant spirit, which take a worthy place beside the masterpieces of all time.

Through Richard Wagner, Germany for the first time took over the leadership in opera. Wagner's influence extended itself to all domains of music, and imitations of his dramas were undertaken not only in Germany, but also in France, although his work experienced no actual continuation. It is too powerful to be transcended. As the fairy tale followed the heroic saga in the historical development of poetry, so one may, perhaps, view Engelbert Humperdinck's fairy-tale opera *Hänsel und Gretel* as a pleasing anticlimax.

In a certain sense, of course, Richard Strauss [18] is a pupil of Richard Wagner. His operas *Salome* (1905), *Elektra* (1909), *Rosenkavalier* (1911), *Ariadne* (1912), *Die Frau ohne Schatten* (The Woman without a Shadow, 1919), *Die ägyptische Helene* (The Egyptian Helen, 1928), *Arabella* (1933), and *Die schweigsame Frau* (The Silent Woman, 1935; libretto by S. Zweig) freely continue the *leitmotif* system. Strauss also merits to be called a pupil of Wagner inasmuch as he has composed only texts that are works of genuine literary value, whether, like Debussy, he chose already existing works, as the *Salome* of Oscar Wilde, or succeeded in winning a distinguished poet for his purposes, as Hugo von Hofmannsthal. The strength of the Strauss music consists in its tonal stimulation and attraction, and in its ability to paint objects and events. In its fiery nature, it also seems to have been influenced by the sparkling glow of C. M. von Weber.

Hans Pfitzner (born 1869) leans strongly toward the romanticists. He is especially famous also as a colorist: *Der arme Heinrich* (Poor Henry, 1891–93); *Palestrina* (1912–15). The operas of Hans Huber (1852–1921) are further after-blooms of romanticism. The peculiarity of this Swiss composer consists in his borrowing from his native scenes. His *Schöne Bellinda* (1916) treats a fairy tale of the Grisons Mountains by Gian Bundi. Max Schillings, in his *Mona Lisa* (1915) follows in the footsteps of Strauss. Friedrich Klose (born in 1862), who called his colorful work *Ilsebill* (1903) a dramatic symphony, has been somewhat influenced by Bruckner. The half-Italian Wolf-Ferrari (born 1876) presents in his

[18] RICHARD STRAUSS (b. Munich, 1864) was the son of a chamber musician (horn-player), pupil of Benno Walter and of the court-conductor F. W. Meyer in Munich. In 1885 he became music-director at the court of Meiningen, 1886 at the court in Munich, 1889 court-conductor in Weimar, 1894 in Munich, 1898 court-conductor and 1908 General Director of Music in Berlin; 1919–24 leader of the Vienna State Opera in conjunction with Schalk. Since then Strauss has devoted himself completely to composition, living either in Garmisch or in Vienna. The instrumental composition of Strauss reaches its climax in his symphonic poems: *Don Juan,* 1889; *Macbeth,* 1890; *Tod und Verklärung* (Death and Transfiguration), 1891; *Till Eulenspiegels lustige Streiche* (The Merry Pranks of Till Eulenspiegel), 1890; *Also sprach Zarathustra* (So spake Zarathustra), 1896; *Don Quichote* (Don Quixote), 1898; *Ein Heldenleben* (The Life of a Hero), 1899; *Sinfonia domestica,* 1904; *Alpensinfonie,* 1915. BIBLIOGRAPHY: H. T. Finck, *Richard Strauss, the Man and His Works.* Little, Brown, & Co., Boston, 1917.—E. Newman, *Richard Strauss.* J. Lane, London & N. Y., 1908.—R. Specht, *Richard Strauss und sein Werk.* E. P. Tal & Co.,Leipzig, 1921.—M. Steinitzer, *Richard Strauss, eine Biographie.* Deutsche Verlagsanstalt, Stuttgart, 1927.

lighter works, with happy effect, all kinds of reminiscences of the old *intermezzo* and the *opera buffa*. His one-act piece *Susannens Geheimniss* (Susanna's Secret), 1909, is charming. Eugen d'Albert (born in 1864) writes according to the Italian *verismo*, with great attention to the external effect, e.g., *Tiefland* (Lowland, 1903); *Tote Augen* (Dead Eyes, 1914). Next to Strauss, he is the most successful among the modern German operatic composers.

The Austrian, Franz Schreker (born in 1878) is a kind of German Debussy, not in the sense of being an imitator, but rather a counterpart, with his scintillating, colorful style, which abandons the symphonic element as the following works show: *Der ferne Klang* (The Distant Sound), 1912; *Der Schatzgräber* (The Treasure-Digger), 1920. Mention should further be made of W. Braunfels (born 1882): *Die Vögel* (The Birds), a lyrical and phantastic piece based upon Aristophanes, 1920; Ferruccio Busoni (1866–1924): *Turandot, Arlecchino;* and E. N. von Reznicek (born 1860): *Ritter Blaubart,* (Knight Bluebeard) 1920. Julius Bittner (born 1874) attempted to create a folk opera, *Das höllisch Gold* (The Hellish Gold), 1916. Ingenious construction characterizes the *Oberst Chabert* (Colonel Chabert) of Wolfgang von Waltershausen (b. 1882).

The Oratorio

In the years 1799 and 1801, respectively, J. Haydn wrote his *Schöpfung* (Creation) and his *Die Jahreszeiten* (The Seasons), and therewith established the German oratorio of large form. He had come to know the monumental works of Handel in London, and was inspired by these, as is very evident in his great choruses. Moreover, the style of Haydn signifies an advance over that of Handel in its greater mobility and in the free union of solos and chorus. The content of both the *Creation* and the *Seasons*, with their nature pictures and *genre* scenes, was sympathetic to Haydn's nature. He was able in these, his last great works, to unfold once more in a brilliant manner the richness, manifoldness, and versatility of his phantasy. The appreciation of nature in that day, which viewed the entire world as a gift of God created and determined for mankind, found its most beautiful and artistic expression in these oratorios.

In the last third of the eighteenth century, an oratorio of small dimensions was developed by C. P. E. Bach and J. H. Rolle (1716–85). The form was revived in a somewhat expanded manner in the nineteenth century by masters such as Carl Löwe, Louis Spohr, and Friedrich Schneider. The *Weltgericht* (The Last Judgment), 1819, of Schneider enjoyed a considerable reputation for a long period. The form received strong stimulus from F. Mendelssohn's *St. Paul* (1836) and *Elijah* (1846), of which the second, at any rate, belongs to world literature. Even though it does not reach the depth of Handel's compositions, it is nevertheless distinguished by its vivid characterization of the prophet and the priests of Baal, who oppose him in a most lively dramatic manner, as well as by a vocability and a sureness and manifoldness in its form.

A school of composers united themselves to Mendelssohn. Numerous smaller musicians followed in his footsteps; and in addition to this, his oratorios, like those of Haydn before him, had a strong influence on the cultivation of choral music.

Robert Schumann entered upon the scene with an original and stimulating work: *Das Paradies und die Peri* (Paradise and the Peri) 1841, a composition written in a characteristically, softly tinted Lied style. The work revived anew the secular oratorio. It was followed by the less picturesque, but more profound, *Szenen aus Goethes Faust* (Scenes from Goethe's Faust). In his *Manfred*, intended as *entr'acte* music for Byron's drama, Schumann wrote most individualistically. The work has been chiefly produced in oratorio form, the music alternating with spoken text.

Schumann found a successful follower in the field of the secular oratorio in Max Bruch (1838–1920): *Odysseus* (1873); *Arminius* (1875), etc. His works found joyful recognition, and were repeatedly produced in the days of the newly founded German *Reich*. Bruch also wrote dramatic cantatas for male choruses, which experienced a revival in the nineteenth century. The best known is *Frithjof* (1864). Friedrich Hegar must also be mentioned here as composer of the oratorio *Manasse* (1888), and as the creator of the ballad for male voices, and the regenerator of male chorus composition.

In France, Hector Berlioz had taken up the oratorio and given it a strongly dramatic turn. His *Damnation de Faust* (Damnation of Faust) 1846, is one of the most brilliant works of this kind through the manifoldness of its colors and its rich orchestration.

Franz Liszt entered upon a new path in the oratorio of churchly tendency, by reviving the saint legend, which had been so popular in its day in the Italian oratorio. Thus he founded a new Catholic oratorio.

Moreover, his *Heilige Elisabeth* (Saint Elisabeth) distinguishes itself not only by its subject matter, but also by its advanced form, by the employment of modern instrumental and harmonic means, and by the introduction of the Wagnerian *Leitmotiv*. Among the numerous successors of *Saint Elisabeth*, the *Saint François* by the Belgian, Edgar Tinel, an oratorio of large proportions, is conspicuous. There is also a characterful and euphonious work, built upon the *Hymn to the Sun* by St. Francis, by the Swiss composer Hermann Suter, entitled *Le Laudi di Francesco d'Assisi* (1924).

More significant than Liszt's *Saint Elisabeth* is his *Christus*. Its characteristic lies in the fact that in it Liszt consciously employs all stylistic forms from the Gregorian chant and the *a cappella* song of the time of Palestrina to the most highly developed modern orchestration. Moreover, Liszt does not merely present copies of the old forms, but rather shows how they can be filled with new spirit, so that his *Christus*, filled with the profoundest religious feeling, is a work that is able to afford the most manifold and deep stimuli.

One may place in this class *Les Béatitudes*, by César Franck,[19] which likewise has a Catholic foundation. In its external effect, it must be admitted, the work is somewhat monotonous. France, which in earlier times devoted its attention only casually to the oratorio, has taken a more active interest in the last decades, through composers like Gounod, Saint-Saëns, Massenet, Gabriel Pierné (born in 1863: *La Croisade des Enfants*, 1902, a musical legend; *Les Enfants à Beethléem*, 1907, a mystery; *Saint François d'Assise*, 1912, oratorio). The Swiss, G. Doret, may also be mentioned here.

Italy also in recent times resumed the composition of oratorios. At the head of the new Italian movement stands Lorenzo Perosi with his oratorio trilogy: *The Passion according to St. Mark*, *The Transfiguration of Christ*, *The Resurrection of Lazarus*, 1897.

England, distinguished by a rich choral tradition, and blessed with

[19] CÉSAR FRANCK (b. Liège, 1822; d. Paris, 1890) studied at the Conservatory in Paris, and settled in that city as teacher of piano playing. In 1853 he became master of the chapel, and in 1859 organist, at the church of Saint Clotilde. In 1872 he became professor of organ at the Conservatory. It was only after his death that his greatness as a composer was fully recognized. His chief works, besides the oratorio *Les Béatitudes*, 1880, and his symphony in D minor, 1889, are his compositions for the organ, especially his *Trois chorals*, 1890, the quartet, the quintet, the sonata for violin, the orchestral works (*Variations symphoniques*, *Eolides*), the piano pieces: *Prélude, aria et final*, 1886; *Prélude, choral et fugue*, 1884. BIBLIOGRAPHY: M. Emmanuel, *César Franck*. Laurens, Paris, 1930.—V. d'Indy, *César Franck*. Alcan, Paris, 16th ed., 1930; Eng. tr. by Rosa Newmarch. J. Lane, London, 1909.

many choral institutions, has presented many oratorios at all times and also possessed its own oratorio composers. But these scarcely ever succeeded in obtaining a general European reputation for their works. Modern English composers of importance are Edward Elgar (1857–1934): *The Dream of Gerontius;* and Frederick Delius (1863–1934): *Sea-Drift; A Mass of Life,* an accompaniment to Nietzsche's *So Spake Zarathustra,* 1905; *A Song of the High Hills,* with a wordless choir.

Church Music

At the head of modern church music stands the *Missa solemnis* of Beethoven. The principle of the composition, which appears to have been applied here for the first time, and which became the leading principle of all modern vocal music, is the minute verbal interpretation of the text, the musical interpretation of its most subtle and recondite nuances. The mobility of expression in the *Missa solemnis* is astounding. No detail, no relationship remains unobserved; everything is reflected in the music and is reproduced with the power and the genius of the mature Beethoven. A similar penetration of the word by the tone can be found later only in the case of Wagner, and in the songs of Hugo Wolf. In church music, the attempt has scarcely been made to attain this degree of finesse. Beethoven himself was persuaded that only a later period would be able to appreciate the *Missa solemnis* properly.

Liszt, indeed, attached himself to Beethoven clearly and consciously. But the only respect in which he was really able to follow him was in his fresh method of presentation which creates the impression of an improvisation; he could not equal him in the profound penetration of his material. His chief work in this style, characterized by its verve and lofty flight, is the Mass which he composed for the dedication of the Cathedral in Gran in 1856 (*Graner Messe*).

In the time of Beethoven, Cherubini also wrote genuine church music (*Missa solemnis in D Minor,* 1821). Franz Schubert (*Mass in A Flat Major*), and R. Schumann (*Mass in C Minor*) also added not unimportant contributions.

In the nineteenth century, with its development of orchestral music, the Requiem offered an especial attraction to composers, because in the sequence "Dies irae," with its presentation of the last judgment, great realistic pictures could be drawn, which, to be sure, are in reality in direct opposition to the spirit of the Requiem. It is to this circumstance that we owe the famous *Requiem*, by Berlioz, with the famous "Tuba mirum" for four wind orchestras, written in 1837, on the occasion of the interment of General Damrémont in the *Invalides* in Paris. The composition is filled with romantic color, and is a work which, though perhaps not always churchly, is of great significance from the first note to the last. A Requiem by the antipode of Berlioz, the already-mentioned Cherubini, which he wrote in 1816 at the command of Louis XVIII for a memorial celebration in honor of the unfortunate Louis XVI, is more serious, and indeed succeeds in maintaining the funereal atmosphere in a remarkably consistent manner.

Verdi wrote his *Requiem* (1874) in memory of the poet Manzoni. In sharp contrast to the usual Italian church music of the day, it towers forth as a dignified work, and reveals the moral greatness of Verdi, who, overcoming the superficiality of his youth, sought to follow the great exemplars of the old Italian church music, and yet remained modern and true to his own individuality.

In this connection, mention may also be made of *Ein deutsches Requiem* (A German Requiem), by Brahms, even though it is no genuine Requiem in the literal sense of the word, but a work freely compiled by the composer himself from scripture passages, written in memory of his mother, and consisting of seven choruses. On the other hand, the beautiful *Requiem* of Gabriel Fauré adopts the traditional form of the Catholic Church, and treats it with a contemplative emotion.

Finally, the Psalms have furnished great subjects to César Franck (Psalm CL, 1888) and more recently to Florent Schmitt (Psalm XLVI, 1904), both works for chorus, orchestra, and organ. Arthur Honegger's *Le Roi David*, an orchestral work with solos and chorus, of great extent, is based on several Psalms, bound together by a dramatic action. More recent works based on the Psalms are those of Zoltan Kodály, *Psalm LV* (Psalmus Hungaricus) in 1923, and of Albert Roussel, *Psalm LXXX*, composed in 1928.

The monumental works of Beethoven, Berlioz, and Verdi are exceptional creations, which scarcely come into consideration so far as use in church is concerned. In the Catholic Church, a reforming reaction took place at the time of romanticism against the kind of church music that prospered in the days of Haydn and Mozart, and indeed flourished in a still more trivial manner until into the second half of the nineteenth century. This reform movement was initiated by the Munich church musicians Aiblinger and Ett, who presented the *Miserere* of Allegri in Munich in the year 1816, and later on compositions by Palestrina. A new enthusiasm arose for the *a cappella* art, and attempts were made to imitate this. A movement arose in church music related to that of the Nazarenes, Veit and Overbeck, in painting. Its leaders were Mitterer, Witt, and Haller. A distinguished work that is often mentioned, written in imitation of the old Italians, was the sixteen-voice Mass of the Berlin musician, Eduard Grell. The movement led to the great reprints of the music of the sixteenth century by Proske and Commer, the complete edition of the works of Palestrina, whose chief editor was the Regensburg musician F. X. Haberl, distinguished for his researches in musicology. In 1867, Franz Witt founded the Cecilia Society for All Lands of German Tongue, which is still efficiently propagating the cause of pure church music. Numerous composers are serving its interests. The most important are Michael Haller (d. Regensburg, 1915) and Franz Nekes (d. Aix-la-Chapelle, 1914). Besides Franz Liszt, Verdi did the most ingenious work in conjunction with the old forms. His *Quattro pezzi sacri*, written at an extreme age, are jewels of church music. A third name must be added to these two, that of Anton Bruckner, who writes in a vein modern for his day, sensually enticing, and yet with child-like piety.

In France, the first one who attempted to give to religious music a less theatrical character was Alex. Choron. In 1817, he established a school of sacred music under the name *Institution royale de musique classique et religieuse*. After the July revolution, that school was dispersed, then restored in 1835 by Niedermeyer, assisted by Ortigue. The school of Niedermeyer, which had the honor of molding Gabriel Fauré, Gigout, A. Messager, and H. Expert, among others, has existed since then.

At the same time in which there was formed the *Société de musique chorale* (1843), the prince of Moskowa prepared the publication of his collections of ancient music, which unfortunately cannot be compared, so far as the exactitude of their texts is concerned, with the great German collections.

Despite these diverse attempts, it can be said that the vocal polyphony of the sixteenth century was scarcely known in France until in 1892 Charles Bordes (1863–1909) founded his *Chanteurs de Saint-Gervais*, and in 1894, in collaboration with Alex. Guilmant and V. d'Indy, the *Schola cantorum*. There is no need to recall the immense work accomplished by these institutions through their spread of Gregorian and

Palestrinian music. An *Anthologie des maîtres religieux primitifs*, begun by Ch. Bordes and completed by Guilmant, presents a repertoire for new societies. These publications, even if they cannot compare with the great critical new editions, render service for practical usage.

Charles Bordes himself renewed the best traditions in writing his motets for diverse combinations of voices. One of the most beautiful of these motets is one on the words of the Gospel: *Domine, puer meus jacet.*[20]

THE LIED [21]

After the accompanied solo *Lied* had reached a first bloom in Germany in the seventeenth century, a strong retrogression took place. About the turn of the century, the productivity ceased completely. The Leipzig poet Sperontes revived it in a strange manner by publishing a large collection of piano pieces with subjoined text, the whole entitled *Singende Muse an der Pleisse* [22] (Singing Muse on the Pleisse), 1736.

The *Lied* made a greater advance through the Berlin school, which began in 1753, and aimed at creating easily singable, popular songs, after the manner of the French chanson. Its ideal, as we have already seen, was realized in the German *Singspiel* of J. A. Hiller and the Viennese of Mozart. But composers also appear who master the small form independently of the theater; indeed, one may designate them as the classicists of the small *Lied*. J. Abr. Peter Schulz [23] published his finely conceived creations in the year 1782. With their vocally expressive declamation and their finely graduated form, they are perfect miniatures. One still hears in Germany *Warum sind der Thränen unterm Mond so viel* (Why Flow the Tears So Freely 'neath the Moon), by Overbeck, and *Der Mond ist aufgegangen, die goldnen Sternlein prangen* (The Moon Has Now Arisen, the Golden Stars Do Shine), by Claudius. Many additional songs of Schulz deserve to be incorporated anew in the *Lied*

[20] Besides his motets, Bordes has left instrumental works, among which are a *Suite basque* for flute and orchestra, and a *Rapsodie basque* for orchestra. Cf. R.M., 1924, Catalogue of the works of Charles Bordes, and *Tribune de Saint Gervais*, XV.

[21] LITERATURE: Max Friedländer, *Das deutsche Lied im 18. Jahrhundert*. 3 vols., Cotta, Stuttgart & Berlin, 1902.

[22] New edition of Sperontes' *Singende Muse an der Pleisse*, ed. by E. Buhle, in the D.d.T., Vols. XXXV–XXXVI.

[23] JOH. ABR. PETER SCHULZ (b. Lüneburg, 1747; d. Schwedt, 1800).—New ed. of 25 songs, ed. by Engelke. Steingräber. BIBLIOGRAPHY: C. Klunger, *J. A. P. Schulz in seinen volkstümlichen Liedern* (Leipzig dissertation). H. M. Brandstetter, Leipzig, 1909.—O. Riess, "J. A. P. Schulzs Leben," Sammelbände der I.M.G., XV.

repertoire of the day. Besides Schulz, must be mentioned J. F. Reichardt,[24] Karl Friedrich Zelter, Johann Rudolf Zumsteeg.[25] The last representative of the simple *Lied* of the Berlin school is Felix Mendelssohn.

The *Lied* composition was tremendously stimulated by the Göttingen *Hainbund* and by Goethe. Reichardt related that his *Lieder* arose virtually spontaneously, by his merely declaiming the poems aloud. As a matter of fact, to a great extent he merely extracted the word melody from the poems. Goethe esteemed the Reichardt settings of his poems highly; in later years, also those of his friend Zelter. The latter was one of the first to apply the method of varying the fundamental melody of a *Lied* according to the context of its different stanzas. In this he became a precursor of Schubert. The Stuttgart composer Zumsteeg also points to the coming great master in his flowing melody and freshly modulating harmony. Yet many others, both great and small, along with Haydn, Mozart, and Beethoven, collaborated in the development of the *Lied*. It found its consummation through the Viennese, Franz Schubert.[26]

---

[24] JOHANN FRIEDRICH REICHARDT (b. Königsberg, 1752; d. Giebichenstein, near Halle, 1814).—New ed. of 30 Goethe *Lieder*, under the editorship of H. Wetzel. Eisoldt & Rohkrämer, Berlin. BIBLIOGRAPHY: Autobiography in *Berlinische musikalische Zeitung*, 1805; reprinted also in Schletterer's biography of Reichardt, *J. F. Reichardt, Sein Leben und seine Werke*. Schlosser, Augsburg, 1865, of which, however, only the first volume appeared; see also, H. M. Schletterer, *J. F. Reichardt, sein Leben und seine musikalische Tätigkeit*. B. & H., Leipzig, 1879.—W. Pauli, *J. F. Reichardt; sein Leben und seine Stellung in der Geschichte des deutschen Liedes*. E. Ebering, Berlin, 1903.

[25] JOHANN RUDOLF ZUMSTEEG (b. Sachsenflur in the Odenwald, 1760; d. Stuttgart, 1802). BIBLIOGRAPHY: Ludwig Landshoff, *J. R. Zumsteeg*. S. Fischer, Berlin, 1902. NEW EDITIONS: Selected *Lieder*, ed. by Landshoff, in the Dreililienverlag, Berlin.—Ballads in the Schubert complete edition.—See E.B., No. 40.

[26] FRANZ SCHUBERT (b. Lichtenthal, near Vienna, 1797; d. Vienna, 1828) was the son of a schoolmaster. He was received into the Vienna court chapel as a soprano, and obtained his early education in the school connected with this institution. His musical instructors were Ruzicka and Salieri. His brief life was uneventful externally. He never obtained a definite music position. He composed incessantly, and reveled in the company of his distinguished friends, the poets Schober, Mayrhofer, Bauernfeld, Grillparzer, von Sonnleithner, the singers Vogl and Baron von Schönstein, the painter Schwind, the musicians Anselm Hüttenbrenner and Franz Lachner.—Schubert left 603 *Lieder*. He himself never heard his two master symphonies. The one in C major was discovered by R. Schumann in 1838, and produced by Mendelssohn; the "Unfinished," in B minor, was first performed in Vienna under Herbeck in 1865. His famous chamber-music compositions are the two string quartets, A minor and D minor (the latter, variations on the *Lied: Der Tod und das Mädchen*), the "Trout" piano quintet (*Forellenklavierquintett*), and the C major quintet for strings. The quartets and choruses for male voices occupy a distinguished place, as do also the four-hand compositions for piano, in which last category, founded by Mozart, Schubert is a specialist. Finally, Schubert also composed a great number of operas, *Singspiele*, cantatas, church works, etc. Complete ed. under the editorship of Eus. Mandyczewski. B. & H.

His greatness rests first of all upon his universality. He is a classical *Lied* composer because he was capable of bringing to expression the rich variety of the poetic individualities. He was stimulated in turn by Matthisson, Goethe, Schiller, the songs of Ossian, Novalis, the two Schlegel, Uhland, Heine, his Austrian fellow countrymen Mayrhofer Schober, J. G. Seidl, and many others; and for each one he finds his special tone.

A new element in the Schubert *Lied* is the great use made of the piano. This would not have been possible without the appearance of the piano-forte, and without the preliminary work of Beethoven. With Schubert, the accompaniment paints the situation. A typical illustration is afforded by the song of Gretchen, from Goethe's *Faust*, composed by Schubert when only seventeen years of age, *Mein Ruh' ist hin* (My Rest Is Gone), with the spinning-wheel accompaniment. The chief idea, of course, is always expressed by the song. It frequently presents a wealth of melody, melody characterized by a singableness and variety of nuances, such as can be found in few other German composers. In addition to this, Schubert also employed all means of declamation and recitative. In popular songs, Schubert expressed verse-structure and rhyme in finest gradations.

BIBLIOGRAPHY: H. Antcliffe, *Schubert*. G. Bell and Sons, Ltd., London, 1910.—G. L. Austin, *The Life of Franz Schubert*. Shepard and Gill, Boston, 1873.—Moritz Bauer, *Die Lieder Franz Schuberts*. Vol. I, B. & H., Leipzig, 1915; by the same author, *Franz Schubert*. Knauer, Frankfurt a. M., 1909.—Oscar Bie, *Schubert;* Eng. tr., *Schubert the Man*, by J. S. Untermeyer. Dodd, Mead, and Co., New York, 1929.—L. A. Bourgault, *Schubert*. Laurens, Paris, 1908.—R. Capell, *Schubert's Songs*. Ernest Benn, London, 1928.—W. Dahms, *Schubert*. Schuster and Loeffler, Berlin and Leipzig, 1912.—O. Deutsch and L. Scheibler, *Franz Schubert, die Dokumente seines Lebens und Schaffens*. 3 vols., G. Müller, Munich and Leipzig, 1913; Eng. tr., *Schubert's Letters and other Writings*, by V. Savile. Faber & Gwyer, London, 1928.—E. Duncan, *Schubert*. J. M. Dent and Co., London, E. P. Dutton and Co., New York, 1905.—W. N. Flower, *Franz Schubert: The Man and His Circle*. Cassell, London, F. A. Stokes, N. Y., 1928.—H. Frost, *Schubert*, S. Low, Marston and Co., Ltd., London, 1881, 1899.—M. Gallet, *Schubert et le Lied*. Perrin, Paris, 1907.—Th. Gérold, *Schubert*. Alcan, Paris, 1923 ("Maîtres de la musique").—W. Wells Harrison, *Schubert's Compositions for Piano and Strings*. The Strad Office, 1915.—W. Heuberger, *Franz Schubert*. "Harmonie," Berlin, 1902; 2d ed., 1908.—W. Klatte, *Franz Schubert*. Marquardt and Co., Berlin, and C. F. W. Siegel, Leipzig, 1907.—H. Koeltzsch, *Franz Schubert in seinen Klaviersonaten*. B. & H., Leipzig, 1927.—H. Kreissle von Hellborn, *The Life of Franz Schubert;* the Eng. tr. by A. D. Coleridge. Longmans, Green, and Co., London, 1869; also Eng. tr. by E. Wilberforce. W. H. Allen, and Co., London, 1866.—P. Landormy, *La Vie de Schubert*. Gallimard, Paris, 6th ed., 1928.—A. Niggli, *F. Schuberts Leben und Werke*. In Waldersees Sammlung musikalischer Vorträge, B. & H., Leipzig, 1880; by the same author, *Schubert*. Reclam, Leipzig, 1890.—R. Pitrou, *Franz Schubert, sa vie intime*. Émile Paul frères, Paris, 1928.—Brent Smith, *Schubert: The Symphonies in C Major and B Minor*. O.U.P., London, 1926; by the same author, *Schubert: The Quartet in D Minor and Octet*. O.U.P., London.—A. H. Fox-Strangways and Steuart Wilson, *Schubert's Songs Translated*. O.U.P., London, 1924.

His perfect organic union of song and clavier is incomparable. His love of nature appears especially strong in his settings of the song cycles by Wilhelm Müller, the *Müllerlieder* and the *Winterreise*. It manifests itself, differently from the expression in Haydn and Beethoven, in a modern way, i.e., in a more or less pantheistic absorption into nature though, to be sure, in Schubert's case quite naïve.

Robert Schumann,[27] who attached himself to Schubert, and adopted

[27] ROBERT SCHUMANN (b. Zwickau, 1810; d. Endenich, near Bonn, 1856) was destined for the law, but turned definitely to music in 1830. He was prevented from carrying out his intention of fitting himself under Wieck in Leipzig for the career of a piano virtuoso by a foolish experiment which was intended to develop independence of the fingers, but in reality lamed one of them. In consequence of this he devoted himself entirely to composition and musical literature. In 1834 he founded in Leipzig the *Neue Zeitschrift für Musik*. His op. 1–23 are exclusively piano compositions. In 1840 he married the piano virtuoso, Clara Wieck, against the will of her father, and after lengthy struggles with him. In the same year Schumann wrote a great number of his *Lieder;* in 1841 his symphonies in B flat major and D minor; soon thereafter the piano quartet, the quintet in E flat major, and the oratorio, *Das Paradies und die Peri* (Paradise and the Peri). In 1843 he became an instructor at the Conservatory in Leipzig, which Mendelssohn founded. After a concert tour with his wife to Russia, he settled in Dresden in 1844. In 1850 he moved to Düsseldorf as municipal director of music. A disease of the brain which had already appeared in 1833, compelled him to discontinue his position, and he was relieved of it in the fall of 1853. In 1854 he attempted suicide in the Rhine, but was rescued. He died in a sanatorium at Endenich. The following larger works remain to be mentioned: Symphony in C Major, 1846; E Flat Major, 1850; *Scenes from Goethe's Faust*, 1844; *Manfred*, 1849. Complete critical edition, B. & H. BIBLIOGRAPHY: His writings, edited by himself, 1854; new edition, Reclam; complete and critical edition, *Gesammelte Schriften*, under the editorship of M. Kreisig. 2 vols., B. & H., Leipzig, 1914; Eng. tr. Fanny Raymond Ritter, *Music and Musicians*, E. Schuberth & Co., N. Y., 1877; 2d series, E. Schuberth & Co., N. Y., Reeves, London, 1880; Fr. tr. of the writings on music and musicians, by H. de Curzon. Vol. I, Fischbacher, Paris, 1898.—K. Storck, *Schumanns Briefe in Auswahl*. Greiner & Pfeiffer, Stuttgart, 1906; Eng. tr., *Letters of R. Schumann*, by H. Bryant. J. Murray, London, A. P. Dutton, N. Y., 1907; *Lettres choisies de Schumann*, Fr. tr. Mme. Mathilde P. Crémieux. 2 vols., Fischbacher, Paris, 1909–12.—G. F. Jansen, *Robert Schumanns Briefe, neue Folge*. 3d ed., B. & H., Leipzig, 1904; Eng. tr. by M. Herbert. R, Bentley & Son, London, 1890.—Clara Schumann, *Jugendbriefe von R. Schumann, Nach den Originalen mitgeteilt*. 4th ed., B. & H., Leipzig, 1910; Eng. tr., *Early Letters of R. Schumann*, by M. Herbert. G. Bell & Sons, London, 1888.—H. Abert, *Robert Schumann*. Schlesische Verlagsanstalt, Berlin, 1920.— V. Basch, *Schumann*. Alcan, Paris, 1926; by the same author, *La Vie douloureuse de Schumann*. Alcan, Paris, 1928; Eng. tr., *Schumann, A Life of Suffering*, by C. A. Phillips, NewYork, A. A. Knopf, 1931.—H. Bedford, *Schumann*. Kegan Paul, London, 1933.—J. A. Fuller-Maitland, *Schumann*. New edition, S. Low, Marston & Co., London, 1913; by the same author, *Schumann's Concerted Chamber Music*. O.U.P., London, 1929; by the same author, *Schumann's Pianoforte Works*. O.U.P., London, 1927.—G. F. Jansen, *Die Davidsbündler*. B. & H., Leipzig, 1883.—D. G. Mason, *The Romantic Composers*. Macmillan Co., New York & London, 1919.—F. Niecks, *Robert Schumann*. Dent & Co., London, 1926.— E. J. Oldmeadow, *Schumann*. G. Bell & Sons, London, 1910.—A. W. Patterson, *Schumann*. Dent & Co., London, 1903.—A. Reissmann, *Robert Schumann, sein Leben und seine Werke*. 3d ed., J. Guttentag, Berlin, 1879; Eng. tr., *The Life and Works of Robert Schumann*, by A. L. Alger. G. Bell & Sons, London, 1886.—Ph. Spitta, *Musikgeschichtliche Aufsätze*. Gebrüder Paetel, Berlin, 1894.—J. von Wasielewski, *Robert Schumann*. B. & H., Leipzig,

his style in some of his *Lieder*, passed beyond him in others, indeed in the majority of his songs, by giving the piano a position of precedence over the song.

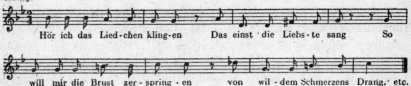

In this song of Heine (Nr. 10 of the *Dichterliebe*), the song merely declaims the verses of the poet, in a manner which to be sure is in consonance with the contents of the words, and which does justice to the structure of the rhymed strophe, but does not say much from the purely musical point of view; the profounder content of the poem is expressed by the piano accompaniment. This style is marked by especial originality and beauty in the songs of Eichendorff, because here the characteristic language of the poet finds its expression in the song also. Besides the phantastic and the ecstatic tone, Schumann especially finds the youthfully fresh note. Storming youth has never been sung more realistically or genuinely than in the familiar song of Justinus Kerner *Wohlauf noch getrunken.*

Karl Loewe,[28] the master of the ballad, might be called the Schubert of the North. The severer form of the ballad corresponds to the colder North. To have given it musical form is the achievement of Loewe. There were ballads before Loewe, but either they were sung balladsinger fashion, all strophes to the same melody—one can imagine what this would be in the case of Bürger's thirty-two strophe *Leonore*—or they were composed throughout in theatrical manner, like the interesting but monstrous creations of Zumsteeg. Loewe preserved the nature of the

---

1858, 4th ed. 1906; Eng. tr. by A. L. Alger. O. Ditson & Co., Boston, C. H. Ditson & Co., N. Y., 1871.

[28] KARL LOEWE (b. Löbejün, near Halle, 1796; d. Kiel, 1869) was a pupil of the distinguished theoretician Türk in Halle, and found his life positions in Stettin, where he became music teacher at the Gymnasium in 1820, and municipal director of music. Loewe sang his own ballads, accompanying himself on the piano. Complete edition of the Ballads and Lieder under the editorship of M. Runze. B. & H., Leipzig, 1899–1900. BIBLIOGRAPHY: H. Bulthaupt, Karl Loewe (Reimann's Berühmte Musiker). "Harmonie," Berlin, 1898.—J. Chantavoine, *Musiciens et Poètes.* Alcan, Paris, 1912.—M. Runze, *Karl Loewe.* Reclam, Leipzig, 1905; by the same author, *Karl Loewe, eine aesthetische Beurteilung.* Waldersees Vorträge, 5th series, B. & H., Leipzig, 1884.

ballad by retaining the strophic form, but he employed several strophe melodies in one and the same ballad, these alternating according to the content of the text, e.g., in the *Harald*, of Uhland, in which the composer uses two melodies, one for Harald and one for the elves. In this way the ballad retains its fundamental character of a narrative song. Loewe is the master of the dramatically animated narrative. One of the chief characteristics of the ballad is that it springs naturally from the soil, and a goodly part of Loewe's greatness lies in the elemental nature of his art. An example is the song of the Erl-King, which is built on the triad only. Its effect is that of a sound of nature. The melody of Loewe is seldom brilliant—the enchanting song of Noeck is an exception—but his melody is always winsome or engaging. He struck the hearty, simple folk tone as did no other composer. He is the Uhland of music.

The greatest representative of the modern *Lied* is recognized today in the long-neglected Hugo Wolf. He has already been referred to in speaking of Beethoven's *Missa solemnis*. Wolf shares with Beethoven and Wagner their passionate absorption in the text. Wolf is not content to allow himself to be inspired by Goethe or Mörike to write independent music, not even by an Italian or a Spanish folk song, but he seeks, by complete immersion in the text, to present everything in tones, and precisely that which the poet thought and felt. To this end he employs not only all the means of song, of melody and declamation, in the most refined gradations, but also instrumental music with all the refinement of expression which it had attained in the nineteenth century, as well as a modern, boundlessly rich harmony.

Brahms, on the other hand, again emphasized much more the purely musical. He took as his point of departure the folk song, sought the fundamental atmosphere of the text, and where this was in consonance with his nature, with its leaning toward an elegiac pathos, he created compositions which are characterized by expansive melodies and profound harmonization, and which belong to the most beautiful music in the domain of the German *Lied*.

Among the very latest composers of the German *Lied*, Richard Strauss has won the greatest success. His *Lieder* dazzle chiefly by means of some brilliant tonal phenomenon.

Finally, one may say that the German *Lied* is as immeasurable as the German forest. Its treasures should be mined much more freely than is done at the present time. One could number hundreds of appealing masters, and there has been no cessation of productivity noticeable in this field even to the most recent times. One need merely mention as additional names: Max Reger, Gustav Mahler, Hans Pfitzner, Felix Weingartner, Max Schillings, Siegmund von Hausegger, Hermann Bischoff; the Swiss composers Hans Huber, Walter Courvoisier, Volkmar Andreae, Othmar Schoeck. Schoeck, of markedly excellent lyrical talent, has lately followed most modern paths. As a representative of the modern style, one might also mention the Austrian, Josef Marx.

In France, the romanza, which had succeeded the old air in the second half of the eighteenth century, maintained itself in favor until the middle of the nineteenth. The melodies of Gounod himself are scarcely less than romanzas with equal couplets and ritornelles.

But between 1868 and 1885 Henri Duparc (1848–1933) wrote his admirable *Lieder* and Gabriel Fauré, about the same time, commenced his series of melodies. The school of the French *Lied* was established. Unlike the German school it did not cultivate simple songs, easily accessible to the people. The lyricism in France is tender and restrained; the composers attenuate still more the poems, already refined. There results a vocal music of rare sensibility, but so subtle that its expression cannot move the public at large. It is for this reason that the musical recreations of the people are, in France, so removed from art. Whereas the *Lieder* of Brahms, in Germany, are sung by all, one must be a musician to interpret the melodies of Duparc.

It is not that his thirteen pieces lack a vigorous inspiration or profundity of feeling. With a sure genius, Henri Duparc knew how to preserve the unity of a piece through the different phases which the text determines. Thanks to the repeated employment of a short motif, or to the reiteration of a rhythm, melodies, even long ones, are compacted into single and poignant dramatic moments.

Ernest Chausson (1855–99), like Duparc a pupil of César Franck, has written vocal works (*Serres chaudes* on the poems of M. Maeterlinck, *Cantique à l'épouse, Chanson perpétuelle, Poème de l'amour et de la mer,* with orchestra) expressing a fine and tranquil emotion.

Gabriel Fauré, whose productivity extended over sixty years, continued to endow his *Lieder* with more originality, more charm, more perspicuity, to free himself from the old types, in order to create more pliant forms. His flexible and tender melody rests upon a harmony frequently indicated by fleeting arpeggios. The bitterness of Verlaine becomes sweet melancholy when it is sung by G. Fauré, and of his anguish, there remains only ardor.

Quite other is the interpretation which Claude Debussy [29] gave of the same poet, when he interpreted him in one of his first works (*Ariettes oubliées*). That in Verlaine which he sought to reproduce, is his instability, his agitation, and the impetuosity of his quickly consumed passion. Debussy found, in interpreting Baudelaire, majestic and colorful tones, for Charles d'Orléans, a knowing naïveté, for poor Villon, restless rhythms, jovial or devout. In each poem he discovered a new manner of reflecting the text in a music as mobile as water. The water is celebrated in a hundred ways in that music; Debussy found exquisite expressions for the rain, the fountain, the waves, the "dreams of the water which slumbers."

The piano there no longer supports the song after the manner of an accompaniment, but as a partner, more free and more rich in resources. Whereas the melodic declamation remains sparing in its accents—that is especially striking in the *Chansons de Bilitis*—the piano not only creates an atmosphere, but it conjures and describes.

[29] CLAUDE DEBUSSY (b. Saint-Germain-en-Laye, 1862; d. Paris, 1918). The principal dates of his productions are the following: 1884, Prix de Rome for the cantata *L'Enfant prodigue;* 1887, *La Damoiselle élue* (The Blessed Damozel), according to D. G. Rossetti; 1888, *Ariettes oubliées* (Forgotten Ariettas), according to Verlaine; 1890, *Cinque poèmes de Baudelaire* (Five Poems of Baudelaire); 1892, *Prélude à l'après-midi d'un faune* (Prelude on the Afternoon of a Faun), according to Mallarmé; 1893, *Quatuor à cordes* (String Quartet); 1898, *Trois chansons de Bilitis* (Three Songs of Bilitis), according to Pierre Louys; 1899, *Trois nocturnes pour orchestre* (*Nuages, Fêtes, Sirènes:* Clouds, Festivals, Sirens); 1902, *Pelléas et Mélisande;* 1905, *La Mer* and *Images* for orchestra; 1911, *Martyre de saint Sébastien*, according to G. d'Annunzio; 1913, *Jeux* (Games), ballet; 1915–17, the three sonatas: for violin and piano; for cello and piano; for viola, flute, and harp. BIBLIOGRAPHY: M. Boucher, *Claude Debussy*. Rieder, Paris, 1930.—A. Coeuroy, *Debussy*. Aux éditions cosmopolites, Paris, 1930.—W. H. Daly, *Debussy*. Methuen Simpson, Edinburgh, 1908.—E. Decsey, *Debussy*. 1933.—J. Durand, *Lettres de Claude Debussy à son éditeur*. A. Durand et fils, Paris, 1927.—M. Emmanuel, *Pelléas et Mélisande*. Mellottée, Paris, 1926.—Ch. Koechlin, *Debussy*. H. Laurens, Paris, 1928.—Louis Laloy, *Claude Debussy*. Les Bibliophiles fantaisistes, Paris, 1909; by the same author, *La Musique retrouvée*. Plon, Paris, 1928.—J. Lépine, *La Vie de Claude Debussy*. A. Michel, Paris, 1930.—F. Liebig, *Claude A. Debussy*. Lane, London, 1908.—Ernest Newman, articles in *Musical Times*, May and August, 1918.—R. Peter, *Claude Debussy*. Gallimard, Paris, 1931.—Romain Rolland, *Musiciens d'aujourd'hui*. Hachette, Paris, 5th ed., 1912; Eng. tr., *Musicians of To-day*, by M. Blaiklock. H. Holt, N. Y., 1915.—F. H. Shera, *Debussy and Ravel*. O.U.P., London, 1925.—A. Suares, *Debussy*. Émile-Paul frères, Paris, 1923.—L. Vallas, *Debussy*. Plon, Paris, 1927; by the same author, *Les Idées de A. Debussy*. Les Éditions musicales de la Librairie de France, Paris, 1928; Eng. tr., *Theories of Debussy*, by Maire O'Brien. O.U.P., London, 1929; by the same author, *C. Debussy et son temps*. Alcan, Paris, 1932; Eng. tr., *Claude Debussy: His Life and Works*, by Maire and Grace O'Brien. O.U.P., London, 1933.

Beside Debussy and after him, Maurice Ravel (*Shéhérazade, Histoires naturelles,* according to Jules Renard, *Trois poèmes de Mallarmé, Chansons hébraïques, Chansons madécasses*), Albert Roussel (*Poèmes d'Henri de Régnier, Poèmes chinois*), and Florent Schmitt, represent in their three different *genres* the modern school of the French *Lied.* Let us mention as further representatives: Reynaldo Hahn, André Caplet, Louis Aubert, P. de Bréville, Lili Boulanger, Erik Satie, Darius Milhaud (*Poèmes juifs, Mélodies populaires hébraïques, Prières journalières*), George Auric, Fr. Poulenc (*Bestiaire*).

PROGRAM MUSIC; BERLIOZ AND LISZT

In the eighteenth century, French composers, apart from Gossec, had done little in the domain of the symphony. Hector Berlioz [30] therefore

[30] HECTOR BERLIOZ (b. Côte-Saint-André in the Dauphiné, 1803; d. Paris, 1869) was the son of a physician and was destined to follow the vocation of his father. However, in Paris he turned from medicine to music against the will of his parents. He became a pupil of Lesueur, won the Prix de Rome at the Conservatory in 1830, and in the same year produced his *Symphonie fantastique,* that original work that became the basis of modern program music. As winner of the *Prix de Rome* he had to sojourn in Rome for three years. His experiences there are reflected in his symphony *Harold en Italie* (1834). There followed the *Requiem* (1837), the symphonic cantata *Roméo et Juliette* (1839), the *Damnation de Faust* (1846). Mention should also be made of the *Enfance du Christ,* a *Te Deum,* the operas *Benvenuto Cellini* (1838), *Béatrice et Benedict* (1862), *Les Troyens à Carthage* (1863), *La Conquête de Troie* (first performance at Karlsruhe in 1890), Berlioz wrote brilliant musical *feuilletons* in the *Journal des débats* and other papers. Although Berlioz achieved passing successes in France, during his life, he never won lasting recognition. He was much more highly esteemed in Germany, Austria, and Russia, whither he undertook journeys in the years 1843–47. His *Traité de l'instrumentation* (1839) is a classical work. Complete edition of his works under the editorship of Malherbe and Weingartner, B. & H. The collected writings of Berlioz appeared during his lifetime in various volumes under the titles: *Voyage musical en Allemagne et en Italie, Les Soirées de l'Orchestre, Les Grotesques de la musique, À travers chants.* His memoirs appeared after his death. There is a complete edition of his writings in German translation. B. & H., 1903–12. BIBLIOGRAPHY: H. Berlioz, *Evenings in the Orchestra;* Eng. tr. by C. E. Roche. Knopf, N. Y., 1929.—Michel Brenet (Marie Bobillier), *Deux Pages de la vie de Berlioz.* L. Vanier, Paris, 1889.—Ad. Boschot, under the title *Histoire d'un romantique.* 3 vols., Plon-Nourrit & cie., Paris, 1906–13.—K. F. Boult, *Berlioz's Life as Written by Himself in His Letters and Memoirs.* Dent & Co., London, 1903.—E. Dannreuther, *The Romantic Period.* Vol. VI of the "Oxford History of Music." O.U.P., London, 1905.—W. H. Hadow, *Studies in Modern Music,* Vol. I; *Hector Berlioz.* Macmillan, N. Y., 10th ed.,1923.—J. L. A. Jullien, *Musique: Mélanges.* Librairie de l'Art, Paris, 1896.—Arthur W. Locke, *Music and the Romantic Period in France.* K. Paul, Trench, Trubner & Co., London, 1920.—Paul Marie Masson, *Berlioz.* Alcan, Paris, 1923.—Ernest Newman, *Musical Studies, Berlioz, Romantic and Classic.* J. Lane, London & N. Y., 1915.—J. G. Prod'homme, *Hector Berlioz.* C. Delagrave, Paris, 2d ed., 1913; Ger. tr. by Frankenstein. Deutsche Verlagsactiengesellschaft, Leipzig, 1906.— Julien Tiersot, *Correspondance d'Hector Berlioz.* 2 vols., Calmann-Lévy, Paris, 1930; by the same author, *La Damnation de Faust.* Mellottée, Paris, 1924; by the same author, *Hector Berlioz et la société de son temps.* Hachette, Paris, 1904.—T. S. Wotton, *Berlioz, Four Works*

towers forth in the nineteenth century like a high mountain from a plain. He is commonly considered the greatest master of instrumentation, as the composer in whom the genius for tone, more or less common to all the French, found its brilliant embodiment.

But Berlioz is more than a mere ingenious mixer of colors. Through the revival of program music and the introduction of the *Leitmotiv*, he gave the nineteenth century most fruitful stimulus. Both as a melodist and as a sketcher of character, he must be classed among the great original creators. He felt himself to be the successor of Beethoven, and with justice, in so far as he could appeal to the Pastoral Symphony, and inasmuch as his *Symphonie fantastique* and his *Harold* symphony are genuine symphonies; they certainly contain at least the spice of symphonic salt in their first movements. Through the introduction of the *Leitmotiv*, or the *idée fixe*, as Berlioz called it, he gave in an ingenious manner to his variegated orchestral presentation that unity which is the presupposition of a really great work of art.

Berlioz's music, like Beethoven's, is strongly subjective. But that which in the case of Beethoven's works we only surmise, and really learn only through biographical investigation, Berlioz himself tells us openly. His works are the immediate deposit of his personal experiences and emotions. Every one of them constitutes a bit of autobiography, clad in the romantic style of Victor Hugo, in a style which was also Berlioz's own literary style, and which he even lived in his personal life, as we know from his memoirs with their strange mixture of the romantic and the grotesque.

Berlioz created nothing new with the introduction of program music. The Greeks, as we saw, already possessed this, and it can be traced with greater or less clearness through the history of music. Formally, the symphonies of Berlioz are a kind of combination of symphonic form and old French ballet. In the *Harold* symphony, the tutti is contrasted with fascinating effect with a solo viola. In *Roméo et Juliette*, song is united with instrumental music after the manner of Beethoven's Ninth Symphony, an undertaking which gave rise to many attempts, which, to be sure, always remained more or less experimental.

Robert Schumann, in his famous review of the *Symphonie fantastique*, called attention to the primal power and beauty of Berlioz's melody, and

(Fantastic Symphony, Overture to "Benvenuto Cellini," "The Captive," Overture to "The Corsair"). O.U.P., London, 1929.

he himself somewhere said that he always attempted to present a great wealth of melodies in his works. Berlioz is a native of the south of France. If one is surprised that for centuries no significant music came from the land of the troubadours, one can at least rejoice in the blessing which Berlioz has bestowed. One need only recall the delightful orchestral love song from *Roméo et Juliette:*

Franz Liszt [31] was so carried away by the *Symphonie fantastique*, that on the same evening on which he had heard it for the first time, he began

[31] Franz Liszt (b. Raiding, near Sopron, Hungary, 1811; d. Bayreuth, 1886) was presented publicly when only nine years of age as a child prodigy. He came to Vienna in 1821, where Beethoven, after his farewell concert, imprinted a kiss upon the forehead of the youthful performer. Czerny was his piano teacher. In 1823, he went to Paris, where he studied theory with Paër and Reicha, and immediately became the fashion as a young virtuoso. Liszt possessed a strong religious vein throughout his life, and he is reported to have been on the verge of becoming a priest when Paganini appeared in Paris and through his successes fired the young Liszt to enter anew upon the career of a virtuoso. In 1835 he fled with his beloved, the Countess d'Agoult (her *nom de plume* was Daniel Stern) to Geneva, and thence began his wanderings through all Europe, celebrating incredible, fabulous triumphs as a virtuoso. In 1842 he became Court-Conductor Extraordinary at Weimar. From 1848 to 1862 he resided there permanently. With this a new period began during which chiefly his orchestral compositions were written, the *Faust-* and the *Dante-Symphony*, the symphonic poems, *Ce qu'on entend sur la montagne* (V. Hugo), *Tasso, Les Préludes, Orpheus, Prometheus, Mazeppa, Festklänge, Héroïde funèbre, Hungaria, Hamlet, Hunnenschlacht* (Battle of the Huns), *Die Ideale, Von der Wiege bis zum Grabe* (From the Cradle to the Grave).—His most important piano compositions are the concertos in A and E flat major, the sonata in B minor, 15 Hungarian rhapsodies, *Années de pélerinage*, masterful transcriptions of works by Beethoven (symphonies), Schubert, and Berlioz for the piano. Mention must be made of Liszt's magnanimous character. There was scarcely a young composer who did not receive encouragement or support from him. A complete edition of Liszt's works is in process of publication through B. & H.—His collected writings were edited by Lina Ramann, 1880–83. Bibliography: M. d'Agoult, *Memoiren, Erinnerungen an Franz Liszt.* 2 vols., edited by Daniel Ollivier, with a preface by S. Wagner; Reissner, Dresden, 1928.—C. Bache, *Letters of Franz Liszt,* collected by La Mara (Marie Lipsius) and tr. by Constance Bache. 2 vols., Grevel & Co., London, 1894.—R. Ledos de Beaufort, *Franz Liszt, the Story of His Life.* O. Ditson Co., Boston, 1910.—*Briefwechsel zwischen Wagner und Liszt.* 2 vols., B. & H., Leipzig, 1887; 2d ed. 1900; Eng. tr. *Correspondence of Wagner and Liszt* by F. Hueffer. 2 vols., Grevel & Co., London, 1888; 2d ed., 1897, with index by W. A. Ellis.—M. D. Calvocoressi, *Franz Liszt.* Laurens, Paris, 1906.—J. Chantavoine, *Franz Liszt.* Alcan, Paris, 5th ed., 1928.—F. Corder, *Liszt.* Kegan Paul, London, 1925; 1933.—K. Grunsky, *Franz Liszt.* Kistner & Siegel, Leipzig, 1924.—A. Hervey, *Franz Liszt and His Music.* John Lane, London & N. Y., 1911.—J. G. Huneker, *Franz Liszt.* C. Scribner's Sons, New York, 1911.—J. Kapp, *Liszt.*

a piano arrangement. As composer, he is the most distinguished successor of Berlioz. In accordance with the latter's example, he wrote two symphonies of large form, the *Faust* symphony in three movements, and the *Dante* symphony in two. Later he founded the symphonic poem of one movement, which develops its musical forms according to the poetic program. With this, Liszt, the great stimulator, pointed out new ways; and numerous composers following in his footsteps, have turned their attention to the symphonic poem.

Liszt did not possess the original creative power of Berlioz, but he was of a poetic nature, who dedicated himself with idealistic flight to the loftiest tasks. His most original contributions lay in the field of harmonic invention, where he discovered genuine new land, and where Richard Wagner himself learned from him. Thus, e.g., he depicts the brooding nature of the hero in the *Faust* symphony (first movement) by means of the augmented triad:

But frequently also, of course, Liszt was dependent upon others in harmonic invention. A characteristic of his tone language is the fact that it frequently seems rather to adumbrate, than actually to express, his meaning, and also that he leaves the best part to the execution. Liszt is also a virtuoso as a composer, in so far as he always demands a virtuoso rendition of his works, virtuoso especially with regard to the expression. If such a performance is really attained, one marvels at the effect, whereas this effect is quite lacking in a mediocre performance. One

Schuster & Loeffler, Berlin, 1920; by the same author, *Liszt Brevier*. B. & H., Leipzig, 1910; by the same author, *Das Dreigestirn, Berlioz, Liszt, Wagner*. Schuster & Loeffler, Berlin, 1920.—F. Liszt, *The Gipsy in Music;* Eng. tr. by Ed. Evans. Reeves, London, 1926.—Sir A. Mackenzie, *Liszt*. T. C. & E. C. Jack, London, F. A. Stokes, N. Y., 1913.—Rosa Newmarch, *Borodin and Liszt;* Eng. version of A. Habets' French version of V. V. Stasov's *A. Borodin*. Digby Long & Co., London, 1895.—Nohl and Gollerich, *Franz Liszt*. Reclam, Leipzig, 1833; Eng. tr. by G. P. Upton, *Life of Liszt*. A. C. McClurg & Co., Chicago, 1897.—P. Raabe, *Franz Liszt*. 2 vols., Cotta, Stuttgart & Berlin, 1931.— L. Ramann, *Franz Liszt als Künstler und Mensch*. 3 vols., B. & H., Leipzig, 1880–94; Eng. tr., *Franz Liszt, Artist and Man*, by E. Cowdery. 2 vols., W. H. Allen & Co., London, 1882.—Ed. Reuss, *Franz Liszt*. C. Reissner, Dresden & Leipzig, 1898; also, H. Seemann, Nachfolger, Leipzig, 1898.—Cosima Wagner, *Franz Liszt*. F. Bruckmann, Munich. 1911.

surmises the significance of a Beethoven composition even in a second-rate interpretation, but Liszt becomes intelligible only through a virtuoso presentation. Of great consequence in Liszt are many details of great finesse. He also frequently employs the recitative, which gains meaning only when it is played in a declamatory manner.

Liszt also transferred program music to the piano, as in his *Années de pèlerinage* (Years of Pilgrimage), the *Saint François d'Assise prêchant aux oiseaux* (The Sermon of St. Francis of Assisi to the Birds), etc. What has just been said concerning the execution is especially pertinent here. These compositions contain a multitude of tonal beauties and great varieties of minutely differentiated expression, but they demand a master hand to extricate them. Liszt combined the tonal achievements of Schumann and Chopin, and enhanced them by means of his virtuosity.

The large form of the program symphony was cultivated after Liszt by J. Raff, J. Rheinberger, C. Goldmark, Ph. Scharwenka, S. von Hausegger, the Frenchman, V. d'Indy, the Belgian, P. Gilson, the Swiss composers, Hans Huber and Herman Suter, the Russians, Tschaikowsky and Rimsky-Korsakov. It is noteworthy that in the case of the Belgians, Swiss, and Russians, national traits often appear.

Among the numerous representatives of the symphonic poem, C. Saint Saëns was especially successful (*Le Rouet d'Omphale, Danse macabre,* etc.) Richard Strauss brought it to a new and great development. He transferred to it the polyphonic style of Richard Wagner, and caused the world to marvel at his new and bold tone pictures.[32]

THE SYMPHONY AND THE PIANO MUSIC OF THE ROMANTICISTS

Haydn, Mozart, and Beethoven were universal spirits who embraced the world. Franz Schubert was a composer of his native hearth. Everywhere in his instrumental music, one hears more or less strongly a Viennese tone. As a classicist in the domain of the song, he belongs in the category of the above-mentioned three, but as a symphonist he was a romanticist. To be sure, the first movement of the symphony in B minor, this incomparable picture of youthful struggles, would have been worthy even of Beethoven in its dramatic vitality; and in his great symphony in C major, Schubert filled with his thought even the monumental form

---

[32] Strauss has written the following symphonic poems: *Don Juan* (1889), *Macbeth* (1890), *Tod und Verklärung* (1890), *Till Eulenspiegels lustige Streiche* (1895), *Also sprach Zarathustra* (1896), *Don Quichote* (1898), *Ein Heldenleben* (1899), *Sinfonia Domestica* (1904), *Alpensinfonie* (1915).

of Beethoven. Nevertheless, Schumann called its style "novellistic." If one wishes to understand what he meant by this, one need only recall the horn melody at the beginning of the C Major Symphony with its Eichendorff evanescence, its uncertain vacillation between major and minor:

It is not a mere introduction and preparation, but a completed picture. It is followed by another melody in the allegro, and this, in turn, by others, as if a story were being related. There is no strict logical development, with a dramatic climax, as with Beethoven.

Schubert, of course, also wrote many sonatas for the piano, but with their lack of formal cohesion, they fall far short of the *Impromptus* and the *Moments musicaux* with which he created the modern "character piece" (*Charakterstück; pièce libre*). From that time the chief emphasis was placed upon this. We also possess precious dances especially *Ländler*, slow waltzes, from his hand. Indeed the character piece itself is dependent upon the dance form. As the seventeenth and eighteenth centuries gave their best on the clavier in the form of poetically composed dances, so also again the nineteenth. It was unable to maintain itself on the lofty plane of the sonata.

The small form constitutes the new root, the *Lied* for the opera, the dance for piano music. At the head, there stands, besides the pieces of Schubert, the *Aufforderung zum Tanz* (The Invitation to the Dance) by C. M. von Weber, which differs from the former in its dramatic flight, as indeed everything that Weber wrote is characterized by dramatic verve. This dramatic character is most ingenious in the fascinating, scintillating *Konzertstück* (Concert Piece) in F Minor, as well as in the piano sonatas, which in reality are no sonatas, but juxtaposed dramatic character pieces.

It is reported that when Weber produced his *Freischütz* in Berlin in 1821, he visited in the home of Mendelssohn, and that he made a profound impression upon the twelve-year-old prodigy, Felix. The impression was determinative. Mendelssohn [33] adopted from Weber the phan-

---

[33] FELIX MENDELSSOHN-BARTHOLDY (b. Hamburg, 1809; d. Leipzig, 1847) was the son of a wealthy banker. He was a pupil of Ludwig Berger and of Zelter in Berlin, whither the family had moved in 1811. After journeys, for the purpose of study, to France, England, and Italy, Mendelssohn became municipal director of music in Düsseldorf in 1834, and conductor of the Gewandhaus Concerts in Leipzig in 1835. He developed an exemplary

tastic side of romanticism. He inherited the magic wand that bade the elves dance, and the magic mirror in which one beholds fairy lands. Time and conditions assisted the artist in developing his inclinations. He came to maturity after the storms of the Napoleonic wars had dissipated themselves, and he died in the year 1847, before the revolution of 1848. He did not experience world catastrophes, and did not concern himself with the unfortunate political conditions. He lived in the phantastic world of romanticism. Thus it was vouchsafed to the seventeen-year-old youth to create a veritable masterpiece in his *Overture to a Midsummer-Night's Dream*, which presents the fantasticality of Shakespeare's work in a most engaging manner. His other overtures (Mendelssohn called them concert overtures) *Hebriden oder Fingalshöhle* (Hebrides or Fingal's Cave), *Die Schöne Melusine* (The Beautiful Melusine), *Meeresstille und glückliche Fahrt* (Calm Sea and Prosperous Voyage) are not less lively, and are brilliant in their orchestral coloring. Mendelssohn pursued a similar direction in his *Scottish Symphony* in A minor, which is distinguished by a characteristic melodiousness, and assumes true symphonic character in its first movement with its fleeting fog and rolling sea. This symphony also reveals a fundamental characteristic of Men-

---

activity, taking cognizance of contemporary talent, as well as introducing historical concerts. Already in 1829 he had produced the *St. Matthew Passion* of Bach in Berlin, thereby giving a strong impetus to the revival of the works of Bach. So far as influence is concerned Bach is a composer of the nineteenth century! (Concerning the Bach movement in the nineteenth century, which was of the greatest significance for the music of the nineteenth century, see the report of H. Kretzschmar in the last volume of the Bach Gesellschaft Edition.) Complete edition of Mendelssohn's works under the editorship of Rietz. B. & H.—Mendelssohn's *Travel-Letters*, 1861, 5th ed., 1832. BIBLIOGRAPHY: C. Bellaigue, *Mendelssohn*. Alcan, Paris, 1907.—V. Blackburn, *Mendelssohn*. G. Bell & Sons, London, 1908.—W. Dahms, *Mendelssohn*. Schuster & Loeffler, Berlin, 1919.—F. G. Edwards, *The History of Mendelssohn's Elijah*. Novello & Co., London, Novello, Ewer & Co., N. Y., 1897.—J. C. Hadden, *Life of Mendelssohn*. W. H. Allen & Co., London, 1888; Jack, London, 1904.—F. Hiller, *F. Mendelssohn-Bartholdy, Briefe und Erinnerungen*. Du Mont-Schauberg, Cologne, 1874; Eng. tr., *Mendelssohn, Recollections and Letters*, by M. E. von Glehn. Church & Co., Cincinnati, Macmillan, London, 1874.—Lampadius, *F. Mendelssohn, ein Gesamtbild seines Lebens und Wirkens*. F. E. C. Leuckart, Leipzig, 1886; Eng. tr., *Life of Felix Mendelssohn Bartholdy*, by Wm. L Gage. O. Ditson & Co., Boston, 1887.—H. J. Moser, *Geschichte der deutschen Musik*, Vol. III,[2] pp. 153–164. Cotta, Stuttgart & Berlin, 1930.—W. S. Rockstro, *Mendelssohn*. S. Low, Marston & Co., London, 1884; 2d enl. ed., 1911.—P. de Stoecklin, *Mendelssohn* (in "Musiciens célèbres"). Laurens, Paris, 1907.— S. S. Stratton, *Mendelssohn*. J. M. Dent & Co., London, E. P. Dutton & Co., N. Y., 1901.— E. Vuillermoz, *Une Heure de musique avec Mendelssohn*. Aux Éditions cosmopolites, Paris, 1930.—C. Winn, *Mendelssohn* (description of "Mid-summer Night's Dream" Music, Violin Concerto, "Hebrides," Prelude and Fugue in E. Minor). O.U.P., London, 1927.—Ernst Wolff, *Felix Mendelssohn-Bartholdy* (in Reimann's "Berühmte Musiker"). "Harmonie," Berlin, 1909.

delssohn in noblest form, namely, his tendency toward sentimentality. Less important are the *Italian Symphony* and the *Reformation Symphony*.

In piano music, Mendelssohn's most original contributions are his *capricci* and *scherzi*, reminding one of the dance of elves; also the justly-named *Variations sérieuses*. In his *Lieder ohne Worte* (Songs without Words), Mendelssohn fulfilled a cultural mission. He presented genuine house-music, a reflection of happy family life, in which he himself was allowed to partake, which he himself was allowed to enjoy.

The *Songs without Words* took the place of less worthy works which had forced their way into the repertoires of the time. Robert Schumann declared war against these, not only by means of original compositions, as did Mendelssohn, but also by spoken and written word. He established the *Neue Zeitschrift für Musik*, and thought out the *Davidsbund* (David's League) which existed only in his own fancy, and to which he reckoned all those who were pursuing the same ends as himself. Concerning its members, the *Davidsbündler*, he said that they should kill the Philistines. These Philistines were the composers of the brand of Herz and Hünten, who were flooding the world with their shallow variations and operatic fantasias, their rondos and polaccas. Like Rossini in the opera, their piano music formed the counterpart to the classical art, and was accepted only too eagerly in the entertainment-seeking period of the Restoration. It had sprung from the Haydn-Mozart school which had deteriorated rapidly, and could show but few able representatives, e.g., Johann Nepomuk Hummel. This deterioration is closely associated with the instrumental virtuosity which was developing at that time, and which reached its climax in Paganini and Liszt. No time had produced so many brilliant, phenomenal executants as that day. The entire piano-playing public made obeisance to a superficial claptrap.

The writings of Schumann have, of course, also a profounder significance. As French music had done long before, so now German music entered consciously into closer relation with the general intellectual culture of the day. Musicians defended their standpoint from an esthetic-philosophical point of view. C. M. von Weber had already preceded Schumann in this. The writings of both still offer much that is stimulating.

As a composer, Schumann was efficacious, like Mendelssohn, by substituting good for bad. His entire creative activity proceeded from the piano. Formally he followed in the path of Schubert. With him he shared the fondness for the *Ländler*, but with the difference that he poetized this still more. In his *Papillons*, in the *Carnival*, in the *Davidsbündler-tänze*, everywhere the *Ländler*, or slow waltz, forms the basis. Schumann's piano works for the most part are in the form of a kind of suite, which, however, is both more free, as well as more organic, than the old suite of the seventeenth and eighteenth century.

As Schumann, from the formal point of view, took the modest dance as his point of departure, spiritually he set out from domestic life. He conducts us into the *bourgeoise* dance hall, into the children's room, into the woods, and to the meadow. He is the Ludwig Richter, or still better the Jean Paul of music. In common with this poet whom he almost deified, he sets out from the commonplaces of daily life, and rises to the heights of idealism, or he immerses himself in philosophic depths. He was thoroughly aware of the essence of his own music. He once wrote to his bride:

" Everything that occurs in the world affects me, politics, literature, humanity. I ponder over everything in my own way, until the thoughts then break forth and clarify themselves in music. But for this very reason many of my compositions are so difficult to understand, because they are associated with remote interests. Often also they are significant, because everything strange moves me, and I must then again express it musically."

And indeed, Schumann converted his meditations into tone in a thoroughly original manner. The piano speaks a language of its own in his compositions. Already in the case of Schubert, one occasionally finds enchanting tones which are altogether peculiar to the piano, and which are evoked primarily through certain arpeggio effects. As the old Italians did with the violin, and Couperin with the clavecin, so Schumann, and beside him especially Chopin and Liszt, made of the pianoforte a unique means of expression, that speaks in an idiom altogether peculiar to itself.

Schumann's manner of composition, which consists in constructing entire sentences, not from complete themes or periods, but only from short motifs, can be explained, in part, by his fondness for the piano, to which it is especially adapted. But with the boldness which was characteristic of Schumann, he transferred it to the orchestra also. As theme for the first movement of the B Flat Major Symphony, he used the short motif:

Allegro molto vivace.

and the first movement of the D Minor Symphony is indeed merely built up on a kind of arabesque. The master was especially strong in the expression of a youthful enthusiasm and revelry, and there is a great directness in his brief formulations. However, beside the fresh Florestan nature, the more feminine Eusebius spirit also finds proper expression in the symphonies. Both of the works just cited will remain for all times artistic symbols of youth.

A large school gathered about Mendelssohn and Schumann, and produced a whole group of able symphonists, e.g., Anton Rubinstein, R. Volkmann, Hermann Götz, Carl Reinecke, A. Dietrich.

As poet of the piano, Frédéric Chopin [34] takes his place beside Schumann. He was a native of Poland, and added a new element to musical composition by taking the melodies and rhythms of his native land as his

[34] FRÉDÉRIC CHOPIN (b. Zelazowa-Wola, near Warsaw, 1810; d. Paris, 1849) was the son of a French father, who had settled in Poland, and of a Polish mother. After completing his studies at the preparatory school, he appeared in public as pianist in Warsaw in 1827; then with great success, in Vienna. He turned to Paris, and settled there permanently, being active as a much-sought-after piano instructor and as composer. A distinguished circle of friends gathered about him: Heine, Balzac, Liszt, Berlioz, Meyerbeer, the violin virtuoso Ernst. His relation to the writer George Sand, whom he revered passionately is well known. BIBLIOGRAPHY: Henri Bidou, *Chopin*. Alcan, Paris, 1925; Eng. tr., *Chopin*, by C. A. Phillips. A. A. Knopf, N. Y., 1927.—H. C. Colles, *The Growth of Music*, Vol. III. O.U.P., London, 1916.—J. C. Hadden, *Chopin*. J. M. Dent & Co., London, E. P. Dutton & Co., N. Y., 1903.—W. H. Hadow, *Studies in Modern Music*, 2d series. Seeley Service, London, 10th ed., 1921; Macmillan, N. Y., 1923.—Ferd. Hoesick, *Chopin*. 3 vols., F. Hoesick, Warsaw, 1912. (Fundamental but in Polish).—J. G. Huneker, *Chopin, the Man and His Music*. C. Scribner's Sons, New York, 1923, Reeves, London.—G. C. A. Jonson, *A Handbook to Chopin's Works*. Heinemann, London, 1905; 2d ed., revised, Reeves, London, 1912.—M. Karasowski, *Friedrich Chopin; sein Leben u. seine Briefe*. 4th ed., Ries & Erler, Berlin, 1914; Eng. tr. by E. Hill. W. Reeves, London, C. Scribner's Sons, N. Y., 1906.—Kelley, *Chopin the Composer*. G. Schirmer, N. Y., 1913.—Hugo Leichtentritt, *Frédéric Chopin*. "Harmonie," Berlin, 1905.—A. W. Locke, *Music and the Romantic Movement in France*. Kegan Paul, London, 1920.—D. G. Mason, *The Romantic Composers*. Macmillan, N. Y., 1906; 1919.—F. Liszt, *Chopin*. Fr., M. Escudier, Paris, 1852; B. & H., Leipzig, 1852; Ger. tr. by La Mara, in "Gesammelte Schriften," Vol. I. B. & H., Leipzig, 1880–83; 5th ed., B. & H., 1906; Eng. tr. by J. Broadhouse. Reeves, London, 1899; 2d ed., 1913.—Fr. Niecks, *Frédéric Chopin as a Man and Musician*. 2 vols., Novello & Co., London, Novello, Ewer & Co., N. Y., 1902.—Elie Poirée, *Chopin*. Laurens, Paris, 1906.—Bernhard Scharlitt, *Chopin*. B. & H., Leipzig, 1919; by the same author, Ger. tr., *Friedrich Chopins gesammelte Briefe* B. & H., Leipzig, 1911.—S. Tarnowski, *Chopin, as Revealed by Extracts from His Diary*; Eng. tr. by N. Janotha, edited by J. T. Tanqueray. Reeves, London, 1905. —Ad. Weissmann, *Chopin*. Schuster & Loeffler, Berlin & Leipzig, 1912.—Ch. Willeby, *F. F. Chopin*. S. Low, Marston & Co., London, 1892.

basis, and domesticating them in European music. To be sure, Polish strains had occurred previously in European music, and indeed not infrequently, especially in German compositions; but in Chopin's case, the national music constitutes the very center about which everything revolves. In the Scandinavian countries, in Bohemia, in Russia, the example set by Chopin was subsequently followed; he stands at the head of a series of more recent, similar developments. Moreover, he was uniquely successful in bringing Polish music to universal European recognition, indeed to a degree unequaled by any other nation. To be sure, Chopin has remained the only Polish composer of consequence, whereas great schools have been formed in the other countries.

Chopin limited himself altogether to the piano. He is a specialist, as Froberger and Couperin were specialists in their days. Polish folk music offered him precious rhythmic material in its dances, in the mazurka, and especially in the polonaise. Chopin added a richly refined harmony. He evoked the most elusive charms from the piano, and revealed himself as an ingenious artist through his poetic application and interpretation of tonal figures, passages, and embellishments, and through his endlessly varied invention of the same.

The National Schools [35]

Italy, France, Germany, England, and Spain were almost the sole furtherers of musical development until the middle of the nineteenth century. As the king's son awakened Sleeping Beauty, so romanticism awakened nations who, to be sure, had dreamed music, but had not hitherto entered the international contest. The Far North was the first to awake. The overture, *Nachklänge aus Ossian* (Reminiscences from Ossian), by the Danish composer, Niels W. Gade,[36] created a sensation

[35] BIBLIOGRAPHY: R. Batka, *Die Musik in Böhmen.* Dürerverlag, Prague, 1906.—Camille Mauclair, *Histoire de la musique européenne, 1850–1914.* Fischbacher, Paris, 1914.— M. Montague-Nathan, *A History of Russian Music.* W. Reeves, London, 1918.—Rosa Newmarch, *The Russian Opera.* E. P. Dutton & Co., N. Y., 1914.—Walter Niemann, *Die Musik seit Richard Wagner.* Schuster & Loeffler, Berlin & Leipzig, 1913; by the same author, *Die Musik Skandinaviens.* B. & H., Leipzig, 1906.—A. Pougin, *Essai historique sur la musique en Russie.* Fischbacher, Paris, 1904.—L. Sabaneyeff, *Modern Russian Composers,* Eng. tr. by J. A. Joffe. International Publishers, N. Y., 1927; Ger. tr. by B. O. von Riesemann. B. & H., Leipzig, 1926.—Soubies, *Précis de l'histoire de la musique russe.* Fischbacher, Paris, 1893.

[36] NIELS WILHELM GADE (b. Copenhagen, 1817; d. there, 1890) was organist and conductor of the concerts of the Copenhagen Concert Society. BIBLIOGRAPHY: Dagmar Gade, *N. W. Gade, Aufzeichnungen und Briefe.* Geering, Basel, 1894; 2d ed., 1912.— Ph. Spitta, "N. W. Gade," in the collected *Aufsätze zur Musik,* 1894.—P. W. Beh-

when it was first performed under Mendelssohn in Leipzig in 1841. His
C Minor Symphony followed in 1843. In the first *allegro* it strikes up the
heroic ballad tone of the North. A Nordic, gently melancholic, veil of
mist hovers over the slow introductory melody:

Gade began with markedly national music. Later he became more and
more an imitator of the style of Mendelssohn. But he created a school,
the chief representatives of which were A. Hamerik (1843–1923) in
Denmark itself, but especially the Norwegians J. S. Svendsen (1840–
1911), Ch. Sinding (b. 1856), and Edward Grieg.[37] Grieg is the most
original among them. His music rests completely on the Norwegian folk
music and its antique tonal system to which the European harmony
adapts itself with difficulty. But Grieg turns this very circumstance to
advantage by introducing new and charming harmonic successions. A
melancholy atmosphere lies spread over the Norwegian folk music much
more than over the Danish. This, in turn, contrasts strangely with the
bold rhythms of the dances. Grieg completely immersed himself in this
strange world of tone, and he succeeded in placing the crude but brilliantly sparkling gems in an artistic setting in which they have a charming effect. This is especially true of his piano compositions and his songs,
but also of his music to the drama *Peer Gynt* by his fellow countryman,

rend, *Niels W. Gade.* B. & H., Leipzig, 1918.—Ch. Kjerulf, *Gade.* Gyldendal, Copenhagen
& Christiania (Oslo), 1917.
[37] EDWARD GRIEG (b. 1843, Bergen; d. there, 1907) studied at the Leipzig Conservatory.
The early deceased, genial Norwegian composer, Richard Nordraak, exerted a decisive
influence upon his creative talent. From 1871–80 he conducted the music society founded
by himself in Christiania (Oslo). Later he lived either in his native city, or sojourned in
Germany or Italy. BIBLIOGRAPHY: H. T. Finck, *Grieg and His Music.* New ed., Dodd,
Mead & Co., New York, 1929.—E. M. Lee, *E. Grieg.* G. Bell & Sons, London, 1908 —
D. G. Mason, *From Grieg to Brahms.* Macmillan, New York, 1902.—W. Niemann, "Ed-
vard Grieg," *Z. f. MW.*, 1932.—Y. Rokseth, *Grieg.* Les Éditions Rieder, Paris, 1933.—J.
Röntgen, *Edvard Grieg.* J. P. Kruseman, 's-Gravenhage, 1930.—G. Schjelderup and
W. Niemann, *Edvard Grieg.* C. F. Peters, Leipzig, 1908.—R. H. Stein, *Grieg.* Schuster &
Loeffler, Berlin, 1921.—P. de Stoecklin, *Grieg.* Alcan, Paris, 1926.

Ibsen. Arranged in the form of suites, this has become a favorite work of the entire musical world, and is a model of good folk music.

Bohemia possesses a still greater musical treasury than the Far North. This country has been blessed musically from olden times. In the eighteenth century it was called the conservatory of Europe, because it sent many musicians into the orchestras of all lands. The Bohemians revere Friedrich Smetana [38] as the father of their national music. He produced a large orchestral work entitled *My Fatherland* in Prague in the year 1875. In the form of a program suite in six parts, it presents scenes from the life and the history of Bohemia. The easily understood musical language which has been learned from the people, the plastic and energetically dramatic diction, and an appealingly rich orchestral color mark the composition as a most significant work of the best type of popular art. It is a counterpart to the suites of Grieg. The same holds true of the operas of Smetana *The Bartered Bride*, *The Kiss*, etc.

Smetana found a talented successor in Anton Dvorak,[39] who first gained recognition through his Slavic orchestral dances, and then showed through his symphonies, among which the third in F major is probably the most significant, and his chamber music, that works in larger form are also susceptible to national treatment. His most popular

[38] BEDRICH (FREDERIC) SMETANA (b. Leitomischl, 1824; d. Prague, 1884) was a pupil of Proksch in Prague and of Liszt. From 1866–74 he was conductor at the national theater in Prague. He had to give up this position on account of deafness. BIBLIOGRAPHY: F. Krejči, *Frederic Smetana.* "Harmonie," Berlin, 1907.—Z. Nejedly, *B. Smetana.* Nakladatelstvi Hijda & Tucek, Prague, 1903; Ger. tr. by Elsa Brod. Orbis, Prague, 1924; Eng. tr. published by Geoffrey Bles, London, 1924; Fr. tr., Bossard, Paris, 1924.—William Ritter, *Frederic Smetana* (in "Maîtres de la musique"). Alcan, Paris, 1907.—E. Rychnowsky, *B. Smetana.* Deutsche Verlagsanstalt, Stuttgart, 1924.—J. Tiersot, *Smetana.* Laurens, Paris, 1926.—B. Wellek, *F. Smetanas Leben und Wirken.* H. Dominicus (T. Gruss), Prague, 1899.
[39] ANTON DVORAK (b. Nelahozeves, 1841; d. Prague, 1904) was a butcher's son, and musically also rose from the ranks, having served as a violinist in a second-rate orchestra in Prague. After 1862 he was viola player in the national theater. In 1873 he received a state allowance and soon became a celebrated composer, also teacher of composition at the Prague Conservatory. In 1892 he went to New York as director of the National Conservatory, but returned to Prague in 1895. Besides his generally known symphonies and chamber pieces, Dvorak wrote several Czecho-Slovakian national operas, as well as cantatas and oratorios. BIBLIOGRAPHY: H. C. Colles, *The Growth of Music*, Vol. III. O.U.P., London, 1916.— W. H. Hadow, *Studies in Modern Music*, Vol. II. Seeley Service, London, 10th ed., 1921; Macmillan, N. Y., 1923.—K. Hoffmeister, *Dvorak;* Eng. tr. by Rosa Newmarch. Lane, London, 1928.—D. G. Mason, *From Grieg to Brahms.* Macmillan, New York, 1927.— L. Ssabanejew, *Geschichte der russischen Musik;* Ger. tr. by B. O. Riesemann. B. & H., Leipzig, 1926; Eng. tr., *Modern Russian Composers*, by J. A. Joffe. International Publishers, New York, 1927.—J. Zubatsky, *Dvorak* (biographical essay in German). Hug, Leipzig, 1886; Eng. tr. by W. H. Hadow in *Studies in Modern Music*, 2d series. 10th ed., Macmillan, New York. 1923.

symphony, in E minor, is entitled *From the New World* (1894). It was written during Dvorak's American period, and in it he used themes borrowed from the American Negro. In very recent times the following have also contributed successfully to the Czecho-Slovakian music: Zdenko Fibich (1850–1900), J. Suk (b. 1874), O. Nedbal (1874–1930), Vitezslaw Novak (b. 1870), W. Stephan (b. 1889), and L. Vycpalek (b. 1882).

While Bohemia was a branch station of European music from very early times, Russia, on the other hand, remained almost altogether in obscurity until the nineteenth century. At the present day, however, it has the richest and most diversified national music school. The fermentation which gave rise to the literary movement, characterized by the names of Pushkin, Turgenev, Tolstoy, Dostoyevsky, also bore fruit in the field of music.[40] The forerunner was the opera *Life for the Czar* by Glinka,[41] which was produced in St. Petersburg in 1836. After this the pianist Balakirev (1837–1910) took over the leadership. In the 1860's, he gathered in his house the composers C. Cui, M. Moussorgsky,[42] N. A. Rimsky-Korsakov,[43] and Alex. Borodin.[44] These famous

[40] Cf. *History of Russian Music*, by M. Montagu-Nathan, W. Reeves, London, 2d ed., 1918; also the work by Sabaneyeff, referred to on p. 306.

[41] MICHAIL IWANOWITSCH GLINKA (b. Novospasskoié, Smolensk, 1804; d. Berlin, 1857) studied piano with John Field in St. Petersburg (Petrograd), and theory with S. W. Dehn in Berlin. In 1830 he made a trip to Italy where homesickness for his native country inspired in him the thought of writing Russian music. His *Life for the Czar*, 1836, the first real Russian opera, was a national success. In 1837 Glinka became master of the choir of the imperial chapel. In 1842 he presented *Rousslan and Ludmilla*. BIBLIOGRAPHY: M. D. Calvocoressi, *Glinka*. Laurens, Paris, 1913.—Montagu-Nathan, *Glinka*. Constable, London, 1916, Duffield, N. Y., 1917.—Rosa Newmarch, *The Russian Opera*. Herbert Jenkins Ltd., London, E. P. Dutton, N. Y., 1914.—O. von Riesemann, *Monographieen zur russischen Musik* (*Die Musik in Russland vor Glinka*, *M. J. Glinka*, etc.). Drei Masken Verlag, Munich, 1923.

[42] MODESTE PETROVITCH MOUSSORGSKY (b. Karew, 1839; d. Petrograd, 1881) spent his life as an official of the Russian administration. He suffered from a nervous malady, and died in a hospital. His chief work, *Boris Godunov*, one of the most lyric dramas of modern times, [*Continued on page 310.*]

[43] NIKOLAI ANDREJEWITSCH RIMSKY-KORSAKOV (b. 1844, Tichwin, Nowgorod; d. Lubensk, department of St. Petersburg, 1908) attended the Marine Academy in St. Petersburg from 1856–62, studying music at the same time. He wrote his first symphony, op. 1, during a [*Continued on page 310.*]

[44] ALEXANDER PORPHYRIÉVITCH BORODIN (b. St. Petersburg, 1834; d. there, 1887) pursued music as an avocation, his real vocation being that of professor of chemistry at the Academy of Medicine at Petrograd. BIBLIOGRAPHY: G. E. H. Abraham, *Borodin, the Composer and His Music*. W. Reeves, London, 1927.—V. V. Stassoff, *A. Borodin*. Fr. tr., *I: Alexandre Borodin, sa vie et ses œuvres. II: Franz Liszt, d'après la correspondance de Borodin*, by A. Habets. Librairie Fischbacher, Paris, 1893; Eng. tr. as *Borodin and Liszt*, by Rosa Newmarch. Digby, Long & Co., London, 1895.

five brought the national movement into action. Rimsky-Korsakov wrote the very first Russian symphony; it was performed in 1865. Moussorgsky's *Boris Godunov* (1874), characterized by great choral scenes, is doubtless the most original national music drama of heroic style that was ever written. His *Kovantchina* also presents choral scenes which introduce the Russian masses. His dramas, as well as his *Lieder* (*Children's-Room, Songs and Dances of Death*, etc.), his symphonic pieces (*Night on the Bald Mountain*, etc.), and his suite for piano entitled *Pic-*

[*Footnote 42, continued from page 309.*]
was completed in 1869, but revised by Rimsky-Korsakov, 1896–98. It is the latter version with which the public in general is familiar. He was unable to finish his *Kovantchina* (completed and instrumentated by Rimsky-Korsakov), as also his other theatrical work, *The Fair at Sorotchinsk* (ed. by Cui and Tscherepnin). BIBLIOGRAPHY: V. M. Belaiev, *Mussorgsky's Boris Godunov and Its New Version;* Eng. tr. by S. W. Pring. O.U.P., London, 1928.—M. D. Calvocoressi, *Moussorgsky.* Alcan, Paris, 3d ed., 1921; Eng. tr. *Moussorgsky, the Russian Musical Nationalist,* by A. E. Hull. London, K. Paul, Trench, Trubner, 1919.— R. Godet, *En marge de Boris Godounof.* 2 vols., Alcan, Paris, J. and W. Chester, Ltd., London, 1926.—J. Handschin, *Moussorgsky.* Neujahrsblatt der Allgemeinen Musikgesellschaft, Zurich, 1924.—J. G. Huneker, *Essays.* Scribner's Sons, New York, 1929. T. W. Laurie, London, 1930.—Montagu-Nathan, *Moussorgsky.* Constable, London, 1916; by the same author, *A History of Russian Music.* Reeves, London, Scribner's, N. Y., 1914; 2d ed., 1918; by the same author, *An Introduction to Russian Music.* Palmer, London, Phillips, Boston, 1916.—P. Rosenfeld, *Musical Portraits.* Harcourt, Brace & Howe, N. Y., Kegan Paul, London, 1920.—O. von Riesemann, *Moussorgsky.* Drei Masken Verlag, Munich, 1926; Eng. tr. by Paul England. A. A. Knopf, New York and London, 1929.— K. von Wolfurt, *Moussorgsky.* Deutsche Verlagsanstalt, Stuttgart, 1927.

[*Footnote 43, continued from page 309.*]
cruise around the world as a midshipman of the Russian fleet. From 1871 until his death he was professor of instrumentation and free composition at the Conservatory at St. Petersburg. From 1886 to 1890 he was conductor of the Russian Symphony Concerts in St. Petersburg. Besides writing the first Russian symphony, he also wrote the first Russian symphonic poem, *Sadko.* His most popular stage works are: *Sniegurotchka* (The Snow-Maiden), 1882, and *Sadko,* the ideal of a folk opera, 1897. BIBLIOGRAPHY: *The History of My Musical Life, 1844–1906;* Eng. tr. by J. A. Joffe, ed. by Carl van Vechten. A. A. Knopf, New York, 1923, Secker, London, 1924; Fr. tr., *Ma vie musicale,* by E. Halpérine-Kaminsky. Lafitte et cie., Paris, 1914; Ger. tr., *N. A. R.-K., Chronik meines musikalischen Lebens,* by Oskar von Riesemann. Deutsche Verlagsanstalt, Stuttgart, 1927; Max Hesse, Stuttgart, Berlin, 1928.—N. van Gilse van der Pals, *Rimsky-Korsakov* (Leipzig dissertation). B. & H., Leipzig, 1914; by the same author, *Rimsky-Korsakovs Opernschaffen nebst Skizze über Leben und Wirken.* W. Bessel, Leipzig and Paris, 1929.—M. Montagu-Nathan, *A History of Russian Music,* pp. 179–236. Reeves, London, 1915; by the same author, *Rimsky-Korsakov.* Constable, London, 1916, Duffield, New York, 1917.—Rosa Newmarch, *The Russian Opera,* pp. 281–333. E. P. Dutton, New York, 1915.—P. Panoff, "Der nationale Stil, N. A. Rimsky-Korsakovs," *Arch. f. MW.,* VIII, 1, 1926; by the same author, *Die nationale Kunstmusik Rimsky-Korsakovs* (Bonn dissertation). 1927.—*The Foundations of Instrumentation,* ed. by M. Steinberg. Russischer Musik Verlag, Berlin, St. Petersburg, 1913; Fr. tr. by M. D. Calvocoressi, *Principes d'orchestration.* 2 vols., "Edition Russe de Musique," Eschig, Paris; Russischer Musik Verlag, Berlin & Moscow, 1914; Eng. tr. by Ed. Agate. *Principles of Orchestration.* "Edition Russe de Musique," Russischer Musik Verlag, Russian Musical Publishing Co., Berlin, New York, etc., 1922.

tures at an Exposition (1874) are characterized by a genuine originality drawn from real life.

As symphonist, Alexander Borodin stands at the head. A peculiarity of the Russian school is the frequent and tireless varying of short motifs, a characteristic which it has apparently taken over from the music of the steppes. It can become quite unbearable, but when applied with imagination, and built upon characteristic motifs, as in the first and last movements of both symphonies of Borodin (E Flat Major and B Minor), pictures full of character, reflections of Russian life, unfold themselves. In his slow movements, Borodin understands how to conjure up the exalted sense of the infinity of the Russian steppes. One easily experiences a bit of this on steeping one's self in the theme of the *adagio* of the B Minor Symphony:

Peter Tchaikovsky,[45] the most distinguished representative of the Russian school, in reality belongs to it only partially. For he writes music also in the style of Berlioz and Schumann. In other words, a certain hybrid nature characterizes his music. Beside profound inspirations of broad outline one often finds trivialities. None the less, Tchaikovsky

[45] Piotr (Peter) Ilyitch Tchaikovsky (b. Votkinsk, Government of Viatka, 1840; d. Petrograd, 1893) was at first a government official, since 1863 a pupil at the Conservatory at St. Petersburg. From 1866 to 1877 he was teacher of theory at the Conservatory at Moscow. After 1877 he devoted himself entirely to composition, having been enabled to do this through the munificence of a patroness, a wealthy widow, Nadezhda Filaretovna von Meck, who gave him an annual pension of 6,000 rubles. He divided his time between Russia and Italy, Switzerland, and Germany. Besides his seven symphonies, one must mention his six orchestral suites and the opera *Eugen Onegin*. Bibliography: E. Blom, *Tchaikovsky's Orchestral Works* ("Romeo and Juliet," First Piano Concerto, Fourth Symphony, "Nutcracker" Suite). O.U.P., London, 1927.—E. Evans, *Tchaikovsky*. J. M. Dent & Co., London, E. P. Dutton & Co., N. Y., 1906, 1921.—K. Hrubý, *Peter Tschaikowsky, eine monographische Studie*. H. Seemann, Leipzig, 1902.—O. Keller, *Peter Tschaikowsky*. B. & H., Leipzig, 1914.—I. Knorr, *Peter Jljitsch Tschaikowsky*. "Harmonie," Berlin, 1900.—E. M. Lee, *Tchaikovski* ("The Music of the Masters"). Brentano, N. Y., 1904, J. Lane, London, 1906.—R. Newmarch, *Tchaikovsky, His Life and Works*. G. Richards, London, 1900; 2d enl. ed., Edwin Evans, William Reeves, London, 1907; Scribner, N. Y., 1908.—R. H. Stein, *Tschaikowskij*. Deutsche Verlagsanstalt, Stuttgart, 1927.—Modest Tchaikovsky, *The Life of Piotr Ilyitch Tchaikovsky*. 3 vols., P. Jurgenson, Moscow, 1900–3; Ger. tr. by P. Juon, *Das Leben Peter Jljitsch Tschaikowsky's*. P. Jurgenson, Moscow and Leipzig, 1901–3; Eng. tr., abridged, by R. Newmarch, as *The Life and Letters of Peter Ilich Tchaikovsky*. J. Lane, London & N. Y., 1906.—For analysis of Tchaikovsky's works see *Tchaikovsky Orchesterwerke erläutert*, No. 14 of Schlesinger's "Meisterführer." Schlesinger, Berlin, 1911.

had a distinguished talent, and his fourth, fifth, and sixth symphonies in F Minor, E Minor, and B Minor (*Pathétique*) respectively, overtower most contemporary productions by the thrilling directness of their expression.

After these great originators, the Russian school was not lacking in composers. Those who ventured with success upon the perilous domain of the symphony are: Alexandre Taneïev, Serge Liapounov (1859–1924), the precocious and fecund Alexandre Glazounov (b. 1865; eight symphonies, six overtures, five orchestral suits, three ballets, five quartets, etc.), comparable to Mendelssohn by the elegance of his form; the genial Alexandre Scriabin (1872–1915), who set out under the influence of Richard Wagner and arrived at the greatest originality (symphonies, *Poem of Ecstasy, Prometheus, The Divine Poem;* ten sonatas for piano) and Serge Rachmaninov (b. 1873; symphonies and concertos for piano and orchestra).

Modern Poland is represented especially by Karol Szymanowsky (b. 1883; sonatas for violin and piano, three symphonies, *Stabat Mater,* 1930, for *soli*, chorus, and orchestra) and Alexander Tansman (b. 1897).

BRAHMS; GERMANY IN RECENT TIMES [46]

Brahms [47] started from the Mendelssohn-Schumann school, but became independent of it. Beethoven and Bach were his guiding stars.

[46] See Rudolf Louis, *Die deutsche Musik der Gegenwart,* 2d ed., 1915.

[47] JOHANNES BRAHMS (b. Hamburg, 1833; d. Vienna, 1897) was the son of a double-bass player in the Hamburg orchestra, and a pupil of E. Marxsen. In 1853 Schumann called attention to the young genius in his *Neue Zeitschrift für Musik* in enthusiastic terms. From 1854 to 1857, Brahms was director of the choir at Detmold. In 1862 he settled permanently in Vienna. From 1872 to 1875 he directed the Vienna *Gesellschaftskonzerte,* otherwise devoting himself entirely to composition. In his younger years, he had appeared as a piano virtuoso. Brahms wrote four symphonies: C minor, 1876; D major, 1877; F major, 1883; E minor, 1885. Besides these, his chamber music is of especial significance: 4 piano trios, 3 string quartets, 2 string quintets, 1 clarinet quintet, 2 string sextets. Besides the German *Requiem,* he wrote the following vocal works with orchestral accompaniment: *Rhapsody,* for alto voice and male chorus; *Schicksalslied* (Song of Destiny); *Nänie; Rinaldo* (male chorus). BIBLIOGRAPHY: H. Antcliff, *Brahms.* G. Bell & Sons, London, 1908.—H. C. Colles, *Brahms.* Lane, London, Brentano, N. Y., 1908; by the same author, *The Chamber Music of Brahms.* O.U.P., London, 1933.—J. L. Erb, *Brahms.* J. M. Dent & Co., London, E. P. Dutton & Co., N. Y., 1905.—G. Ernest, *Brahms.* Deutsche Brahms Gesellschaft, Berlin, 1930.— Ed. Evans, Sr., *Johannes Brahms.* Vol. I, the vocal works. W. Reeves, London, 1912.— M. Friedländer, *Brahms' Lieder: Einführung in seine Gesänge.* Simrock, Berlin, 1922; Eng. tr., *Brahms's Lieder, An Introduction to the Songs for One and Two Voices,* by Leese. O.U.P., London, 1928.—J. A. Fuller-Maitland, *Brahms.* J. Lane, N. Y., Methuen & Co., Ltd., London, 1911.—W. Hammermann, *Johannes Brahms als Liedkomponist* (Leipzig dissertation). Spamer, Leipzig, 1912.—D. E. Hecht, *Recollections of Johannes Brahms.* Seely & Co., London, 1899, being a translation of A. Dietrich, *Erinnerungen an Johannes Brahms*

From the former he took over the great periodic structure, which allows of a firmer basis for the symphony than the Schumann motif technique; from Beethoven also, the strictly thematic development. In a certain sense he employs the *Leitmotif;* he is fond of using a motif as the basis of an entire movement or even of an entire symphony, a motif which constantly binds the parts together, and like an Ariadne thread, shows the way. In the first and second symphonies, these motifs are short chromatic successions; in the third, the brief thought:

which introduces it as a kind of superscription, and resounds repeatedly throughout. As actual theme the following great period follows:

In his extensively contrapuntal development, and in his orchestration, not mobile as with Haydn, but constantly ponderous and full, Brahms stood under the influence of Bach and of the older period in

in Briefen, bes. aus. s. Jugendzeit. O. Wigand, Leipzig, 1898; and J. V. Widmann, *Johannes Brahms in Erinnerungen.* Gebrüder Paetel, Berlin, 1898; 3d ed., 1910.—G. Henschel, *Personal Recollections of Johannes Brahms.* R. G. Badger, Boston, 1907.—Max Kalbeck, *Johannes Brahms.* 4 vols., Deutsche Brahms-Gesellschaft, Berlin, 1904–14; by the same author, *Brahms Briefwechsel mit H. & L. von Herzogenberg.* Deutsche Brahms-Gesellschaft, Berlin, 1907; Eng. tr., *Johannes Brahms—The Herzogenberg Correspondence,* by Hannah Bryant. E. P. Dutton, N. Y., Murray, London, 1909.—P. Landormy, *Brahms.* Alcan, Paris, 1921.—E. M. Lee, *Brahms, The Man and His Music.* S. Low, Marston & Co., Ltd., London, 1916; by the same author, *Brahms's Orchestral Works.* O.U.P., London, 1931.—Daniel Gregory Mason, *From Grieg to Brahms.* Macmillan, New York, 1927.—Florence May, *The Life of Johannes Brahms.* E. Arnold, London, 1905, 1911; Ger. tr. by L. Kirschbaum. B. & H., Leipzig, 1912.—W. Nagel, *Johannes Brahms.* J. Engelhorns Nachfolger, Stuttgart, 1923.—W. Niemann, *Brahms.* Deutsche Verlagsanstalt, Stuttgart, Berlin, 13th ed. 1922; Eng. tr., by C. A. Phillips. A. A. Knopf, N. Y., 1930.—J. Pulver, *Johannes Brahms.* K. Paul, Trench, Trubner & Co., Ltd., London, 1926.—H. Reimann, *Johannes Brahms.* Schlesische Verlagsanstalt, Berlin, 6th ed., 1922.—Sophie Charlotte von Sell, *Johannes Brahms, Ein deutscher Künstler.* J. F. Steinkopf, Stuttgart, 1931.—R. Specht, *Johannes Brahms.* J. M. Dent & Sons, London, E. P. Dutton & Co., N. Y., 1930.

general. He was fond of contrasting the instruments, not individually, but in entire choirs; his style is weighty and massive, but in these very characteristics, of a peculiar beauty. This full-bloodedness, which also expresses itself everywhere in the character of the themes, and to which is added a decided preference for serious moods, is specifically North German. Mendelssohn's and Schumann's works have conquered the world for themselves; Brahms is much more decidedly national than these two, and hence also the spread of his works has been proportionately slower.

Brahms is especially great in his use of the variation form. He reminds one of the old North German organ masters. He wrote a special orchestral piece in this form in his *Variations on a Theme by Haydn*. He used the form on the greatest scale in the finale of his Fourth Symphony, in E minor, in which, after the manner of the *passacaglia*, he developed a mighty, monumental work from a few bass notes. This finale represents the consummation, or crown, of the entire symphonic movement. What Mozart and Beethoven had already occasionally attempted, namely, to develop a symphony or sonata to a greater and greater climax to the very end, as over against the rule of the jovial or cheerful conclusion as in the case of Haydn and the Italians, Brahms here set up as his principle in a more energetic and emphatic manner.

Max Reger [48] is more one-sided than Brahms, and is given to certain

[48] MAX REGER (b. Brand, Bavaria, 1873; d. Leipzig, 1916) was the son of a schoolmaster who was transferred to Weiden in 1874. Reger studied with H. Riemann, taught counterpoint and composition at the Royal Academy in Munich, 1905–06, and from 1907 to his death, at the Leipzig Conservatory. From 1911 to 1914 he was court *Kapellmeister* at Meiningen, and undertook numerous concert tours with his orchestra. Reger's organ compositions are of especial importance beside his chamber music and orchestral works. BIBLIOGRAPHY: G. Bagier, *Max Reger*. Deutsche Verlagsanstalt, Stuttgart, 1923.—Harvey Grace, "The Late Max Reger as Organ Composer," in M.T., June, 1916.—Karl Hasse, *Max Reger*. C. F. W. Siegel, Leipzig, 1921.—M. Hehemann, *Max Reger, eine Studie über moderne Musik*. R. Piper & Co., Munich, 1911; 2d ed., 1917.—H. Holle, *Regers Chorwerke*. Halbreiter, Munich, 1922.—R. Huesgen, *Der junge Reger und seine Orgelwerke*. (Freiburg dissertation), 1932.—E. Isler, *Max Reger*. Hug, Zurich, 1917.—S. Kallenberg, *Max Reger*. Reclam, Leipzig, 1929.—H. Keller, *Reger und die Orgel*. O. Halbreiter, Munich, 1923.—A. Lindner, *Max Reger, ein Bild seines Jugendlebens und künstlerischen Werdens*. J. Engelhorns Nachfolger, Stuttgart, 1923.—H. M. Poppen, *Max Reger*. B. & H , Leipzig, 1921.—H. E. Rahner, *Die Orgelfantasieen Regers* (Heidleberg dissertation), 1933.—Elsa (von Bagenski) Reger. *Mein Leben mit und für Max Reger*. Koehler & Amelang, Leipzig, 1930.—Eugen Segnitz, *Max Reger, Abriss seines Lebens und Analyse seiner Werke*. P. Schraepler, Leipzig, 1922.—Fritz Stein, *Max Reger* (in preparation). Athenaion, Potsdam.—Clara Ebert Stockinger, "Max Reger," in *Helden des Willens*, pp. 178–194. Strecker & Schröder, Stuttgart, 1930.—Hermann Unger, *Max Reger*. Drei Masken Verlag, Munich, 1921.—A German Max Reger Gesellschaft has been located in Stuttgart since 1920. There is also an

mannerisms. He writes a contrapuntally artistic style, which operates extensively with chromaticism, which latter fact has its inner ground in the frequently gloomy mood to which the composer is fond of surrendering himself. Contrasted with this, however, in jovial movements with bold rhythms and sudden transitions, a certain Bavarian jollity makes itself manifest. Reger is at his greatest in his organ compositions; characteristic or original, also, in many chamber-music works. On the other hand, in his orchestral compositions he did not attempt the great form of the symphony, but only the variation, according to the model of Brahms, and the suite. This last he sometimes treats with effervescent humor.

A further word must be devoted to the suite. Its revival was a result of the renaissance of the works of Bach. J. Raff deserves the credit of having founded the suite anew. The most successful of the composers of orchestral suites was Franz Lachner, who succeeded in striking healthy, popular tones, a privilege seldom granted to the modern German composers. Robert Volkmann, however, also discovered this vein in his serenades for string orchestra. The title *Serenade* is taken from the suite music of the time of Haydn and Mozart, and indicates that the music in question is of a jovial and sociable nature. Brahms also wrote two orchestral serenades (D major and A major), which contain delightful material in individual movements, but taken in their entirety they are too diffuse and uniform or monotonous. J. O. Grimm and S. Jadassohn have written suites in archaic style, which, by their consistent application of the canon form, have carried the imitation of the ancients to the extreme. Recent composers have turned with predilection to the suite, e.g., E. N. von Reznicek, F. Busoni, W. Braunfels, B. Sekles, E. von Dohnányi, H. Rietsch, Georg Schumann, and the Swiss composers Volkmar Andreae, Joseph Lauber, and Karl Heinrich David. The following should also be mentioned, as having followed more or less, in most recent times, in the footsteps of Brahms with successful symphonies of classical form: Felix von Weingartner, Hugo Kaun, Ewald Strässer, Fritz Volbach, Georg Göhler, F. Hummel, Paul Juon, Georg Schumann. Still more fruitful than these, the Swiss composer Hans Huber worked the symphonic field in manifold ways. He is

---

Austrian Society in Vienna. There are Reger Archives in Weimar. In 1934 the Max Reger-Gesellschaft began the publication of a thematic index of the composer's works (B. & H., Leipzig).

followed very recently, with works of classical structure, with no program, by his countryman Fritz Brun. As a fine-feeling, late romanticist the Freiburger, Julius Weismann, active in the most varied fields, must also be mentioned.

The distinguished symphonist, Anton Bruckner,[49] stands in a certain contrast to Brahms. He introduces his Austrianism into his symphonies as no other had done since Schubert. While at the time of romanticism, the leaders were all North Germans and Leipzig formed the center, in the second half of the nineteenth century the center again shifted more southward. Reger and Richard Strauss are native Bavarians; Bruckner and his follower, Mahler, are Austrians; and, strange to say, the native Hamburger, Brahms, lived and labored in Vienna, and often borrowed from the Viennese and the Hungarian folk music.

Bruckner inherited above all, as a precious heirloom, the Austrian tonal sense, but he possessed more than merely this. He understood how to invent great song themes, and to invest them in brilliant orchestral garb. A deep, childlike piety speaks from his adagios, often a warm appreciation of nature reveals itself. Bruckner modifies the form of the symphonic movements according to his ideas and needs. To this, of course, there can be no objection, but there is objection to the occasional diffuseness, which stands in contradiction to the principle of the symphony.

Gustav Mahler [50] proceeded from the school of Bruckner. He adopted

[49] ANTON BRUCKNER (b. Ansfelden, Upper Austria, 1824; d. Vienna, 1896) was the son of a schoolmaster, and himself became a schoolmaster in 1845 in St. Florian, being organist of the foundation at the same time. In 1856 he became organist of the Cathedral in Linz; in 1867, organist of the imperial chapel in Vienna, and teacher of counterpoint at the Vienna Conservatory. His life work consists of his nine symphonies: C minor, 1865, produced in 1868; C minor, produced in 1873; D minor, 1877; E flat major (the *Romantic*), 1880; B flat major, 1878, produced in 1894; A major, 1833, produced in its entirety, 1899; E. major, 1884; C minor, 1892; D minor (unfinished), 1894, produced in 1903; a string quintet, 3 Masses, a *Te Deum*, a Psalm, and smaller choral compositions. BIBLIOGRAPHY: Ernst Decsey, *Anton Bruckner*. Deutsche Verlagsanstalt, Stuttgart & Berlin, 1922.—G. Engel (Jean Poueigh), *The Life of Anton Bruckner*. Roerich Museum Press, New York, 1931.— August Göllerich, *Anton Bruckner*. 3 vols., G. Bosse, Regensburg, 1922–32 (completed by M. Auer).—E. Kurth, *Anton Bruckner*. 2 vols., M. Hesse, Berlin, 1926; the most important work on Bruckner.—H. Rietsch, necrology in the *Biographisches Jahrbuch und deutscher Nekrolog*. Vol. I, pp. 302–319. G. Reimer, Berlin, 1897.—Erich Schwebsch, *Anton Bruckner*. Bärenreiter Verlag, Cassel, 1927.—A complete edition of Bruckner's works, edited by Robert Haas, has been begun in Vienna (Musikwissenschaftlicher Verlag).

[50] GUSTAV MAHLER (b. Kalischt, Bohemía, 1860; d. Vienna, 1911) studied at the University and at the Conservatory in Vienna, was kapellmeister at various places, Laibach, Olmütz, Leipzig; became director of opera at Pest in 1888, was first opera kapellmeister in Hamburg, 1891–97, kapellmeister and later director of the court opera at Vienna. From

from his teacher the grandeur of the conception and the beauty of tonal development and display. But spiritually he tended in quite a different direction. His symphonies are dramatically-planned, colossal paintings, which he handled in a realistic manner with all the means at his disposal. Mahler did not hesitate to apply trivial themes, if he deemed it necessary, or, quite naïvely, he introduced a long post-horn solo in the midst of a symphony, in order to create a definite atmosphere. The unity, of course, is thus jeopardized, but, nevertheless, in all of Mahler's symphonies there are significant passages, tones that are at times overwhelming, at times enchanting. By drawing upon solo and choral song, they frequently expand into powerful cantatas, or they are genuine choral works, like the *Lied der Erde* (Song of the Earth) or the Eighth Symphony, E Flat Major, the *Symphony of the Thousand*, so-called from the number of participants required.

INSTRUMENTAL MUSIC IN FRANCE [51]

In the first half of the nineteenth century, Berlioz alone represented the symphony in France. About 1870, some artists of high standing, C. Saint-Saëns, E. Lalo, César Franck, Ernest Chausson, directed the

---

1907 to 1909 he sojourned in New York as conductor at the Metropolitan Opera. His symphonies are the following: D major, 1891; C minor, 1895; D minor, 1896; G major, 1901; D minor, 1904; A minor, 1906; E minor, 1908; E flat major (Symphony of the Thousand), 6 parts, 2 movements with soli and chorus, 1910; D major (posthumous), and the *Lied der Erde* (Song of the Earth) with tenor and alto solo. Mahler also completed C. M. von Weber's sketches for the opera *Die drei Pintos*. BIBLIOGRAPHY: G. Adler, *Gustav Mahler*. Universal Edition, Leipzig & Vienna, 1916; enl. ed., 1920.— P. Bekker, *Die Sinfonien Gustav Mahlers*. Schuster & Loeffler, Berlin, 1921.—E. Combe, "Les symphonies de Mahler." R.M., 1922.—G. Engel, *Gustav Mahler, Song Symphonist*. Bruckner Soc. of America, New York, 1933.—R. Mengelberg, *Gustav Mahler*. B. & H., Leipzig, 1923.—R. Specht, *Gustav Mahler*. Schuster & Loeffler, Berlin, 1913.—P. Stefan-Gruenfeldt, *Gustav Mahler, eine Studie über Persönlichkeit und Werk*. Piper & Co., Munich, 1910; 4th ed. 1921; Eng. tr., *Gustav Mahler, a study of his personality and work* by T. E. Clark. Schirmer, New York, 1913.

[51] BIBLIOGRAPHY: G. J. Aubry, *La Musique française d'aujourd'hui*. Perrin, Paris, 1916.— Jean Chantavoine, *De Couperin à Debussy*. Alcan, Paris, 1921.—A. Coeuroy, *La Musique française moderne*. Delagrave, Paris, 1922.—Romain Rolland, *Musiciens d'aujourd'hui*, Paris, 1914; Eng. tr., 1915.—Octave Séré, *Musiciens français d'aujourd'hui*. Mercure de France, Paris, 7th ed., 1921; contains biographies, and indices of the works, of the following composers: Georges Bizet, Charles Bordes, Alfred Bruneau, Alexis de Castillon, Emmanuel Chabrier, Gustave Charpentier, Ernest Chausson, Camille Chevillard, Claude Debussy, Léo Delibes, Paul Dukas, Henry Duparc, Gabriel Fauré, César Franck, Vincent d'Indy, Paul Ladmirault, Edouard Lalo, Guillaume Lekeu, Jules Massenet, André Messager, Gabriel Pierné, Jean Poueigh, Maurice Ravel, Albert Roussel, Camille Saint-Saëns, Florent Schmitt, Déodat de Séverac.—J. Tiersot, *Un Demisiècle de musique française (1870–1917)*. Alcan, Paris, 2d ed.. 1924.

French taste toward the forms of pure music which had been neglected until then.

Charles Camille Saint-Saëns gives artistic expression in his symphonies to old French qualities: clarity, elegance, graceful mobility, and solemn pathos. His works, perfect in form, have little of the personal element, but they are, nevertheless, of value on account of their beautiful presentation and their French characteristics. The same must be said of the aristocratic, knightly symphony in B Flat Major by Ernest Chausson. The Symphony in G Minor, by Edouard Lalo (1885), has contributed to the creation of the French symphonic style.

The young composers view César Franck as the founder and leader of the modern national school. He was a Belgian by birth, and began with the organ as his point of departure. In his compositions, something of the pious mysticism of the old Netherlands school again makes its appearance. His chief work is his Symphony in D Minor, in three movements. The theme of the slow introduction:

reveals clearly the character of Franck's music, a profound, searching seriousness, that at times loses itself in brooding. In addition, it has clearly constructed French form. Franck's harmony, which is fond of utilizing chords of the ninth, especially serves the expression of his mysticism. The symphony gains greatness through its unity, which is brought about technically by reiterated motifs, but which exists inwardly as well.

Vincent d'Indy, the most celebrated of Franck's disciples, emphasizes the French national standpoint even more than Franck in all his works, including his symphonies. One need merely call attention to his *Symphonie sur un chant montagnard français*, 1886, which is based on folk music of the Cevennes; *Jour d'été à la montagne*, 1905; *Poème des Rivages*, 1921; *Diptyque méditerranéen*, 1927. The Breton, Guy Ropartz (b. 1864), another pupil of Franck, also frequently uses themes from his homeland (*Symphonie sur un chant breton*).

The suite gained special significance. Its renewal by G. Bizet was also founded on a nationalistic basis. In his two famous *Arlesienne suites*, originally composed as theater music for Daudet's drama, *L'Arlésienne*, Bizet abandons the folk music of southern France, and creates, with superior taste and perfect art, gripping character pieces which can only be compared with the old suites of the seventeenth century or the Norwegian ones of Grieg or the Bohemian ones of Smetana. Doubtless it was because, here, as well as there, the ultimate source was genuine, that such true, popular music could arise. Its national character is noteworthy. It is scarcely duplicated to such a degree in the new French suite which took on a great lease of life as the result of the inspiration of Bizet and the eager cultivation by such composers as Saint-Saëns, Massenet, Godard, Charpentier, the Swiss composers, Jaques-Dalcroze, Joseph Lauber, and many others.

The modern orientation of the French music is especially indebted to Emmanuel Chabrier (1841–94), whose bold spirit has created scintillating works: the Spanish rhapsody, *España*, the operas, *Gwendoline* and *Le Roi malgré lui* (The King in Spite of Himself), 1887, his piano pieces whose harmonic freedom and subtle technique have created a school. Whether he chose to base his music on an operatic libretto, or whether, as in his free works, he allowed all the youthfulness of his phantasy to sparkle, his orchestra preserves an animation, a sprightliness, and a richness which are ravishing.

Claude Debussy, in his works for orchestra (*Après-midi d'un faune*, 1893, *Nocturnes*, 1899, *La Mer*, 1905, *Images*, 1909), at times—as in the second of the nocturnes, *Fête*, or in the *Images*—not only produced a color effect as marvellous as that of Chabrier, but in addition to this, he understood how to paint sadness and the world of dreams; he possessed a taste, a delicate sense of nature, a finesse of expression, which were lacking in Chabrier. He directed orchestral music into new channels with his impressionistic style, which employs its harmonies, preferably dissonances, for color effects, and gains peculiar charms through their intermixture and concentration. He builds up his melodies extensively on the whole-tone scale of exotic music (e.g., C D E F♯ G♯ B♭ C). His bizarre effects, of course, also rest upon this device. To be sure, he adds to this, as by no means the least significant element in his music, the old talent of the French for fine-nerved, piquant rhythm, without which all harmonic skill remains ineffective.

The most original representatives of the French symphonic school after Debussy, although they did not all write regular symphonies, are

Paul Dukas (*Symphony in C Major*, 1896; *L'Apprenti sorcier*, 1897; *La Péri*, 1912); Maurice Ravel (*Rapsodie espagnole*, 1907; *Daphnis et Chloé*, 1906–11; *La Valse*, 1919; *Boléro*, 1928; etc.); Albert Roussel (b. 1869; *Evocations*, 1919; *Pour une fête de printemps*, 1921; *Symphony in G Minor*, 1922); Florent Schmitt (b. 1870; *La Tragédie de Salomé; Antoine et Cléopâtre*). These are surrounded, or succeeded, by numerous artists of talent, among whom are G. M. Witkowski (b. 1867), Roger-Ducasse (1873), Louis Aubert (1877), J. Ibert (1890), G. Migot (1891), etc.

The first works of French chamber music were created by César Franck. His trios (after 1841), quintet (1878), and quartet (1889), laid the foundation for a renaissance. This renaissance was furthered by G. Fauré,[52] Ernest Chausson, V. d'Indy, Guillaume Lekeu (1870–94), Gabriel Pierné. The Quartet in G major of Debussy (1893), his three sonatas, the Quartet in F major (1902); the trio (1915) of Maurice Ravel, and his sonata for violin and violoncello (1922); the quintet for piano and strings of Florent Schmitt (1905); the sonatas for violin of Albert Roussel, and his trio for flute, viola, and violoncello (1929), are works which have become classics.

Finally, the music of the piano was revived at the same time, both in its technical and serious aspects, thanks to the numerous and charming works of G. Fauré, to the *Préludes* of Debussy, to the music of Déodat de Séverac (1873–1921), who reflects with feeling and freshness the life of the Languedocian countryside, to the *Sonatinas* of Ch. Koechlin (b. 1867), with a novel tone, to the *Promenades* of Albéric Magnard (1865–1914), to the *Variations sur un thème de Rameau* of P. Dukas, to the *Suite* and *Sonatina* of Albert Roussel, and especially to the compositions for piano of Maurice Ravel (*Miroirs, Sonatine, Gaspard de la Nuit*, etc.).

[52] GABRIEL FAURÉ (b. Pamiers, 1845; d. Paris, 1924) was appointed professor of composition at the Paris Conservatory in 1896, and director in 1905. He was the teacher of Ravel, Fl. Schmitt, Koechlin, L. Aubert, etc. Throughout almost his entire life he occupied positions as organist. He composed, especially, 2 sonatas for violin and piano, 2 for violoncello and piano, 2 quartets, 2 quintets, more than 100 songs, the dramatic music: *Prométhée*, 1900, *Pénélope*, 1913, and the suite for orchestra: *Pelléas et Mélisande*. BIBLIOGRAPHY: L. Aguettant, *Fauré*. Lyon, 1924; by the same author, *Le Génie de Gabriel Fauré* (conference held at Lyons the 17th of October, 1924). "Aux deux collines," Lyon.—A. Bruneau, *La Vie et les œuvres de Gabriel Fauré*. Charpentier et Fasquelle, Paris, 1925.—Ph. Fauré-Frémiet, *Fauré*. Rieder, Paris, 1929.—Ch. Koechlin, *Fauré* (in "Les Maîtres"). Alcan, Paris, 1927.—G. Servières, *Fauré*. Laurens, Paris, 1930.—See also the special number of the R.M, Oct., 1922.

MUSIC IN ITALY, SPAIN, ENGLAND, AND AMERICA [53]

Italy, which took the lead in European music from the sixteenth to the eighteenth century, assumed a secondary place in the nineteenth, because it failed to participate in the development of instrumental music. For several decades now, however, the Italians are also endeavoring to call into life a symphonic music of their own. G. Sgambati (1843–1914), took the lead; he was followed by G. Martucci (1856–1909), Enrico Bossi (1861–1925), and Orefice (1865); Leone Sinigaglia (1868) and Franco Alfano (1877) have written symphonies; Ottorino Respighi (b. 1879) has brought to performance symphonic poems, Sinfonia drammatica, a quartet, and sonatas;[54] Ildebrando Pizzetti (b. 1880), a quartet, sonatas for violin, for violoncello, the Poème Émilien for violin and orchestra. The young generation, brilliantly represented by Alfredo Casella (1883), Francesco Malipiero (1883), Francesco Santoliquido (1883), Vincenzo Tommasini (1880), are conversant with all the modern harmonic discoveries, and one may well anticipate a renaissance of pure music in Italy, analogous to that which has taken place in France in the last fifty years, and which has placed France among the foremost musical nations.

Spanish music [55] has preserved the most original accent of all, that which is nearest the soil and the people. Although Isaac Albeniz (1860–1909) studied in France, his works preserve all the melancholy and the passion of the songs of his country. Claude Debussy has said concerning him, that without exactly reproducing the popular themes, he has drawn upon them for his music in such a way that one is unable to perceive a line of demarcation. A pupil of Liszt and a piano virtuoso, Albeniz has endowed Spanish music with a spirited technique, and one well adapted to its character. The dozen pieces for piano which constitute the collection entitled Iberia have a savor all their own. The greatest among the modern Spanish composers, Felipe Pedrell (1841–1922), Enrique Granados (1867–1916), Joaquin Turina (1882), Conrado del Campo (1879), Bartolomeo Perez Casas (1873), Federico Mompou (1895), have

---

[53] Cf. G. Jean-Aubry, La Musique et les nations. Editiones de La Sirène, Paris; J. & W. Chester, Ltd., London, 1922.
[54] Among Respighi's chief works are the following: Le fontane di Roma (1917), I Pini de Roma (1924), Concerto Gregoriano for violin and orchestra (1922), Trittico Botticelliano for chamber orchestra (1927), Feste di Roma (1928).
[55] See Carl van Vechten, The Music of Spain. A. A. Knopf, 1918; with preface and notes by P. G. Morales. Kegan Paul, London, 1920.

written music in which the severe and passionate Spain always shines through.

Among continental composers, let us cite also, among the Swedes, Kurt Atterberg (b. 1887); among the Swiss, Konrad Beck (b. 1901), Robert Blum (b. 1900), Henri Gagnebin (b. 1886); in Germany and in Austria, Willi Moellendorf (b. 1872), Erich Korngold (b. 1897), Joseph M. Hauer (b. 1883), Anton von Webern (b. 1883), and Egon Wellesz (b. 1885); and in Finland, Jean Sibelius.[56]

Since the days of Handel, England [57] has had no great international

[56] JEAN SIBELIUS (b. Tawastehus, 1865) originally studied law in Helsingfors. Turning to music, he studied under Becker in Berlin, and Goldmark and Rob. Fuchs in Vienna. He is living in Järvenpää, Finland. Sibelius derives his inspiration especially from the sagas and myths of the Finnish people. He has created a style of his own which is related to Finnish folk music. From early program music, Sibelius has turned to the "absolute" forms. He has written seven symphonies, symphonic poems, among them the well-known *Finlandia*, orchestral suites, serenades for violin and orchestra, a string quartet, an opera, "The Maiden in the Tower," male choruses, songs, piano pieces, etc. BIBLIOGRAPHY: Rosa Newmarch, *Jean Sibelius, a Finnish Composer*. B. & H., Leipzig, 1906; Ger. tr. by L. Kirschbaum. B. & H., Leipzig, 1906.—Walter Niemann, *Jean Sibelius*. B. & H., Leipzig, 1917.
[57] BIBLIOGRAPHY AND COLLECTIONS: H. Orsmond Anderton, *Early English Music*. Published at the Offices of "Musical Opinion," London, 1920.—G. Becking, *Englische Musik*. Handbuch der Englandkunde, II, 1929.—Lucy E. Broadwood and J. A. Fuller-Maitland, *English County Songs*. The Leadenhall Press, London, C. Scribner's Sons, N. Y., 1893.— Charles Burney, *History of Music*. Printed for the author, London, 1776–89.—G. Cecil, *The History of Opera in England*. Barnicott & Pearce, Taunton, 1930.—Henry Davey, *History of English Music*. J. Curwen & Sons, London, 1921.—E. Dent, *The Foundations of English Opera*. Cambridge University Press, Cambridge, 1928.—*English Folk Dance and Song Society Journal*. O.U.P., London, 1914 ff.—Grattan Flood, *A History of Irish Music*. Browne & Nolan, Dublin, 1906.—C. Grey, *Contemporary Music*. O.U.P., London, 1924.— W. H. Hadow, *English Music*. Longmans, Green & Co., London & New York, 1931.—John Hawkins, *History of Music*. T. Payne & Son, London, 1776.—Marjorie Kennedy-Fraser, *Songs of the Hebrides*. Boosey & Co., London, 1909–c. 1921.—Marjorie Kennedy-Fraser and Kenneth Macleod, *From the Hebrides*. Paterson's Publications, Glasgow, 1925; by the same authors, *Sea Tangle*. Boosey & Co., London, 1913.—A. Mackenzie, *A Musician's Narrative*. Cassell, London, 1927.—J. A. Fuller-Maitland & W. Barclay Squire, *Fitzwilliam Virginal Book*. B. & H., London & Leipzig, 1899.—Willibald Nagel, *Geschichte der Musik in England*. 2 vols., K. J. Trübner, Strassburg, 1894–97.—(The) *Oxford History of Music*. O.U.P., 1901– 29; 2d ed., 1929–32.—(The) *Petrie Collection: The Complete Collection of Irish Music*, edited by George Petrie. Dublin, 1855; new edition, edited by C. V. Stanford. Boosey & Co., London, 1902–5.—Playford, *The Dancing Master;* new editions: a modern reprint was edited and published (1933) by Hugh Mellor. 10 Bolt Court, Fleet Street, London; cf. also Elise van der Ven-ten Bensel, *30 Contra-Dansen*. Selections from "The English Dancing Master." "De Spieghel," Amsterdam, 1931; Nellie Chaplin, *Court Dances and Others*. J. Curwen, London, 1911; G. Götsch & R. Gardiner, *Alte Kontra-Tänze; übertragen aus* "The English Dancing Master." G. Kallmeyer, Wolfenbüttel & Berlin, 1928; Mary J. Woolnoth, *Playford's Country Dances*. J. Curwen, London, 1913.—Th. Ravenscroft, *Pammelia* (MS copy in N. Y. Public Library); *Pammelia and Other Rounds and Catches*. O.U.P., London, 1928; by the same author, *Deuteromelia* (MS copy in N. Y. Public Library); by the same author, *Melismata*.—Stafford Smith, *Musica antiqua*. Preston, London, 1812.—Stokoe and Reay, *Songs of Northern England*. Walter Scott, Newcastle-

figure in music. This, however, does not mean that she has not cultivated an active musical life and produced composers of genuine merit. Even to the present day, England may well boast of its choirs, its choruses, and its church music.

Some of Handel's contemporaries are worthy of mention even in a work which primarily scales the mountain tops and means to present but a bird's-eye view of the outstanding movements and figures in musical history.

William Croft or Crofts,[58] the composer of the splendid hymn tunes "St. Anne," "St. Matthew," and "Hanover," wrote some excellent church music in a collection entitled *Musica sacra* which he published in the year 1724.

Maurice Greene,[59] a musician of great natural genius, began the great collection of church music which was completed after his death by his pupil, William Boyce.[60] The latter's fame rests chiefly upon this excellent collection, in three folio volumes, of cathedral music of the sixteenth and seventeenth centuries. Boyce's work was continued by Samuel Arnold (1740–1802) who collected a large quantity of English ecclesiastical music of the seventeenth and eighteenth centuries, and by the publication of John Page (d. 1812), *Harmonia sacra*, a collection of anthems in score, selected from the most eminent masters of the sixteenth, seventeenth, and eighteenth centuries, three folio volumes.

Thomas Augustine Arne devoted himself to secular music of a "dainty tunefulness," primarily connected with the stage, writing incidental music to adaptations of Milton's *Comus*, Shakespeare's *As You Like It*, and *The Tempest*. He also wrote the oratorios *Abel* and *Judith*, and the opera *Artaxerxes*. He is the composer of the musically undistinguished "Rule Britannia," an extract from his music to the masque *Alfred*.

on-Tyne, 1899.—*Tudor Church Music*. O.U.P., London, 1922–25.—Ernest Walker, *A History of Music in England*. O.U.P., London, 1924.—Ph. Warlock (Ph. Heseltine) & Ph. Wilson, *English Ayres* (XVII cent.). 6 vols., O.U.P., London, 1927–31.—H. E. Wooldridge, *Old English Popular Music*. 2 vols., Chappell & Co., London, 1893. In the section on English music the editor has been primarily dependent upon the work by Ernest Walker.

[58] WILLIAM CROFT or CROFTS (c. 1678–1727) was organist of Westminster Abbey, "Master of the Children," and organist and composer to the royal chapel. He is buried in Westminster Abbey.

[59] MAURICE GREENE (1695–1755) was organist of St. Paul's Cathedral, organist and composer to the Chapel Royal (succeeding Croft); professor of music at Cambridge, and "Master of the King's Musick."

[60] WILLIAM BOYCE (1710–79) was a pupil of William Greene, composer to the Chapel Royal, "Master of the King's Musick," conductor of the Three Choirs Festivals at Gloucester, Worcester, and Hereford, founded at Gloucester in 1724.

Especially familiar are his Shakespeare settings "Where the Bee Sucks," "Under the Greenwood Tree," and "Blow, Blow, Thou Winter Wind."

The outstanding English composers under the later Georges were Benjamin Cooke (1734–93), organist of Westminster Abbey; Jonathan Battishill (1738–1801), whose "O Lord, Look Down from Heaven" represents the best in English church music between Greene and the younger Wesley; the already-mentioned Samuel Arnold; Thomas Atwood,[61] John Clarke Whitfield (1770–1836), William Crotch (1775–1847) whose oratorio *Palestine* has been called "the one and only even moderately outstanding English oratorio in the century between Arne's *Judith* and Bennett's *The Woman of Samaria*";[62] Samuel Wesley, the outstanding musician of the period, and, finally, John Field.

Samuel Wesley[63] was recognized as the leading organist of his day and was the first outstanding protagonist of J. S. Bach in England, being also coeditor of an English edition of the latter's *Well-Tempered Clavichord*. Wesley must be reckoned among the great English composers by virtue of his best religious productions. His finest works were his motets and antiphons, written for the Roman ritual, such as the eight-voice *In exitu Israel*, the *Exultate Deo*, and the *Dixit Dominus*. Concerning a number of his great compositions it has been said "nothing by any other Englishman since the days of Byrd is so full of that dim, introspective tender austerity that marks the great masterpieces of the old Catholic composers."[64]

Although John Field[65] wrote seven piano concertos, his fame rests chiefly upon his nocturnes which gained great historical importance through the further development of this species by Chopin and subsequent composers. Field was the virtual founder of this category of musical composition and also, apparently, invented the name. It has been said that the nocturnes of Field and the motets of Wesley "are by

[61] THOMAS ATWOOD (1765–1838) was organist at St. Paul's Cathedral, one of the founders of the Philharmonic Society, and one of the first professors at the Royal Academy of Music.
[62] ERNEST WALKER, *A History of Music in England*, p. 245.
[63] SAMUEL WESLEY (1766–1837) was the son of the famous hymn writer and nephew of the founder of Methodism. An accident in early manhood which made him subject to attacks of mental aberration unfitted him for a regular position. He wrote four Masses and shorter works for the services of the Roman Church, and a number of Anglican anthems, services, etc.
[64] ERNEST WALKER, *loc. cit.*, p. 242.
[65] JOHN FIELD (1782–1837) was an Irishman by birth, a pupil of Clementi in London and lived in Russia from 1804 to 1832, where, after extensive travels, he died.

far the most artistically self-subsisting specimens of English music of the period." [66]

In addition to the names mentioned above, Muzio Clementi (1752–1832), though an Italian by birth, may be reckoned among the English composers on account of his long residence in London. His fame rests, to be sure, primarily upon the fact that he was one of the originators of piano technique in his well-known *Gradus ad Parnassum*. He had as pupil John Baptist Cramer (1771–1858), a native German, but for many years also a resident of England, who, in his piano studies, followed his master in the development of piano technique. The studies are still used and respected.

Toward the end of the eighteenth century, "glee clubs" sprang into existence in great numbers for both social and artistic purposes. The "glee" which these clubs cultivated was a compromise. "It was more definitely melodious and rhythmical than the madrigal, and more especially laid out for solo male voices, while at the same time it preserved the artistic interests of more or less continuous rather than strophic design and a certain amount of contrapuntal elaboration, as well as the homogeneity of tone resulting from the absence of accompaniment." [67] The English glee distinguishes itself from the male-voice music of other countries by the important part assigned to the high counter-tenor or male alto—a development of falsetto singing which has continued in the English cathedral choirs from the time of Charles II to the present day. It is unknown on the continent.

In 1776, Sir John Hawkins published his *History of Music*. Charles Burney's appeared from 1776 to 1789. While contemporary opinion by far preferred Burney, subsequent judgment has given preference to Hawkins. In 1812, Stafford Smith published a collection of nearly two hundred pieces, chiefly English, under the title *Musica antiqua*, which forms an important supplement to the examples given in Hawkins and Burney.

Among the early Victorian composers, the names of John Goss (1800–80), Samuel Sebastian Wesley, George Alexander Macfarren, Henry Hugo Pierson, and William Sterndale Bennett deserve especial mention.

As Samuel Wesley was the dominating figure in English church music

[66] ERNEST WALKER, *loc. cit.*, p. 255.
[67] ERNEST WALKER, *loc. cit.*, p. 237.

at the beginning of the nineteenth century, his son Samuel Sebastian [68] dominated the early Victorian period. He has been called "the Anglican composer *par excellence*" [69] and "one of the very foremost names in English artistic history in the nineteenth century." [70] Among his great anthems may be mentioned "Thou wilt keep him in perfect peace" and "Cast me not away." His chief characteristics are good part writing, melodiousness, and sense of proportion. He also deserves attention as a prolific composer of hymn tunes.

The grip of Handel upon English musical life was somewhat loosened by the influence of Mendelssohn whose *Elijah* was first performed at Birmingham in 1846. Both Macfarren and Bennett show his influence. The latter followed in the footsteps of Samuel Wesley in making propaganda for J. S. Bach in England. Macfarren [71] wrote an oratorio, *St. John the Baptist*, and a cantata for female voices, *Songs in a Cornfield*. Bennett [72] wrote an oratorio, *The Woman of Samaria*, and a cantata, *The May Queen*. In the instrumental field, mention should be made of Bennett's C minor and F minor piano concertos, his "Parisina" overture, his overture entitled "The Naiads," and that entitled "The Wood-nymph," and the "Water-Color Sketches" for piano—*The Lake*, *The Millstream*, and *The Fountain*. Schumann dedicated his "Études symphoniques" to Bennett.

Although Bennett is the more pleasing of the two, the orchestral works of Henry Hugo Pierson [73]—*Romeo and Juliet*, *Macbeth*, and *Faust* —show greater originality. He has been called "a sort of early Richard Strauss." [74]

The best writer of unaccompanied secular music of the time, the best imitator of the classical madrigal, was Robert Lucas Pearsall (1795–1856).

---

[68] SAMUEL SEBASTIAN WESLEY (1810–76) was a member of the Chapel Royal, organist of Hereford Cathedral, Leeds Parish Church, and of Winchester and Gloucester cathedrals.
[69] ERNEST WALKER, *loc. cit.*, p. 263.
[70] ERNEST WALKER, *loc. cit.*, p. 265.
[71] GEORGE ALEXANDER MACFARREN (1813–87) was university professor at Cambridge and principal of the Royal Academy of Music.
[72] WILLIAM STERNDALE BENNETT (1816–75) was chorister in King's College Chapel at Cambridge, student at the Royal Academy of Music, friend of Mendelssohn and Schumann in Leipzig, university professor at Cambridge, and principal of the Royal Academy of Music.
[73] HENRY HUGO PIERSON (1815–73)—the name was originally Pearson, the spelling being changed after residence in Germany—attended Harrow and Cambridge, studied music chiefly in Germany, became Reid professor at Edinburgh, but resided in Germany during most of his later life.
[74] ERNEST WALKER, *loc. cit.*, p. 282.

Among the later Victorian composers the outstanding names are those of Arthur Sullivan, Arthur Goring Thomas (1850-92), John Stainer (1840-1901), Joseph Barnby (1838-96), John Bacchus Dykes (1823-76) and the quintet, frequently grouped together, Alexander Campbell Mackenzie, Charles Hubert Hastings Parry, Frederick Hymen Cowen, Charles Villiers Stanford, and Edward Elgar.

Arthur Sullivan [75] was probably the most popular composer that England ever produced. His light operas, with librettos by W. S. Gilbert, may be considered classic in their *genre*, trivial though the music be. They have not ceased to be popular where the English language is spoken.

Thomas wrote two operas, *Emeralda* and *Nadeshda*, which are his two most important works. His music is characterized by a refined technique, is of a Parisian aristocratic type, but lacking in individuality.

Stainer, organist at St. Paul's Cathedral and professor of music at Oxford, Barnby, organist at Eton and principal of the Guildhall School of Music, and Dykes, precentor at Durham Cathedral, represent a large school of rather sentimental, Victorian hymn, anthem, and service composers. As has been said they exemplify "Gounod's ideal in terms of Protestantism." [76]

The most important choral work of Mackenzie [77] is the oratorio *The Rose of Sharon* (1884), based on the "Song of Solomon." He also wrote the operas *Colomba* and *The Troubadour*, and the cantatas *The Story of Sayid* and *The Dream of Jubal;* also the *Scottish Rhapsodies for Orchestra* and an orchestral ballad to Keat's poem *La Belle Dame sans Merci*. His work at its best, it has been said, is characterized by "a sort of quiet but nevertheless warm picturesqueness." [78]

Cowen,[79] whose music may be described generally as "frankly pretty,"

[75] ARTHUR SEYMOUR SULLIVAN (1842-1900) studied at the Royal Academy and the Leipzig Conservatory. He was Principal of the National Training School of Music, 1876-81. BIBLIOGRAPHY: T. F. Dunhill, *Sullivan's Comic Operas, a Critical Appreciation*. E. Arnold, London, 1928.—B. W. Findon, *Sir Arthur Sullivan—His Life and Music*. J. Nisbet, London, 1904.—W. S. Gilbert, *The Savoy Operas*, the texts. Macmillan, London, 1926.— A. Godwin, *Gilbert & Sullivan*. Dent, London, 1926.—I. Goldberg, *The Story of Gilbert & Sullivan, or the Complete Savoyard*. Simon & Schuster, N. Y., Murray, London, 1928.— H. Saxe-Windham, *Sullivan*. Kegan Paul, London, 2d ed., 1926.—H. Sullivan & N. Flower, *Sir Arthur Sullivan*. Cassell, London, 1927.

[76] ERNEST WALKER, *loc. cit.*, p. 307.

[77] ALEXANDER CAMPBELL MACKENZIE (b. 1847), after residence in Germany and Italy, became principal of the Royal Academy.

[78] ERNEST WALKER, *loc. cit.*, p. 298.

[79] FREDERICK HYMEN COWEN (b. 1852) studied at the Leipzig Conservatory, and at the

wrote the not infrequently polished and charming *Sleeping Beauty*, *The Water Lily*, the oratorio *Ruth*, and the operas *Thorgrim*, *Signa*, and *Harold*. His cantata, a setting of Collins' *Ode to the Passions* (1898), is probably the chief work among his oratorios and cantatas. He wrote also an "Idyllic," a "Scandinavian," and a "Welsh" symphony.

Stanford, Parry, and Elgar compose the trio which stands at the head of modern English music. Stanford,[80] a native Irishman, not only edited Irish folk songs, but wrote original works that amount virtually to Irish folk music, as the opera *Shamus O'Brien* and the choral ballad *Phaudrig Crohoore*. *Shamus O'Brien* has been termed "one of the most deliciously 'open-air' works in all British music." [81] It is a *Singspiel* according to the old model, i.e., with spoken dialogue. *Shamus O'Brien* and *Much Ado About Nothing* are Stanford's best stage works. Among other important works, are his two oratorios *The Three Holy Children* and *Eden*, a Requiem, *Te Deum*, a Mass in G, a cantata entitled *The Veiled Prophet*, choral settings of Elizabethan pastorals, of great delicacy and polish, a setting of Whitman's *Ode to Death*, the so-called "Sea-Music" consisting of *The Revenge* and *The Voyage of Maeldune* (both settings of poems by Tennyson), a setting of Henley's *The Last Post*, a *Stabat Mater*, the masterpiece of all the larger choral compositions. Among the instrumental compositions, mention should be made of the *Irish Symphony*, in F minor, and of the *Irish Fantasies* for violin. Stanford has been termed the most versatile and prolific of the latter Victorian composers, combining Irish tunefulness, Tennysonian romanticism and vivid imagination. His best works are among "the permanently notable achievements of English art." [82]

Chas. Hubert Parry [83] is perhaps the greatest of the quintet referred

---

Stern Conservatory in Berlin, was conductor of the Philharmonic Society, the Hallé Orchestra, and other instrumental and choral organizations.

[80] CHARLES VILLIERS STANFORD (b. Dublin, 1852; d. London, 1924) became organist of Trinity College, Cambridge, university professor, and professor of composition at the Royal College of Music. See Stanford, *Studies and Memories*. Constable, London, 1908; also Stanford, *Interludes, Records, and Reflections*. Murray, London, 1922.

[81] ERNEST WALKER, *loc. cit.*, p. 302.

[82] ERNEST WALKER, *loc. cit.*, p. 304.

[83] CHARLES HUBERT HASTINGS PARRY (1848–1918) studied at Eton, was director of the Royal College of Music, and university professor of music at Oxford. His *The Evolution of the Art of Music* was published by D. Appelton & Co., London, in 1908; his *J. S. Bach*, by G. P. Putnam's Sons, N. Y., 1909; and his *Style in Musical Art*, by Macmillan and Co., London, 1911. See also Parry, *College Addresses*, edited by H. C. Colles. Macmillan, London, 1926; and Graves, *Hubert Parry*. 2 vols., Macmillan, London, 1926.

to above. It has been said that if a birthday were to be celebrated for modern English music it would doubtless be Sept. 7, 1880—the day on which Parry's *Prometheus Unbound* (Shelley), a work full of lyrical rapture, was first produced, at the Gloucester Festival. Splendid works, too, are his setting of Shirley's Ode, *The Glories of Our Blood and State*, from "The Contention of Ajax and Ulysses," of *L'Allegro* and *Il Penseroso*, *De Profundis*, *Invocation to Music*, *Ode to Music*, *The Lotus Eaters*, *Te Deum*, *St. Cecilia's Day*, *Blest Pair of Sirens* (Milton), the oratorios *Judith*, *Job*, and *King Saul*, *The CXXX Psalm*, *The Pied Piper of Hamlin* (Browning), *A Song of Darkness and Light*, *War and Peace*, *Voces Clamantium*, and *The Love That Casteth out Fear*. Among his instrumental works mention must be made of his *Cambridge Symphony*, *Symphonic Variations for Orchestra*, the *B Minor Trio for Piano and Strings:* but Parry is at his best when writing for chorus and orchestra, not in instrumental writing.

In addition to his music compositions, Parry has written a work entitled *The Evolution of the Art of Music*, a book on *J. S. Bach*, and a treatise on *Style in Musical Art*. The masterpieces of his career are motets for unaccompanied chorus entitled *Songs of Farewell*, in which he reaches "heights of massive and tranquil spiritual dignity." [84] His unison choral songs include the setting "England," one of the noblest of the British patriotic tunes. Parry's music is characterized by nobility of manner, dignified climaxes, massiveness, intellectualism, spaciousness, and sincerity. He has been called "one of the truest and most single-minded leaders of our modern art." [85]

Elgar [86] wrote the oratorios *The Dream of Gerontius* (1900), first presented in Westminster Catholic Cathedral in 1903, *The Apostles* (1903), and *The Kingdom* (1906), the so-called "Enigma Variations" for orchestra, perhaps his best work, an overture *In the South*, and *Introduction and*

[84] ERNEST WALKER, *loc. cit.*, p. 364.
[85] ERNEST WALKER, *loc. cit.*, p. 301.
[86] EDWARD ELGAR (1857–1934) was a native of Worcester and was almost completely autodidact. In later life he was appointed university professor at Birmingham, ultimately becoming King's Musician. BIBLIOGRAPHY: R. J. Buckley, *Sir Edward Elgar*. Lane, London, 1905 ("Living Masters of Music").—Louise Dyer, *Edward Elgar*, "Music by British Composers." O.U.P., London, 1931.—Cecil Gray, *Contemporary Music*. O.U.P., London, 1924.—D. G. Mason, *Contemporary Composers*. Macmillan, N. Y., 1918.—Ernest Newmann, *Elgar*. J. Lane, London, 3d ed., 1922 ("Music of the Masters").—J. F. Porte, *Elgar and His Music*. I. Pitman and Sons, Ltd., London, 1933.—A. J. Sheldon, "Edward Elgar," in *Musical Opinion*. London, 1932.—F. H. Shera, *Elgar's Instrumental Works*. O.U.P., London, 1931.

Allegro for orchestra of strings, some fine *Sea Pictures* for contralto and orchestra, two symphonies, a program orchestral work, *Falstaff*, concertos for violin and violoncello, an orchestral composition entitled *Carillon*, a short choral suite, *The Spirit of England*, an Ode entitled *The Music Makers*, which ranks highest among his later choral works, a piano quintet, a string quartet, and a violin sonata. Elgar's music is characterized by a strong feeling for color, subtle orchestration, mysticism, sensuousness rather than sternness, and, even in his later works, a certain lightness of weight as compared with the classics.

Among other very modern British composers mention should be made of Frederick Delius (1863–1934), Granville Bantock (b. 1868), Walford Davies (b. 1869), Ralph Vaughan Williams (1872), Gustav Holst (1874–1934), Samuel Coleridge Taylor (1875–1912), Frank Bridge (b. 1879), John Ireland (b. 1879), Cyril Scott (b. 1879), and Arnold Trevor Bax (b. 1883).

Frederick Delius is an extremely individualistic composer, fond of evanescent exotic harmonies and of half lights. Among his chief compositions are the orchestral poems *Brigg Fair* and *In a Summer Garden*, the orchestral *Lebenstanz* (Life's Dance), the *Messe des Lebens* (A Mass of Life), with Nietzsche's poem "Tiefe Ewigkeit" as its finale, the setting of Whitman's *Seadrift*, the wordless choral songs *To Be Sung on a Summer Night on the Water*, his chief opera *Romeo und Julia auf dem Dorfe* (A Village Romeo and Juliet), and his violin concerto.

Granville Bantock is at his best in his orchestral tone poems based on Shelley's *Witch of Atlas* and Ernest Dawson's *Pierrot of the Minute*, respectively, in his *Hebridean Symphony*, and in his choral work *Omar Khayyam*, or the choral ballet *Pan in Arcady*. Among other works are a tone poem on Browning's *Fifine at the Fair*, a part song *On Himalay*, and the *Sappho* song cycle. Bantock is impulsive and brilliant, but inclined to be short-breathed.

Sir Walford Davies, who succeeded Elgar as musician to the King, has set *The Song of St. Francis* and the medieval morality play *Everyman*.

Vaughan Williams has been influenced strongly by English folk music, in the collecting and arranging of which he has been assiduous. Among his most important works are his settings of Stevenson's *Songs of Travel*, of Whitman's *Toward the Unknown Region* and *Sea Symphony*, of Herbert's *Mystical Songs*, Houseman's *On Wenlock Edge*, the *Choral Fantasia on Christmas Carols*, the *Pastoral Symphony*, a *Fantasia on a Theme by*

Tallis, for strings, and the *London Symphony*, the last-named generally considered his masterpiece. Williams's compositions are characterized by individuality, warmth, mysticism, at times humor, and at times also by archaic mannerisms.

Gustav Holst fostered an individual harmonic language which occasionally tends to archaic mannerism like that of Vaughan Williams. His style is characterized by austerity, Indian mysticism, and massiveness. His chief works are some first class ballet music, the orchestral *Beni Mora Suite*, the *Hymn of Jesus* (a setting of a Gnostic ritual), an orchestral suite *The Planets*, the *Rigveda Hymns*, and music for Whitman's *Ode to Death*, called "one of the chief landmarks of modern English music." [87]

Samuel Coleridge Taylor, produced in the cantata *Hiawatha's Wedding Feast* (1898) a naïvely beautiful and charmingly childlike work. This was supplemented by the sequels *The Death of Minnehaha* and *Hiawatha's Departure*. His masterpiece is *The Orchestral Ballade in A Minor*.

Frank Bridge is at his best in his chamber music, having written a string sextet in E flat, a quartet in G minor, and a piano quartet phantasy in F sharp minor. He has also written an orchestral suite, entitled *The Sea*.

John Ireland's songs are among the finest of the present day, though his style tends more toward the bitter than the sweet. His writing is strong and individualistic, but not infrequently rough-edged. Among his principal works are his setting of Symons's *The Adoration*, the orchestral poem *The Forgotten Rite*, the second violin-and-piano sonata in A minor, and some piano solos as *The Rhapsody*, *The Island Spell*, and *Chelsea Reach*.

Cyril Scott has written good piano music, such as the five *Poems*, though his best work is probably his setting of Crashaw's *Nativity Hymn*, for soli, chorus, and orchestra. It has been said: "the restlessly rich harmonic and rhythmic idioms often end in a nervous monotony of effect." [88]

Arnold Bax is perhaps at his best in the orchestral poem *November Woods*, the *Phantasy* for viola and orchestra, the eight-voice motet *Mater*, *Ora filium*, and the piano sonata in G major. His style is impressionistic and at times exotic.

A word should be added concerning the collections of British folk music. Among early collections mention must be made of Ravenscroft's

[87] ERNEST WALKER, *loc. cit.*, p. 372.   [88] ERNEST WALKER, *loc. cit.*, p. 376.

Pammelia, Deuteromelia, and *Melismata,* of Playford's *The Dancing Master,* first published in 1650 in several voluminous editions, and reprinted in enlarged form eighteen times to 1728. Much labor has been bestowed upon the collecting of such material in more recent times. Outstanding collections are William Chappell's *Popular Music of the Olden Time* (also a revised edition by H. E. Wooldridge entitled *Old English Popular Music*), *Somerset Folksongs,* the *Folksong Society's Journal, English County Songs,* Stokoe and Ray's large collection of *Songs of Northern England,* the *Petrie Collection,* the so-called "Irish tunes" (mostly English) in the *Fitzwilliam Virginal Book,* and the collection of *Hebridean Folksongs,* edited by Marjorie Kennedy-Fraser, in addition to the collections already mentioned on pages 322 to 323. It has been said that Irish folk music is, on the whole, the finest that exists; that for sheer beauty of melody, Schubert, Mozart, and Irish folk songs constitute "a triad unchallenged in the whole range of the art." [89]

In connection with English folk music, a word should be said concerning the English hymn tune. The first collection of so-called "English church-tunes," unharmonized, was *Sternhold's Psalter* of the year 1556. The *Allison Psalter* of the year 1599 was entirely Allison's own work, and represents the Elizabethan style at its purest. The last of its kind was *Playford's Psalter* of the year 1677. A lofty level was maintained by the mixed collections of Day, Este, and Ravenscroft, and this was furthered by the excellent work of Clarke and Croft. But after 1860 a rapid decline took place through the efflorescence of the so-called "devotional hymn tune" of the Victorian period as represented by Stainer, Barnby, and Dykes. To be sure, some good tunes, as certain ones by Parry and Stanford, have continued to make their appearance—a good example is the very fine *Sine nomine* by Vaughan Williams. Fortunately, at the present day, a new appreciation of the best in hymn tunes is again manifesting itself, though, to be sure, rather in the form of recognition of the valuable in the old, than in original composition.

If one wishes to divide English music into definite periods, it falls naturally into the following phases: in the thirteenth century, represented by the "Sumer is i-cumen in" canon, English music seems to stand unrivaled; after a relapse it again comes to the fore in the first half of the fifteenth century with the distinguished name of Dunstable; after another eclipse it again blossoms forth under Netherland influence

[89] ERNEST WALKER, *loc. cit.,* p. 336.

in the brilliant Elizabethan period from c. 1540 to c. 1620; another period
of eclipse is followed by the very brief Purcellian period, about twenty
years in duration only, revealing French and Italian influence; a very
long period of dearth is followed by the later Victorian days, revealing
German influence; this period again is followed by the modern one in
which genuine originality reveals itself.

For a long time America [90] contented itself with importing from Europe

[90] BIBLIOGRAPHY: William Francis Allen and Lucy McKim Garrison, *Slave Songs*. N. Y.,
1867; reprint, P. Smith, N. Y., 1929.—Th. Baker, *Über die Musik der nordamerikanischen
Wilden* (Leipzig dissertation). B. & H., Leipzig, 1882.—W. H. Barnes, *The Contemporary
American Organ*. J. Fischer & Bro., N. Y., 1933.—F. C. Bennett, *History of Music and Art
in Illinois*. Historical Publishing Co., Philadelphia, 1904.—Bailey Birge, *History of Public
School Music in U. S. A.* O. Ditson Co., Boston, C. H. Ditson, N. Y., 1928.—F. H. Botsford,
Collection of Folksongs I: from America. G. Schirmer, N. Y., 1930.—Howard Brockway and
Lorraine Wyman, *Lonesome Tunes: folksongs from the Kentucky mountains*. H. W. Gray,
N. Y., 1916; by the same authors, *Twenty Kentucky Mountain Songs*. O. Ditson Co., Boston,
1920.—Frederick R. Burton, *American Primitive Music*. Moffat, Yard, and Co., N. Y.,
1909.—S. N. Coleman, *A Children Symphony*. (Columbia University dissertation). Bureau
of Publications of Teachers College, Columbia University, N. Y., 1931.—J. H. Cox, *Folksongs of the South*. Harvard University Press, Cambridge, 1925.—Natalie Curtis (Mrs. Burlin), *Songs of Ancient America*. G. Schirmer, N. Y., 1905; by the same author, *The Indian's
Book*. Harper Bros., N. Y. & London, 1907.—A. T. Davison, *Music Education in America*.
Harper Bros., N. Y. & London, 1926.—P. W. Dykema, *Music for Public School Administrators*. Teachers College Publications, Columbia University, N. Y., 1931.—L. C. Elson, *The
History of American Music*. Revised by Arthur Elson. Macmillan, N. Y., 1924; by the
same author, *The National Music of America*. L. C. Page, Boston; new rev. ed., 1924.—
A. Farwell, *Music in America* in the series *The Art of Music*.—Alice C. Fletcher, *A Study
of Omaha Indian Music*. Peabody Museum, Cambridge, Mass., 1893; by the same author,
Indian Story and Song from North America. Small, Maynard & Co., Boston, 1900.—
E. Gagnon, *Chansons populaires du Canada*. Beauchemin, Montreal, 5th ed., 1908.—G. B.
German, *Cowboy Campfire Ballads*. S. Dak., Yankton, 1929.—Roland Palmer Gray,
Songs & Ballads of the Maine Lumberjacks. Harvard University Press, Cambridge, 1924.—
K. Hackett, *The Beginnings of Grand Opera in Chicago, 1850–1859*. The Laurentian Pub-
lishers, Chicago, 1913.—*The Harvard Musical Association, 1837–1912*. G. H. Ellis, Boston,
1912.—W. C. Handy, *Memphis Blues*. T. C. Bennett Co., N. Y., 1912; by the same author,
Collection of Blues. Robbins Engel, N. Y., 1925; by the same author, *Blues: an anthology*.
A. & C. Boni, N. Y., 1926.—E. E. Hipsher, *American Opera and Its Composers*. Theodore
Presser Co., Philadelphia, 1927.—J. T. Howard, *Studies of Contemporary American Composers*. J. Fischer and Bro., N. Y., 1927–29; by the same author, *Our American Music* (300
years of it). T. Y. Crowell, N. Y., 1931.—M. A. Howe, *Music Publishers in New York before
1850*. Printed at the New York Public Library, 1917.—M. A. de W. Howe, *The Boston Sym-
phony Orchestra, 1881–1931*. Houghton Mifflin, Boston, 1931.—Rupert Hughes, *American
Composers*. Page and Co., Boston, 1914.—J. R. Johnson, *Utica Jubilee Singers' Spirituals*.
O. Ditson Co., Boston, 1930.—Pierre Key, *International Music Year Book 1929–1930*.
P. Key, Inc., N. Y., 1925 ff.—E. C. Krohn, *A Century of Missouri Music*. Privately printed,
St. Louis, 1924.—H. C. Lahee, *Annals of Music in America* (since 1740). Marshall Jones
Co., Boston, 1922.—M. Larkin, *Singing Cowboy*. A. A. Knopf, N. Y., 1931.—F. A. H.
Leuchs, *The Early German Theater in New York, 1840–72*. Columbia University Press,
N. Y., 1928.—John A. Lomax, *Cowboy Songs and other Frontier Ballads*. Macmillan, N. Y.,
1922.—D. G. Mason, *Tune in America*. A. A. Knopf, N. Y., 1931.—Frank J. Metcalf,
American Psalmody (Catalogue of American Songbooks from 1721 to 1820). C. F. Heart-

both music and musicians. To be sure there were early, even though quite feeble, attempts at original composition. In the period between 1620 and 1800 there were the Psalmodists of New England, but so far as we know, these did not write music of their own until the time of William Billings (1746–1800) in the latter part of the eighteenth century. There were no secular composers until Francis Hopkinson (1737–91). American program music for orchestra was written by Anton Philipp Heinrich (1781–1861). In the period between 1800 and 1860 Stephen Collins Foster (1826–64) wrote the songs that have virtually become folk music. In the period between 1860 and the present day America began to produce composers of its own, especially the so-called "Boston group." Only the music composed after 1860 in America merits consideration in a work such as this.

The first native composer whose reputation as a writer in the larger forms has survived is John Knowles Paine (1839–1906). It has been said that American music begins with him. He is also significant as having been the first incumbent of a chair in music at an American university, having been professor of music at Harvard for thirty years, 1875–1905. A Mass in D by Paine was performed at the Singakademie in Berlin in

man, N. Y., 1917.—F. J. Metcalf, *American Writers and Compilers of Sacred Music.* The Abingdon Press, N. Y., Cincinnati, 1925.—*Church Music and Musical Life in Pennsylvania in the 18th Century.* Printed for The Society of Colonial Dames, Philadelphia, 1926 ff.—J. Mursell and M. Glenn, *The Psychology of School Music Teaching.* Silver, Burdett, and Co., Boston, and N. Y., 1931.—G. C. D. Odell, *Annals of the New York Stage.* Columbia University Press, N. Y., 1927–31.—Odum and Johnson, *Negro Workaday Songs.* University of North Carolina Press & O.U.P., 1926.—Mrs. Winthrop B. Palmer, *American Songs for Children.* Macmillan, N. Y., 1931.—Louise Pound, *American Ballads and Songs.* Scribners, N. Y., 1922; by the same author, *Folk-song of Nebraska and the Central West.* Nebraska Academy of Sciences, Lincoln, 1915.—E. Reinbach, *Music and Musicians in Kansas.* Kansas Hist. Soc., Topeka, 1930.—C. Reis, *American Composers of Today.* International Soc. for Contemporary Music, U. S. Section, N. Y., 1930.—Franz Rickaby, *Ballads and Songs of the Shantyboy.* Harvard University Press, Cambridge, 1926.—E. Roggeri, *Musicisti Americani.* Fratelli Bocca, Turin, 1931.—P. Rosenfeld, *An Hour with American Music.* Lippincott, Philadelphia and London, 1929.—E. Russell, *The American Orchestra and Th. Thomas.* Doubleday, Page & Co., N. Y., 1927.—Carl Sandburg, *The American Songbag.* Harcourt, Brace & Co., N. Y., 1927.—G. O. Seilhamer, *History of the American Theater, 1749–97.* Globe Printing House, Philadelphia, 1888–89.—O. G. Sonneck, *Fr. Hopkinson (1737–91) and J Lyon (1735–94).* Printed for the author by H. L. McQueen, Washington, D. C., 1905; by the same author, *Early Concert Life in America, 1731–1800,* B. & H. Leipzig, 1907; by the same author, *Bibliography of Early Secular American Music.* Washington, for the author, 1905; by the same author, *Early Opera in America.* G. Schirmer, N. Y., 1915; L. Stringfield, *America and Her Music.* University of North Carolina Press, Chapel Hill, N. C., 1931.—W. T. Upton, *Art Song in America.* O. Ditson and Co., Boston and N. Y., Lyon and Healy, Chicago, 1930.—O. Wegelin, *M. Hawkins.* Privately printed, N. Y., 1917; reprinted, W. Abbott, Tarrytown, N. Y., 1927. In the following survey the editor has been primarily dependent on the work by John Tasker Howard, *Our American Music.*

1867. Two symphonies, one in C minor, the other in A major, known as "The Spring" symphony, were both played by Theodore Thomas. Paine further composed an oratorio *St. Peter;* four cantatas, *A Song of Promise, Phoebus Arise, The Realm of Fancy* (Keats), and *The Nativity* (Milton); two symphonic poems, *An Island Fantasy*, and *The Tempest;* an "Ocean Fantasy," *Poseidon and Aphrodite;* an overture, *As You Like It;* and incidental music to Sophocles' *Oedipus Tyrannus* (which won a gold medal at an international concert at the unveiling of the monument to Wagner in Berlin) and to Aristophanes' *Birds.*

Arthur William Foote (b. 1853) received his entire musical training in America. His music is the expression of a nature of refined sensibility. His masterpiece is perhaps his symphonic prologue to *Francesca da Rimini* (Dante). In addition to this he has written three orchestral suites; three cantatas, *The Farewell of Hiawatha, The Wreck of the Hesperus,* and *The Skeleton in Armor; Four Character Pieces after Omar Khayyam,* for orchestra; a number of good compositions of chamber music, and many piano and organ pieces, as well as songs.

George Whitfield Chadwick (1854–1932) is significant, not only as composer, but also on account of his long tenure of the position of director of the New England Conservatory at Boston. A pupil of Reinecke, Jadassohn, and Rheinberger, Chadwick wrote for the most part in a conservative style. His music not infrequently shows vivid imagination, strength, and melodic inventiveness, and at times a sense of humor. He has also employed the idioms of Negro songs. Chadwick has written in almost all forms. Among his chief works are his ode for the opening of the Columbian exposition (Chicago, 1893), *The Viking's Last Voyage;* his *Phoenix Expirans;* six overtures, *Rip Van Winkle, Thalia, The Miller's Daughter, Melpomene, Adonais,* and *Euterpe; Symphonic Sketches;* a symphonic ballad, *Tam o' Shanter;* the *Suite Symphonique;* a lyric drama, *Judith;* a comic opera, *Tabasco;* an operetta, *Love's Sacrifice;* an opera, *The Padrone;* incidental music to Walter Browne's morality play *Everywoman;* the *Dedication Ode, Ecce jam noctis;* a pastoral, *Noel;* and especially his setting of Sidney Lanier's *Ballad of Trees and the Master.* He has also written three symphonies and a sinfonietta.

Arthur Bird (1856–1923) is really an expatriate, having lived in Germany since 1886. He wrote *Karnevalszene* for orchestra; a symphony; a ballet, *Rübezahl;* a comic opera, *Daphne;* two *Decimettes* for wind instruments; *Oriental Scenes* for concert organ, etc.

Edgar Stillman Kelley (b. 1857) remained truer to his native hearth than his almost exact contemporary Bird, although he spent eight years, long after his European student days, teaching piano and composition in Berlin. He has written a Chinese orchestral suite, *Aladdin;* the *New England* symphony; an oratorio, *The Pilgrim's Progress;* a symphonic poem, *The Pit and the Pendulum;* and a symphonic suite, *Alice in Wonderland,* and music for *Ben Hur.*

Frank van der Stücken (1858–1929), a student of Reinecke and Grieg, director of the college of music in Cincinnati, conductor of the symphony orchestra there, and of the Cincinnati Festival from 1905 to 1912, wrote a prologue to Heine's tragedy *William Ratcliff;* incidental music to Shakespeare's *Tempest;* a symphonic prologue, *Pax triumphans;* the *Festival Hymn* for men's voices, etc.

Edward MacDowell [91] is considered by many the ablest composer that America has produced. He has often been compared with Grieg. His music is perhaps as individualistic as that of Grieg. Although it is often bold and strong in its expression, it is also frequently gentle and sensitive in detail. Like many other romanticists, not a little of MacDowell's music is characterized by a certain short-breathedness. This does not mean, however, that he could not probe the depths and scale great peaks. He does the latter especially in his four piano sonatas, *Tragica, Eroica, Norse,* and *Celtic,* which reveal passion, dignity, and breadth. Mac-

[91] EDWARD ALEXANDER MACDOWELL (b. New York, 1861; d. there, 1908) studied music with Carreño, with Marmontel in Paris, and Lebert, Ehlert, and Raff in Germany. In 1881 he was teacher at the conservatory in Darmstadt, in 1882 he resided in Wiesbaden. After his marriage in America in 1884, he returned to Germany where he resided at Frankfort and at Wiesbaden. In 1888 he returned to America, settling in Boston. From 1895 to 1904 he was professor of music at Columbia University, the first incumbent of the chair of music at that institution. Since his death his widow transferred to The MacDowell Memorial Association the property at Peterboro, N. H., which had been his summer home, as a "centre of interest to artists working in varied fields, who, being there brought into contact, may learn to appreciate fully the fundamental unity of the separate arts." The idea had been MacDowell's own, and at this summer colony artists gather for work and intercourse. Since 1910 an annual festival, chiefly musical, has been held there. BIBLIOGRAPHY: C. Adams, *What the Piano Writings of Edward MacDowell Mean to the Piano Student.* Clayton F. Summy Co., Chicago, 1913.—R. W. Brown, *Lonely Americans.* Coward-McCann, N. Y., 1929.—T. P. Currier, "MacDowell as I Knew Him." *Musical Quarterly,* G. Schirmer, Jan., 1915.—Lawrence Gilman, *Edward MacDowell, a Study.* John Lane Co., New York and London, 1909.—E. F. Page, *Edward MacDowell, His Works and Ideals.* Dodge, N. Y., 1910.—J. F. Porte, *Edward MacDowell, a Great American Tone Poet.* K. Paul, Trench, Trubner & Co., London, 1922.—O. G. Sonneck, *Catalogue of First Editions of Edward MacDowell.* Libr. of Congress Publ., 1917.—*The Critical and Historical Essays* by MacDowell have been edited by W. J. Baltzell. A. P. Schmidt, Boston, 1912; 2d ed., 1931.

Dowell composed five symphonic poems, *The Saracens*, *The Lovely Alda*, *Hamlet and Ophelia*, *Lancelot and Elaine*, and *Lamia* (Keats); two orchestral suites, the second known as *The Indian Suite;* two piano concertos; groups of piano pieces under the titles, *Woodland Sketches*, *Sea Pieces*—perhaps his best work—*Fireside Tales*, and *New England Idyls*. He also wrote more than forty songs, a book of *Verses*, and *Critical and Historical Essays*.

Charles Martin Loeffler (1861–1935) was a native Alsatian, but he lived in America since 1881. His music approaches French impressionism, reveals modal influences, and is characterized frequently by mysticism and a fastidious orchestration. The best known of his orchestral pieces are *La Mort de Tintagiles* (Maeterlinck) and *A Pagan Poem* (Virgil, eighth Eclogue). He has also written a symphony in one movement with men's chorus, *Hora mystica;* a symphonic poem, *Memories of My Childhood;* a suite for violin and orchestra, *Les Veillés de l'Ukraine* (after Gogol); a symphonic fantasy, *La Villanelle du diable* (Rollinat); and a setting for solo voice and chamber orchestra of St. Francis's *Canticum fratris solis* (Canticle of the Sun).

Horatio William Parker (1863–1919), a pupil of Rheinberger, contests, in the minds of some, with Edward MacDowell for the palm as America's ablest composer. As a matter of fact, he was extremely uneven in his work. His oratorio, *Hora novissima* (Bernard de Morlaix's "Rhythm of the Celestial Country") well expresses the mysticism of the text, and his opera *Mona* has been classed with "Salomé" and "Pelléas et Mélisande;" but at times Parker became extremely trivial. He was at his best in his choral compositions, the chief of which were the cantatas *The Dream King and His Love*, *A Wanderer's Psalm*, *The Legend of St. Christopher*, *A Star Song*. For the bicentennial celebration of Yale University, where Parker was professor of music, he composed a Greek ode for chorus and orchestra. A second opera, *Fairy Land*, should also be mentioned, as well as a concerto for organ and orchestra. His choral compositions, religious and secular, exceed forty in number.

Gustav Strube (b. 1867), though a German by birth, has lived in America since 1890. He has written three symphonies, four symphonic poems, three overtures, two rhapsodies and four preludes, besides chamber music, etc. He is the founder and conductor of the Baltimore symphony orchestra.

Frederick Shepherd Converse (b. 1871) wrote the first opera by an

American to be produced at the Metropolitan Opera House in New York, *The Pipe of Desire* (March 18, 1910). To compete with Honegger's *Pacific 231* he wrote *Flivver Ten Million*. American also is his tone poem, *California*, suggested by the fiesta at Santa Barbara. He has written three symphonies; two concert overtures, *Youth* and *Euphrosyne;* two symphonic poems, *Ormazd* and *Ave atque Vale;* etc.

Henry Kimball Hadley (b. 1871) has written four symphonies: the first, *Youth and Life;* the second, *The Four Seasons;* the third, unnamed; the fourth, *North, East, South, West*. He considers his tone poem *Salome* his best work. Other tone poems are *Lucifer* and *The Ocean*. He has written the concert overtures, *In Bohemia* and *Othello;* a rhapsody for orchestra, *The Culprit Fay;* an Oriental suite; and much chamber and choral music. He has also been quite active in the operatic field, having written some five operas, the best being, probably, *Cleopatra's Night*.

Edward Burlingame Hill (b. 1872), member of the division of music at Harvard University, has written two symphonies; an orchestral poem, *Lilacs* (Amy Lowell); a symphonic poem, *The Fall of the House of Usher;* two symphonic pantomimes; a suite for orchestra, *Stevensonia;* and four pieces after poems from Robert Louis Stevenson's "Child's Garden of Verse." Hill has indulged in "the sport of the musically polite" by writing a *Jazz Study* for two pianos.

Daniel Gregory Mason (b. 1873), MacDowell Professor of Music at Columbia University, comes from a musical family, being a grandson of Lowell Mason, one of the early protagonists of public-school music in America, and a nephew of William Mason, a distinguished pianist and piano pedagogue. Mason might be termed a modern conservative, being a follower of the classicists and romanticists rather than of the impressionists. He has written some thirty works, among them two symphonies, the *Festival Overture*, the *String Quartet on Negro Themes*, and a song cycle, *Russians*.[92]

[92] Mention should also be made of the important books which Mason has written on musical subjects, such as *Appreciation of Music*. 5 vols., H. W. Gray, N. Y., Novello, London, 1907–25.—*A Student's Guide to Music*. H. W. Gray, N. Y., 1909.—*Great Modern Composers*. H. W. Gray, N. Y., Novello, London, 1916.—*Contemporary Composers*. Macmillan, N. Y., 1918.—*The Romantic Composers*. Macmillan, N. Y., 1919.—*A Guide to Music for Beginners*. H. W. Gray, N. Y., 1922.—*Music and the Plain Man*. H. W. Gray, N. Y., 1924.—*From Song to Symphony—a Manual of Music Appreciation*. O. Ditson Co., Boston, 1924.—*Artistic Ideals*. W. W. Norton, N. Y., 1927.—*From Grieg to Brahms*. Macmillan, N. Y., 1927.—*The Dilemma of American Music*. Macmillan, N. Y., 1928.—*Beethoven and His Forerunners*. Macmillan, N. Y. & London, 1930.—*Tune in America*. A. A. Knopf, N. Y., 1931.—*The Chamber Music of Brahms*. Macmillan, N. Y., 1933.—Mason

John Alden Carpenter (b. 1876) is conspicuously a humorist in music. Although he leans strongly toward French impressionism, Walter Damrosch has called him one of the most American of our composers. His humor in no wise conflicts with a tender sentiment and grace. He understands also how to fill many of his works with color. He has written: *Adventures in a Perambulator*, describing the sensations of a baby wheeled along the sidewalks by his nurse; *Concertino* for piano and orchestra, depicting the conversation of two friends who have become a bit garrulous; a symphony; a ballet, *The Birthday of the Infanta; Krazy Kat*, a jazz pantomime parodying the comic strip of the American newspaper; *Skyscrapers*, presenting the cacophonic noises of our American streets and other phases of American life; and the song cycles, *Gitanjala* (Tagore), *Watercolors* (four Chinese tone poems), and *Improving Songs for Anxious Children*, revealing real children in every mood.

Ernest Schelling (b. 1876) has written a symphony in C minor; the *Fantastic Suite* for pianoforte and orchestra; *Impressions from an Artist's Life*, for piano and orchestra—a set of variations, each variation depicting one of the artist friends of the composer; the *Symphonic Legend;* and an orchestral fantasy, entitled *A Victory Ball* (Alfred Noyes), a war composition.

David Stanley Smith (b. 1877) succeeded Horatio Parker as professor of music at Yale University. He has written three symphonies; the *Prince Hal* overture; *A Poem of Youth* for orchestra; *Fête galante* for orchestra with flute obligato; *Impressions*, an orchestral suite; *Five Melodies for Orchestra; The Fallen Star*, for chorus and orchestra; *Rhapsody of St. Bernard* for chorus, semichorus, soli, and orchestra, his most important choral work; and a considerable quantity of chamber music.

Charles Tomlinson Griffes (1884–1920), who died at the early age of thirty-six, had a rare and original talent, a fine, sensitive, and fastidious musical nature. His chief compositions were *The Pleasure Dome of Kubla Khan* (Coleridge), a tone poem for orchestra, his most important work; a *Poem* for flute and orchestra; *Roman Sketches* for piano.

Deems Taylor (b. 1885) has written *Through the Looking Glass*, a suite from Lewis Caroll's *Alice in Wonderland; The Siren Song*, a rhapsody for strings, wind, and piano; *The Portrait of a Lady*, a rhapsody for

was also editor-in-chief of *The Art of Music*. 14 vols., National Society of Music, New York, 1914–17.

strings, wind, and piano; *Jurgen*, a symphonic poem; *Circus Day*, a suite; and two choral cantatas, *The Chambered Nautilus* and *The Highwayman*. He is best known by his two operas, both of which have been produced at the Metropolitan Opera House, *The King's Henchman* (Edna St. Vincent Millay) and *Peter Ibbetson* (Collier). At the time of its production *The King's Henchman* was proclaimed "the best American Opera." [93]

Although Ernest Bloch (b. Switzerland, 1880) did not come to America until he was thirty-six years of age, he wrote an epic rhapsody *America*, which endeavors to depict the ideals of the country, "the future credo of all mankind," "the common purpose of widely diversified races ultimately to become one race, strong and great." For the most part, however, Bloch expresses himself in a strongly Jewish idiom. His music often reveals some of the poetry and the passion, the sorrow and the exaltation of the Judaism of the Old Testament. His form has been termed rhapsodic rather than symphonic. A number of the titles of his compositions themselves indicate the Hebraic nature of the music. Thus, beside his chief operatic work, *Macbeth*, he has written an opera *Jezabél; Trois poèmes juifs;* a rhapsody, *Schelomo;* a symphony, *Israel;* a poem for pianoforte, *Jeremiah; Three Psalms* (CXXXVII, CXIV, XXII), for voice and orchestra; and a liturgical setting for the synagogue service. He has also written two symphonies, one of them called *La Montagne;* symphonic poems: *Vivre-aimer, Hiver-printemps;* chamber music, etc.

Howard Hanson (b. 1896), director of the Eastman School of Music at Rochester, N. Y., may be described as a conservative modernist. His orchestral works have been performed repeatedly, and his opera *Merry Mount* (R. L. Stokes) was presented at the Metropolitan Opera House in 1934. His chief orchestral works are: two symphonies, the first called the *Nordic*, the second, the *Romantic; North and West;* a symphonic poem, *Lux Aeterna;* a tone poem for orchestra, *Pan and the Priest;* four shorter orchestral numbers, *Before the Dawn, Exaltation*, a symphonic *Rhapsody*, and a *Symphonic Legend;* two choral works, *Lament for Beowulf*, and an *Heroic Elegy*.

Three further recent operas, finally, have evoked considerable comment as being indicative of present-day American trends, namely, *The*

[93] Lawrence Gilman in The New York *Tribune*. Quoted by John Tasker Howard in *Our American Music*, p. 489.

Emperor Jones (based on Eugene O'Neill's drama), by Louis Gruenberg; *Helen Retires* (text by John Erskine), by George Antheil; and *Four Saints* (text by Gertrude May Stein), by Virgil Thompson.

America being both a young and an agglutinative nation, the subject of the American folk song, especially that of the legitimacy of the title, on account of the questions of actual derivation, presents many problems. Without entering into a discussion of these questions, we may include under this general heading, in addition to the virtual folk songs of Stephen Foster already alluded to, the songs of the Indian, of the Negro, of the mountaineers of Kentucky, Tennessee, the Carolinas, and Virginia, of the cowboys, of the lumberjacks, and the hillbilly songs of the Ozark mountains.

The first scientific work on Indian music was written by Theodore Baker, the editor of the *Biographical Dictionary of Music* (Schirmer), as a doctor's thesis at the university of Leipzig. The work, entitled *Über die Musik der nordamerikanischen Wilden,* was based on investigations made personally among the Seneca Indians of the State of New York. Alice C. Fletcher has written *A Study of Omaha Indian Music* (1893), and *Indian Story and Song from North America* (1900). Frederick R. Burton presented his study of Indian music in his book entitled *American Primitive Music* (1909). Natalie Curtis (Mrs. Burlin) published her investigations of more than eighteen tribes in *The Indian's Book* (1907), a collection of 200 songs. She also published a work entitled *Songs of Ancient America.* One of the outstanding authorities on Indian music is Frances Densmore of the Bureau of American Ethnology of the Smithsonian Institution at Washington.

Whether the Indian has a keener, more complicated sense of rhythm and a range of more minute intervals than the white man are questions which are answered both affirmatively and negatively. Those who answer in the negative insist that the so-called complexity of rhythm is in reality lack of rhythmic sense, and that the so-called smaller intervals are the result of faulty intonation and bad musical ears. As in other primitive music, the pentatonic scale plays an important part. The instruments used were flutes, whistles, drums, and rattles.

It has been said that "Negro music has probably made a deeper impression on American life than has any other class of songs. First, through its cousin the minstrel song, then by way of rag-time, and lately through the blues and jazz, the Negroid manner has permeated our popular music." [94] To these lower forms must be added the so-called "spiritual," the Negro's religious song. The search after, and cultivation of, the "spiritual" has developed into a veritable vogue, fostered especially by the traveling Negro singers from Fiske University, Hampton, Tuskegee, and other institutions. To what extent the Negro music is original and to what extent it has been influenced by the white man's music are moot questions. One of its chief characteristics, of course, is syncopation. The pentatonic scale again plays an important rôle. Both features are also characteristic of native African music, as well as an ability for part singing. Collections of Negro songs have been made by J. R. Johnson, *Utica Jubilee Singers' Spirituals;* by Odum and Johnson, *Negro Workaday Songs;* by William Francis Allen and Lucy McKim Garrison, *Slave Songs*, 1867; by W. C. Handy, *Memphis Blues*, 1912. Among the secular songs, Howard lists [95] "work songs, for cotton picking, corn shucking, stevedoring; railroad songs of the section gang; steamboat songs; prison songs of the chain gang and the rock pile; bad men's songs; devil songs (many unprintable); and then, of course, the 'blues' which have been carried into our modern jazz." The so-called "blues" are a result of a self-pity vein; they are a species of lamentations or sorrow songs. To be sure, when the singer drowns his sorrow in carousing or merriment, or persuades himself that his situation is perhaps not so bad after all, the "blues" may assume a right jovial character. The importance of "jazz" as a contribution to modern music is also a greatly debated question. To be sure, it has invaded the ranks of the musically elite.

The isolation of the mountaineers in Kentucky, Tennessee, the Carolinas and Virginia, explains the survival of uncorrupted folk music in these localities, although it is primarily traditional English ballad music brought over by the settlers from their European homes and handed down to their progeny. The debt has been clearly pointed out and listed in Cecil Sharp's *English Folk Songs from the Southern Appalachians.* Other collections are: Howard Brockway and Loraine Wyman, *Lonesome Tunes*, and *Twenty Kentucky Mountain Songs;* J. H. Cox, *Folk-Songs of the South.* A type of dulcimer is found as an accompanimental instrument in Kentucky.

Cowboy songs have been collected by John A. Lomax in *Cowboy Songs and Other Frontier Ballads*, Macmillan; lumberjack songs from the woods

[94] John Tasker Howard, *Our American Music*, p. 416.
[95] *Loc. cit.*, p. 423.

of Michigan, Wisconsin, and Minnesota have been collected by Franz
Rickaby in *Ballads and Songs of the Shanty-Boy*, Harvard University
Press; and Roland Palmer Gray collected *The Songs and Ballads of the
Maine Lumberjacks*. Further collections of folk songs are Louise Pound's
American Ballads and Songs, and Carl Sandburg, *The American Songbag*.

MacDowell in his *Indian Suite* and possibly Dvorak in his *New World
Symphony* blazed the path in the use of native material. Henry Franklin
Belknap Gilbert (1868–1928) followed the example with the *Comedy
Overture on Negro Themes*, the *Negro Rhapsody*, the *Dance in the Place
Congo*, and *Americanesque*. Charles Wakefield Cadman (b. 1881) wishes
to be known as something more than an arranger of Indian melodies,
though he has devoted much of his time to this subject. His Indian opera,
Shanewis was produced at the Metropolitan Opera House in 1918. The
Indian Dances of Charles Sanford Skilton (b. 1868) have won wide
popularity. Frederick Jacobi (b. 1891) has written the *String Quartet on
Indian Themes* which was performed both by the Flonzaley Quartet and
at the International Festival of Chamber Music at Zürich. John Powell
(b. 1882) has written the *Rhapsodie nègre*, one of the most extensively
played of the larger orchestral compositions by American composers, a
work depicting the ultimate tragedy of the Negro race; a *Sonata vir-
ginianesque*, presenting views of plantation life in Virginia; and a series
of piano pieces entitled *At the Fair*. Finally, mention may be made of
David Guion's group of piano pieces entitled "Cowboys' and Old
Fiddlers' Breakdowns," including *Turkey in the Straw, Sheep and Goat
Walkin' to Pasture*, and the *Arkansas Traveller*. John Powell has ranked
these settings higher than Beethoven's "Country Dances," and Percy
Grainger has termed *Turkey in the Straw* a cosmopolitan masterpiece.[96]
Rubin Goldmark (b. 1872), who wrote a *Requiem* for orchestra, suggested
by Lincoln's Gettysburg address, also wrote the *Negro Rhapsody* which
was published in Vienna.

Not even a cursory sketch of American music would be complete
without a word concerning the symphony orchestras which have played
such an important part in American musical education and life. The
Philharmonic Society of New York, which was raised to the highest fame
through the conductorship of Toscanini, was founded in 1842. Theodore
Thomas, the great pioneer in the spread of musical taste in America,
to whom America owes a lasting debt of gratitude, and who finally be-

[96] Quoted by John Tasker Howard, *loc. cit.*, p. 456.

came the great conductor of the Chicago Symphony Orchestra, organized his own orchestra in New York City in 1862. The Symphony Society of New York, made famous by Leopold and Walter Damrosch (the organization has now been merged with the Philharmonic Society) was founded in 1878; the Boston Symphony Orchestra, in 1881; the present Chicago Orchestra, in 1891; Cincinnati, in 1895; Los Angeles, in 1897; Philadelphia, in 1900; Minneapolis, in 1903; St. Louis, in 1907; San Francisco, in 1909; Cleveland, in 1918; and Detroit, in 1919. Pierre Key's *International Music Year Book* for 1929–30 lists seventy-three permanent symphony orchestras in America, eleven in Group I, and sixty-two in Group II.

The number of opera companies in America is far smaller than that of the orchestral organizations, due doubtless, to a great extent, to a lack of native artists and the excessive cost of importations. To be sure, the Metropolitan Company of New York probably presents opera on a higher plane of virtuosity than that attained by any other stage.

Key enumerates 576 choral organizations. The Handel and Haydn Society of Boston, with one exception the oldest choral organization in America, was founded in the year 1815. The New York Oratorio Society was organized for Leopold Damrosch in 1874. Key also cites 122 festival organizations. The Worcester Festival was founded in 1858; the first Cincinnati Festival, under Theodore Thomas, took place in 1873; the Bethlehem Bach Festival, under J. Fred Wolle, in 1900—to mention but a very few of the outstanding ones.

The Argentine Republic has not remained indifferent to the contemporary musical movement, and has experienced, during the last few decades, a nationalistic resurrection to which Alberto Williams (b. 1862) and Pascal de Rogativo especially contributed. Brazil is represented by H. Villa-Lobos and Chile, by Humberto Allende.

VIII

THE TWENTIETH CENTURY

PRESENT TENDENCIES IN MUSIC [1]

TODAY the music of all countries presents the same picture: on the entire front it stands under the banner of revolt. Our day is similar to the beginning of the seventeenth century; revolutionary tendencies are making themselves felt, something new at any price is sought after. It seems impossible to fill the old forms with new spirit. Their content exhausted itself through their over-expansion; romanticism destroyed itself through its exaggeration. The World War also contributed its share in altering spiritual disposition and spiritual tendencies. It awoke the artists from the dream-world of phantasy and philosophical speculation, and transported them to a world of rough reality. There is much realism in modern music. It again wishes to be music, nothing else, above all to make effective its chief elements, dynamics, rhythm, tone. In order not to remain bound to the old spirit by the old forms, it is seeking new paths. Or still better, it is battering at the old foundations, indeed it is already pulling them down. The unique thing about the new music is the fact that it is discarding the old tonal system which has prevailed for centuries, and whose sanctity, but fifty years ago, only a barbarian or a bungler would have dared to question, while it is replacing it with other foundations that are molded according to the varying situations.

It is a breach with tradition, which, to be sure, like all historical events did not occur overnight, but followed a long development. Liszt, who introduced the minor scale of the Gypsies, must be mentioned as one of the stimulators toward the new development. The re-introduction of the old ecclesiastical modes by Russian composers and Max Reger also prepared the way for changes. Pupils of Reger, e.g., the Swiss, Rudolf Moser, still employ them. The application of dissonance as a pictorial

---

[1] BIBLIOGRAPHY: René Dumesnil, *La Musique contemporaine en France.* 2 vols., Colin, Paris, 1930.—H. Erpff, *Entwicklungszüge in der zeitgenössischen Musik.* G. Braun, Karlsruhe, 1922.—Lotte Kallenbach-Greller, *Geistige und tonale Grundlagen der modernen Musik.* B. & H., Leipzig, 1930.—Ch. Koechlin, article in the Enc. Lav., Part 2, Vol. I, pp. 591–760.

means by Richard Strauss, and the mass effects of Gustav Mahler also led to the overdrawing of the bow.

But among the foregoing, tonality in the old sense everywhere still prevails. Claude Debussy took the decisive step by employing the whole-tone scale, which he found in use among the Chinese, as the basis of his compositions. Next one must mention the Russian, Alexandre Scriabin,[2] for whom a chord of six tones constituted by fourths serves as foundation. Arnold Schönberg[3] proceeds still further, and brings us to absolute atonality. As leader and teacher he drew numerous younger composers in his wake. His procedure approximately consists in using the semi-tones of the traditional system as a basis, but in such manner that none of them has tonic or ground-tone function, and there is no relation between the chords. Heinrich Kaminski,[4] proceeding from Reger, also writes atonally. Besides instrumental music, he especially cultivates the field of sacred music, in which department he may be viewed as one of the leading masters in Germany.

Still another method in modern composition is the simultaneous employment of two or three tonalities in one work, the so-called bi-tonality or poly-tonality. The Frenchmen, Albert Roussel, Charles Koechlin, and

[2] ALEXANDRE NICOLAÏEVITCH SCRIABIN (b. Moscow, 1872; d. there, 1915) was professor of piano at the Moscow Conservatory from 1898–1903. Besides his 3 symphonic poems cited above, p. 312, one should mention 3 symphonies and 10 sonatas for piano, the last 5 of which contain his purest and sublimest musical thought. BIBLIOGRAPHY: A. E. Hull, *Scriabin, a Great Russian Tone Poet.* K. Paul, Trench, Trubner and Co., Ltd., London, 2d ed., revised, 1925; by the same author, "A Survey of the Pianoforte Works of Scriabin," in *Mus. Quart.*, October, 1916; by the same author, "The Pianoforte Sonatas of Scriabin," in *M.T.*, November and December, 1916.—M. Montague-Nathan, *A Handbook of the Pianoforte Works of Scriabin.* J. & W. Chester, London, 1916 & 1922.—Rosa Newmarch, "Scriabine and Contemporary Russian Music," in *The Russian Review*, February, 1913.

[3] ARNOLD SCHOENBERG (b. Vienna, 1874) directed a class in composition at the "Hoch-schule für Musik" in Berlin, and has written a treatise on harmony. He has composed works for piano, orchestra, both chamber and grand, songs, and ballads. Mention should especially be made of his symphonic poem, *Pelléas et Mélisande*, his song suite, *Pierrot lunaire*, for semideclamation with accompaniment of string quartet, flute, and clarinet; his drama with music *Die glückliche Hand* (The Fortunate Hand). BIBLIOGRAPHY: A. E. Hull, "Schoenberg Explained," in *Monthly Mus. Record*, March–July, 1914.—J. G. Hune-ker, "Schoenberg,' in *Ivory, Apes and Peacocks.* Scribner's Sons, New York, 1926.—Egon Wellesz, *Arnold Schoenberg.* Tal & Co., Leipzig, 1921; Eng. tr. by W. H. Kerridge, J. M. Dent, London, E. P. Dutton, New York, 1925.

[4] HEINRICH KAMINSKI (b. Thiengen, near Waldshut in the Black Forest, 1886) is the son of a pastor of the Old Catholic Church. He is devoting his time to composition in Ried in the Isar valley, near Munich. He has written music for an arrangement by W. Schmidt-bonns of an old French Mystery of the Passion, Munich, 1920; the 69th Psalm for soli, choir, and orchestra; motets, and chamber music. BIBLIOGRAPHY: S. Günther, Musik XXII, 7.—Erh. Krieger, Z. f. MW., 1933.—H. Mersmann, Kammermusik IV, 138 ff. C. F. Schmidt, Heilbronn.—H. J. Moser, Z. f. MW., 1929.

Darius Milhaud employ this method. The Hungarian, Zoltan Kodály, moreover, builds upon two characteristic fundamental chords, or upon individual, prominent, representative tones, his "tone-symbols."

Even at this stage the tones which have been at our disposal for centuries, and which each of our familiar instruments is capable of producing are still employed. This tonal material, however, no longer suffices for other innovators, so that they increase it by introducing intervals smaller than the semitone. Ferruccio Busoni proposes intervals of one-third of a whole tone; the Czecho-Slovakian, Alois Haba (b. 1893), who is proceeding with the greatest energy, and causing the greatest comment, employs quarter tones. To be sure, oriental music has used such intervals at all times and still uses them, but this music is homophonic, and it is questionable whether a polyphonic system can be built upon quarter tones. Haba found the quarter tones in the folk music of his home, and thus hit upon the thought of introducing them into art music also. This fact is noteworthy: while Schönberg doubtless discovered the new way solely through his own artistic intuition and deliberation, in other cases the suggestion or stimulation almost invariably proceeded from folk music and primitive music.

In his notes on his friend Igor Stravinsky,[5] C. F. Ramuz, the author of the text, *The Story of the Soldier*, relates that Stravinsky is interested in all elemental tone phenomena, the stroke on a kettle, the beat on a drum, etc. He is especially concerned with the development of elementary rhythms and sounds, and with their striking combinations. He is stimulated by the life of nature and the native Russian folk music. At times the works of this composer, so remarkably fertile in ideas, seem to consist of nothing but rhythms and sounds; but this is an illusion, for these rhythms and sounds are of such musical texture, the works are penetrated with a substance so musical, that an unwritten melody resounds above them as it does above a chordal prelude of Bach.

[5] IGOR STRAVINSKY (b. Oranienbaum, near Petrograd, 1882) was a pupil of Rimsky-Korsakov. He is living in France. His chief works are the following: *L'Oiseau de feu* (The Fire-bird), 1910; *Petrouchka*, 1911; *Le Sacre du printemps* (The Rites of Spring), 1913; *Renard*, 1917; *Pulcinella*, 1919; *Symphony for Wind-Instruments*, 1920; *Mavra*, 1922; *Octet for Wind-Instruments*, 1923; *Concerto*, 1924; *Oedipus-Rex*, 1927; *Apollon Musagète*, 1927; *Le Baiser de la fée*, 1928; *Capriccio*, 1929; *Symphonie de psaumes*, 1930. BIBLIOGRAPHY: M. Montagu-Nathan, *Contemporary Russian Composers*. C. Palmer & Hayward, London, F. A. Stokes, N. Y., 1917.—A. Schaeffner, *Igor Stravinsky*. Rieder, Paris, 1931.—C. van Vechten, "Igor Stravinsky, a New Composer," in *Music After the Great War*. G. Schirmer, N. Y., 1915.—C. S. Wise, "Impressions of Igor Stravinsky," *Mus. Quart.*, April, 1916.

The relation of the Hungarian composer, Béla Bartók, to the treasury of the folk music of his home is especially characteristic. His great folk-song collections are model accomplishments of scientific scholarship. In his compositions, he utilizes the melodic treasure in a contrapuntal style of fearless severity.

Everywhere the folk song acts as a stimulus. In England, the modern national movement grew forth, not only from the old familiar Scotch and Irish element, but especially also from the newly discovered English folk song. In Spain, the folk music has long been utilized in art music. Oscar Esplá (b. 1886) bases his compositions on scales derived from the folk music of Alicante. The ballets of Manuel de Falla (*Amor*, *The Magician*, 1915; *The Three Cornered Sombrero*, 1919) also show national influence, particularly the folklore of Andalusia.

Since Bizet's *Carmen*, Spanish echoes are frequently heard in French music. They are introduced for the sake of picturesque effects, the attainment of which was always one of the aims of French music. The *Rapsodie espagnole* and the *Boléro* of Maurice Ravel [6] renew the French tradition of descriptive music. Ravel is fecund in new tonal effects, even on the piano. His compositions are characterized by genuine French elegance and the greatest finesse in workmanship; indeed, he displays such mastery in these respects that he has been called a second Couperin.

The first one to oppose the impressionism which ruled in France after Debussy was Erik Satie (1866–1925; *Parade*, 1917; *Socrate*, 1918). He has exercised a great influence. His most immediate heirs are Georges Auric (b. 1899), Francis Poulenc (b. 1899), Germaine Tailleferre, Henri Sauguet, and Maxime Jacob. Georges Auric's works include ballets: *Les Fâcheux* (The Bores) 1924; *Les Matelots* (The Sailors) 1925; and

[6] MAURICE RAVEL (b. Ciboure, Dep. Basses-Pyrénées, 1875) was a pupil at the Conservatory at Paris. Mention has already been made of his quartet, his trio, his sonata for violin, his sonata for violoncello, his piano pieces, and his songs. His most important orchestral works are: *Rapsodie espagnole*, *Daphnis et Chloé*, and *Valse*. For the stage he has written: *L'Heure espagnole* (The Spanish Hour), *L'Enfant et les Sortilèges* (The Infant and the Sorceries; on a text by Colette). BIBLIOGRAPHY: G. Jean Aubry, *La Musique française d'aujourd'hui*. Perrin et cie., Paris, 1916.—A. Coeuroy, *La Musique française moderne*. Delagrave, Paris, 1922.—G. Dyson, *The New Music*. O.U.P., London, 1926.—C. Gray, *A Survey of Contemporary Music*. O.U.P., London, 1925.—E. Burlingame Hill, *Mus. Quart.*, January, 1927.—R. Manuel, *Maurice Ravel et son œuvre*. Durand, Paris, 1914; by the same author, *Maurice Ravel et son œuvre dramatique*. Les Éditions musicales de la Librairie de France, Paris, 1928.—J. Marnold, *Musique d'autrefois et d'aujourd'hui*. Dorbon-ainé, Paris, 1912.—H. Prunières, in *Cinquantes ans de musique française de 1874 à 1925;* Vol. II: Portraits et médaillons. Les Éditions musicales de la Librairie de France, Paris, 1929.—R.M., special Ravel number, April, 1925.—O. Séré, *Musiciens français d'aujourd'hui*. Mercure de France, Paris, 7th ed., 1921.—Shera, *Debussy and Ravel*. O.U.P., London, 1925.

La Pastorale, 1926. Francis Poulenc composed a ballet, *Les Biches* (The Hind) 1924; *Concert champêtre* (The Rural Concert) for harpsichord and orchestra, 1929.

A figure of other timber is Arthur Honegger, born in France in 1892 of Swiss parents. In the place of a glimmering impressionism, he places a powerful constructive expressionism. When he takes a locomotive as the subject of a composition, as in *Pacific 231*, he not only presents the impression which such a marvel of modern mechanism makes upon a sensitive, artistic temperament, but he represents the thing in reality; he makes the object really visible. In his dramatic Psalm, *Le Roi David*, the choruses of the young Israelites veritably roar their lamentations or their rejoicings. Another oratorio, *Judith* (1925), deserves to be mentioned, as well as the symphonic poems, *Horace victorieux* (1921), *Rugby* (1928), and the opera, *Antigone* (1929).

Darius Milhaud (b. 1892) has interwoven in his music an echo of Brazilian folklore in such compositions as *Le Boeuf sur le toit* (The Ox on the Roof), 1919; and *Saudades*, 1921, and of the Negro jazz band, in *Creation du monde* (The Creation of the World), 1923; he has also expressed profoundly Jewish feeling.

His exceedingly exuberant and extremely fertile personality shows itself in his seven quartets, his six symphonies for small orchestra, his seven operas, his five ballets, and his scenic music for the works of Claudel (*Protée*, and *Orestie* of Aeschylus).

Negro jazz is, of course, a stimulus coming from primitive art. The craving for primitive art is quite general. Its changing, leaping rhythms have an invigorating effect upon the somewhat somnolent European music. As to whether the new American dances can, and will, be as fructifying as were, in their day, the minuets, the sarabands, and gavottes of the epoch of Lully, remains to be seen. American jazz makes its appearance on the stage, with quite sufficient breadth, in Ernst Krenek's opera, *Jonny spielt auf* (Johnny Plays up).

The jazz accents also show themselves in some of the compositions of Paul Hindemith.[7] In connection with this young German composer who,

---

[7] PAUL HINDEMITH (b. Hanau, 1895) plays the violin, viola, and the viola d'amour. From 1915 to 1922 he was concert master of the opera orchestra in Frankfurt-on-the-Main. He has written sonatas for violin, viola, violoncello, string quartets, numerous concertos, and for the theater *Cardillac* and *Neues vom Tage* (News of the Day). BIBLIOGRAPHY: H. Strobel, *Paul Hindemith*. Melosverlag, B. Schotts Söhne, Mainz, 2d ed., 1931.—K. Westphal, *Die Moderne Musik*. B. G. Teubner, Leipzig and Berlin, 1928.

besides Schönberg, thanks to his rich rhythmic invention, is beginning to assume the leadership, another innovation must be mentioned, perhaps the most important and most fruitful of all, namely, the unlimited independence of the voice leading. This, of course, is not a break with the past, but a development. Through the revival of Bach, polyphony again reappeared. Brahms returned to the still older counterpoint. Erwin Lendvai and Kurt Thomas also draw valuable inspiration from this in their *a cappella* works. Thomas has written an *a cappella* setting of the Passion history, a form which was admired in the fifteenth and sixteenth centuries. Instrumental composition, moreover, goes back still further, and renews the polyphony of the Middle Ages, that severe and bold polyphony of Leoninus, Perotinus, and Machaut, which took no cognizance of the general euphony, but sought only rhythmic and tonal balance.

Finally, one must mention the fondness for parody and burlesque effects. The still brief chapter of musical humor has been genuinely enriched by modern composers, such as Darius Milhaud and Felix Petyrek.

If the question be raised as to the kinds of composition in modern music, the answer is that, as always at the beginning of a new stylistic period, brief forms are favored. During the time of romanticism every composer who respected his own ability wrote several symphonies. Today this great form is seldom used. Even when, in chamber music, we find quartets and sonatas, they are, for the most part, decidedly brief. The renaissance movement, which can be observed since the time of romanticism, continues its course. There is fondness for the *Concerto grosso* (Kaminski). As in the days of Bach, solo concertos with the accompaniment of but a small chamber orchestra are written. Stravinsky has written two concertos for the piano; Prokofiev,[8] three for piano and one for violin. Hindemith has composed numerous concertos with orchestra, for violin, viola, piano, organ, and wind instruments.

Everywhere in the theater, not only in France, the ballet with pantomime is cultivated. The dance is the most elementary form of music. It best answers the will for elemental expression, and indeed the renewal of music is going hand in hand with the art of the dance. But composers

---

[8] SERGE PROKOFIEV (b. Gouvernement Jekaterinoslaw, Russia, 1891) was a pupil at the Conservatory at Petrograd. He has written 3 ballets for orchestra, the chief among which are *Chout*, 1921, and *Le Pas d'acier*, 1927; 4 operas, the principal one being the *Amour des trois oranges* ("The Love for Three Oranges"), 1921; numerous piano pieces, among them the *Visions fugitives*, 5 sonatas, 3 concertos, etc. His boldest work is *Sarcasmes*.

are not stopping at the ballet. The opera also is to be modeled according to the new ideas. In Germany, more or less successful attempts have been made by Alban Berg (b. 1885; opera *Wozzeck*, completed in 1922), Ernst Toch, Heinrich Kaminski, and Paul Hindemith. In Italy, where the opera constantly occupied the center of interest, the movement is perhaps making the deepest inroads on the stage. One of the chief works in the new direction is Ildebrando Pizzetti's *Fedra*, composed on a text of the nationalistic poet Gabriele d'Annunzio. In France, the young composers have turned aside from grand opera to the advantage of the music of the theater, of the *opéra comique* and of the operetta.[9] Stravinsky, at the head of the musical movement in all these matters, brings about a fusion of the opera with the ballet, the cantata, or the oratorio in such works as *Renard, Noces*, and the opera oratorio, *Oedipus-Rex*.

It is sometimes difficult for the unprepared listener to feel at home or to come to terms with the dissonances of modern music. But of course one must remember that innovations have always aroused opposition, and that it has always been necessary for the ear to accustom itself to new kinds of tone. It would therefore be wrong, indeed narrowminded, simply to assume an attitude of opposition. On the contrary, the duty devolves upon every lover of music to explain to himself and clarify for himself the modern efforts. There is no modern music *per se*, but here, too, original creations and weak imitations. Here, too, the motto should be: "Prove all things; hold fast that which is good." To be sure, it is not easy to separate the chaff from the wheat. But the grains of wheat are present and constitute a sowing which promises a new harvest.[10]

We have pursued the development of music to the present time. In this brief introduction, we had for the most part to content ourselves with the mention of works of art without being able to enter upon a discussion of the history of the cultivation of music. In the nineteenth century especially, attention should have been called to the development of orchestras, the rise of the great amateur choruses, the male-chorus movement, the founding of conservatories, etc.

The history of the cultivation of music, like that of composition, is very instructive. In pursuing this, one constantly observes that, where

[9] Among recent French theatrical works one may cite: *Le Poirier de misère*, 1927, *Le Fou de la dame*, 1928, by Marcel Delannoy; *Angélique*, 1927, by Jacques Ibert. Vincent d'Indy has written an operetta: *Le Rêve de Cinyras*, 1927.

[10] Cf. H. Kretzschmar, *Musikalische Zeitfragen*, Peters, Leipzig, 1903.

song is cultivated in the schools, where conservatories, choruses, orchestras and opera houses are present, the art of music develops and prospers, and especially also, that talents are awakened that would otherwise waste away.

We shall conclude with the lesson which this recognition teaches. Whatever course the musical composition of the future takes, it will surely thrive, if all those who love music will endeavor to provide it with the means of self-expression; if everyone in his own station will contribute his share to the furtherance of its cultivation.

ADDENDA TO BIBLIOGRAPHICAL
FOOTNOTES

ADDENDA TO BIBLIOGRAPHICAL
FOOTNOTES

The numbers at the left are the numbers of the pages to which these items are related.

3 Harding, R. E. M., *Origins of Musical Time and Expression*. O. U. P., N. Y., 1938.

4 Kirby, P. R., *The Musical Instruments of the Native Races of South Africa*. O. U. P., London, 1934.

5 Andersen, J. C., *Maori Music, with Its Polynesian Background*. "Polynesian Society, Turnbull lib." Wellington, New Zealand, 1934.

5 Galpin, F. W., *The Music of the Sumerians and Their Immediate Successors, the Babylonians and Assyrians*. Cambridge [Eng.] U. P., 1937.

5 Varley, D. H., *African Native Music: an Annotated Bibliography*. "Royal Empire Society Bibliographies," No. 8. Royal Empire Society, London, 1936.

6 Farmer, H. G., *The Arabian Influence on Musical Theory*. H. Reeves, London, 1925.

6 —— *Historical Facts for the Arabian Musical Influence*. "Studies in the Music of the Middle Ages." W. Reeves, London, 1930.

6 Schlesinger, Kathleen, *The Greek Aulos*. Methuen, London, 1939.

14 Robertson, A., *The Interpretation of Plainchant; a Preliminary Study*. O. U. P., London, 1937.

27 Pillet, A., *Bibliographie der Troubadours-ergänzt, weitergeführt und herausgegeben von Dr. Henry Carstens*. "Schriften der Königsberger gelehrten Gesellschaft." Sonderreihe, Bd. 3. M. Niemeyer, Halle, 1933.

37 Gennrich, F., *Grundriss einer Formenlehre des mittelalterlichen Liedes als Grundlage einer musikalischen Formenlehre des Liedes*. M. Niemeyer, Halle, 1932.

37 Meier, John, *Deutsche Volkslieder mit ihren Melodien*. Bd. I–II, 1. W. de Gruyter, Berlin, 1935, 1937.

37 Müller-Blattau, J. M., *Das deutsche Volkslied*. M. Hesse, Berlin-Schöneberg, 1932.

37 Pulikowski, J. V., *Geschichte des Begriffes Volkslied im musikalischen Schrifttum*. C. Winter, Heidelberg, 1933.

57 Husmann, H., *Die dreistimmigen Organa der Notre-Dame Schule*. Frommhold & Wendler, Leipzig, 1935. Berlin dissertation.

57 Schmidt, H., *Die drei- und vierstimmigen Organa*. Bärenreiter, Kassel, 1933. Vienna dissertation, 1930.

60 Two facsimiles of music of the Notre Dame school have been published: Baxter, J. H., *An Old Saint Andrews Music Book* (Cod. Helmst. 628). O. U. P., London, 1931. Facsimile.

60 Rokseth, Yvonne, *Polyphonies du XIIIe siècle; le manuscrit H 196* . . . *de Montpellier*. 4 vols. Ed. de l'Oiseau Lyre, Paris, 1935–36. Facsimile and complete transcription. Vol. IV (Commentary) in preparation.

66 Apel, W., *Accidentien und Tonalität in den Musikdenkmälern des 15. und 16. Jahrhunderts*. Triltsch & Huther, Berlin, 1936.

71 Georgiades, T., *Englische Diskanttraktate aus der ersten Hälfte des 15. Jahrhunderts*. "Schriftenreihe d. Musikwissenschaftlichen Seminars d. Univ. München." Bd. 3. Musikwiss. Seminar d. Univ. München, München, 1937. Munich dissertation, 1935.

71 *The Old Hall Manuscript*. Transcribed and ed. by the Rev. A. Ramsbotham. Pts. I–III. The Plainsong & Medieval Music Society, Faith Press, London, 1930–38.

74 Stephan, W., *Die burgundisch-niederländische Motette zur Zeit Ockeghems*. "Heidelberger Studien zur Musikwissenschaft," Bd. VI. Bärenreiter, Kassel, 1937.

80 Osthoff, *Die Niederländer und das deutsche Lied (1400–1640)*. Junker und Dünnhaupt, Berlin, 1938. "Neue deutsche Forschungen, Abteilung Musikwissenschaft," Bd. 7.

91 Coates, Henry, *Palestrina*. Dutton, N. Y., 1938.

91 Jeppesen, K., *Counterpoint; the Polyphonic Vocal Style of the Sixteenth Century*. Translated, with an introduction by Glen Haydon. Prentice-Hall, N. Y., 1939.

99 Moser, H. J., *Die mehrstimmige Vertonung des Evangeliums*. B. & H., Leipzig, 1931.

99 Zenck, H. F., *Sixtus Dietrich; ein Beitrag zur Musik und Musikanschauung im Zeitalter der Reformation*. B. & H., Leipzig, 1928. Publik. älterer Musik Jahr. 3, T. 2.

104 Jeppesen, K., *Die mehrstimmige italienische Laude um 1500*. Lewin & Munksgaard, Kopenhagen; B. & H., Leipzig, 1935.

104 Pratt, W. S., *The Music of the French Psalter of 1562; a historical survey and analysis with the music in modern notation*. "Columbia University Studies in Musicology." Columbia Univ. Press, N. Y., 1939.

109 Eppstein, H., *Nicolas Gombert als Motettenkomponist*. R. Mayr, Würzburg, 1936. Bern dissertation, 1934.

168 Michaelis, O., *Heinrich Schütz-eine Lichtgestalt des deutschen Volkes*. G. Schloessmann, Leipzig, 1935.

168 Moser, H. J., *Heinrich Schütz, sein Leben und Werk*. Bärenreiter, Kassel, 1936. A monumental work.

168 Works on H. Schütz: see *Jahrbuch der Musikbibliothek Peters*, for 1935, p. 160; also 1936, p. 148.

173 Grusnick, B., *Dietr. Buxtehude*. Bärenreiter, Kassel, 1937.

173 Ludwig, H., *Marin Mersenne und seine Musiklehre*. Buchhandlung des Waisenhauses, Halle, Berlin, 1935.

173 Stahl, W., *Buxtehude*. Bärenreiter, Kassel, 1937.

179 Westrup, J. A., *Purcell*. "Master Musicians." E. P. Dutton & Co., N. Y., 1937.

186 Büttner, H., *Das Konzert in den Orchestersuiten G. Ph. Telemanns*. R. Noske, Borna-Leipzig, 1935. Leipzig dissertation.

186 Hoerner, H., *Georg Philipp Telemanns Passionsmusiken; ein Beitrag zur Geschichte der Passionsmusiken in Hamburg*. R. Noske, Borna-Leipzig, 1933. Kiel dissertation, 1931.

186 Schmuck, Frau Käte (Schaefer), *G. Ph. Telemann als Klavierkomponist*. R. Noske, Borna-Leipzig, 1934. Kiel dissertation, 1934.

186 Valentin, E., *G. Ph. Telemann (1681–1767)–eine Biographie*. A. Hopfer, Burg bei Magedeburg, 1931.

189 Meyer, E. H., *Die mehrstimmige Spielmusik des 17. Jahrhunderts in Nord- und Mittel-Europa*. "Heidelberger Studien zur Musikwissenschaft," Bd. II. Bärenreiter, Kassel, 1934.

190 Mohr, E., *Die Allemande*. Gebr. Hug & Co., Zürich und Leipzig, 1932.

194 Hunicken, R., *Samuel Scheidt, ein althallischer Musikus; Sein Leben und Wirken*. "Hallische Nachrichtenbücherei," Vol. XVI. Hallische Nachrichten, Halle a. S., 1934.

194 *Samuel Scheidt, Festschrift aus Anlass des 350 Geburtstages, 1587–1937*. Kallmeyer, Wolfenbüttel, 1937.

197 Pincherele, M., *Corelli*. "Les Maîtres de la musique." F. Alcan, Paris, 1933.

209 Ulrich, B., *Die altitalienische Gesangsmethode-die Schule des Belcanto*. F. Kistner und C. F. W. Siegel, Leipzig, 1933.

215 Mann, A., *"Die Lehre vom Kontrapunkt" von Joh. Jos. Fux*. H. Moeck, Celle, 1938.

216 Laurencie, L. de la, *Rameau, Biographie Critique*. "Les musiciens célèbres." H. Laurens, Paris, 1926.

218 Dent, E. J., *Handel*. "Great Lives" [42]. Duckworth, London, 1934.

218 *Georg Friedrich Händel; Abstammung und Jugendwelt*. Festschrift zur 250. Wiederkehr des Geburtstages Georg Friedrich Händels. Gebauer-Schwetschke, Halle, 1935.

218 Müller-Blattau, J., *G. F. Händel*. "Die grossen Meister der Musik." Athenaion, Potsdam, 1933.

218 Williams, C. F. A., *Handel*. "Master Musicians." E. P. Dutton & Co., N. Y., 1935.

219 Taut, K., *Verzeichnis des Schrifttums über Georg Friedrich Händel*. Händel-Jahrbuch, Jhrg. 6, 1933. B. & H., Leipzig, 1934.

222 Gray, C., *The 48 Preludes and Fugues of J. S. Bach*. O. U. P., N. Y., 1938.

222 Moser, H. J., *J. S. Bach*. Klassiker der Musik. Hesse, Berlin, Schöneberg, 1935.

222 Schering, A., *J. S. Bachs Leipziger Kirchenmusik, Studien und Wege zu Ihrer Erkenntniss*. Neue Bachgesellschaft, Vereinsj. 36, 2. B. & H., Leipzig, 1936.

222 Steglich, R., *J. S. Bach*. "Die grossen Meister der Musik." Athenaion, Potsdam, 1935.

222 Williams, C. F. A., *Bach.* "Master Musicians." E. P. Dutton & Co., N. Y., 1934.

232 Pfäfflin, C., *Pietro Nardini, seine Werke und sein Leben; ein Beitrag zur Erforschung vorklassischer Instrumentalmusik.* F. Find Söhne, Plieningen-Stuttgart, 1935. Tübingen dissertation.

234 Gerstenberg, W., *Die Klavierkompositionen Domenico Scarlattis.* Forschungsarbeiten des Musikwissenschaftlichen Instituts der Universität. Leipzig, Bd. 2. G. Bosse, Regensburg, 1933.

234 Sitwell, S., *A Background for Domenico Scarlatti.* Faber and Faber, London, 1935.

234 Valabrega, C., *Il clavicembalista Domenico Scarlatti: il suo secolo — la sua opera; con 233 esempi musicali.* Guanda, Modena, 1937.

235 Gagey, E. M., *Ballad Opera.* Columbia Univ. Press, N. Y., 1937. Columbia University dissertation.

240 Einstein, A., *Gluck.* Tr. by Eric Blom. "Master Musicians." E. P. Dutton & Co., N. Y., 1936.

248 Schmid, E. F., *Carl Ph. Em. Bach und seine Kammermusik.* Bärenreiter, Kassel, 1931.

249 Hadden, J. C., *Haydn.* "Master Musicians." E. P. Dutton & Co., N. Y., 1934.

252 Anderson, E., *The Letters of Mozart and His Family; chronologically arranged, translated and edited with an introduction, notes, and indices.* 3 vols. Macmillan, London, 1938.

252 Blom, E., *Mozart.* "Master Musicians." E. P. Dutton & Co., N. Y., 1935.

252 Brunner, H., *Das Klavierklangideal Mozarts und die Klaviere seiner Zeit.* "Veröffentlichungen des Musikwissenschaftlichen Instituts der deutschen Universität in Prag," Bd. 4. R. M. Rohrer, Brünn, 1933. Prague dissertation, 1931.

252 Gheon, H., *In Search of Mozart.* Sheed and Ward, N. Y., 1934. Tr. by Alexander Dru.

252 Köchel, Ludwig Ritter von, *Chronologisch- thematisches Verzeichnis sämtlicher Tonwerke Wolfgang Amade Mozarts, nebst Angabe der verlorengegangenen, angefangenen, übertragenen, zweifelhaften und unterschobenen Kompositionen.* 3. Aufl. bearbeitet von Alfred Einstein. B. & H., Leipzig, 1937.

252 Turner, W. J., *Mozart, the Man and His Works.* A. A. Knopf, N. Y., 1938.

252 Wyzewa, T. de, and Saint-Foix, G. de, *W.-A. Mozart: sa vie musicale et son œuvre, de l'enfance à la pleine maturité.* 3 vols. Desclée, de Brouwer, Paris, 1937.

260 Bücken, E., *Ludwig van Beethoven.* "Grosse Meister." Athenaion, Potsdam, 1934.

260 *Beethoven und die Gegenwart; Festschrift des Beethovenhauses Bonn, Ludwig Schiedermair zum 60. Geburtstag.* Hrsg. von Arnold Schmitz. F. Dümmler, Berlin, 1937.

260 Korte, W., *L. van Beethoven, eine Darstellung seines Werkes.* "Klassiker der Musik." M. Hesse, Berlin, Schöneberg, 1936.

260 Riezler, Walter, *Beethoven.* E. P. Dutton & Co., N. Y., 1938.

260 Scott, M. M., *Beethoven.* "Master Musicians." E. P. Dutton & Co., N. Y., 1934.

260 Shepherd, A., *The String Quartets of Ludwig van Beethoven; Historic and Analytic Commentaries.* H. Carr, The Printing Press, Cleveland, 1935.

266 Toye, F., *Rossini; a Study in Tragi-Comedy.* A. A. Knopf, N. Y., 1934.

274 Kroll, E., *Carl Maria von Weber.* "Grosse Meister." Athenaion, Potsdam, 1934.

276 Goslich, S., *Beiträge zur Geschichte der deutschen romantischen Oper, zwischen Spohrs "Faust" und Wagners "Lohengrin."* "Schriftenreihe des Staatlichen Instituts für deutsche Musikforschung," I. Fr. Kistner & C. F. W. Siegel, Leipzig, 1937.

276 Killer, E., *Albert Lortzing.* Athenaion, Potsdam, 1938.

277 Fehr, M., *R. Wagners Schweizer Zeit.* Bd. I: 1849–55. H. R. Sauerländer & Co., Aarau & Leipzig, 1934.

277 Ganzer, K. R., *Richard Wagner, der Revolutionär gegen das 19. Jahrhundert.* F. Bruckmann, München, 1934. Munich dissertation.

277 Gilman, L., *Wagner's Operas.* Farrar and Rinehart, N. Y., 1937.

277 Jacobs, R. L., *Wagner.* "Master Musicians." E. P. Dutton & Co., N. Y., 1935.

277 Leroy, L. A., *Wagner's Music Drama of the Ring.* N. Douglas, London, 1925.

277 Pourtalès, G. de, *Richard Wagner: the Story of an Artist.* Tr. from the French by Lewis May. Harper & Bros., N. Y., 1932.

277 Stemplinger, E., *R. Wagner in München (1864–70); Legende und Wirklichkeit.* Knorr & Hirth, München, 1933.

277 Tiersot, J., *Lettres françaises de R. Wagner.* B. Grasset, Paris, 1935.

281 Berrsche, A., *Hans Pfitzner; Verzeichnis sämmtlicher erschienenen Werke; mit einem Vorwort "Hans Pfitzner und die absolute Musik."* Leuckart, Leipzig, 1938.

281 Gysi, F., *R. Strauss.* "Grosse Meister." Athenaion, Potsdam, 1934.

284 Haag, H., *César Franck als Orgelkomonist.* "Heidelberger Studien zur Musikwissenschaft," Bd. IV. Bärenreiter, Kassel, 1936. Heidelberg dissertation.

288 Moser, H. J., *Das deutsche Lied seit Mozart.* 2 vols. Atlantis Verlag, Berlin-Zürich, 1937.

289 Bates, R., *Franz Schubert.* D. Appleton-Century, N. Y., 1935.

289 Duncan, E., *Schubert.* "Master Musicians." E. P. Dutton & Co., N. Y., 1934.

289 Kahl, W., *Verzeichnis des Schrifttums über Franz Schubert, 1828–1928.* "Kölner Beiträge zur Musikforschung," Bd. I. G. Bosse, Regensburg, 1938.

289 Porter, E. G., *The Songs of Schubert.* William and Norgate, London, 1937.

289 Vetter, W., *Franz Schubert.* "Grosse Meister." Athenaion, Potsdam, 1934.

291 Gertler, W., *R. Schumann in seinen frühen Klavierwerken*. Kallmeyer, Wolfenbüttel, 1931. Freiburg dissertation.

291 Patterson, A. W., *Schumann*. "Master Musicians." E. P. Dutton & Co., N. Y., 1934.

293 Bieri, G., *Die Lieder von Hugo Wolf*. "Berner Veröffentlichungen zur Musikforschung." Hft. 5. P. Haupt, Bern & Leipzig, 1935. Bern dissertation.

295 Lockspeiser, E., *Debussy*. "Master Musicians." E. P. Dutton & Co., N. Y., 1936.

295 Thompson, Oscar, *Debussy: Man and Artist*. Dodd, Mead & Co., N. Y., 1937.

296 Elliot, J. H., *Berlioz*. "Master Musicians." E. P. Dutton & Co., N. Y., 1938.

296 Wotton, T. S., *Hector Berlioz*. O. U. P., London, 1935.

298 Liszt, F., *Correspondance de Liszt et de la Contesse d'Agoult, 1833 à 1840*. Publiée par Daniel Ollivier. B. Grasset, Paris, 1933.

298 Newman, E., *The Man Liszt; a Study of the Tragi-Comedy of a Soul Divided against Itself*. Scribner, N. Y., 1935.

298 Raabe, P., *Franz Liszt*. 2 vols. J. G. Cotta, Stuttgart and Berlin, 1931.

298 Sitwell, S., *Liszt*. Houghton Mifflin, Boston and N. Y., 1934.

301 Stratton, S. S., *Mendelssohn*. "Master Musicians." E. P. Dutton & Co., N. Y., 1934.

301 Thompson, Mrs. F. A. H., *Mendelssohn and His Friends in Kensington; Letters from Fanny and Sophy Horsley, written 1833–36*. O. U. P., London, 1934.

305 Maine, B., *Chopin*. "Great Lives." Macmillan, N. Y., 1933.

305 Murdoch, W. D., *Chopin; His Life*. Macmillan, N. Y., 1935.

305 Ottich, M., *Chopins Klavierornamentik*. Kallmeyer, Wolfenbüttel and Berlin, 1938. Berlin dissertation.

309 Abraham, G. E. H., *Studies in Russian Music*. Scribner, N. Y., 1936.

309 Federov, V., *Moussorgsky*. "Les Musiciens célèbres." H. Laurens, Paris, 1935.

311 Bowen, C. S. D., and von Meck, B., *Beloved Friend; the Story of Tchaikowsky and Nadejda von Meck*. Random House, N. Y., 1937.

312 Billroth, Gottlieb O., *Billroth und Brahms im Briefwechsel*. Urban und Schwarzenberg, Berlin und Wien, 1935.

312 Browne, P. A., *Brahms: the Symphonies*. "The Musical Pilgrim." O. U. P., London, 1933. Analyses.

312 Ehrmann, A. von, *J. Brahms: Weg, Werk, und Welt*. B. & H., Leipzig, 1933.

312 —— *Johannes Brahms; thematisches Verzeichniss seiner Werke*. B. & H., Leipzig, 1933. Supplement to *Johannes Brahms; Weg, Werk, und Welt*.

312 Erb, J. L., *Brahms*. "Master Musicians." E. P. Dutton & Co., N. Y., 1934.

312 Evans, E., *Handbook to the Chamber and Orchestral Music of Johannes Brahms*. 2 vols. W. Reeves, London, 1933–35.

312 Geiringer, C., *Brahms*. Tr. from the German by H. B. Wiener and Bernard Miall. Houghton Mifflin, Boston, 1936.

312 Geiringer, K., *J. Brahms; Leben und Schaffen eines deutschen Meisters.* R. M. Rohrer, Wien, 1935.

312 Hill, R., *Brahms; a Study in Musical Biography.* D. Archer, London, 1933.

312 Murdock, W. D., *Brahms; with an analytical study of the complete piano-forte works.* Rich and Cowan, London, 1933.

312 Stephenson, K., *Johannes Brahms' Heimatbekenntmiss in Briefen an seine Hamburger Verwandten.* P. Hartung, Hamburg, 1933.

314 Lindner, A., *Max Reger; ein Bild seines Jugendlebens und künstlerischen Werdens.* 3d ed. "Deutsche Musikbücherei," Bd. XXVII. G. Bosse, Regensburg, 1938.

314 Rahner, H. E., *Max Regers Choralfantasien für die Orgel.* "Heidelberger Studien zur Musikwissenschaft," Bd. V. Bärenreiter. Kassel, 1936.

314 Stein, F., *Max Reger.* "Grosse Meister." Athenaion, Potsdam, 1939.

316 Haas, R., *Anton Bruckner.* "Grosse Meister." Athenaion, Potsdam, 1934.

316 Walter, Bruno, *Gustav Mahler.* Tr. from the German by James Galston. Kegan Paul, Trench, Trubner & Co., London, 1937.

320 Jomkélévitch, V., *Gabriel Fauré et ses mélodies avec 172 citations musicales dans la texte.* Plon, Paris, 1938.

322 Delius, C., *Fredrick Delius: Memories of My Brother.* I. Nicholson and Watson, London, 1935.

322 Ekman, K., *Jean Sibelius: His Life and Personality.* Wilmer, London, 1936.

322 Fenby, Eric, *Delius as I Knew Him.* G. Bell & Sons, London, 1937.

322 Gray, C., *Sibelius: the Symphonies.* "Musical Pilgrim." O. U. P., London, 1935.

322 Holst, I., *Gustav Holst.* O. U. P., N. Y., 1938.

322 Howes, F., *The dramatic works of R. V. Williams.* "The Musical Pilgrim." O. U. P., N. Y., 1937.

322 Törne, Bengt de, *Sibelius: a Close-up.* Houghton Mifflin, Boston, 1937.

322 Williams, I. A., *English Folk-Song and Dance.* "English Heritage Series." Longmans, Green & Co., N. Y., 1935.

322 Williams, R. V., *National Music.* Mary Flexner Lectures, Vol. 2. O. U. P., N. Y., 1934.

325 Burney, C., *A General History of Music from the Earliest Ages to the Present Period (1789); with critical and historical notes by Frank Mercer.* 2 vols. Harcourt, Brace, N. Y., 1935.

327 Dunn, G. E., *A Gilbert and Sullivan Dictionary.* G. Allen & Unwin, Ltd., London, 1936.

327 Pearson, H., *Gilbert and Sullivan. A Biography.* Harper & Brothers, N. Y., 1935.

329 Maine, B., *Elgar; His Life and Works.* 2 vols. G. Bell & Sons, London, 1933.

333 Henry, M. E., *Folk-Songs from the Southern Highlands.* J. J. Augustin, N. Y., 1938.

333 Howard, J. T., *Stephen Foster, America's Troubadour.* T. Y. Crowell Co., N. Y., 1935.

333 ——— *Our American Music.* Crowell, N. Y., 1939.

333 Hudson, A. P., *Folksongs of Mississippi and Their Background.* Univ. of North Carolina Press, Chapel Hill, 1936.

333 Korson, G. G., *Minstrels of the Mine Patch; Songs and Stories of the Anthracite Industry.* Univ. of Pennsylvania Press, Philadelphia, 1938.

333 Locke, A., *The Negro and His Music.* Bronze Booklet, No. 2. Associates in Negro Folk Education, Washington, D. C., 1936.

333 Lomax, J. A., and A., comps., *American Ballads and Folk Songs.* Foreword by George Lyman Kittredge. Macmillan, N. Y., 1934.

333 Morris, H., *Contemporary American Music.* The Rice Institute, Houston, Texas, 1934.

333 Scarborough, D., *A Song Catcher in Southern Mountains; American Folksongs of British Ancestry.* Columbia Univ. Press, N. Y., 1937.

333 Scholes, P. A., *The Puritans and Music in England and New England.* O. U. P., London, 1934.

333 Underhill, R. M., *Singing for Power; the Song Magic of the Papago Indians of Southern Arizona.* Univ. of California Press, Berkeley, 1938.

344 Schianca, A. C., *Historia de la Música Argentina. Origen y Características.* Establecimiento gráfico argentino, Buenos Aires, 1933.

345 Bauer, M. E., *Twentieth Century Music; How It Developed; How to Listen to It.* Putnam, N. Y., 1933.

345 Krenek, Ernest, *Ueber neue Musik; sechs Vorlesungen zur Einführung in die theoretischen Grundlagen.* Ringbuchhandlung, Wien, 1937.

345 McNaught, W., *A Short Account of Modern Music and Musicians.* H. W. Gray Co., N. Y., 1937.

345 Slonimsky, N., *Music since 1900.* 2d ed. W. W. Norton & Co., N. Y., 1938.

345 Veloz, Frank and Yolanda, *Tango and Rumba.* Harper, N. Y., 1938.

346 Dickenmann, P., *Die Entwicklung der Harmonik bei A. Skrjabin.* P. Haupt, Bern, 1935. Bern dissertation, 1931.

347 Evans, Edwin, *Stravinsky: the Fire-Bird and Petrushka.* "The Musical, Pilgrim." O. U. P., London, 1933.

347 Handschin, J., *Igor Strawinsky-Versuch einer Einführung.* Hug & Co., Zürich, 1933.

347 Stravinsky, Igor, *Chronicle of My Life.* Tr. from the French. V. Gollancz, London, 1936.

347 ——— *Stravinski; an Autobiography.* Simon and Schuster. N. Y., 1936.

349 Hindemith, P., *Unterweisung im Tonsatz.* B. Schott's Söhne, Mainz, 1937.

349 ——— *Opera: Mattis der Maler.* B. Schott's Söhne, Mainz, 1934.

349 Nelson, S. R., *All about Jazz.* Heath, Cranton, London, 1934.

349 Panassié, H., *Hot Jazz; the Guide to Swing Music.* Tr. from the French *Le Jazz Hot.* M. Witmark & Sons, N. Y., 1936.

349 Tappolet, W., *Arthur Honegger.* Hug & Co., Zürich-Leipzig, 1933.

350 Beaumont, C. W., *Complete Book of Ballets.* G. P. Putnam, N. Y., 1938.

350 ——— *A Bibliography of Dancing.* The Dancing Times, London, 1929.

350 Calvocoressi, Michel, *Musicians Gallery: Music and Ballet in Paris and London.* Faber and Faber, London, 1933.
350 Magriel, P. D., *A Bibliography of Dancing.* H. W. Wilson, N. Y., 1936.
350 Sachs, C., *World History of the Dance.* W. W. Norton & Co., N. Y., 1937.
350 Valois, N. de, *Invitation to the Ballet.* J. Lane, London, 1937.

GENERAL BIBLIOGRAPHY

GENERAL BIBLIOGRAPHY

INTRODUCTORY TEXTS

Aber, Adolf, *Handbuch der Musikliteratur*. B. & H., Leipzig, 1922.

Bernstein, M., *An Introduction to Music*. Prentice-Hall, N. Y., 1937.

Blom, Eric, *General Index to Modern Musical Literature*. Curwen, London, 1927.

Davies, W., *The Pursuit of Music*. T. Nelson & Sons, N. Y., 1935.

Mackinney, H. D., and Anderson, W. R., *Discovering Music*. American Book Co., N. Y. and Cincinnati, 1934.

Mies, Paul, *Noten und Bücher*. Ein Wegweiser durch die musikalische Buch- und Notenliteratur für den Musikfreund. Tonger, Cologne, 1926.

Müller-Blattau, Joseph, *Einführung in die Musikwissenschaft*. Vieweg, Berlin, 1932.

Schering, Arnold, *Tabellen zur Musikgeschichte*. 4th ed. B. & H., Leipzig, 1934.

Schiedermair, Ludwig, *Einführung in das Studium der Musikwissenschaft*. Kurt Schröder, Bonn, 1930.

Tovey, D. F., *Essays in Musical Analysis*. O. U. P., London, 1935.

DICTIONARIES

Baker, Theodore, *Biographical Dictionary of Musicians*. 3d ed., G. Schirmer, New York, 1919.

—— *Dictionary of Musical Terms*. 18th ed., G. Schirmer, New York, 1918.

Brenet, Michel (Bobillier, Marie), *Dictionnaire pratique et théorique de la musique*. Colin, Paris, 1926.

Bücken, Ernst, *Handbuch der Musikwissenschaft*. Athenaion Verlag, Potsdam, 1928–31.

Clément et Larousse, *Dictionnaire des opéras*. Revised by A. Pougin. Larousse, Paris, 1897.

Darrell, R. D., *The Gramophone Shop Encyclopedia of Recorded Music*. Gramophone Shop, N. Y., 1936.

Eaglefield-Hull, A., *A Dictionary of Modern Music and Musicians*. 2 vols., J. M. Dent and Sons, Ltd., London, 1924.

Einstein, Alfred, *Das neue Musiklexikon* (German edition of A. Eaglefield-Hull's *Dictionary of Modern Music and Musicians*). Hesse, Berlin, 1926.

Eitner, Robert, *Quellenlexikon der Musiker und Musikgelehrten*. (Extends to the middle of the 19th century.) B. & H., Leipzig, 1900–1904.

Fetis, F. J., *Biographie universelle des musiciens et bibliographie générale de la musique*. 2d ed., edited by A. Pougin, 10 vols., Firmin-Didot, Paris, 1867–81.

Frank, P., *Kurzgefasstes Tonkünstler-Lexikon für Musiker und Freunde der Musik; neu bearbeitet und ergänzt von Wilhelm Altmann*. Bosse, Regensburg, 1936.

Grove, George, *A Dictionary of Music and Musicians.* 3d ed., edited by H. C. Colles, 5 vols., London, 1927–28.

Hull, A. Eaglefield, *see* Eaglefield-Hull, A.

Keller, G., and Kruseman, P., *Geïllustreerd Muzieklexicon.* J. P. Kruseman, Gravenhage, 1932.

Moser, H. J., *Musiklexikon.* Max Hesse Verlag, Berlin, 1932.

Poidras, Henri, *Dictionnaire des luthiers anciens et modernes.* 2 vols., Imprimerie de la Vicomté, Rouen, 1924–29.

Refardt, Edgar, *Historisch-biographisches Musikerlexikon der Schweiz.* Hug & Co., Zürich, 1928.

Riemann, Hugo, *Musik-Lexikon.* 11th ed., edited by A. Einstein. Max Hesse, Berlin, 1929; nouvelle édition française. Payot, Paris, 1931.

Sachs, Curt, *Reallexikon der Musikinstrumente.* Bard, Berlin, 1913.

Scholes, P. A., *The Oxford Companion to Music.* O. U. P., N. Y., 1938.

Thompson, O., *The International Cyclopedia of Music and Musicians.* Dodd, Mead & Co., N. Y., 1939.

Weissenback, A., *Sacra Musica; Lexikon der katholischen Kirchenmusik.* Augustinus-Druckerei, Klosterneuburg bei Wien, 1937.

GENERAL HISTORIES OF MUSIC

Abraham, G., *A Hundred Years of Music.* Knopf, N. Y., 1938.

Adler, Guido, *Handbuch der Musikgeschichte.* 2d ed., 2 vols., H. Keller, Berlin, 1930.

Ambros, A. W., *Geschichte der Musik.* 5 vols., Leuckart, Leipzig, 1852–78; 2d ed., 1880–82. Only to the beginning of the 17th century.

Besseler, H., *Die Musik des Mittlealters und der Renaissance.* "Handbuch der Musikwissenschaft." Ed. by E. Bücken. Athenaion, Potsdam, 1931–34.

Blume, F., *Die evangelische Kirchenmusik.* "Handbuch der Musikwissenschaft," ed. E. Bücken. Athenaion, Potsdam, 1931–34.

Borrel, E., *L'Interprétation de la musique française; de Lully à la Révolution.* "Les Maîtres de la musique." F. Alcan, Paris, 1934.

Bukofzer, M., *Geschichte des englischen Diskants und des Fauxbourdons nach den theoretischen Quellen.* Heitz und Co., Strassburg, 1936. Basel dissertation.

Combarieu, J., *Historie de la musique, des origines au début du XXe siècle.* 3 vols., Colin, Paris, 1913–19.

Douglas, W., *Church Music in History and Practice.* Scribner, N. Y., 1937.

Eichenauer, R., *Musik und Rasse.* J. F. Lehmann, München, 1932.

Einstein, A., *A Short History of Music.* A. A. Knopf, N. Y., 1938. Tr. from the German. 2d American ed., revised, with addition of 39 musical examples, almost identical with his *Beispielsammlung zur Musikgeschichte.*

Fellerer, K. G., *Der gregorianische Choral im Wandel der Jahrhunderte.* "Kirchenmusikalische Reihe," Hft. 3. F. Pustet, Regensburg, 1936.

Gastoue, A., et al., *La Musique française du Moyen Âge à la Revolution.* "Éditions des Bibliothèques Nationales de France." E. Dacier, Paris, 1934.

Gérold, T., *La Musique au Moyen-Âge.* H. Champion, Paris, 1932.

Gérold, T., *Histoire de la musique des origines à la fin du XIVe siècle*. Renouard, Paris, 1936.

Kinsky, G., *Geschichte der Musik in Bildern* (History of Music in Pictures). B. & H., Leipzig, 1929.

Kretzschmar, Hermann, *Führer durch den Konzertsaal*. Part One: *Sinfonie und Suite*. 6th ed., B. & H., Leipzig, 1921; Part Two, Vol. I: *Kirchliche Werke*, 5th edition, 1921; Vol. II: *Oratorien und weltliche Chorwerke*, 4th edition, 1920.

Führer durch den Konzertsaal; begonnen von Hermann Kretzschmar. B. & H., Leipzig.

Die Orchestermusik, Bd. I–II: "Sinfonie und Suite," 7th ed., 1932. Bd. III: H. Engel, "Das Instrumentalkonzert," 1932.

Vokalmusik, Bd. I: "Kirchliche Werke," 5th ed., 1921. Bd. II: "Oratorien und welthiche Chorwerke," 5th ed., 1939.

Die Kammermusik, by Hans Mersmann. 4 vols. 1930–33.

Lavignac, A., et Laurencie, L. de la, *Encyclopédie de la musique*. Part One: *Histoire*. 5 vols., with the collaboration of Romain Rolland, André Pirro, A. Gastoué, L. de la Laurencie, etc., Delagrave, Paris, 1913–22. Part Two: *Technique et pédagogie*. 6 vols., *ibid.*

Moser, H. J., *Corydon, das ist: Geschichte des mehrstimmigen Generalbass-Liedes und des Quodlibets im deutschen Barock*. 2 vols. H. Litolff, Braunschweig, 1933.

Müller-Blattau, J., *Geschichte der deutschen Musik*. C. F. Vieweg, Berlin, 1938.

Oxford History of Music. 6 vols., Oxford University Press, 1901–5. Published with the collaboration of Wooldridge, Parry, Fuller-Maitland, W. H. Hadow, and Dannreuther.

Prunières, H., *Nouvelle histoire de la musique*. 3 vols. Rieder, Paris, 1934, 1936. Vol. III not yet published.

Riemann, Hugo, *Handbuch der Musikgeschichte*. Vol. I, Part One: Antiquity. B. & H., Leipzig, 1904; Vol. I, Part Two: Middle Ages, 1905. Vol. II, Part One: Renaissance, 1907; Vol. II, Part Two: The Period of the Basso Continuo, 1912; Vol. II, Part Three: The 18th and 19th centuries, 1913.

Robertson, D. H., *Sarum Close; A History of the Life and Education of the Cathedral Choristers for 700 Years*. J. Cape, London, 1938.

Schering, A., *Handbuch der Musikgeschichte bis zum Ausgang des 18. Jahrhunderts*. 4th to 6th ed. of the work, under the same title, by A. von Dommer. B. & H., Leipzig, 1923.

—— *Aufführungspraxis alter Musik*. Quelle und Meyer, Leipzig, 1931.

Schneider, Marius, *Geschichte der Mehrstimmigkeit*. 2 vols. J. Bard, Berlin, 1934–35.

Schünemann, G., *Geschichte der deutschen Schulmusik*. 2d ed. Kistner & Siegel, Leipzig, 1931.

Smijers, A., *Algemeene Muziekgeschiedenis*. Uitgeversmaatschappij W. de Haan N. V., Utrecht, 1938.

Werner, A., *Vier Jahrhunderte im Dienste der Kirchenmusik*. C. Merseburger, Leipzig, 1933.

Special Histories of Music

America
   Howard, J. Tasker, *Our American Music*. T. Y. Crowell Co., New York, 1930.
England
   Davey, Henry, *History of English Music*. J. Curwen & Sons, London, 2d ed.,
   1921.
   Walker, Ernest, *A History of Music in England*. Oxford University Press,
   2d ed., London, 1924.
Germany
   Moser, Hans Joachim, *Geschichte der deutschen Musik*. 3 vols., J. G. Cotta'sche
   Buchhandlung Nachfolger, Stuttgart & Berlin, 1928.

Principal Collections of Monographs

Chefs-d'oeuvre de la musique, Les, published under the direction of Paul Lan-
   dormy. Mellottée, Paris.
Handbücher der Musikgeschichte, published under the direction of H. Kretz-
   schmar. B. & H., Leipzig:
   Dirigieren, Schünemann, 1913.
   Instrumentalkonzert, Schering, 1907.
   Kantate und geistliches Konzert, Eug. Schmitz, 1914.
   Lied (Das neue deutsche), Kretzschmar, I, 1911.
   Messe, Peter Wagner, I, 1913.
   Motette, H. Leichtentritt, 1908.
   Musikinstrumentenkunde, C. Sachs, 1920.
   Musikliteratur, A. Aber, 1922.
   Notationskunde, Joh. Wolf, 2 vols., 1913 & 1919.
   Oper, Kretzschmar, 1919.
   Oratorium, Schering, 1911.
   Ouverture, Botsiber, 1913.
   Sinfonie und Suite, K. Nef, 1921.
Maîtres de la musique, Les, published under the direction of Jean Chantavoine.
   Alcan, Paris.
Maîtres de la musique ancienne et moderne, published under the direction of
   André Coeuroy. Rieder, Paris.
Musiciens célèbres, Les, published under the direction of André Pirro. Laurens,
   Paris.

Periodicals

Archiv für Musikwissenschaft. Kistner & Siegel, Bückeburg & Leipzig, 1918–26.
Bulletin de la Société française de musicologie. 1917 ff. Since 1922 published
   under the title: *Revue de musicologie*. Fischbacher, Paris.
Jahrbuch der Musikbibliothek Peters. 1895 ff.
Kirchenmusikalisches Jahrbuch. F. Pustet, Regensburg, 1885 ff.
Monatshefte für Musikgeschichte, edited by R. Eitner. B. & H., Leipzig, 1869–
   1904.

Musical Quarterly. G. Schirmer, New York, 1915 ff.

Musical Times. Novello, London, 1844 ff.

Revue de la S.I.M. (Société internationale de musique). Ch. Delagrave, Paris, 1907–14.

Revue de musicologie, 1922 ff.; 1917–21 published under the title *Bulletin de la Société française de musicologie.* Fischbacher, Paris.

Revue d'histoire et de critique musicale; founded by P. Aubry, J. Combarieu, M. Emmanuel, L. Laloy, and R. Rolland; editor: H. Welter. Rue Bernard Palissy, 4, 1901–10. Merged with S.I.M., 1911.

Revue musicale; director, H. Prunières; editor in chief: André Coeuroy. 132–136 Boulevard Montparnasse, Paris, 1920 ff.

Rivista musicale italiana. Bocca, Turin, 1894 ff.

Sammelbände der Internationalen Musikgesellschaft (S.I.M.G.). B. & H., Leipzig, 1899–1914.

Studien zur Musikwissenschaft, supplements to the *Denkmäler der Tonkunst in Österreich.* Universal Edition, Vienna, 1913 ff.

Vierteljahrsschrift für Musikwissenschaft. B. & H., Leipzig, 1885–94.

Zeitschrift der Internationalen Musikgesellschaft (I.M.G.). B. & H., Leipzig, 1899–1914.

Zeitschrift für Musikwissenschaft. B. & H., Leipzig, 1918 ff.

PRINCIPAL MODERN COLLECTIONS OF OLDER MUSIC

Anthologie des maîtres religieux primitifs, edited by Charles Bordes. Répertoire des chanteurs de Saint Gervais. Bureau d'Edition de la Schola cantorum, Paris, 19–?

Archives des maîtres de l'orgue des XVIᵉ, XVIIᵉ, et XVIIIᵉ siècles, edited by A. Guilmant and A. Pirro. 10 vols. Durand, Paris, 1897–1910.

Arte musicale in Italia, L', edited by L. Torchi. Ricordi & Co., Milan, 1900 ff.

Chorwerk, Das, edited by Fr. Blume. Kallmeyer, Wolfenbüttel, Berlin, 1929.

Collectio operum musicorum Batavorum saec. XVI, edited by Commer. 12 vols., Schott, Mainz, 1840 ff.

Collection of the "Société de musique vocale religieuse et classique" (founded in Paris in 1843), edited by Prince de la Moscowa (Joseph Napoléon Ney). Published by the society. 11 vols., Pacini, Paris (c. 1843–   ).

Denkmäler der Tonkunst, edited by Fr. Chrysander. Expedition der Denkmäler, H. Weissenborn, Bergedorf, 1869–90.

Denkmäler der Tonkunst in Bayern (Monuments of Music in Bavaria). B. & H., Leipzig, 1900 ff.

Denkmäler der Tonkunst in Österreich (Monuments of Music in Austria). Artaria & Co., later, Universal Edition, Vienna, 1894 ff.

Denkmäler deutscher Tonkunst (Monuments of German Music). B. & H., Leipzig, 1892 ff.

Maîtres musiciens de la Renaissance française, Les, edited by H. Expert. Leduc, Paris, 1894 ff.

Monuments de la musique française au temps de la Renaissance, edited by H. Expert. Senart, Paris, 1924 ff.

Musica divina, edited by K. Proske. 4 vols., as *Annus primus*, Pustet, Regensburg, 1853–63; *Selectus novus missarum*, Pustet, Regensburg, 1855–59. *Annus secundus*, edited by Schrems and Haberl. 4 vols., Pustet, Regensburg.

Musica sacra XVI/XVII saec., edited by Commer. 28 vols., Weingart, Erfurt, 1839–87; continued by A. Neithardt.

Musikalische Werke schweizerischer Komponisten des XVI. XVII. und XVIII. Jahrhunderts, edited by Karl Nef. Vol. I: Sacred Works of the XVI Century, edited by W. Merian. Edition Henn, Geneva, 1927.

Nouveau Répertoire des Chanteurs de St. Gervais, edited by Leon Saint Réquier. Biton, St. Laurent-sur-Sèrra (Vendée), 1912, 1913.

Publikationen älterer Musik der deutschen Musikgesellschaft, under the general editorship of Th. Kroyer. B. & H., Leipzig, 1926 ff.

Publikationen der Gesellschaft für Musikforschung, edited by R. Eitner, 29 vols., B. & H., Leipzig, 1873–1905.

Publications de la Société française de Musicologie. Droz, Paris, 1925 ff.

Sammlung vorzüglicher Gesangstücke vom Ursprung gesetzmässiger Harmonie bis auf die Neuzeit, edited by J. F. Rochlitz. 3 vols., Schott, Mainz, 1838–40. Vol. I: from Dufay to G. Gabrieli and Praetorius; Vol. II: from Caccini to B. Marcello and J. J. Fux; Vol. III: from Bach and Handel to M. Haydn and Vallotti.

Trésor musical: Collection authentique de musique sacrée et profane des anciens maîtres belges, edited by R. J. van Maldeghem. 29 vols., Librairie Européene de C. Muquardt, Brussels, 1865–93.

Tribune de St. Gervais, edited by Charles Bordes. Bureau d'Edition de la Schola Cantorum, Paris, 1895 ff.; new series under the editorship of A. Gastoué.

A detailed, although by no means complete, bibliography of reprints and new editions will be found in Carl August Rau's *Geschichte der Musik in Tabellenform*. Sammlung Kösel, Kempten and Munich, 1918.

ANTHOLOGIES

Einstein, Alfred, *Beispielsammlung zur Musikgeschichte*. 4th ed., B. G. Teubner, Leipzig and Berlin, 1930.

Riemann, Hugo, *Musikgeschichte in Beispielen*, mit Erläuterungen von Arnold Schering. 3d ed., B. & H., Leipzig, 1925.

Schering, Arnold, *Geschichte der Musik in Beispielen*. B. & H., Leipzig, 1930.

Steinitzer, Max, *Musikgeschichtlicher Atlas*. Ruckmich, Freiburg, i/Br., 1908.

Wolf, Johannes, *Sing- und Spielmusik aus älterer Zeit*. Quelle & Meyer, Leipzig, 1926.

MUSICAL INSTRUMENTS

Closson, E., *La Facture des instruments de musique en Belgique*. Presses des établissements Degrace à Huy, Brussels, 1935.

Galpin, F. W., *A Textbook of European Musical Instruments; Their Origin, History and Character.* E. P. Dutton & Co., N. Y., 1937.

Menke, Werner, *History of the Trumpet of Bach and Handel; a New Point of View and New Instruments.* Englished by Gerald Abraham. W. Reeves, London, 1934.

Sachs, C., *Geist und Werden der Musikinstrumente.* D. Reimer, Berlin, 1929.

—— *Handbuch der Instrumentenkunde.* 2d ed. Leipzig, 1930. "Kleine Handbücher," Vol. XII.

Schultz, Helmut, *Instrumentenkunde.* "Bücherei prakt. Musiklehre." B. & H., Leipzig, 1931.

Schwartz, H. W., *The Story of Musical Instruments from Shepherd's Pipe to Symphony.* Doubleday, Doran & Co., Garden City, N. Y., 1938.

Van der Straeten, E., *The History of the Violin; Its Ancestors and Collateral Instruments from Earliest Times to the Present Day.* 2 vols. Cassell, London, 1933.

THE ORGAN

Adlung, J., *Musica mechanica organoedi,* hrsg. von Christhard Mahrenholz. Bärenreiter, Kassel, 1931. Facsimile.

Dietrich, F., *Geschichte des deutschen Orgelchorals im 17. Jahrhundert.* "Heidelberger studien zur Musikwissenschaft," Bd. I: Bärenreiter, Kassel, 1932. Heidelberg dissertation, 1928.

Dufourcq, N., *Esquisse d'une histoire de l'orgue en France de XIIIᵉ au XVIIIᵉ siècle.* Larousse, Paris, 1935.

—— *Documents inédits relatifs à l'orgue français (XIVᵉ–XVIIIᵉs.).* 2 vols. E. Droz, Paris, 1934. Published also as Tome V–VI of "Publications de la Société française de musicologie," Seconde serie.

Fellerer, K. G., *Orgel und Orgelmusik.* B. Filser, Augsburg, 1929.

Frotscher, G., *Geschichte des Orgelspiels und der Orgelkomposition.* 2 vols. Max Hesse, Berlin, 1935.

Hickmann, H., *Das Portativ; ein Beitrag zur Geschichte der Kleinorgel.* Bärenreiter, Kassel, 1936.

Klotz, H., *Das Buch von der Orgel.* Bärenreiter, Kassel, 1938.

—— *Ueber die Orgelkunst der Gotik, der Renaissance und des Barock.* Bärenreiter, Kassel, 1934. Issued in 4 parts, 1931–34.

Mahrenholz, C., *Die Berechnung der Orgelpfeifenmensuren von Mittelalter bis zur Mitte des 19. Jahrhunderts.* Bärenreiter, Kassel, 1938.

—— *Die Orgelregister, ihre Geschichte und ihr Bau.* Bärenreiter, Kassel, 1930.

Schlick, A., *Spiegel der Orgelmacher und Organisten.* In modern German, ed. by E. Flade and P. Smets, Mainz, 1932; in original form, ed. by P. Smets. Rheingold, Mainz, 1937.

MISCELLANEOUS

Lott, W., *Verzeichniss der Neudrucke alter Musik, 1936–* Herausgegeben im Auftrage des Staatlichen Instituts für deutsche Musikforschung, Hofmeister, Leipzig, 1937–

Bibliographie des Musikschrifttums, 1936– Hrsg. im Auftrage des Staatlichen
  Instituts für deutsche Musikforschung, von K. Taut. 3 vols. Hofmeister,
  Leipzig, 1936–38.
    Jhrg. 1. [Pt. 1]: Jan.–June, 1936.
    Jhrg. 1. [Pt. 2]: July–Dec., 1936.
    Jhrg. 2: Jan.–Dec., 1937.
Das Erbe deutscher Musik. Various German publishers.
    Reihe I: Reichsdenkmale. 1935–
    Reihe II: Landschaftsdenkmale. 1936–
    (Hrsg. im Auftrage des Staatlichen Instituts für deutsche Musikforschung.)
Moser, H. J., *Tönende Volksaltertümer.* M. Hesse, Berlin-Schöneberg, 1935.
Tillyard, H. J. W., *Handbook of the Middle Byzantine Musical Notation.* Levin
  & Munksgaard, Copenhagen, 1935.
Wolf, J., *Musikalische Schrifttafeln; für den Unterricht in der Notations-Kunde.*
  Siegel, Bückeburg, 1923.

INDEX

A

Abaco, Felice dall', 231
Abert, H., 10
Absalon, fili mi, 170
Académie royale de musique, 174, 175, 176
A cappella style, 91 ff., 167; new enthusiasm for, 287
Accent, 19; determines rhythm, 33
Accentus, 16 ff.
Ach Elslein, liebes Elselein, 84, 85
Acoustics, Chinese measurements, 5; place in Greek tonal system, 7
Adagio, Beethoven's, 265
Adam and Eve, 185
Adam de la Halle, 28, 59
Adam of St. Victor, 24
Adieu mes amours, 139
Adoramus te Christe, 97
Adoration, The, 331
Adriansen, Emmanuel, 134
Adventures in a Perambulator, 339
Affections, doctrine of the, 10
Africaine, L', 270
Agnus Dei, 16, 72, 98
Ahi, che la pena mia mi guida a morte, 211, 212
Ahle, Johann Rudolf, 173
Aïda, 268
Albeniz, Isaac, 321
Albert, Eugen d', 282
Albert, Heinrich, 181, 183, 184
Alceste, 242
Aldhelm, Bishop, 55
A l'entrada del tems clar, 31
Alexander's Feast, 221
Alfano, Franco, 268, 321
Alfonso the Wise, 37
Alfred, 323
Algarotti, Count, 241
All Creatures Now Are Merry-Minded, 125
Allegri, G., 97, 287
Alleluia, 13, 18
Allemande (dance), 190, 193
Allen, William Francis, 342
Allende, Humberto, 344
Allison Psalter, 332
All' Mein Gedanken, die ich han, 44, 48
Alma Redemptoris Mater, 79
Alme Deus, 94

Alouette, L', 108
Als ich auf meiner Bleiche ein Stückchen Garn begoss, 255, 256
Alldeutsches Liederbuch, 41
Altfranzösische Romanzen und Pastourellen des 12. und 13. Jahrhunderts, 46
Amberbach, Bonifacius, 81
Ambrose, Bishop of Milan, 13; hymns composed by, 14
Ambrosian Hymn of Praise, 14
America, 340
American Ballads and Songs, 343
Americanesque, 343
American music, 333–44; two able composers, 337; folk music, 341–43; symphony orchestras, 343; opera companies: other organizations, 344
American Primitive Music, 341
American Songbag, The, 343
Amfiparnaso, L', 120
Amor, 348
"*Amorire, per servar giustizia e fede...*," 165
Amours merchi de trestout mon pouvoir, 73, 74
Ancient civilizations, music of, 5–6
Andreae, Volkmar, 294, 315
Anerio, F., 97
Anerio, G. Francesco, 162
Anfänge der Musik, Die, 3
Anglican High Church, Gregorian chant preserved by, 15
Animuccia, Giovanni, 149
Anke von Tharau, 183
Années de pélerinage, 300
Annelein, 128
Annunzio, Gabriele d', 351
Antheil, George, 341
Anthologie des maîtres religieux primitifs, 288
Antico, 79
Antiphonal singing of groups of voices, 98
Antiphonary, 15; of Gregory, 18; in St. Gall, 18
Antiphons, 18
Apassionata, adagio of the, 265
Apollo Hymn, Delphic, 11
Après-midi d'un faune, 319
Aquinas, Thomas, *Lauda Sion Salvatorem*, 25